Surveying Fundamentals and Practices

SIXTH EDITION

Jerry Nathanson, M. S., P. E.
Professor Emeritus, Engineering Technology
Union County College
Cranford, New Jersey

Michael T. Lanzafama, P. E., P. L. S., P. P.
Adjunct Instructor, Surveying
Union County College
Cranford, New Jersey

Philip Kissam, C. E.
Late Professor Emeritus
Princeton University
Princeton, New Jersey

Prentice Hall
Boston   Columbus   Indianapolis   New York   San Francisco   Upper Saddle River
Amsterdam   Cape Town   Dubai   London   Madrid   Milan   Munich   Paris   Montreal   Toronto
Delhi   Mexico City   Sao Paulo   Sydney   Hong Kong   Seoul   Singapore   Taipei   Tokyo

Editor in Chief: Vernon R. Anthony
Acquisitions Editor: David Ploskonka
Editorial Assistant: Nancy Kesterson
Director of Marketing: David Gesell
Marketing Manager: Derril Trakalo
Senior Marketing Coordinator: Alicia Wozniak
Marketing Assistant: Les Roberts
Project Manager: Holly Shufeldt
Senior Art Director: Jayne Conte
Cover Designer: Karen Salzbach
Cover Photo: iStock
Full-Service Project Management/Composition: Integra Software Services, Ltd.
Printer/Binder: Edwards Brothers, Inc.
Cover Printer: Demand Production Center
Text Font: 10/12, Minion

Many of the designations by manufacturers and seller to distinguish their products are claimed as trademarks. Where those designations appear in this book, and the publisher was aware of a trademark claim, the designations have been printed in initial caps or all caps.

Library of Congress Cataloging-in-Publication Data

Nathanson, Jerry A.
　Surveying fundamentals and practices / Jerry Nathanson, Michael T.
Lanzafama, Philip Kissam.—6th ed.
　p. cm.
Includes bibliographical references and index.
ISBN-13: 978-0-13-500037-3 (alk. paper)
ISBN-10: 0-13-500037-8 (alk. paper)
　1. Surveying.　I. Lanzafama, Michael T.　II. Kissam, Philip　III. Title.
TA545.N28 2011
526.9—dc22

　　　　　　　　　　　　　　　　2009050875

10 9 8 7 6 5 4

Prentice Hall
is an imprint of

www.pearsonhighered.com

ISBN 10:　　0-13-500037-8
ISBN 13: 978-0-13-500037-3

Dedication

To the courageous men and women who are serving or have served in the armed forces of the United States of America, for the defense of freedom and democracy at home and abroad.

PREFACE

Surveying Fundamentals and Practices is an introductory textbook for use in colleges or technical schools where a basic but practical approach to surveying is desired. It is of value primarily to students in civil and civil/construction technology programs. It is also useful for self-instruction and for on-the-job training of surveying technicians. Others who may find this a useful book are students and practitioners of architecture, geology, geography, forestry, real estate, and related subjects in which the measurement and mapping of natural land features, boundary lines, buildings, roads, and other infrastructure on the ground are important aspects.

This textbook is written in a clear and easy-to-read style, presenting the fundamentals of surveying at a level quickly grasped by most beginning students. In some colleges, the traditional field of *surveying* may now be called *geomatics*, or *geometronics*, largely due to the changes in both field and office practice resulting from computer technology applications, and the infusion of GNSS (global navigational satellite systems) and GIS (geographic information systems) into the topic. But the basic concepts remain the same. A technician in this discipline who lacks a firm grasp of the fundamentals of its scientific and mathematical underpinnings is working on shaky ground. This book provides the necessary solid foundation.

In this textbook, the subject matter is organized into three major sections: Part 1, Basic Concepts in Surveying; Part 2, Surveying Equipment and Field Methods; and Part 3, Surveying Applications. A review of basic mathematics, including geometry and trigonometry, is included in Part 1, rather than in the appendix, because of the importance of these topics for technicians. Without a firm understanding of the underlying mathematics, all the computer technology in the world will be of little use to a practitioner in surveying technology. The acronym GIGO (garbage in, garbage out) is of great significance with regard to the many coordinate geometry (COGO) and computer-aided design (CAD) programs that are commercially available. It is essential that technicians working on tasks related to surveying know the basic concepts related to the operation of surveying instruments, and the analysis (reduction) of surveying data, to avoid major blunders. Appendix A provides information on the use of traditional survey equipment and methods.

NEW TO THIS EDITION

- Chapter objectives at the beginning of each chapter
- Coverage of construction layout techniques that use electronic equipment, current computer software, and RTK (real-time kinematic) field procedures
- Description of computer modeling of data files
- Updated descriptions of GPS (global positioning system), GLONASS (global navigation satellite system), and Galileo (Galileo radio navigation satellite system)

In short, this textbook is designed as a reliable point of beginning for those who will work with surveyors or who will have to use or interpret surveying data in their careers, as well as for those who may choose to continue their academic study of surveying at a more advanced level. It includes both examples and practice problems using Systéme International (SI) metric units as well as U.S. Customary units of measurement, reflecting the current state of practice in the United States. Appendix B summarizes units and conversions often used by the surveyor. End-of-chapter review questions are provided and practice exercises are arranged in pairs of similar problems, with answers to the even-numbered problems given in Appendix F and answers to the odd-numbered problems in a solutions manual available from the publisher to instructors teaching a course.

INSTRUCTOR RESOURCES

To access supplementary materials online, instructors need to request an instructor access code. Go to www.pearsonhighered.com/irc, where you can register for an instructor access code. Within 48 hours after registering, you will receive a confirming email, including an instructor access code. Once you have received your code, go to the site and log on for full instructions on downloading the materials you wish to use.

ACKNOWLEDGMENTS

The underlying foundation of this textbook was firmly established by the late Philip Kissam, Professor Emeritus of Civil Engineering, Princeton University, whose very valuable contribution to surveying education is gratefully acknowledged. Professor Jerry A. Nathanson prepared the fourth edition of Philip Kissam's popular textbook *Surveying Practice*, which was published in 1988. This new textbook, a derivative of the fourth edition of *Surveying Practice*, has been updated with the input of Mr. Michael T. Lanzafama, a licensed professional surveyor, engineer, and planner, who has many years of experience in private practice as well as in teaching.

Mr. Michael T. Lanzafama and I thank the individuals who reviewed the manuscript of this new book for offering many helpful comments regarding its contents: Paul Lonie, Temple University; Robert M. McMillan, Sacramento City College; and Hesham Mahgoub, South Dakota State University. We also thank the editorial and production team at Prentice Hall, whose guidance and encouragement helped us greatly. Of course, we remain fully responsible for any errors that may be found, and we welcome any constructive comments or suggestions for the book's improvement from those who use it.

Jerry A. Nathanson, M.S., P.E.
Union County College, Cranford, NJ
nathanson@ucc.edu

Michael T. Lanzafama, P.E., L.S., P.P.
Casey & Keller Inc., Millburn, NJ
landman84@aol.com

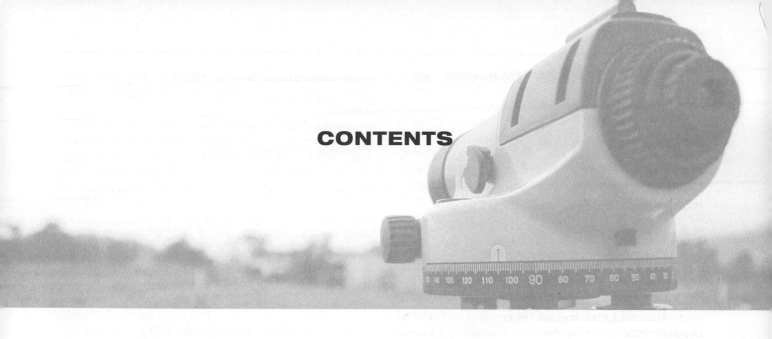

CONTENTS

BASIC CONCEPTS
IN SURVEYING

CHAPTER ONE

INTRODUCTION

CHAPTER OUTLINE

This textbook is intended to serve as an introduction to the fundamentals of surveying. The purposes of this chapter, and the following two chapters of Part 1, are to present a broad overview of the surveying method, to discuss the importance of surveying as a profession, and to cover some basic concepts regarding measurement, computation, and surveying mathematics. This will give the beginning student a foundation for effective study of the traditional and modern surveying instruments, field and office procedures, and surveying applications that are presented in the following parts of the book.

1-1 THE ART AND SCIENCE OF SURVEYING

Simply stated, surveying involves the measurement of *distances* and *angles*. The distances may be horizontal or vertical in direction. Similarly, the angles may be measured in a horizontal or vertical plane. Usually distances are measured on a slope, but they must eventually be converted to a corresponding horizontal distance. Vertical distances are also called *elevations*. Horizontal angles are used to express the directions of land boundaries and other lines.

There are two fundamental purposes for measuring distances and angles. The first is to *determine the relative positions of existing points* or objects on or near the surface of the earth. The second is to lay out or *mark the desired positions of new points* or objects that are to be placed or constructed on or near the earth's surface. There are many specific applications of surveying that expand upon these two basic purposes; these applications are outlined in Section 1-3.

Surveying measurements must be made with *precision* to achieve a maximum of *accuracy* with a minimum expenditure

of time and money. (We will discuss the terms *precision* and *accuracy* in more detail in Section 2-4.)

The practice of surveying is an art because it is dependent upon the skill, judgment, and experience of the surveyor. Surveying may also be considered an applied science because field and office procedures rely upon a systematic body of knowledge, related primarily to mathematics and physics. An understanding of the *art and science of surveying* is, of course, necessary for surveying practitioners, as well as for those who must use and interpret surveying data (architects, construction contractors, geologists, and urban planners, as well as civil engineers).

Basis of Surveying

Surveying is based on the use of precise measuring instruments in the field and on systematic computational procedures in the office. The instruments may be traditional or electronic. The computations (primarily of position, direction, area, and volume) involve applications of geometry, trigonometry, and basic algebra.

Electronic handheld calculators and digital computers are used to perform office computations. In the past, surveyors had to perform calculations using trigonometric and logarithmic tables, mechanical calculators, and slide rules. Today, the availability of relatively low-cost electronic calculators, desktop computers, and surveying software (computer programs) relieves the modern-day surveyor from many hours of tedious computations. But it is still very important for the surveyor to understand the underlying mathematical procedures and to be able to perform the step-by-step computations by applying and solving the appropriate formulas.

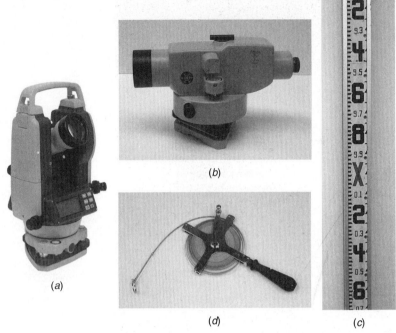

FIGURE 1-1. Traditional surveying instruments: (*a*) Theodolite (*Courtesy of CST/Berger, Illinois*), (*b*) level, (*c*) a level rod, and (*d*) a steel tape.

The traditional measuring instruments used in the field are the *transit* or *theodolite* (to measure angles), the *level* and *level rod* (to measure vertical distances or elevations), and the *steel tape* (to measure horizontal distances). They are illustrated in Figure 1-1. The use of these types of instruments is described in detail in subsequent chapters.

Electronic measuring devices have largely replaced traditional instruments in surveying field work. One of the most advanced of these modern instruments is the *electronic recording tacheometer*, or *total station*, as it is also called (see Figure 1-2*a*). It comprises an electronic distance measuring (EDM) device, an electronic theodolite to measure angles, and an automatic data recorder. Many companies provide a "field-to-finish" system (Figure 1-2*b*), complete with the computer hardware and software needed to analyze and plot the survey data.

The total station and other modern instruments will be discussed again later on in the text. But the fundamental principles of surveying remain the same, whether the electronic or the more traditional instruments are used. The beginning student must still learn these basic principles before using sophisticated modern instruments. In any event, the steel tape, the transit, and the level are still used for many construction and small-scale surveys. In fact, we shall see later on that the steel tape is more accurate than most electronic devices when it comes to measuring relatively small horizontal distances.

With skillful use of surveying instruments and with proficient application of field and office procedures, almost

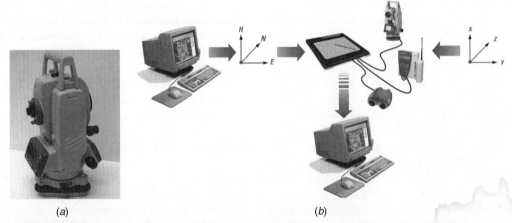

FIGURE 1-2. (*a*) An electronic total-station surveying instrument that can be used to measure and record distances and angles and compute coordinates. (*Courtesy of Leica Geosystems, Inc.*) (*b*) In a field-to-finish system, data may be stored electronically. The data can be "dumped" into the office desktop computer for computations and plotting or printing.

FIGURE 1-3. Practically every line recorded on this photograph was laid out with a transit, a steel tape, and a level—the primary equipment of the surveyor. (*Courtesy of New Jersey Department of Environmental Protection*)

any measurement problem can be solved. Conversely, it is difficult to solve any problem requiring relatively large and accurate measurements without resorting to proper surveying methods and instruments.

Importance of Surveying

Surveying plays an essential role in the planning, design, layout, and construction of our physical environment and infrastructure. The term *infrastructure* is commonly used to represent all the constructed facilities and systems that allow human communities to function and thrive productively.

Surveying is the link between design and construction. Roads, bridges, buildings, water supply, sewerage, drainage systems, and many other essential public-works projects could never be built without surveying technology. Figure 1-3 shows a bird's-eye view of a typical urban environment that depends on accurate surveying for its existence. Nearly every detail seen on that photograph was positioned by surveying methods.

In addition to its customary applications in construction and land-use projects, surveying is playing an increasingly important role in modern industrial technology. Some activities that would be nearly impossible without accurate surveying methods include testing and installing accelerators

for nuclear research and development, industrial laser equipment, and other sensitive precision instruments for manufacturing or research. The precise construction of rocket-launching equipment and guiding devices is also dependent on modern surveying.

Without surveying procedures, no self-propelled missile could be built to the accuracy necessary for its operation. Its guiding devices could not be accurately installed; its launching equipment could not be constructed; it could not be placed in position or oriented on the pad; and its flight could not be measured for test or control. Moreover, its launch position and the position of its target would be a matter of conjecture. Surveying is an integral part of every project of importance that requires actual construction.

1-2 THE SURVEYING METHOD

The earth, of course, is spherical in shape. This fact, which we take for granted today, was an issue of great debate only a few hundred years ago. But despite the unquestionable roundness of the earth, most surveying activities are performed under the tacit assumption that measurements are being made with reference to a flat horizontal surface. This requires some further explanation.

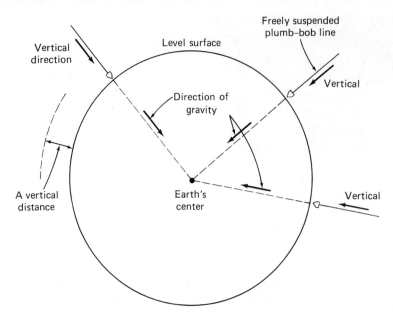

FIGURE 1-4. The vertical direction is defined as the direction of the force of gravity.

Defining Horizontal and Vertical Directions

The earth actually has the approximate shape of an *oblate spheroid*, that is, the solid generated by an ellipse rotated on its minor axis. Its polar axis of rotation is slightly shorter than an axis passing through the equator. But for our purposes, we can consider the earth to be a perfect *sphere* with a constant diameter. In fact, we can ignore, for the time being, surface irregularities like mountains and valleys. And we can consider that the surface of the sphere is represented by the average level of the ocean, or *mean sea level.*

By definition, the curved surface of the sphere is termed a *level surface.* The direction of gravity is perpendicular or normal to this level surface at all points, and *gravity* is used as a reference direction for all surveying measurements. The direction of gravity is easily established in the field by a freely suspended *plumb line*, which is simply a weight, or *plumb*

bob, attached to the end of a string. The direction of gravity is different at every position on the earth's surface. As shown in Figure 1-4, the direction of all plumb lines converge at the center of the earth; at no points are the plumb lines actually parallel.

The *vertical direction* is taken to be the direction of gravity. Therefore, it is incorrect to define vertical as simply "straight up and down," as many beginning students tend to do. The vertical direction varies from point to point on the earth's surface. The only common factor is the direction of gravity.

By definition, the *horizontal direction* is the direction perpendicular (at an angle of 90°) to the vertical direction of gravity. Because the vertical direction varies from point to point, the horizontal direction also does. A horizontal length or distance, then, is not really a perfectly straight line. It is curved like the surface of the earth. This is illustrated in Figure 1-5.

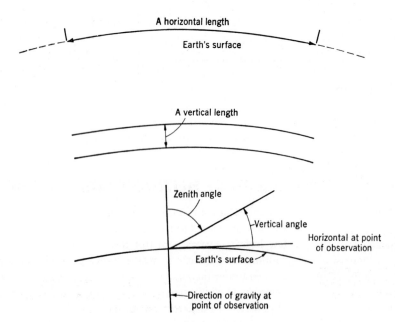

FIGURE 1-5. A true horizontal distance is actually curved, like the surface of the earth.

Measuring Distances and Angles: An Overview

As shown in Figure 1-5, a *horizontal distance* or *length* is measured along a level surface. At every point along that length, the line tangent to the level surface is horizontal. Horizontal distances may be measured by stretching a steel tape between a series of points along a horizontal line. Electronic distance meters, which use infrared light waves and measure very long distances almost instantaneously, are also used. For most surveys, the curvature of the earth can be neglected, as will be discussed in more detail in the next section. Taping and the use of EDM instruments are discussed in Chapter 4.

A *vertical distance* is measured along the direction of gravity and is equivalent to a difference in *height* between two points. When the height is measured with reference to a given level surface such as mean sea level, it is called an *elevation*.

Vertical distances are usually measured with wooden or fiberglass rods held vertically and graduated in centimeters or hundredths of a foot. An instrument called a *level* is used to observe the rod at different points. A level consists of a telescopic line of sight, which can be made horizontal by adjusting an attached sensitive spirit bubble. The instrument can be turned in various directions around a stationary vertical axis. As shown in Figure 1-6, the difference in the readings on the rod at two points is equivalent to the difference in height or elevation between the points.

The relative vertical positions of several points separated by long distances can be determined by a continuous series of level rod observations, as illustrated in Figure 1-7. This procedure is called *leveling*. The line of sight of the level is horizontal at each observation. Because most level rod observations are made with relatively short line-of-sight distances (less than about 300 ft or 90 m), the effect of the earth's curvature is not at all noticeable. This is explained more thoroughly in the following discussion of plane surveying. In any case, proper leveling methods will compensate for the effects of curvature, as well as for possible instrumental errors. Leveling theory and field procedures are discussed in detail in Chapter 5.

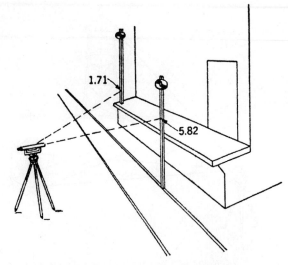

FIGURE 1-6. Measuring a difference in height between a rail and a platform. The difference here is $5.82 - 1.71 = 4.11$ ft.

A *horizontal angle* is measured in a plane that is horizontal at the point of measurement, as illustrated in Figure 1-8. When a horizontal angle is measured between points that do not lie directly in the plane, like points A and B in Figure 1-8, it is measured between the perpendiculars extended to the plane from those points. (Actually, angles are measured between lines, not points. We will discuss this more thoroughly in the part of the book on angular measurement.)

A *vertical angle* is measured in a plane that is vertical at the point of observation or measurement. Either the horizontal direction (horizon) or vertical direction (zenith) may be used as a reference line for measuring a vertical angle. In Figure 1-8, V_1 is the vertical angle between the horizon and the instrument line of sight to point A, and V_2 is the vertical angle between the horizon and the line of sight to point B. Both vertical and horizontal angles are discussed in more detail in Chapter 6.

Horizontal and vertical angles are measured with an instrument called a *transit* or *theodolite*. This type of instrument consists essentially of an optical line of sight, which is perpendicular to and is supported on a horizontal axis.

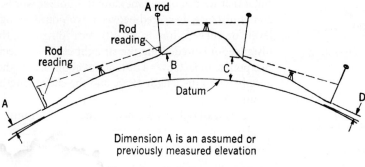

A rod

Rod reading

Rod reading

B

C

Datum

A

D

Dimension A is an assumed or previously measured elevation

Dimensions B, C, D are computed from the rod readings by addition and subtraction and are known as elevations

FIGURE 1-7. The relative vertical positions of two or more points are determined by leveling.

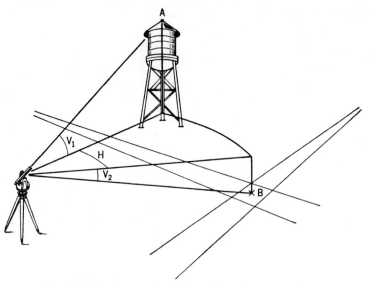

H   is the horizontal angle between A and B
V₁ is the plus vertical angle from the transit to A
V₂ is the minus vertical angle from the transit to B

FIGURE 1-8. Measurement of horizontal and vertical angles.

Theodolites are generally finer in quality and performance (and are more expensive) than transits.

As shown in Figure 1-9, the horizontal axis of the instrument is perpendicular to a vertical axis, about which it can rotate. Spirit levels are used to make the vertical axis coincide with the direction of gravity. Modern instruments use an electronic leveling system. In older instruments, graduated metal circles with verniers or glass circles with micrometers are used to read the angles. In modern theodolites, the circles are scanned electronically, and the value of the angle is displayed digitally.

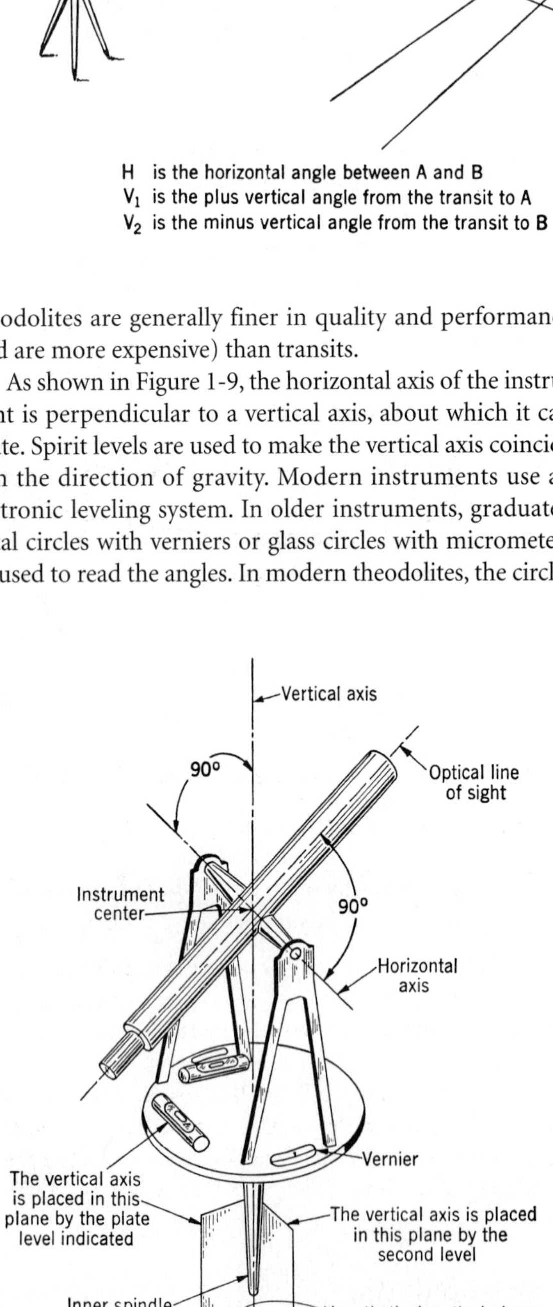

Plane and Geodetic Surveying

We mentioned in the preceding section that most surveying measurements are carried out as if the surface of the earth were perfectly flat. In effect, this means that we make our measurements as if the lines of force due to gravity were everywhere parallel to each other, and as if underneath the irregular ground surface there existed a flat, horizontal reference plane. This is illustrated in Figure 1-10.

The method of surveying based upon this assumption is called *plane surveying*. In plane surveying, we neglect the curvature of the earth, and we use the principles of plane geometry and plane trigonometry to compute the results of our surveys.

The use of plane surveying methods simplifies the work of the surveyor. And for surveys of limited extent, very little accuracy is lost. Within a distance of about 12 mi, or 20 km, the effect of the earth's curvature on our measurements is so small that we can hardly measure it. In other words, a horizontal distance measured between two points along a truly level (or curved) line is, for practical purposes, the same distance measured along the straight *chord* connecting the two points. In fact, over a distance of about 12 mi, the difference between the length of arc and the chord length is only about 0.25 in.

This textbook is designed primarily as an introduction to plane surveying, which, for the reason described previously, is suitable for surveys extending over distances less than about 12 mi. But as it turns out, the vast majority of ordinary private surveys are performed well within these limits. Certain public surveys, however, are conducted by federal or state agencies and cover large areas or distances.

[Figure 1-9 labels:]
← Vertical axis
90°
Optical line of sight
Instrument center
90°
Horizontal axis
Vernier
The vertical axis is placed in this plane by the plate level indicated
The vertical axis is placed in this plane by the second level
Inner spindle
Hypothetical vertical planes

FIGURE 1-9. Transit essentials. Schematic diagram of an *alidade,* which is the upper part of a transit.

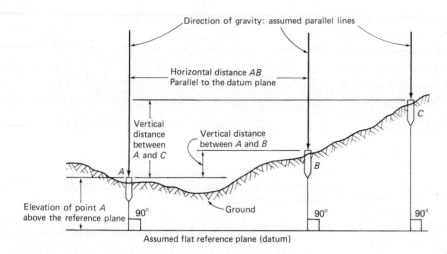

FIGURE 1-10. In plane surveying, the curvature of the earth is neglected and vertical distances are measured with reference to a flat plane.

Such large-scale surveys must account for the true shape of the earth so that the required degree of accuracy is not lost in the results.

A survey that takes the earth's curvature into account is called a *geodetic* survey. These types of surveys are usually conducted by federal agencies such as the U.S. Geological Survey and the U.S. National Geodetic Survey. Various river basin commissions and large cities also perform geodetic surveys. Such surveys generally use very precise instruments and field methods and make use of advanced mathematics and spherical trigonometric formulas to adjust for curvature. In some cases, the instruments and field methods used in a geodetic survey do not differ from those used in a plane survey, but spherical trigonometry must always be used to reduce the geodetic survey data.

The geometry and trigonometry of figures on a curved surface differ considerably from the geometry and trigonometry of plane or flat figures. For example, in a plane triangle, the interior angles always add up to 180°. But this is not the case with a triangle on a curved surface. The triangle shown on the sphere in Figure 1-11, for instance, must contain more than 180°. The sides of that triangle change direction by 90° at each corner, A and B, on the equator. With angle C added to A and B, the sum is clearly more than 180°. Spherical trigonometry, then, takes into account the properties of geometric shapes on curved surfaces.

Geodetic surveying methods are generally used to map large areas and to establish large-scale networks of points on the earth for horizontal and vertical control. The relative positions of these points are measured with a high degree of precision *and* accuracy, both in longitude and in latitude,* as well as in elevation. They are used as points of reference for many other local surveys that require a lower degree of accuracy.

Longitude is the angular distance of a point on the earth's surface, measured east or west of the prime meridian at Greenwich, England. *Latitude* is the angular distance of a point on the earth's surface, measured north or south of the equator.

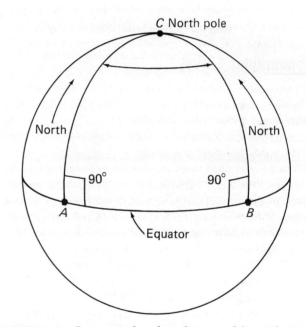

FIGURE 1-11. On a curved surface, the sum of the angles in a triangle is more than 180°.

1-3 SURVEYING APPLICATIONS

As we mentioned at the beginning of this chapter, the two fundamental purposes for surveying are to determine the relative positions of *existing* points and to mark the positions of *new* points on or near the surface of the earth.

Within this framework, many different kinds of surveys are performed. Some specific applications or types of surveys are outlined briefly in this section and are discussed in more detail in Part 3 of the text. Generally, these different types of surveys require different field procedures and varying degrees of precision for carrying out the work.

Property Survey

A *property survey* is performed to establish the positions of boundary lines and property corners. It is also referred to as a *land survey*, *title survey*, or a *boundary survey.* Property surveys are usually performed whenever land ownership is to be transferred or when a large tract of land is to be subdivided into smaller parcels for development. Also, before the design and construction of any public or private land-use project can get under way, it is necessary to accurately establish the legal boundaries of the proposed project site. Constructing a structure on what later is found to be property that belongs to someone else can be a very expensive mistake.

Any survey for establishing or describing land boundaries must be performed under the supervision of a licensed land surveyor. Land surveys in urban areas must be conducted with particular care because of the very high cost of land. In rural areas, less accuracy may be acceptable. Land surveys done to actually mark property corners with permanent monuments are sometimes informally referred to as "stakeout," "outbound," or "bar job" surveys. The results of a property survey may be written into a deed or may be prepared as a drawing called a *plat*, as illustrated in Figure 8-2.

Topographic Survey

A topographic survey is performed to determine the relative positions (horizontal and vertical) of *existing* natural and constructed features on a tract of land. Such features include ground elevations, bodies of water, vegetation, rock outcrops, roads, buildings, and so on.

A topographic survey provides information about the "shape of the land." Hills, valleys, ridges, and the general slope of the ground can be depicted graphically. The data obtained from a topographic survey are plotted and drawn as a suitably scaled map, called a *topographic map*, or *topo map*. Figures 9-1 and 9-2 are examples of topo maps.

The shape of the ground is shown with *contours*, or lines of equal elevation. Because a topo map is always needed before the engineering and architectural design of any building or other project can begin, a topo survey may also be referred to as a *preliminary survey*. Of course, an accurate property survey must always precede the topo survey to establish the boundaries of the project site.

Construction Survey

A construction survey, also called a *layout* or *location survey*, is performed to mark the position of *new points* on the ground. These new points represent the location of building corners, road centerlines, and other facilities that are to be built. These positions are shown on a *site plan*, which is essentially a combination of the property survey and topo survey, along with the newly designed facilities. This may also be called a *plot plan*.

A site plan shows the location dimensions that are to be measured with reference to boundaries or other control points. Vertical heights are given by elevations. Sometimes horizontal positions may be given by coordinates. Wooden stakes are used by the surveyor to mark the positions of the buildings, roads, and other structures. An example of a drawing that includes location dimensions is shown in Figure 1-12.

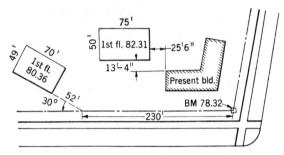

FIGURE 1-12. Typical location dimensions found on engineering or architectural plans, for use during a stakeout survey.

The wooden stakes serve as reference points for the construction contractor who actually builds the project. They may be centerline stakes, offset stakes, or grade stakes. Carpenters, masons, and other skilled trades transfer measurements directly from the survey points. The procedure of placing the markers is called *staking out*. Another term used, especially for pipelines and roads, is *giving line and grade*.

Control Survey

There are two kinds of control surveys: horizontal and vertical. In a horizontal control survey, several points are placed in the ground by the surveyor, using wooden stakes or more permanent markers such as iron bars and concrete monuments. These points, called *stations*, are arranged throughout the site or area under study so that they can be easily seen and surveyed.

The relative horizontal positions of these points are established, usually with a very high degree of precision and accuracy; this is done using *traverse* or global navigation satellite systems (GNSS) survey methods.

In a vertical control survey, the elevations of relatively permanent reference points are determined by *precise leveling* methods. Marked or *monumented* points of known elevation are called elevation *benchmarks* (BMs).

The network of stations and benchmarks provides a framework for horizontal and vertical control, upon which less accurate surveys can be based. For example, boundary surveys or construction surveys can be *tied* into nearby control survey stations and benchmarks. This minimizes the accumulation of errors and the cost of making all the measurements precise.

Existing topographic features and proposed points or structures are connected to the control network by surveying measurements of comparatively low precision. A steel tape and a builder's level may be used in some cases. An example of a control survey network is shown in Figure 1-13. When local surveys are tied into a control survey, a permanent reference is established that can be retraced if the construction stakes or property corners are obliterated for any reason.

Large-scale or geodetic control surveys must account for the curvature of the earth in establishing relative horizontal and vertical positions. Geodetic control surveys include astronomic observations to determine latitude and longitude and the direction of astronomical north. Modern

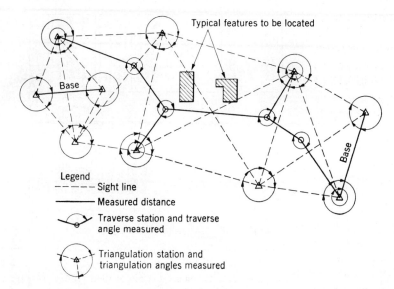

Typical features to be located

Base

Legend
- - - - - Sight line
———— Measured distance
Traverse station and traverse angle measured
Triangulation station and triangulation angles measured

Base

FIGURE 1-13. A horizontal control survey network showing traverse and triangulation stations (points) and courses (lines).

geodetic control surveys can be performed using signals from satellites, which are received by instruments called *global navigation satellite systems* (GNSS).

Route Survey

A route survey is performed to establish horizontal and vertical control, to obtain topographic data, and to lay out the positions of highways, railroads, streets, pipelines, or any other "linear" project. In other words, the primary aspect of a route survey is that the project area is very narrow compared with its length, which can extend up to several kilometers or miles. An example of the results of a route survey—the plan and profile of a proposed road—is shown in Figure 1-14. Plane geometry is used to compute the horizontal and vertical *alignment* of the road.

Other Types of Surveys

A *hydrographic survey* is a preliminary survey applied to a natural body of water. It serves to gather data for mapping the shoreline and for charting the water depths of a river, lake, or harbor. In effect, an underwater topo map is prepared from a hydrographic survey. Navigation and water resources planning projects depend upon data obtained from hydrographic surveys.

A *reconnaissance survey* is a preliminary survey conducted to get very rough data regarding a tract of land. Distances may be approximated by pacing, and spot elevations may be obtained with the use of only a hand level. Examination of aerial photographs may also serve as part of a reconnaissance survey. *Photogrammetric surveying* uses relatively accurate methods to convert aerial photographs into useful topographic maps. A control survey on the ground is still necessary when utilizing photogrammetry to produce accurately scaled maps.

A *cadastral survey* is a boundary survey applied specifically to the relatively large-scale rectangular U.S. Public Lands Survey system. It also refers to the surveying and identification of property in political subdivisions.

Other types of specialized surveys include *mine surveys*, *bridge surveys*, *tunnel surveys*, and *city surveys*. Surveying applications also range from monitoring very small movements of the earth over long periods of time (such as earthquakes and other geological studies) to tracking the orbits of satellites and space vehicles.

Surveying, an activity with roots in antiquity, is now a modern and continually evolving technical discipline and profession.

1-4 HISTORICAL BACKGROUND

Surveying probably has its origins in ancient Egypt, as far back as 5000 years ago. Some type of systematic measurements must have been made, for example, to accurately and squarely lay out the Great Pyramid with respect to the true meridian (the north-south direction line). And the annual floods of the Nile River, which obliterated land boundary markers used for taxation purposes, made it necessary for ancient surveyors to relocate and replace the lost boundaries.

Those early surveyors used ropes that were knotted at uniform intervals to measure distance; the surveyors were, appropriately enough, called *rope stretchers*. The interval between the knots, called a *cubit*, was taken to be the length of the human forearm. The cubit, which, of course, could vary depending on whose forearm was used to establish it, was the basic unit of length used at that time.

It is likely that the subject of geometry (which means "earth measurements") developed primarily because of the need to conduct surveys of the land. Since ancient times, historical records show the development of surveying as an applied science, one that evolved as measuring instruments, as well as computational methods, gradually improved. It is of value for the beginning student of surveying to have at least a general perspective of this historical development. Students may wish to go to *www.surveyhistory.org* for images and explanations of ancient surveying tools.

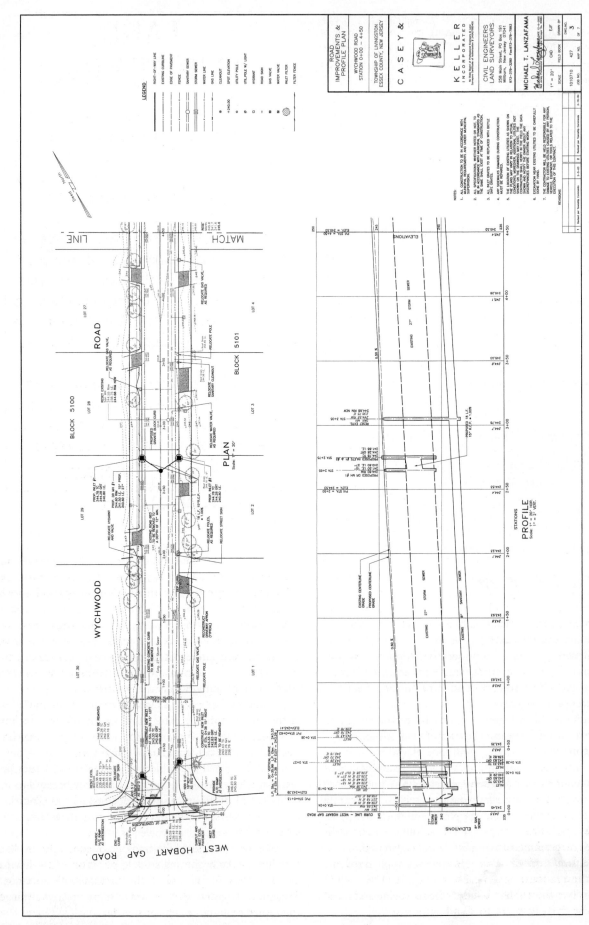

FIGURE 1-14. A typical plan and profile of a section of roadway, prepared from route survey data. (*Courtesy of Casey & Keller, Inc.*)

Perhaps the earliest device used to establish a level line was a triangular A-frame with a plumb line and weight suspended from the apex, called the *libella*. A mark at the center lower bar indicated the proper position of the plumb line for the bar to be horizontal. The position of the mark on the bar could also have been "calibrated" by aligning it with a free water surface.

Ancient Roman engineering accomplishments include roads, aqueducts, and buildings. One of the instruments used by Roman surveyors, who were called *agrimensores* ("land measurers"), was the *groma*. It comprised a pair of crossarms attached at right angles to each other and supported on a vertical staff. Plumb lines suspended from the end of each arm were used to establish perpendicular or right-angle lines of sight. The Romans also used a device called a *chorobate*, a timber beam with a narrow groove on top to hold water, as a leveling instrument; the water surface established a level line of sight.

The magnetic compass was first used as a surveying instrument in the thirteenth century to establish the directions of boundary lines. By the beginning of the sixteenth century, a sighting device similar to the transit, with graduated scales to measure vertical and horizontal angles, was in use. It was improved considerably, in the middle of the seventeenth century, with the addition of the telescope and cross hairs for establishing a line of sight. Also around that time, a device for reading small subdivisions of a graduated scale was invented by Pierre Vernier. The *vernier*, as it is called, is still used today to increase the accuracy of reading angles on most traditional engineering transits.

The development and gradual improvement of surveying instruments continued through the eighteenth century, and the nineteenth century was one of continuing refinement in field methods as well as in instrumentation. It was at the end of the eighteenth century that a systematic survey of the entire public domain in the United States was begun. This large-scale public land survey, as well as the construction of railroads and canals throughout the nation, led to many advancements in surveying procedures.

Several famous Americans, including George Washington, Thomas Jefferson, Daniel Boone, and the writer-philosopher Henry David Thoreau, earned their living as surveyors for a while. George Washington was licensed as a land surveyor by the College of William and Mary. Even Abraham Lincoln served briefly as a "deputy surveyor." And the main character in the symbolic novel *The Castle*, by Franz Kafka, was portrayed as a land surveyor.

The surveying profession, then, has some notable associations with literature and famous personalities. Of course, the study or practice of surveying will not guarantee us fame or fortune. But it is such a practical and down-to-earth subject that knowledge of its basic principles can only serve an individual well, irrespective of his or her future career path.

Since the twentieth century, surveying has emerged as a dynamic and modern technical discipline. The two world wars, as well as the military conflicts in Korea, Vietnam, and the Middle East, have led to significant developments in

LAND SURVEYING

Of all kinds, according to the best methods known; the necessary data supplied, in order that the boundaries of Farms may be accurately described in Deeds; *Woods* lotted off distinctly and according to a regular plan; *Roads* laid out, &c., &c. Distinct and accurate Plans of Farms furnished, with the buildings thereon, of any size, and with a scale of feet attached, to accompany the Farm Book, so that the land may be laid out in a winter evening.

Areas warranted accurate within almost any degree of exactness, and the Variation of the Compass given, so that the lines can be run again. Apply to

Henry D. Thoreau

Facsimile of a Handbill announcing Thoreau's availability as a surveyor, circa 1850.

surveying technology. In fact, the use of electronics and computers in surveying is largely an offshoot of what were, initially, military reconnaissance and mapping applications.

Nonmilitary needs for the inventory and management of natural resources, such as surface water and timberland, have also been a catalyst for advancements in surveying. And the increasing use of aerial photography, GNSS, and photogrammetric surveying is attributable to military as well as peacetime needs for large-scale and accurate surveys.

In the 1980s, the application of space-age technology to surveying practice began to accelerate rapidly, in what may be characterized as a technological revolution. Electronic instruments for distance and angular measurement, automatic data-recording devices, microprocessors for data reduction and computer mapping, laser-leveling devices, remote sensing and surveying of the earth by satellite photographs, and GNSS have all become a part of contemporary surveying practice.

But for now and for many years to come, the study of surveying must begin with the application of traditional instruments, field methods, and computational procedures. These are still in use today. In any case, an understanding of traditional methods using the steel tape, the level and level rod, the transit, and the handheld electronic calculator will provide a solid foundation for keeping up with the latest technological developments in the surveying profession.

1-5 THE PROFESSION OF SURVEYING

A profession may be defined simply as a career activity that requires specialized training in a particular discipline or subject matter. A "professional" must acquire knowledge and skill beyond those of the craftsperson. For the so-called learned professions, such as medicine and law, an academic training comprising many years of college education is generally required. Engineering, engineering technology, and surveying are also learned professional disciplines, although the extent of required college preparation is generally less than that for medicine or law.

Professionals in any discipline must follow a code of ethical conduct that places regard for the safety, health, and welfare of the public above and beyond monetary considerations.

Surveying has long been associated with the profession of civil engineering. The planning, design, and construction of buildings and public-works facilities depend so heavily upon surveying activities that civil engineers and technicians, architects, and construction managers have always had to be skilled and knowledgeable in surveying principles and methods. And they will still have to be so in the future. But in recent years, surveying has emerged as an independent professional discipline, and the requirements for an appropriate college education in surveying are gradually increasing in the United States.

The Licensed Professional Land Surveyor

In addition to the requirement for specialized training, one of the hallmarks of a true profession is that it provides a unique service for people and for society as a whole. To protect the public from possible harm when supposedly "professional" services are offered by unqualified persons, a system of professional Licensure laws has been established in each state of the nation. These laws are meant to safeguard the public welfare by ensuring that only qualified persons engage in offering professional services to the public.

To engage in the practice of land surveying in any state, it is necessary to become licensed by the appropriate board of professional engineers and/or land surveyors in that state. (In most states, licensure requirements for engineers and surveyors are encompassed under the same law.) A surveyor is then licensed to offer his or her services to the public as a professional *land surveyor*, or *LS*, in that state. A person who practices land surveying without a valid license can be fined or even put in jail.

It is important to note that these Licensure laws apply only to the practice of land or boundary surveying, and not to construction surveying or any other activity that does not involve the marking or description of property lines. According to the New Jersey State Board of Professional Engineers and Land Surveyors, for example, the practice of land surveying includes "surveying of areas for their correct determination and description, and for conveyancing, and for the establishment or reestablishment of land boundaries and the plotting of lands and subdivisions thereof, and such topographic survey and land development as is incidental to the land survey."

Employment as a surveyor, then, does not depend upon acquiring a license, as long as the work does not involve setting or measuring the positions of property corners. Only a licensed LS, however, has the authority to sign and affix a seal to survey plats, plot plans, or other boundary descriptions. Most surveyors gain their first years of experience working under the supervision of a professional land surveyor. Anyone who intends to establish a private surveying firm must, of course, have an LS license.

The level of education and work experience required to become licensed as an LS varies from state to state. It is generally necessary to have several years of surveying experience and an appropriate college degree, but many states allow the applicant to substitute additional years of work experience for the formal educational requirements. In an effort to upgrade the status of the surveying profession, there is a trend in some states to make the bachelor's degree a definite and formal educational requirement.

Meeting the state requirements for education and experience qualifies the surveyor to sit for a written examination. The LS license is awarded upon the successful completion of the exam. Many states are adopting a uniform national LS examination. Most of the exam covers basic surveying principles, but a portion of it focuses upon local land-surveying practice and laws, which vary from state to state. A surveyor who becomes an LS in one state can, depending on state law, obtain a license in many other states by the principle known as *reciprocity*, without the need to take another written examination.

1-6 FIELD NOTES

All surveys *must be free from mistakes or blunders*. A potential source of major mistakes in surveying practice is the careless or improper recording of field notes. *Blunders in field records can and must be avoided.* The art of eliminating blunders is one of the most important elements in surveying practice.

Naturally, a blunder in either a boundary or a layout survey may result in high costs for altering, or removing and rebuilding, finished construction. One of the most important rules for avoiding costly blunders in surveying work is to be neat, thorough, and accurate in recording the results of field measurements, sketches, and related observations. Also, the quality and appearance of the field notes are a direct reflection of the entire surveying effort.

The proper taking of field notes, then, is a very important skill for the surveyor, one that cannot be overemphasized. It may sound like a trivial task to an inexperienced surveying technician or student, but it generally is one of the more elusive skills for the beginner. It takes much practice, patience, and concentration to be able to write legible notes and to record meaningful sketches in a handheld notebook, especially if the weather conditions are not the best.

It may seem easier to quickly jot down some figures and rough sketches on a scrap of paper in the field and, later on or the next day, in the comfort of the office, to copy the information neatly into a notebook. *But this is just what must be avoided!* Not only is the copying of notes a waste of valuable time but also it increases the chance for blunders to occur. A legitimate set of survey field notes must contain the original data that were *recorded at the time and place of measurement.* (Sometimes, though, certain data may be copied from one set of notes for use in another survey, but the copied notes must be clearly marked as such.)

A survey party or crew might include three or four members, although two-person crews are more common with the use of electronic equipment. Even one-man crews are now possible with robotic or reflectorless total station instruments. Generally, one member of the field crew, usually called the *party chief,* is responsible for coordinating the survey and for recording the field notes.

An experienced party chief fully appreciates the need for neat, accurate, and thorough field notes. The notes are later used as the basis for office computations and plat or map preparation, often by a technician or engineer who was not at the project site during the survey. The notes obviously must be in a legible and organized form that allows for a clear and definite interpretation.

Often, field notes from one job are referred to, months or years later, in reference to a new job in the same vicinity. If the data were not properly recorded at the time of survey, it is most unlikely that the party chief or other crew members would remember the important facts and figures. And once in a while, the surveyor must present field notes in court, if, for example, there is a dispute over property lines. Obviously, incomplete, illegible, altered, copied, or otherwise improper field notes would not be suitable, or even acceptable, as legal evidence.

Field Notebooks

Most surveyors use a pocket-size, bound field notebook. These surveying field books have appropriate column and grid lines to guide the organized recording of measurements. Field notes must be taken in a consistent and orderly form, as illustrated in Figure 5-23c; other illustrations of typical field book records for distance and angular measurements are presented in appropriate sections of the textbook.

Some surveyors prefer to use small loose-leaf notebooks (particularly for relatively small surveys) so that the field records can be removed and kept in a single file folder for that particular job. A few surveyors may even use a pad and clipboard. The use of loose-leaf notebooks or pads may present problems, though, with respect to lost sheets or to validity as evidence in court (since "cooked-up" notes can easily be inserted into the record).

Rules for Field Notes

1. Record all field data carefully in a field book *at the moment they are determined.* The note keeper must never allow any member of the field party to call out numbers faster than they can be accurately and neatly written down.

2. All data should be checked at the time they are recorded. If possible, two members of the field crew should take the same reading independently. The note keeper should call out the recorded number so that the field party can hear it for verification.

3. An incorrect entry of *measured data* should be neatly lined out and the correct number entered next to or above it. This is particularly important if the notes ever have to be used in court as legal evidence.

4. Field notes should not be altered, and even data that are crossed out should still remain legible. Some surveyors will erase mistakes in descriptions or numerical computations (but not measurements) and neatly rewrite the correct information. In general, though, it is best *never to erase a field book entry.*

5. Original field records should never be destroyed, even if they are copied for one reason or another. *It is unpardonable to lose a field book.*

6. A well-sharpened medium-hard (2H to 4H) pencil should be used for all field notes. All entries should be neatly printed.

7. Sketches should be clearly labeled, including the approximate north direction. Do not crowd sketches together on a page. Although not drawn to scale, freehand sketches should be proportional to what is observed in the field. When possible, use a straightedge and circle template.

8. Show the word VOID on the top of pages that, for one reason or another, are invalid; put a diagonal line across the page. Show the word COPY on the top of copied pages.

9. The field book should contain the name, address, and phone number of the owner, in ink, on the cover. At least one page at the front of the book is reserved for a table of contents. Pages should be numbered throughout the field book.

10. Each new survey should begin on a new page. The left-hand pages of the book generally are used for columns of numerical data. The right-hand pages generally are used for sketches and notes.

11. For each day of work, the project name, location, and date should be recorded in the upper corner of the right-hand page. The names of the crew members and their duties should also be recorded.

12. It is good practice to record the instrument type and serial number, as well as the weather conditions on the day of the survey. This information can be helpful when it is necessary to adjust for instrumental or natural errors or to judge the accuracy of the survey.

FIGURE 1-15. Tripod Data Systems' Ranger data collector. (*Courtesy of Tripod Data Systems, Inc.*)

In summary, it is important to remember that good field notes must be neat and legible, complete and clear, and accurate. The quality of the field notes reflects the quality of the whole survey.

Electronic Data Collectors

Electronic desktop computer technology has added an entirely new dimension to the recording and processing of survey data. Electronic recording devices, such as the one shown in Figure 1-15, are used to automatically collect, store, and display the data acquired by the electronic surveying instruments to which they are attached. This helps to eliminate possible blunders that may occur when data are manually transcribed into a field book. Measurements can also be entered manually via the keyboard, as shown in Figure 1-16. These *data collectors*, as they are called, serve as a

FIGURE 1-16. One-person crew using a robotic instrument and data recorder. (*Courtesy Leica Geosystems, Inc.*)

FIGURE 1-17. An electronic field book that collects and stores information from surveying instruments; notes that identify stations can also be entered or displayed. The stored information can be "dumped" into an office computer for computations. (*Courtesy of Tripod Data Systems, Inc.*)

direct link between the electronic total station and the office computer used for data reduction. The reduced or processed data can then be automatically printed, and/or survey plats or maps can be plotted (see Figure 1-2b).

A so-called electronic field book is illustrated in Figure 1-17. Data can be stored directly from appropriate electronic survey instruments, and they can also be entered manually via the keyboard. In addition, descriptive notes or written text can be keyed in by the operator, displayed, and stored in this electronic device.

The use of data collectors and electronic field books will not completely replace the conventional field book. The surveyor must still make sketches and record descriptive observations that are not entered into the electronic record (e.g., "Station 5 in the NE corner of lot 27"). Also, as unlikely as it may be, there is a chance that the stored data can inadvertently be lost in a "puff of electronic smoke." Conventional field books, then, will be used by most surveyors for some time to come, at least to record backup information and field sketches.

1-7 GEOGRAPHIC INFORMATION SYSTEMS (GIS)

A geographic information system (GIS) is a configuration of computer hardware and software capable of storing, manipulating, analyzing, and displaying (mapping) a large amount and wide variety of geographically referenced data. It is a valuable tool in environmental projects, planning studies, infrastructure analysis, and public safety. It provides a rapid way of mapping, modeling, and analyzing all types of data. Locations for various features can be given

x, y, and z coordinates of longitude, latitude, and elevation. It is here, in the location of physical features, that the surveyor plays a key role. The database that makes up the GIS is constructed from the United States Geological Survey (USGS) maps, aerial photographs, and other sources of vector-based maps. These maps are developed from survey lines and measurements and "fit" to aerial images. Any quality GIS must be based upon data on geographic locations prepared to accuracy standards, which only the surveying profession can provide. In addition to location data, physical attributes that describe various characteristics of the network components and other geographical features are included as part of the database stored in the GIS.

One of the key features of a GIS is its ability to layer several kinds of information on top of each other, at the same location. The layers can be viewed as a set of "transparencies" that can be depicted individually or in combination. For example, one layer could simply be a street map. Another layer could depict property boundaries. Yet another layer could show various land uses. These layers can be viewed separately or together, with the dwellings superimposed on the street map. Multiple layers can be superimposed, and the GIS user can manipulate the order in which they appear. A set of GIS layers is depicted schematically in Figure 1-18.

In a GIS, all objects shown on a map (features) can have information associated with them (attributes). In a municipal taxation map, for example, the individual lots and neighborhoods are the features. The number of dwellings, type of land use, the taxes paid, and the assessed value are some of the attributes associated with the corresponding features. Each type of feature can be stored and displayed as a layer. Clicking on a particular feature will display its unique attributes.

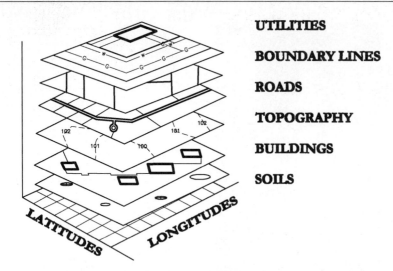

UTILITIES

BOUNDARY LINES

ROADS

TOPOGRAPHY

BUILDINGS

SOILS

GIS: GEOGRAPHICAL INFORMATION SYSTEMS

FIGURE 1-18. Schematic illustration of mapping layers used in GIS technology.

Questions for Review

1. Give a brief definition of surveying and describe its two fundamental purposes.

2. Briefly describe why surveying may be characterized as both an art and a science.

3. Why is surveying an important technical discipline?

4. Define and briefly discuss the terms *vertical* and *horizontal*.

5. What is a plumb line?

6. Is a horizontal distance a perfectly straight line? Why?

7. What is meant by the term *elevation*?

8. What is meant by the term *leveling*?

9. What surveying instruments are used to measure angles?

10. What is the basic assumption for plane surveying?

11. How does geodetic surveying differ from plane surveying? Under what circumstances is it necessary to conduct a geodetic survey?

12. Give a brief description of the following types of surveys: property survey, topographic survey, construction survey, control survey, and route survey. List six other types of specific surveying applications.

13. Briefly outline the historical development of surveying.

14. Is surveying an independent profession? Why?

15. What is the basic purpose of statewide professional licensure laws?

16. Is licensure as an LS necessary for all types of surveying work? Explain.

17. Contact the board of examiners that has jurisdiction over the practice of surveying in your state. Find out what the education and experience requirements are for admission to the LS examination.

18. Why is the proper recording of field notes a very important part of surveying practice?

19. What is one of the most important rules with regard to survey field notes? Why is it so important? List three other important rules.

20. Give two disadvantages of using loose-leaf notebooks for recording surveying data.

21. What general information should a field book contain?

22. What is the basic advantage of using a data collector or an electronic field book for recording surveying measurements? Will these devices completely replace conventional field books?

23. Explain how GIS helps communities plan for the future.

24. Explain the difference between a "feature" and an "attribute" in a GIS.

CHAPTER TWO

MEASUREMENTS AND COMPUTATIONS

CHAPTER OUTLINE

Measurement of distances and angles is the essence of surveying. One of the purposes of this chapter is to discuss the appropriate units of measure for those, and for other related quantities (such as area and volume). Surveyors in the United States must now be able to work with both U.S. Customary units and metric units.

Computation (or data reduction) is also an essential part of surveying; the surveyor must understand the concept of significant figures in the computed, as well as in the measured, quantities. These subjects, as well as the use of modern tools for computation, are discussed in this chapter. We will also discuss the basic types of mistakes and errors that a surveyor must eliminate or minimize in field work. And because no measurement is perfect, we must clarify the meaning and use of the terms *accuracy* and *precision*.

2-1 UNITS OF MEASUREMENT

Most countries of the world use SI metric units of measurement; SI stands for "Système International." In the United States, a gradual transition from the English or U.S. Customary units to SI units is still in progress. This transition will have a continuing impact on surveying practice. Surveyors in the United States must be able to work in both systems and readily convert from one to the other.

Most measurements and computations in surveying are related to the determination of angles (or directions), distance, area, and volume. The appropriate units of measure for these quantities are discussed here briefly.

Angles

An *angle* is simply a figure formed by the intersection of two lines. It may also be viewed as being generated by the rotation of a line about a point, from an initial position to a terminal position. The point of rotation is called the *vertex* of the angle. Angular measurement is concerned with the *amount of rotation* or the space between the initial and terminal positions of the line.

In surveying, of course, the lines do not actually rotate—they are defined by fixed points on or near the ground. It is the *line of sight* of a transit or theodolite that is rotated about a vertical (or horizontal) axis, located at the vertex of the angle being measured. Angles must be identified properly and labeled clearly, as illustrated in Figure 2-1, to avoid confusion.

Degrees, Minutes, and Seconds   There are several systems of angular measurement. The most common is the *sexagesimal system*, in which a complete rotation of a line (or a circle) is divided into 360 *degrees of arc*. In this system, 1 degree is divided into 60 *minutes*, and 1 minute is further divided into 60 *seconds* of arc.

The symbols for degrees, minutes, and seconds are °, ', and ", respectively. Some theodolites can measure an angle as small as 1 second of arc. An angle measured and expressed to the nearest second would, for example, be written as 35° 17' 46" (35 degrees, 17 minutes, 46 seconds). A *right angle*,

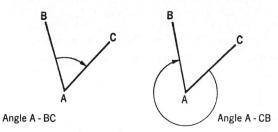

Angle A - BC   Angle A - CB

FIGURE 2-1. The designation *A-BC* or *A-CB* shows which of the two angles at point *A* is being measured or referred to. Clockwise rotation is generally assumed. To simply write "angle *A*" is usually not sufficient.

the space between two *perpendicular* lines, is equal to exactly 90° 00′ 00″.

If two angles such as 35° 17′ 46″ and 25° 47′ 36″ are to be added together, the degrees, minutes, and seconds are first combined separately, resulting in 60° 64′ 82″. But this must be converted to 61° 05′ 22″ because 82″ = 01′ 22″ and 65′ = 1° 05′. When subtracting angles, it may be necessary to first "borrow" 60 minutes from a degree and 60 seconds from a minute. For example, to subtract 35° 17′ 46″ from 90° 00′ 00″, we must write

$$\begin{array}{r} 89°\,59′\,60″ \\ -35°\,17′\,46″ \\ \hline 54°\,42′\,14″ \end{array}$$

Some handheld calculators accept angular values expressed directly in degrees, minutes, and seconds. With many calculators, however, it is necessary to convert degrees, minutes, and seconds to degrees and decimal parts of a degree, or vice versa. For example, an angle of 35° 30′ is equivalent to 35.5°, since 30′/60′ = 0.5°. Likewise, an angle of 142.125° is equivalent to 142° 07′ 30″, since 0.125° = 0.125 × 60′ = 7.5′ and 0.5 = 0.5′ × 60″ = 30″.

Grads   The *centesimal system* of angular measurement is used in some countries. Here, a complete rotation is divided into 400 grades, or *grads*, written as 400^g. The grad is subdivided into 100 parts called *centigrads* (1^g = 100^c), and the centigrad is further subdivided into *centi-centigrads* (1^c = 100^{cc}). A right angle (90°) is equivalent to 100^g. For an angle expressed as 139.4325^g, the first two digits after the decimal point are centigrads (0.43^g = 43^c), and the second pair of digits represents centi-centigrads (0.0025^g = 25^{cc}).

Modern scientific handheld calculators can work with angles expressed in degrees or grads; the mode of angle measurement is usually displayed by the calculator as DEG or GRAD. It is most important, of course, to preset the appropriate mode of angle when using the calculator for computations. For conversions, 1^g = 0.9°.

Another mode of angular measurement programmed into most calculators is the *radian*, or *rad*. By definition, one radian is equivalent to the angle formed between two radii in a circle, when the arc length between the radii is the same as the radius. Since the circumference of a circle is equal to $2\pi R$ (see Section 3-2), there must be 2π (about 2 × 3.14 = 6.28) rad in a circle. Therefore, 6.28 rad = 360° and 1 rad = 57.3°. Radians are used primarily in mathematical formulas and certain surveying computations, but not in field work.

There are other systems for angular measurement that find use in astronomy, navigation, and military applications. In astronomical observations, for example, angles may be measured in terms of hours, minutes, and seconds of time (as a function of the rotation of the earth). This is of significance to the surveyor when "shooting" the sun, or the North Star, and making measurements to determine astronomical north. For military use, the mil is used, where one full circumference is equal to 6400 mils.

Distance

In the U.S. Customary system, the basic unit for distance or length is the *foot*, abbreviated as *ft*. A foot is divided into inches and fractions of an inch (1 ft = 12 in), but when the U.S. Customary system is applied in surveying practice, decimal fractions of a foot are typically used instead of inches and fractions of an inch. A distance of 75 ft 3 in, for example, would be expressed by a surveyor as 75.25 ft, since 3 in = 0.25 ft. (There is a distinction between the *U.S. Survey foot* and the *international foot*, discussed below.)

In the international or SI system of units, the basic unit of length or distance is the *meter*, abbreviated as *m*. Divisions of the meter include the *decimeter* (dm), which equals 0.1 m, the *centimeter* (cm), which equals 0.01 m, and the *millimeter* (mm), which equals 0.001 m. Decimal fractions of a meter are typically applied in surveying practice, rather than the units of decimeters and centimeters. For example, a distance would be expressed as 26.75 m rather than 27 m 75 cm. Relatively large distances are typically expressed in units of *kilometers*, abbreviated as km (1 km = 1000 m). A distance of 123,400 m, for example, may be expressed as 123.4 km (see Appendix B on units and conversions).

The international meter was originally defined in 1791 by the French Academy of Sciences as being equivalent to one ten-millionth (1/10,000,000) of the distance from the Earth's equator to the North Pole. With improvements in technology, the definition of the meter has evolved over time. In 1983, the meter was officially defined by scientists to be the distance traveled by light in a vacuum in 1/299,792,458 second; this provides a very precise, constant, and universal standard of length for scientists as well as surveyors.

In the United States, the SI system of units is mandatory only for the design of federal government facilities and for geodetic surveys conducted by federal agencies such as the National Geodetic Survey. Many states also use the SI system for highway design and construction layout, but by and large, switching from Customary units to SI units is a voluntary process by surveying and mapping practitioners in the U.S. Because of this, it is often necessary for surveyors to convert distances and coordinates from one system of units to another.

Originally, the conversion relationship between the foot and the international meter was 1 ft = 1200/3937 m = 0.03048006096 m. That is called the U.S. Survey foot. In 1959, the relationship was redefined to be 1 ft = 0.3048 m (exactly). That is called the international foot. The difference between the two standards is very small (about 2 parts per million or 8 inches in 60 miles), and is of little or no consequence for ordinary plane surveys. Although this textbook is primarily concerned with plane surveying methods, it is important for students to be aware of these refinements in standards of linear measure.

They must be taken into account when making unit conversions related to the coordinates and elevations of points in horizontal and vertical control surveys.

One of the disadvantages of the U.S. Customary system of units is the wide variety of terms used for linear measure. The *Gunter's chain*, for example, has long been used as a unit of linear measure for land surveys in the United States. One chain is equivalent to 66 ft. One quarter of a chain is called a *rod, perch,* or *pole*; each is equivalent to 16.5 ft. The chain contains exactly 100 *links*.

In the past, the standard width of public roads was set at 2 rd, or 33 ft. Many old deeds state the distances of land boundaries in terms of chains and its fractions, and the entire U.S. Public Land Survey is based on Gunter's chain (see Section 8-1). And in the southwest part of the United States, another unit, called the vara (equivalent to about 33 in), was used in many past surveys.

Following are the relationships among several units of distance in the U.S. Customary system. (These, along with other metric relationships and conversions, are also tabulated in Appendix B for easy reference.)

1 foot (ft) = 12 inches (in.)

1 yard (yd) = 3 feet

1 mile (mi) = 5280 feet = 80 chains (ch)

1 chain = 66 feet

1 rod (rd) = 0.25 chain = 16.5 feet

1 link (lk) = 0.01 chain = 7.92 inches = 0.66 feet

Metric Prefixes   In the SI metric system, certain prefixes are used along with the meter to define different lengths. For example, the prefix *kilo* stands for 1000 and the prefix *milli* stands for 1/1000, or 0.001. The following SI relationships are useful in surveying practice:

1 kilometer (km) = 1000 meters (m)

1 millimeter (mm) = 0.001 meter

1 centimeter (cm) = 0.01 meter

1 decimeter (dm) = 0.1 meter

1 m = 10 dm = 100 cm = 1000 mm

Area

The unit for measuring area, which expresses the amount of two-dimensional space encompassed within the boundary of a closed figure or shape, is derived from the basic unit of length. In the U.S. Customary system, this is the square foot (sq ft or ft²). For land areas, the more common U.S. term for area is the *acre* (ac), where 1 ac = 43,560 ft².

An acre is also equivalent to 10 sq ch, that is, the area encompassed in a rectangle that is 1 ch wide and 10 ch long (66 ft × 660 ft = 43,560 ft²). Very large areas are generally expressed in terms of square miles (sq mi or mi²). The square yard (sq yd or yd²) may be used to express areas for earthwork computations.

In SI metric units, the basic unit for area is the square meter (m²). Large land areas may be expressed in terms of either square kilometers (sq km or km²) or by hectares (ha), where 1 ha is equivalent to 10,000 m². Another metric unit

for area is the *are*, where 1 are = 100 m². The following is a summary of the relationships pertaining to area:

1 square mile (mi²) = 640 acres (ac)

1 acre = 10 square chains (sq ch) = 43,560 square feet (ft²)

1 square yard (yd²) = 3 ft × 3 ft = 9 square feet (ft²)

1 hectare (ha) = 100 ares = 10,000 square meters (m²)

1 square kilometer (km²) = 100 hectares = 1,000,000 square meters (m²)

The following approximate conversions are useful in surveying applications:

1 km² = 0.386 mi²

1 ha = 2.47 ac

1 m² = 1.2 yd² = 10.76 ft²

In Figure 2-2, the relationship between the acre and the hectare is shown to scale. For surveyors in the United States, it is important to "think metric," and to develop an ability to quickly visualize such relationships between the two systems of units. It is better to remember approximate relationships between U.S. and SI units; the exact conversions can always be looked up in a table.

Volume

The U.S. Customary unit of measure for the volume of a solid is *cubic feet* (ft³), or, more often in surveying, *cubic yards* (yd³). Volume is also expressed in terms of *cubic meters* (m³) in the SI system. Measurement and computation of earthwork volumes to determine the amount of excavation (cut) and embankment (fill) needed for a roadway or site development project constitute a common surveying task. (When the expression "yards" of excavation or fill is used, it really means cubic yards.) It is important to note

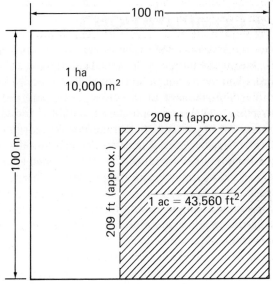

FIGURE 2-2. Think metric! There are roughly 2.5 ac in 1 ha of area.

that $1 \text{ yd}^3 = 3 \text{ ft} \times 3 \text{ ft} \times 3 \text{ ft} = 27 \text{ ft}^3$. Many beginning students make the mistake of using 9 as a volume conversion factor from yards to cubic feet. Formulas for computation of volumes are given in Section 3-1.

Conversion to SI Metric

In 1976 the U.S. Geological Survey (USGS) began to produce topographic maps in SI units, and recently, the U.S. Bureau of Reclamation used SI metric lengths, areas, and volumes when it advertised for bids on a major construction project. But the SI conversion recommendations are not yet being followed by all public agencies or private surveyors.

There is still some resistance to the SI changeover by many professional surveyors, as well as by some people in the construction trades and legal and real estate professions. Because past surveys have been done using conventional U.S. units, that system can never really be completely abandoned.

Example 2-1
Convert an area of 125.55 ac to an equivalent area expressed in hectares.

Solution

$$125.55 \text{ ac} \times \frac{1 \text{ ha}}{2.471 \text{ ac}} = \frac{125.55}{2.471} \frac{\text{ac} \times \text{ha}}{\text{ac}} = 50.81 \text{ ha}$$

Note that because 1 ha = 2.471 ac, the ratio of 1 ha/2.471 ac is equal to 1 or unity. All conversions can be done by setting up appropriate ratios like this and then multiplying by the given value. Also, the units of acres in the numerator and denominator cancel out, leaving the desired unit of hectares. By writing out the dimensions like this and canceling, we can avoid mistakes such as multiplying acres by 2.471 (when we really must divide) to get hectares.

The answer to this problem, 50.81 ha, was *rounded off* from the answer displayed by an electronic calculator; rounding off is discussed further in the next section.

2-2 COMPUTATIONS

Surveying practice involves both field work and office work. Measurements are made in the field, and the data are recorded in a field book and/or stored electronically. Usually, the data are used in the office to prepare a deed description, a plat, or a topo map; to establish locations (coordinates) of points; to determine land area; or to estimate earthwork volume. The data must first be converted into a form that will be suitable for the intended application. This involves mathematical computations in a process called *data reduction*.

In addition to presenting the fundamentals of surveying field practice, a primary purpose of this book is to introduce some of the basic computational methods for surveying data reduction. Specific applications are covered throughout the chapters of Parts 2 and 3. The objective of this particular section is to lay the foundation for accurate computation and problem solving by the beginning student.

Tools for Computation

Modern surveying computations are done with the aid of handheld electronic calculators or with digital computers. Desktop computers and handheld programmable calculators are readily available at reasonable prices. To remain competitive, the professional surveyor must make efficient use of these computational tools. The biggest difficulty is usually choosing from among the wide variety of hardware (calculators and computers) and software (programs or internal instructions for the hardware) that are on the market.

Calculators In addition to the four basic arithmetic functions $(+, -, \times, \div)$, the *scientific calculator* includes keys for trigonometric (trig) and inverse trig functions [sin (x), cos (x), tan (x)]; natural and common logarithmic (log) functions [ln (x) and log (x)]; exponential functions (e^x, y^x); square root; and several other functions and constants. It is expected that the beginning surveying student will own or have access to a scientific calculator rather than to the simpler "four-function" calculator.

A wide variety of handheld scientific calculators is available. The algebraic-entry type allows data to be entered just as they would be written in an algebraic expression. For example, to subtract 5 from 9, the data are entered simply as $9 - 5 =$, and the answer 4 is displayed immediately after the equal $(=)$ key is pressed. But in the RPN (reverse polish notation) type of calculator, there is no equal key. The 9 key is pressed first and then a key marked ENTER is pressed, followed by the 5. Finally, the minus $(-)$ key is pressed and the answer 4 is displayed.

Use of the algebraic-entry type of calculator may seem more natural than the RPN type, but in many instances the RPN type uses fewer keystrokes to solve problems and, in a short time, a person becomes accustomed to its use. The beginning student should experiment with both types before purchasing a calculator.

Most scientific calculators have one or more memory registers and some are actually programmable. With a handheld programmable calculator, it is possible to set up a sequential set of instructions for computation that the machine will "remember." After the program has been stored, keying in the data in the proper order is sufficient to obtain the problem solution.

Some programmable calculators are available with specialized surveying programs or Application Pacs, comprising plug-in modules or magnetic cards on which the programs are stored. These kinds of programming packages are sometimes referred to as *canned software*. The calculators can be used in the field or can be connected to printers and other peripheral devices in the office, including a larger computer.

Computers The development of high-speed personal computers has provided the surveyor with a powerful office tool for data reduction, plotting, and mapping.

Programs and data are stored magnetically in memory in the form of binary digits (zeros or ones). Each binary digit, or bit, is represented by the direction of magnetization at the bit location on a tiny integrated circuit chip. Numbers entered in the more familiar decimal system, which uses digits from 0 to 9, are converted into the binary number system by the computer. Letters of the alphabet are also converted into a coded sequence of binary digits.

The *central processing unit* (CPU) of a computer includes a master control unit, an arithmetic logic unit, and an input-output (I/O) controller. Like memory, the CPU is contained on small integrated circuit chips inside the computer case. These miniaturized CPUs are also called microprocessors. In microprocessor systems, memory may be in the form of random access memory (RAM) or read-only memory (ROM). The ROM is used to store operating systems (programs that only coordinate or direct the interactions among the various computer units), as well as fixed program subroutines, common mathematical functions, and constants like π. ROM data can only be read out, not entered, and they are a permanent part of the computer system.

In RAM, new data can be either entered into or read out of the unit. RAM is used to store new operating programs and the data used in those programs. Memory retrieval in RAM is faster than in ROM, but information stored in RAM is not permanent. When the computer is turned off, the data in RAM are lost.

Several high-level programming languages are used to give instructions to the computer. A computer program comprises a logical procedure for solving a particular problem, called an algorithm. The algorithm is generally written out as a series of individual steps or program statements, expressed in one of the high-level languages. These statements are translated internally into machine language statements and ultimately into binary numbers. The computer "understands" these statements and carries out the given instructions at lightning speed.

In addition to performing computations for data reduction and problem solving, computers can display images graphically. In fact, the computer can transmit data and control a plotting machine that will produce a finished plat or map. This is often referred to as computer-aided drafting (CAD). An example of a CAD drawing is shown in Figure 8-9.

Electronic calculators and desktop computers are powerful, high-speed computational aids. They can significantly improve efficiency and productivity in surveying practice. But it is still necessary for the user of this equipment to have a firm grasp of the underlying surveying concepts and computational procedures.

In fact, it would be very difficult to interpret and understand the instruction manuals for commercially available software without having first done the computations manually, that is, by solving the appropriate formulas step by step. It is also important to develop a sense of proportion and judgment with regard to the quantities that are measured and computed before relying completely on the output of a programmed calculator or desktop computer.

Significant Figures

A measured distance or angle is never exact; the "true" or actual value cannot be determined primarily because there is no perfect measuring instrument. The closeness of the observed value to the true value depends upon the quality of the measuring instrument and the care taken by the surveyor when making the measurement.

For example, a measured distance might be estimated roughly as 80 ft "by eye," 75 ft by counting footsteps or paces, or 75.2 ft with a steel tape graduated in feet. With a surveyor's tape graduated in feet, tenths, and hundredths of a foot, the same distance may be observed to be 75.27 ft. With a little more care, a distance of 75.275 ft may be measured with the same tape. With a finer measuring device, perhaps 75.2752 ft could be measured. But an exact measurement of the true distance can never be obtained.

The number of *significant figures* in a measured quantity is the number of sure or certain digits plus one estimated digit. This is a function primarily of the least count or graduation of the measuring instrument. For example, with a steel tape graduated only in increments of feet, we can be certain of the foot value, like 75, but we can only estimate the one-tenth point.

An observed distance of 75.2 ft has three significant figures. It would be incorrect to report the distance as 75.200 ft (which has five significant figures) because that would imply a greater degree of exactness than can be obtained with the measuring instrument. As illustrated in Figure 2-3,

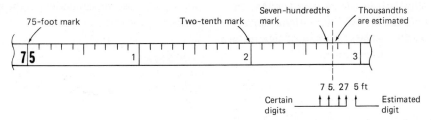

FIGURE 2-3. Because the smallest interval on the steel tape is one-hundredth of a foot, a thousandth of a foot (the third decimal place) must be an estimated digit. (In the United States, most surveyor's tapes are graduated in decimals of a foot—not in feet, inches, and fractions of an inch.)

the observed distance of 75.275 ft using a tape graduated to hundredths of a foot has four certain digits and one estimated digit; that number has five significant figures.

Rules   As mentioned earlier, the number 75.200 has five significant figures. In general, zeros placed at the end of a decimal number are counted as significant. Zeros between other significant digits are also counted as significant. For example, 17.08 has four significant figures and 150.005 has six. But zeros just to the right of the decimal in numbers smaller than unity (1) are not significant. For example, the number 0.000123 has only three significant figures as does the number 0.0123. Also, trailing zeros to the right of the digits in a number written without a decimal are generally not significant.

Here are some other examples of significant figures.

25.35	Four significant figures
0.002535	Four significant figures
12034	Five significant figures
120.00	Five significant figures
12,000	Two significant figures

If the trailing zeros in the preceding 12,000 were actually significant digits, we could write 12,000; the decimal would indicate that the number has five significant figures instead of two. But in cases like this, it is preferable to use scientific notation, that is, 1.2000×10^4, to indicate the significance of the trailing zeros.

When numbers representing measured quantities are added, the sum cannot be any more exact than any of the original numbers. The least number of decimals is generally the controlling factor. For example,

$$
\begin{array}{r}
4.52 \\
+23.4 \\
+468.321 \\
\hline
\text{Sum} = 496.241
\end{array}
$$

$\longrightarrow$ exact only to tenths—this controls

$\longrightarrow$ round off to 496.2, the nearest tenth

When subtracting one number from another, it is best first to round off to the same decimal place. For example, 123.4 minus 2.345 may be computed as $123.4 - 2.3 = 121.1$, to the nearest tenth.

The rule for multiplication (or division) is that the product (or quotient) should not have more significant figures than the number with the least amount of significant figures used in the problem. For example,

$$\frac{1.2345 \times 2.34 \times 3.4}{6.78 \times 7.890} = 0.18 \longrightarrow \text{rounded off to two significant figures}$$

The number 3.4, with two significant figures, controls here.

Rounding Off Numbers   When doing the preceding computation with a handheld calculator, the answer displayed is 0.1836028, with seven significant digits after the decimal. Many beginning students tend to report all computed results using as many significant figures as are displayed by their calculators. But this is often incorrect because such an answer may imply more exactness than is warranted or is even possible to be measured. Use of too many significant figures is usually a sign that the surveyor or technician is inexperienced and does not fully understand the nature of the measurement or of the computation being performed.

To round off 0.1836028 to two significant figures, we simply dropped the extra digits after the 0.18 in the original solution. In general, if the first extra digit is less than 5, we drop it along with any additional digits to the right. But, if the first extra digit is 5 or more, after we drop it we must add 1 to the last digit of our rounded solution. For example, 0.1836028 rounded off to three significant figures would be 0.184 because the first extra digit after the third is greater than 5. Some additional examples are as follows:

3456 becomes 3500 rounded off to two significant figures.

0.123 becomes 0.12 rounded off to two significant figures.

4567 becomes 4570 rounded off to three significant figures.

987.432 becomes 987 rounded off to three significant figures.

234.545 becomes 234.5 rounded off to four significant figures.

2-3 MISTAKES AND ERRORS

No measurement can be perfect or exact because of the physical limitations of the measuring instruments as well as limits in human perception. Even the finest and costliest surveying instruments cannot be manufactured or adjusted with absolute perfection. And there is a limit to how closely any surveyor can read a graduated scale, no matter how good his or her vision is.

The difference between a measured distance or angle and its true value may be due to mistakes and/or *errors*. These are two distinct terms. It is necessary to eliminate all mistakes and minimize all errors when conducting a survey of any type. All surveyors, and any user of surveying data, must have a clear understanding of the nature and sources of mistakes and errors.

Blunders

A blunder is a significant mistake caused by human error. It may also be called a gross error. Generally, it is due to the inattention or carelessness of the surveyor, and it usually results in a large difference between the observed or recorded quantity and the actual or true value. Blunders may also be caused by a lack of judgment or knowledge; this type of mistake can be avoided only by a thorough understanding of the principles of surveying. But even the most experienced of surveyors must take care to eliminate blunders due to occasional inattention to the work at hand.

A typical mistake or blunder is the misreading of a number on the surveying instrument itself. For example, the reading on a level rod may be taken as 4.90 when it actually was 3.90. Even when the number is read correctly and called out to the note keeper, it may be incorrectly recorded; a common mistake is to transpose the digits, for example writing 5.30 instead of 3.50. Also, the number may be placed in the wrong position in the field book or it may be incorrectly labeled. Following the rules of good note keeping (Section 1-6) will help to eliminate these types of blunders.

Mistakes may be caused by sighting on a wrong target with the transit when measuring an angle or by taping to an incorrect station. They may also be caused by omitting a vital piece of information, such as the fact that a certain measurement was made on a steep slope instead of on a horizontal surface. And when measuring a distance with a tape, there may be a miscount of the number of full tape lengths in the measurement. A really embarrassing blunder for a surveyor is to stake out the wrong lot on a block or even on the wrong street.

The possibilities for mistakes are almost endless. But they are only caused by occasional lapses of attention; they can and must be eliminated by careful checking of the work in progress. Unless they are negligible, or if two blunders happen to cancel each other (a rare occurrence), mistakes can be discovered at the time they are made. The surveyor must be continually alert and constantly examine and check the observed quantities to eliminate careless mistakes.

Systematic and Accidental Errors

An error is the difference between a measured quantity and its true value, caused by imperfection in the measuring instrument, by the method of measurement, by natural factors such as temperature, or by random variations in human observation. It is not a mistake due to carelessness. Errors can never be completely eliminated, but they can be minimized by using certain instruments and field procedures and by applying computed correction factors.

There are two basic types of errors: systematic errors and accidental errors. A surveyor must understand the distinction between these types of errors to be able to minimize them.

Systematic Errors   Repetitive errors that are caused by imperfections in the surveying equipment, by the specific method of observation, or by certain environmental factors, are systematic errors. They are also referred to as mechanical or cumulative errors.

Under the same conditions of measurement, systematic errors are constant in magnitude and direction or sign (either plus or minus). They usually have no tendency to cancel, and if corrections are not made, they can accumulate to cause significant differences between the measured and actual or true quantities. The surveyor must carefully consider the possible causes of systematic errors and take appropriate steps to minimize their effects on the results of the survey.

For example, suppose that a 30-m steel tape is the correct length at 20°C and that it is used in a survey when the outdoor air temperature is, say, 35°C. Because steel expands with increasing temperature, the tape will actually be longer than it was at 20°C. The surveyor must decide whether or not the error that will result is large enough to be important; this depends on the purpose and extent of the survey. If it is important, the surveyor must correct all the length measurements accordingly. If the tape was used several times in the course of measuring a single line, a seemingly small error in one tape length could have accumulated into a more significant overall error.

Measurements made with levels may be subject to various systematic errors. For example, the axis of the spirit bubble with which the instrument is leveled and the line of sight through the telescope may not be parallel as they should be. This will result in a constant error of vertical distance measurement unless the instrument is adjusted or certain field procedures are followed.

Transits, theodolites, and even electronic distance-measuring instruments (EDMIs) are also subject to systematic errors. The horizontal axis of rotation of the transit, for instance, may not be exactly perpendicular to the vertical axis. And changes in barometric air pressure may affect the electronic distance measuring (EDM) signal frequency, thereby causing an error in the recorded distance. Systematic errors related to the various pieces of surveying equipment are discussed in more detail in the appropriate sections of this book.

Accidental Errors   An *accidental* or *random error* is the difference between a true quantity and a measurement of that quantity that is free from blunders or *systematic errors.* Accidental errors always occur in every measurement. They are the relatively small, unavoidable errors in observation that are generally beyond the control of the surveyor. Greater skill coupled with better-quality surveying equipment and methods will, however, tend to reduce the magnitude and overall effects of accidental errors.

These random errors, as the name implies, are not constant in magnitude or direction (plus or minus). One measurement may be slightly larger and the very next reading of the instrument may be slightly smaller, but because the errors are not of equal size, they do not cancel out completely. Accidental errors follow the laws of chance and their analysis is based on the mathematical theory of statistics and probability.

One example of a source of accidental errors is the slight motion of a plumb-bob string, which occurs when using a tape to measure a distance. The tape is generally held above the ground and the plumb bob (simply a suspended weight on a string) is used to transfer the measurement from the ground to the tape.

It is impossible to keep the string line from swaying slightly, especially on a windy day. There will always be a difference, then, between the distance measured with the plumb bob and the actual, or true, distance. In a series of measurements to the same point, these differences will vary in size and direction. Sometimes the plumb bob will swing beyond the true point and sometimes it will swing short of the point.

Most Probable Value   If two or more measurements of the same quantity are made, usually different values are obtained due to random errors. As long as each measurement is equally reliable, the average value of the different measurements is taken to be the true or most probable value. The average, or arithmetic mean, is computed simply by summing all the individual measurements and then dividing the sum by the number of measurements. For example, if a distance was measured four times, resulting in values of 55.63, 55.78, 55.55, and 55.81 m, then the most probable value of the distance would be taken as $(55.63 + 55.78 + 55.55 + 55.81) \div 4 = 55.69$ m.

The 95 Percent Error   Using appropriate statistical formulas, it is possible to test and determine the probability of different ranges of random errors occurring for a variety of surveying instruments and procedures. The most probable error is that which has an equal chance (50 percent) of either being exceeded or not being exceeded in a particular measurement. It is sometimes designated as E_{50}.

In surveying, the 95 percent error, or E_{95}, is a useful criterion for rating survey methods. For example, suppose a distance of 100.00 ft is measured. If it is said that the 95 percent error in one taping operation, using a 100-ft tape, is ± 0.01 ft ($\pm$ is read as "plus or minus"), it means that the likelihood is 95 percent that the actual distance is within the range of 100.00 ± 0.01 ft. Likewise, there will remain a 5 percent chance that the error will exceed 0.01 ft. The E_{95} is sometimes called the maximum anticipated error, but as was just pointed out, there is still a 1-in-20 chance that it will be exceeded.

By using statistics and probability concepts in this manner, it is possible to rate surveying instruments and procedures with regard to anticipated or probable errors on the basis of data from surveys previously performed. With this information, a proper choice of instruments and procedures can be made when a future survey is planned. Generally, a survey should be planned so that 95 percent of the work will be acceptable because it is less expensive to redo 5 percent of the work than to attempt to reach perfection throughout.

The 95 percent error can be estimated from surveying data using the following formula from statistics:

$$E_{95} = 1.96 \times \sqrt{\frac{\Sigma (\Delta)^2}{n(n - 1)}} \tag{2-1}$$

where Σ = sigma, "the sum of"

$\quad \Delta$ = delta, the difference between each individual measurement and the average of n measurements

$\quad n$ = the number of measurements

Example 2-2

A distance was measured five times (by pacing) as follows: 75.3, 76.2, 75.7, 75.5, and 75.8 m. Compute the most probable distance and the 95 percent error of that procedure.

Solution

The most probable distance is the average distance. The average, or arithmetic mean, is computed as

$$\frac{7.53 + 76.2 + 75.7 + 75.5 + 75.8}{5} = 75.7 \text{ m}$$

The value of $\Sigma (\Delta^2)$ may be computed by taking the difference between each measurement and the average, squaring those differences, and summing:

$$(75.3 - 75.7)^2 = 0.16$$
$$(76.2 - 75.7)^2 = 0.25$$
$$(75.7 - 75.7)^2 = 0.00$$
$$(75.5 - 75.7)^2 = 0.04$$
$$(75.8 - 75.7)^2 = \underline{0.01}$$
$$\Sigma (\Delta)^2 = 0.46$$

From this and Equation 2-1, we get

$$E_{95} = 1.96 \times \sqrt{\frac{0.46}{5(5 - 1)}} = \pm 0.30 \text{ m}$$

We can now say that the maximum anticipated error from this survey procedure is ± 0.30 m and that we are 95 percent sure that the true distance is within the range of 75.7 ± 0.30 m.

How Accidental Errors Add Up   Consider the problem of measuring and marking a distance of 900 ft between two points using a 100-ft long steel tape. Assume that the maximum probable error for measuring 100 ft was determined to be ± 0.010 ft. What would be the maximum probable error for measuring the total distance of 900 ft with the same tape and the same procedure?

To measure the distance, we have to use the tape several times; there would be 9 separate measurements of 100 ft, each with a maximum probable error of ± 0.01 ft. It is tempting simply to say that the total error will be $9 \times (\pm 0.01) = \pm 0.09$ ft. But this would be incorrect. Because some of the errors would be plus and some would be minus, they would tend to cancel each other out. Of course, it would be very unlikely that the errors would completely cancel and so there will still be a remaining error at 900 ft.

A fundamental property of accidental or random errors is that they tend to accumulate, or add up, in proportion to the square *root* of the number of measurements in which they occur. (It is often assumed that the number of measurements is directly proportional to the length of a survey.) This relationship, called the law of compensation, can be expressed mathematically in the following equation:

$$E = E_1 \times \sqrt{n} \tag{2-2}$$

where E = the total error of n measurements

E_1 = the error for one measurement

n = the number of measurements

Applying Equation 2-2 to the preceding problem, we get

$$E = \pm 0.010 \sqrt{9} = \pm 0.010 \times 3 = \pm 0.030 \text{ ft}$$

In other words, we can expect the total accidental error when measuring a distance of 900 ft to be within a range of ± 0.030 ft, with a confidence of 95 percent. Of course, we do not know exactly what the error will be. And there is still a 5 percent chance that the error will exceed 0.030 ft.

It must be kept in mind that this type of analysis assumes that the series of measurements are made with the same instruments and procedures as for the single measurement for which the maximum probable error is known. Finer (and more expensive) instruments, along with better (and more time-consuming) procedures, can reduce the size of the maximum probable error for any measurement.

Overview of Mistakes and Errors The surveyor must constantly be aware of the possibilities for mistakes and errors in survey work. The following statements review the basic principles:

1. Blunders can, and must, be eliminated.
2. Systematic errors may accumulate to cause very large errors in the final results. They can be recognized only by an analysis of the principles inherent in the equipment and methods, and they must be eliminated by applying computed corrections or by changing the field procedure.
3. Accidental errors are always present, and they control the quality of the survey. They can be reduced at a higher cost by using better field equipment and more time-consuming field procedures.
4. Accidental errors of the same kind accumulate in proportion to the square root of the number of observations in which they are found. This rule makes it possible to rate past surveys and to select survey procedures for a desired quality of survey. The number of observations is proportional to the total distance of the survey.

2-4 ACCURACY AND PRECISION

Accuracy and precision are two distinctly different terms that are of importance in surveying. They require some discussion and clarification about their meaning and use.

Surveying measurements must be made with an appropriate degree of precision to provide a suitable level of accuracy for the problem at hand. In the preceding discussion of accidental errors of measurement, it was said that the maximum anticipated error could be reduced with the use of improved surveying instruments and procedures. This implies the possibility of different levels of precision and accuracy in survey work. What is the difference between accuracy and precision and how do we characterize the different levels?

Because no measurement is perfect, the quality of the results obtained must be characterized by some numerical standard of accuracy. *Accuracy* refers to the degree of perfection obtained in the measurement—in other words, how close the measurement is to the true value. (In this regard, we assume that all blunders have been eliminated and systematic errors have been corrected; the accuracy of a survey depends only on the size of the accidental errors.)

When the accuracy of a survey is to be improved or increased, we say that greater precision must be used. Precision, then, refers to the degree of perfection used in the instruments, methods, and observations—in other words, to the level of refinement and care of the survey. In summary,

Precision → Degree of perfection used in the survey

Accuracy → Degree of perfection obtained in the results

In a series of independent measurements of the same quantity, the closer each measurement is to the average value, the better is the precision. High precision is costly but is generally necessary for high accuracy. The essential art of surveying is the ability to obtain the data required, with a specified degree of accuracy, at the lowest cost. The specified degree of accuracy depends on the type and the purpose of the survey.

For example, a geodetic control survey requires much higher accuracy and, therefore, better precision in the instruments and work than does a preliminary topographic survey for a small building. Likewise, a construction survey for locating a bridge pier requires higher accuracy and precision than does a construction survey for a storm sewer.

Suppose that one surveyor measures a distance between two points and obtains a value of 750.1 ft. Another surveyor measures the same distance but obtains a value of 749.158 ft. The second surveyor obviously used greater precision. But if the true distance is known to be exactly 750.11 ft, the first measurement of 750.1 ft is obviously more accurate than the second. It would seem that there was a blunder or some systematic error in the second measurement. High precision, then, is not always a guarantee of high accuracy if blunders and systematic errors have not first been eliminated from the work.

To further clarify the distinction between accuracy and precision, again consider the measurement of a distance between two points. Suppose we know that the actual distance is exactly 300.00 m and that three different survey crews are to make the measurement using different instruments and methods. Each crew measures the distance five times. The results of their measurements are shown graphically in Figure 2-4.

The work of the first crew shows good precision but poor accuracy. The measurements are clustered together, but the average value of those measurements would be significantly different from the actual 300.00 m. The work of the

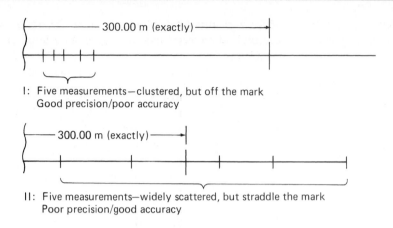

I: Five measurements—clustered, but off the mark
Good precision/poor accuracy

II: Five measurements—widely scattered, but straddle the mark
Poor precision/good accuracy

III: Five measurements—clustered close to the true value
Good precision/good accuracy

FIGURE 2-4. It is important to understand the difference between accuracy and precision in surveying measurements.

second crew shows poor precision because of the wide scatter of the measurement values. But the accuracy is good because the average of the data, which is the best estimate of the true value, will be pretty close to 300.00. Finally, the work of the third survey crew demonstrates both good precision and good accuracy. All their measurements are closely clustered around the actual, or true, distance.

Error of Closure and Relative Accuracy

The difference between a measured quantity and its true, or actual, value is called the *error of closure* or just *closure*. In some cases, the closure can be taken simply as the difference between two independent measurements. For example, suppose a distance from point A to point B is first determined to be 123.25 m. The line is measured a second time, perhaps from B to A, using the same instruments and methods. A distance of 123.19 m is obtained. The error of closure is simply $123.25 - 123.19 = 0.06$ m. It is due to accidental errors, as long as blunders have been eliminated and systematic errors corrected.

Suppose the actual distance was known to be 123.30 m from some other source, such as a previous governmental control survey. The closure would be determined as the difference between the average measured value and the known true value. In this example, the average measured value is $(123.25 + 123.19) \div 2 = 123.22$ m. The error of closure would be $123.30 - 123.22 = 0.08$ m.

Yet another way to determine closure, from a series of independent measurements of the same quantity, is to use the maximum anticipated error. For instance, in Example 2-2 we could say that the error of closure for the average distance of 75.7 m was 0.25 m. (But if we did know the true, or actual, distance from some other source, say 75.9 m, our closure would be taken as the difference between 75.9 and 75.7, or 0.2 m.)

Relative Accuracy   For horizontal distances, the ratio of the error of closure to the actual distance is called the *relative accuracy*. (In some other textbooks, it is also referred to as the *degree of accuracy*, *order of accuracy*, *accuracy ratio*, *relative precision*, or just plain *precision*. No matter what it is called, the concept is essentially the same.)

Relative accuracy is generally expressed as a ratio with unity as the first number or numerator. For example, if a distance of 500 ft were measured with a closure of 0.25 ft, we can say that the relative accuracy of that particular survey is 0.25 ft per 500 ft (0.25/500), or 1/2000. This is also written as 1:2000. Basically, this means that for every 2000 ft measured, there is an error of 1 ft. The relative accuracy of a survey can be compared with a specified allowable standard of accuracy to determine whether the results of the survey are acceptable.

Relative accuracy can be computed from the following formula:

$$\text{Relative accuracy} = 1: \frac{D}{C} \qquad (2\text{-}3)$$

where D = distance measured

C = error of closure

Example 2-3

A distance of 577.80 ft is measured by a surveying crew. The true distance is later found to be 577.98 ft from another source. What is the relative accuracy of the measurement?

Solution

The error of closure is

$$577.80 - 577.98 = -0.18 \text{ ft}$$

Using Equation 2-3, we get

$$\text{Relative accuracy} = \frac{1:577.80}{0.18} = 1:3200$$

Note that we used the absolute value of the closure (no minus sign) and that we rounded off the ratio (relative accuracy need not be computed with great precision). As we will discuss in Chapter 4, ordinary surveys with a steel tape give an accuracy of between 1:3000 and 1:5000.

A ratio with a large second number or denominator implies better accuracy than a ratio with a small number or denominator. For example, a relative accuracy of 1:6000 is better than that of 1:3000. In other words, an error of 1 ft will be expected when measuring a distance of 6000 ft, as compared with an error of 1 ft in half that distance. If a distance of 600 m was measured with a relative accuracy of 1:6000, we could expect an error of $\pm (1/6000)(600) = \pm 0.1$ m; if the same distance were measured with an accuracy of 1:3000, we could expect an error of $\pm (1/3000)(600) = \pm 0.2$ m.

As we have already discussed, accidental errors tend to increase in proportion to the square root of the distance measured (or the number of observations made) and not to the actual distance itself. Therefore, when the same *precision* (that is, equipment and care) is applied, the relative accuracy of a long survey will be better than that of a short survey. In Example 2-3, if the survey were four times as long, the estimated error of closure would be

$$0.18 \times \sqrt{4} = 0.36 \text{ ft}$$

and the relative accuracy would be

$$1:(4 \times 577.80)/0.36 = 1:6400$$

presumably twice as accurate.

In general, for a set of similar measurements, to double the accuracy of a particular survey, four times the number of original observations or measurements must be taken; to triple the relative accuracy, nine times as many observations must be made; and so on.

Distance measurements of very high precision, such as are made with certain EDMIs, may be characterized in terms of *parts per million* (ppm) of accuracy. For example, a relative accuracy of 5 ppm is equivalent to the ratio 5:1,000,000, or 1:200,000. In a distance of, say, 1 km, or 1000 m, an accuracy of 5 ppm would be caused by an error of 5 mm [i.e., 1:(1000 m/5 mm) = 1:(1,000,000 mm/5 mm) = 1:200,000].

Standards of Accuracy In the United States, allowable accuracies for control surveys have been specified by the Federal Geodetic Control Subcommittee. For many years these standards included three different levels, or *orders*: first, second, and third order, for both horizontal and vertical control surveys. The orders were further broken down into classes. Three new orders of accuracy were added in 1985 for GPS surveys: AA, A, and B. In 1998 the Federal Geodetic Control Subcommittee released new standards that used a term called *Relative Positional Accuracy*. This standard is independent of the method of survey and is based upon a 95 percent confidence level. Relative positional accuracy is defined as a value that represents the uncertainty of the location of a point in a survey relative to any other point in the same survey at a 95 percent confidence level. What this means is that if we measure a distance of 1000 ft with a stated reliability of plus or minus 0.10 ft at a 95 percent confidence level, we can be confident that a measurement of that line will be between 999.90 ft–1000.10 ft 95 out of 100 times.

The accuracy of a particular survey may be characterized according to the appropriate range of federal standards. A summary of the standards, as well as a comparison of the earlier standards to the current standards, is given in Table 2-1.

Choice of Survey Procedure The required relative accuracy for a survey may be specified by the surveyor's employer or client, or it may be established by experience and judgment. Sometimes the order of accuracy is specified. In any case, a maximum allowable closure can be determined for a particular survey. The surveyor should choose equipment and methods that have a rating or maximum anticipated error closely equal to that for maximum allowable closure. For traverse surveys (discussed in more

Table 2-1. Selected Federal Standards for Traverse Surveys

GPS Order	Traditional Surveys Order and Class	Relative Accuracy Required Between Points
Order AA		1 part in 100,000,000
Order A		1 part in 10,000,000
Order B		1 part in 1,000,000
	First Order	1 part in 100,000
	Second Order	
	Class I	1 part in 50,000
Order C	Class II	1 part in 20,000
	Third Order	
	Class I	1 part in 10,000
	Class II	1 part in 5000

detail in Chapter 7), the most convenient value to use for rating the survey is the E_{95} for 1000 ft.

Example 2-4

A horizontal control traverse survey is required to close with a 1:5000 accuracy. The total distance of the traverse is about 10,000 ft. What is the required rating or maximum anticipated error per 1000 ft for the survey method to be used?

Solution

In 10,000 ft, the maximum error of closure is 1/5000 × 10,000 = 2 ft.

On the basis of the law of compensation (Equation 2-2) and the fact that the number of measurements or observations is proportional to the length of a survey, we can write the following expression:

$$\frac{E_{95} \text{ for } 1000 \text{ ft}}{\sqrt{1000}} = \frac{2}{\sqrt{10\,000}}$$

from which we get

$$E_{95} \text{ for } 1000 \text{ ft} = \frac{2 \times \sqrt{1000}}{\sqrt{10\,000}} = \frac{2}{\sqrt{10}} = 0.63 \text{ ft}$$

From this, a survey procedure known to have a maximum anticipated error (E_{95}) equal to or less than 0.63 ft in 1000 ft would be chosen.

Check: $0.63 \times \sqrt{\dfrac{10\,000}{1000}} = 0.63 \times \sqrt{10} = 2 \text{ ft}$

Questions for Review

1. Briefly describe two different types of units for angular measurement.

2. What is meant by the phrase data reduction?

3. Name two basic types of handheld scientific calculators.

4. What do the following abbreviations stand for: CPU, RAM, ROM, CAD?

5. In a measured quantity, the number of certain digits plus one estimated digit is called the number of _____.

6. Is it good practice always to report all the digits displayed by a calculator in an answer to a problem? Why?

7. Define the term *blunder*, and give three typical examples in surveying.

8. Define the term *error* as it pertains to surveying work. How does it differ from a blunder?

9. What are the basic differences between a systematic error and an accidental error?

10. Indicate by A (accidental), S (systematic), or B (blunder) the type of error or mistake the following would cause:

    a. Swinging plumb bob while taping
    b. Using a repaired (spliced) tape
    c. Aiming the transit at the wrong point
    d. Recopying field data
    e. Surveying with a transit that is not level
    f. Reading a 9 for a 6
    g. Reading the transit scale without a magnifying glass
    h. Working in poor light
    i. Not aiming the transit carefully
    j. Not focusing the transit carefully

11. Indicate by an A, S, or B whether the following would cause accidental errors, systematic errors, or blunders:

    a. Using a level rod that is inaccurately graduated
    b. Having too long a sight distance between the level and level rod

    c. Carelessly centering the bubble of the spirit level in a level instrument when leveling
    d. Using a level instrument that is out of adjustment so that the line of sight is not horizontal when the bubble is centered
    e. Failing to check a reading
    f. Failing to correct for temperature when measurements are made with a steel tape on a very hot or cold day
    g. Failing to hold the level rod on the correct point
    h. Leveling when "heat waves" make it difficult to read the level rod
    i. Using the wrong end of the tape for measurement
    j. Working without glasses if you normally wear them

12. What is meant by the 95 percent error?

13. Accidental errors accumulate in proportion to the _____ of the _____.

14. What is the basic difference between accuracy and precision? Is good precision always a guarantee of good accuracy?

15. Show by a sketch of the distribution of several rifle shots on a bull's-eye target the following results: (a) both good precision and good accuracy, (b) poor precision but good accuracy, and (c) good precision but poor accuracy.

16. Define error of closure, and give three ways in which it might be determined.

17. Define relative accuracy, and give two examples of how it is expressed or written. Which of your examples represents better accuracy?

18. When the same precision is used, would the relative accuracy of a long survey be the same as, better than, or worse than the accuracy of a shorter survey? Why?

19. To double the accuracy of a particular survey, must the number of observations or measurements be halved,

doubled, or tripled? What must be done to triple the relative accuracy?

20. What does ppm refer to with respect to accuracy?

21. What is meant by standard of accuracy?

Practice Problems

1. Convert the following angles to decimal degree form:
   a. 35° 20′ (use two decimal places)
   b. 129° 35′ 15″ (use four decimal places)

2. Convert the following angles to decimal degree form:
   a. 00° 45′ (use two decimal places)
   b. 77° 23′ 49.5″ (use five decimal places)

3. Convert the following angles to degrees, minutes, and seconds:
   a. 45.75° (to the nearest minute)
   b. 123.1234° (to the nearest second)

4. Convert the following angles to degrees, minutes, and seconds:
   a. 86.65° (to the nearest minute)
   b. 27.54329° (to the nearest tenth of a second)

5. What is the sum of 25° 35′ and 45° 40′? Subtract 85° 56′ from 137° 32′.

6. What is the sum of 45° 35′ 45″ and 65° 50′ 22″? Subtract 45° 52′ 35″ from 107 °32′ 00″.

7. Convert the angles in Problem 1 to centesimal units.

8. Convert the angles in Problem 3 to centesimal units.

9. Convert the following angles to the sexagesimal system:
   a. 75^g
   b. 125.75^g
   c. 200.4575^g

10. Convert the following angles to the sexagesimal system:
   a. 23^g
   b. 75.245^g
   c. 150.7654^g

11. Convert the following distances, as indicated:
   a. 125.25 ft to meters
   b. 75.525 m to feet
   c. 35 ch 1 rd 10 lk to feet
   d. 2.75 mi to kilometers

12. Convert the following distances as indicated:
   a. 67.35 ft to meters
   b. 246.864 m to feet
   c. 75 ch 3 rds 20 lk to feet
   d. 1.23 mi to kilometers

13. Convert the following areas as indicated:
   a. 100,000 ft^2 to acres
   b. 5.75 ac to hectares
   c. 5.75 ha to acres

d. 1000 ac to square miles
   e. 3.5 mi^2 to square kilometers

14. Convert the following areas as indicated:
   a. 75,500 ft^2 to acres
   b. 10.5 ac to hectares
   c. 10.5 ha to acres
   d. 750 ac to square miles
   e. 5.3 mi^2 to square kilometers

15. Convert the following volumes as indicated:
   a. 270 ft^3 to cubic yards
   b. 100 yd^3 to cubic meters

16. Convert the following volumes as indicated:
   a. 500 ft^3 to cubic yards
   b. 150 yd^3 to cubic meters

17. How many significant figures are there in the following:
   a. 0.00123
   b. 1.00468
   c. 245.00
   d. 24,500
   e. 10.01
   f. 45.6
   g. 1200
   h. 1200
   i. 54.0
   j. 0.0987

18. How many significant figures are there in the following:
   a. 0.906
   b. 2.468
   c. 460.00
   d. 42,710
   e. 20.005
   f. 1.23
   g. 2400
   h. 4500
   i. 504.0
   j. 0.03570

19. Round off the sum of 105.4, 43.67, 0.975, and 34.55 to the appropriate number of decimal places.

20. Round off the sum of 0.8765, 1.23, 245.567, and 34.792 to the appropriate number of decimal places.

21. Express the product of 1.4685 × 3.58 to the proper number of significant figures.

22. Express the quotient of 34.67 ÷ 0.054 to the proper number of significant figures.

23. Round off the following numbers to the three significant figures: 357.631, 0.97531, 14,683, 34.55, and 10.087.

24. Round off the following numbers to three significant figures: 45.036, 245,501, 0.12345, 251.49, and 34.009.

25. A distance was taped six times with the following results: 246.45, 246.60, 246.53, 246.35, 246.39, and 246.55 ft. Compute the 95 percent error for that survey.

26. A distance was taped six times with the following results: 85.87, 86.03, 85.80, 85.95, 86.06, and 85.90 m. Compute the 95 percent error for that survey.

27. With reference to Problem 25, what would be the maximum anticipated error for a survey that was twice as long if the same precision was used?

28. With reference to Problem 26, what would be the maximum anticipated error for a survey that was three times as long if the same precision was used?

29. A distance of 345.75 ft is measured by a survey crew. The true distance is known to be 345.82 ft. What is the relative accuracy of the measurement?

30. A group of surveying students measures a distance twice, obtaining 67.455 and 67.350 m. What is the relative accuracy of the measurements?

31. With reference to Problem 29, what would be the relative accuracy if a survey four times as long were done using the same precision?

32. With reference to Problem 30, what would be the relative accuracy if a survey three times as long were done using the same precision?

33. Determine the accuracies of the following:

Error, ft	Distance, ft
10.00	23,361
0.50	3005
1.27	14,000
0.09	1002
1.00	25,000
0.84	8400

34. Repeat Problem 33 for the following:

Error, ft	Distance, ft
8.00	30,560
0.07	2000
1.32	8460
0.13	1709
1.00	17,543
0.72	1800

35. What is the maximum error of closure in a measurement of 500 m if the relative accuracy is 1:3000?

36. What is the maximum error of closure in a measurement of 2500 ft if the relative accuracy is 1:5000?

37. A horizontal control traverse survey is required to close with a 1:10,000 accuracy. The total distance of the traverse is about 15,000 ft. What is the required rating or maximum anticipated error per 1000 ft?

38. A horizontal control traverse survey is required to close with a 1:10,000 accuracy. The total distance of the traverse is about 3 km. What is the required rating or maximum anticipated error per 100 m?

CHAPTER THREE

BASIC MATHEMATICS FOR SURVEYING

Surveying is an applied science that depends very much on mathematics for solutions to many problems. But most surveying problems do not require the use of mathematics beyond the level of algebra, geometry, and trigonometry. It is generally assumed that surveying students have a good background in these subjects and are prepared to apply that knowledge. Many, though, can benefit from a brief review of fundamentals, particularly those who may have been out of school for a while before beginning their study of surveying.

This chapter is presented to serve as a refresher in geometry and trigonometry. It is intended primarily for review by self-study. Some users of this text may already be well prepared and will want to skip directly to Chapter 4 in Part 2 of the text. Others may want to review only certain parts of the chapter. In either case, it is important that beginners in surveying have a good understanding and working knowledge of elementary mathematics before proceeding with their studies.

3-1 GEOMETRY AND MENSURATION

Geometry ("earth measurement") is perhaps the oldest branch of mathematics, and as mentioned in Section 1-4, it originated from the need to measure (or survey) the land in ancient times. It is concerned with the properties of and relationships among lines, angles, surfaces, and solids. *Mensuration* refers to the process of measuring and computing lengths or distances, surface areas, and volumes of solids. The practice of surveying, of course, depends heavily on applications of geometry and mensuration.

Several basic geometric properties, relationships, and formulas that are used to solve surveying problems, and that will be discussed further in later chapters, are outlined and

illustrated in the following sections. They are presented here without proof. Students who are interested in seeing the actual geometric proofs can refer to any introductory textbook on plane geometry.

Lines and Angles

1. A *straight line* is the shortest line joining two points. If two straight lines intersect, the opposite angles are equal (Figure 3-1, $\angle a = \angle c$ and $\angle b = \angle d$).

2. Two angles whose sum is equal to a *right angle* (90°) are said to be *complementary* angles; that is, one is the *complement* of the other. Two angles whose sum is equal to the sum of two right angles are said to be *supplementary* angles; that is, one is the *supplement* of the other. If two adjacent angles are supplementary, their exterior sides are in the same straight line; a straight line forms an angle of 180°, called a *straight angle* (Figure 3-2, $\angle a + \angle b = 180°$).

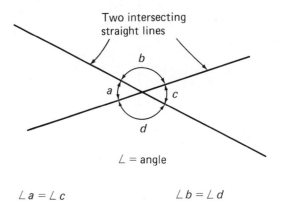

$\angle a = \angle c$ $\angle b = \angle d$

FIGURE 3-1. The opposite angles between intersecting straight lines are equal.

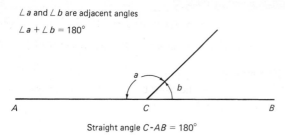

∠ a and ∠ b are adjacent angles

∠ a + ∠ b = 180°

Straight angle C-AB = 180°

FIGURE 3-2. Angle *a* and angle *b* are supplementary angles.

3. A *perpendicular line* drawn from a point to another given line forms two right angles at the intersection of the two lines. It is the shortest distance from the point to the given line (Figure 3-3).

4. A *bisector* is a line that divides another line (or an angle) into two equal parts. Any point on the perpendicular bisector of a line is equally distant from the two ends of the line (Figure 3-4, *AC = CB*).

5. Any point on the bisector of an angle is equally distant from the two sides of the angle (Figure 3-5, *BD = DF*).

6. Straight lines in the same plane that do not meet, no matter how far they are extended, are *parallel lines*. If two parallel lines are intersected by another straight line, the *alternate-interior angles are equal* (Figure 3-6, ∠ *a* = ∠ *b*; ∠ *c* = ∠ *d*). The two interior (and exterior)

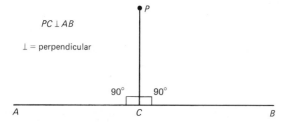

PC ⊥ AB

⊥ = perpendicular

90°   90°

FIGURE 3-3. The perpendicular distance *PC* from point *P* to line *AB* is the shortest distance from *P* to *AB*. Line *PC* forms two right angles (90°) at its intersection with *AB*.

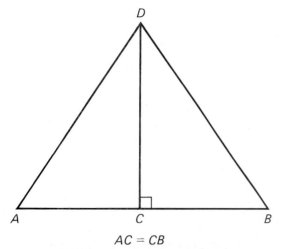

AC = CB

FIGURE 3-4. Line *DC* is a perpendicular bisector of line *AB*. The length of line *AD* equals the length of line *BD*.

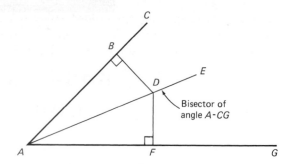

FIGURE 3-5. Distance *BD* = distance *DF*.

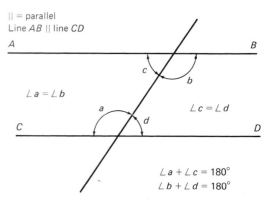

|| = parallel
Line *AB* || line *CD*

∠ a = ∠ b

∠ c = ∠ d

∠ a + ∠ c = 180°
∠ b + ∠ d = 180°

FIGURE 3-6. Alternate interior angles between parallel lines are equal.

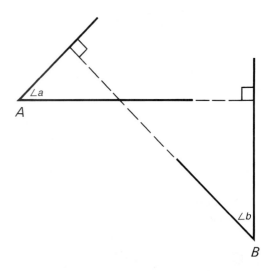

FIGURE 3-7. Angle *A* = angle *B*.

angles on the same side of the intersecting line are supplementary.

7. If the sides of two angles are perpendicular, each to each, the angles are equal (Figure 3-7, ∠ *a* = ∠ *b*).

Some Properties of Polygons

A *polygon* is a closed plane figure with three or more straight sides. The *perimeter* of a polygon is equal to the sum of the lengths of each of the sides.

Triangles A triangle is a three-sided polygon that encloses an area equal to one-half its base times its height (Figure 3-8). As a formula, the area is expressed as follows:

$$A = \frac{1}{2} \times b \times h \qquad (3\text{-}1)$$

Equation 3-1 may also be written as $bh/2$. (Remember, in the product of algebraic symbols, the $\times$, or times sign, may be omitted so that the expression bh implies the product $b \times h$.)

The symbol b is the *base*, and h is the *height*, or *altitude*, of the triangle. The height must be measured perpendicular to the base, but it can be either inside or outside the triangle. Any side of a triangle may be taken as the base.

If the sides of a triangle are given as a, b, and c, then its area may also be expressed by the following formula:

$$A = \sqrt{s(s - a)(s - b)(s - c)} \qquad (3\text{-}2)$$

where s is equal to half the sum of the sides, or $s = (a + b + c)/2$.

Example 3-1

Compute the area enclosed by a triangle with sides equal to 50, 120, and 130 m.

Solution

$$s = \frac{50 + 120 + 130}{2} = 150$$

Using Equation 3-2, we get

$$A = \sqrt{150(150 - 50)(150 - 120)(150 - 130)}$$
$$= \sqrt{150(100)(30)(20)}$$
$$= \sqrt{9,000,000} = 3000 \text{ m}^2$$

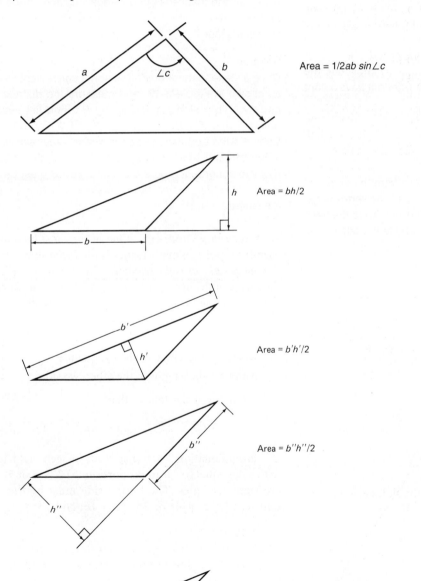

Area = 1/2$ab \sin \angle c$

Area = $bh/2$

Area = $b'h'/2$

Area = $b''h''/2$

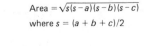

Area = $\sqrt{s(s-a)(s-b)(s-c)}$
where $s = (a + b + c)/2$

FIGURE 3-8. The area of a triangle can be computed by any of the three formulas given here.

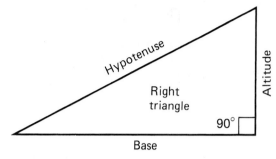

Area = 1/2 (base × altitude)

FIGURE 3-9. In a right triangle, the side opposite the right angle is always the longest side and is called the *hypotenuse*.

The sum of interior angles of any plane triangle *always* equals 180°, or a straight angle. A *right triangle* contains one interior angle of 90° and two complementary *acute* (less than 90°) angles. The side opposite the right angle, called the *hypotenuse*, is always the longest side of the triangle (Figure 3-9). The other two sides are called the *legs* of the triangle. (The area of a right triangle is simply half the product of its legs.) An *oblique triangle* does not have a right angle (or a hypotenuse).

An *equilateral* triangle has three equal sides (and three equal angles, each of 60°). If two sides of a triangle are equal, but the third is different, it is called an *isosceles triangle*.

In an isosceles triangle, the angles opposite the equal sides are equal. Also, the altitude drawn from the vertex of an isosceles triangle bisects (divides in half) the vertex angle as well as the base (Figure 3-10). If a line parallel to the base of a triangle bisects one side, it also bisects the other side; that line is half the base in length.

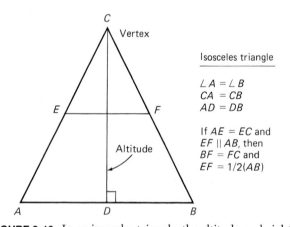

FIGURE 3-10. In an isosceles triangle, the altitude, or height, bisects the vertex angle *C* and the base *AB*.

Two triangles are said to be *congruent* if the corresponding parts (three sides and three angles) of each are exactly equal. It is not necessary to know that all six parts of the triangles are equal. If it is known that three parts of one, including at least one side, are the same as three corresponding parts of the other, then the two triangles must be congruent, that is, identical.

If two angles of one triangle equal two angles of another, the triangles have the same essential shape and are said to be *similar* (Figure 3-11). The corresponding sides of similar triangles are proportional; that is, the *ratios of the corresponding sides are equal* (e.g., *CB/AB* and *FE/DE* in Figure 3-11). This very important property of triangles is the basis of trigonometry, which is discussed in the next section.

Example 3-2

How can the inaccessible distance *AB*, across the pond, be measured by simple linear measurement using only a surveyor's tape?

Solution

Drive a stake to mark point *X* at some convenient location, as shown in Figure 3-12, and measure the distances *AX* and *BX*. Sight along lines *AX* and *BX*, and set stakes at points *Y* and *Z*, so that distances *AX = XY* and *BX = XZ*. Because the opposite angles at *X* are equal and the two sides of each triangle are equal, the triangles *XAB* and *XYZ* are congruent. Therefore, distance *AB* must be equal to distance *ZY*, which is accessible and can be easily measured.

Pythagorean Theorem   One of the most famous (and useful) formulas in mathematics is the *Pythagorean theorem.* It *applies only to right triangles.* The theorem states that the square of the hypotenuse equals the sum of the squares of the other two sides, or legs. As a formula, it is written

$$c^2 = a^2 + b^2 \qquad (3\text{-}3)$$

where c = the length of the hypotenuse

a and b = the lengths of the other two sides

From this, it also follows that

$$a = \sqrt{c^2 - b^2} \qquad \text{and} \qquad b = \sqrt{c^2 - a^2} \quad (3\text{-}4)$$

From Equation 3-4, it may easily be seen that triangles with sides equal to (or in proportion to) 3, 4, 5 or 5, 12, 13 are right triangles. The longer side must be the hypotenuse: $5^2 = 3^2 + 4^2$ or $25 = 9 + 16$; and $13^2 = 5^2 + 12^2$

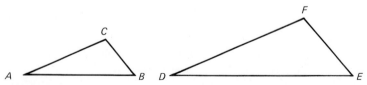

FIGURE 3-11. $\angle A = \angle D$ and $\angle C = \angle F$; therefore, triangles *ABC* and *DEF* are similar.

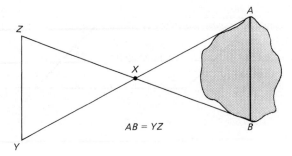

FIGURE 3-12. Illustration for Example 3-2.

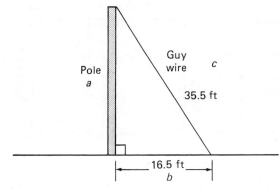

FIGURE 3-14. Illustration for Example 3-4.

or $169 = 25 + 144$. These right triangles were used by ancient surveyors to lay out square corners.

Example 3-3

A tract of land has the shape of a right triangle, with road frontage along the longer side, or the hypotenuse (Figure 3-13). The other two sides are measured to be 75.55 and 95.25 m. What is the length of road frontage for that tract?

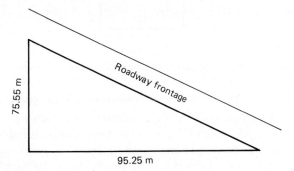

FIGURE 3-13. Illustration for Example 3-3.

Solution

Applying the Pythagorean theorem, we get

$$c^2 = (75.55)^2 + (95.25)^2 = 14{,}780.365$$

Taking the square root of both sides, we get

$$c = \sqrt{14{,}780.365} = 121.6\,\text{m} \quad \text{(rounded off)}$$

(*Note:* The intermediate result of 14,780.365, as displayed on a handheld calculator, does not actually have to be written down and should not be rounded off; only the final answer is rounded.)

Example 3-4

A guy wire that supports a telephone pole is 35.5 ft long and is anchored to the ground at a distance of 16.5 ft from the base of the pole (Figure 3-14). If the pole is perpendicular to the ground, what is its height?

Solution

In reference to Figure 3-14, the pole height is represented as *a* and the guy-wire length as *c*. Applying the Pythagorean theorem, we can write

$$a = \sqrt{c^2 - b^2} = \sqrt{35.5^2 - 16.5^2} = \sqrt{988} = 31.4\,\text{ft}$$

Quadrilaterals and Parallelograms A quadrilateral is a closed plane figure with four sides and four angles. The sum of the interior angles in any quadrilateral is 360°, or one complete rotation.

A *trapezoid* is a four-sided figure with only one pair of opposite sides parallel (Figure 3-15). The two parallel sides are the *bases* of the trapezoid. The area enclosed in a trapezoid equals the average length (half the sum) of the two bases, *a* and *b*, times the *altitude*, or perpendicular distance, *h*, between them.

In equation form, the area of a trapezoid is expressed as follows:

$$A = \frac{(a + b)}{2} \times h \quad \text{or} \quad \left[\left(\frac{1}{2}\right) \times (a + b) \times h\right] \quad (3\text{-}5)$$

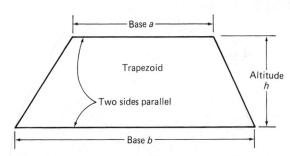

FIGURE 3-15. The area of a trapezoid is $\dfrac{(a + b)}{2} \times h$.

Example 3-5

A parcel of land has the shape shown in Figure 3-16. The value of the land is $50,000 per hectare. How much is the parcel worth?

Solution

The parcel of land has the shape of a trapezoid because only two sides are parallel. The altitude is 50.00 m and the two bases are 116.90 and 60.00 m in length. Applying the formula for the area of a trapezoid, we get the following:

$$A = \frac{(116.90 + 60.00)\,50.00}{2} = 4422.50\,\text{m}^2$$

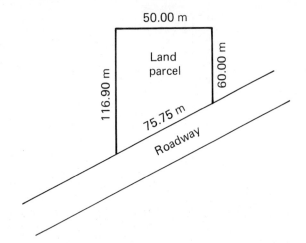

FIGURE 3-16. Illustration for Example 3-5.

Because 1 ha = 10,000 m², we get the following:

$$4422.50 \, m^2 \times \frac{1 \, ha}{10,000 \, m^2} \times \frac{\$50,000}{ha} = \$22,112.50$$

A quadrilateral in which no two sides are parallel is called a *trapezium*. The area of a trapezium can be determined by drawing a diagonal line between two opposite vertices and adding the areas of the two triangles that are formed (Figure 3-17a). It can also be determined by using Equation 3-6 (Figure 3-17b). The trapezium shown in Figure 3-17b is the basic shape of a roadway cross section. In practice, a device called planimeter can be used to measure the area of a trapezoid drawn to scale. The "coordinate method" may also be used (see Section 10-7) and CAD systems can quickly compute the area as well.

$$A = \frac{dh}{2} + \frac{(h' + h'')b}{4} \tag{3-6}$$

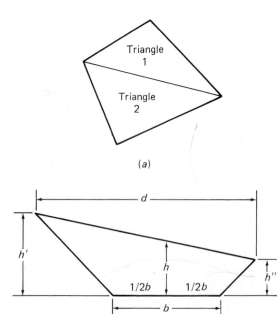

FIGURE 3-17. Two different forms of a trapezium.

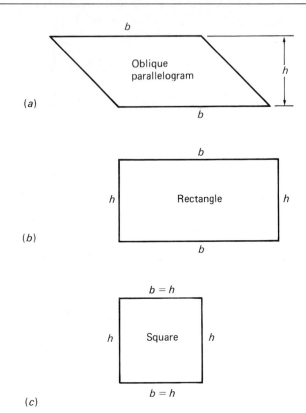

FIGURE 3-18. Three forms of a parallelogram: (*a*) oblique, (*b*) rectangular, and (*c*) square.

A *parallelogram* is a quadrilateral with each pair of opposite sides parallel (Figure 3-18). A *rectangle* is a parallelogram with four right angles, and a *square* is a rectangle with four equal sides. A line perpendicular to the parallel bases of any parallelogram is called its *altitude*. In an *oblique parallelogram* (not a rectangle or square), the altitude should not be confused with a side.

The opposite sides of a parallelogram are always equal in length and the *diagonal* (a line that joins opposite vertices of the figure) divides the parallelogram into two congruent triangles. Also, the two diagonals of a parallelogram bisect each other.

The area of a parallelogram equals the product of its base and its altitude, or in equation form

$$A = bh \tag{3-7}$$

where *b* = the base

h = the *altitude* of the figure

For a rectangle, the area is simply the product of its dimensions, or length times width. For a square figure, it is simply the algebraic square of a side.

Example 3-6

A rectangular parcel of land is sold for $10,000. The land is 652.55 ft long and 220.00 ft wide. What is the price per acre of land?

Note that 652.55 × 220.00 = 143,561 ft²; however, the product cannot have any more significant digits than the least significant digits of what is being multiplied. Therefore, 652.55 × 220.00 = 143,560 ft².

Solution

The area equals

$$652.55 \times 220.00 = 143{,}560 \text{ ft}^2$$

$$143{,}560 \text{ ft}^2 \times \frac{1 \text{ ac}}{43{,}560 \text{ ft}^2} = 3.296 \text{ ac}$$

The price per acre is

$$\frac{\$10{,}000}{3.296 \text{ ac}} = \$3034 \text{ per acre}$$

Sum of Interior Angles   A polygon may have any number of sides. A *pentagon*, for example, has five sides; a *hexagon* has six sides. For any polygon, *the sum of the interior angles is the number of straight angles that is two less than the number of sides.* In formula form, we can write

$$\text{Sum of interior angles} = 180° \times (n - 2) \qquad (3\text{-}8)$$

where n = the number of sides (or angles) of the polygon.

A triangle, for example, has $n = 3$ sides and, as we already know, the sum of the interior angles is $180 \times (3 - 2) = 180°$. A quadrilateral has four sides, and the sum of angles is $180 \times (4 - 2) = 180 \times 2 = 360°$. (What is the sum of interior angles for a pentagon? For a hexagon?)

Some Properties of the Circle

The very familiar closed plane figure called a *circle* is formed by a curved line, every point of which is equally distant from a single point inside the figure. That point, of course, is called the *center,* and a line from the center to any point on the circle is called the *radius* of the circle.

Any straight-line segment that has its ends on the circle is called a *chord* (Figure 3-19). A straight line that passes

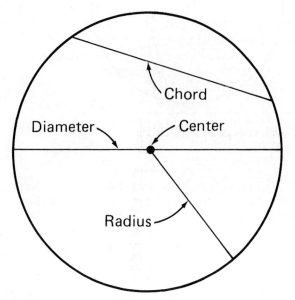

FIGURE 3-19. Any straight line with both ends on the circle is a chord.

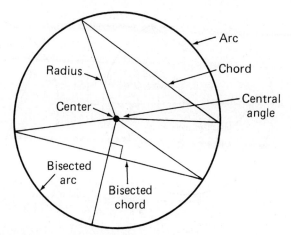

FIGURE 3-20. A radius drawn perpendicular to a chord bisects the chord and the intercepted arc.

through the center and has its two ends on the circumference of the circle is called the *diameter.* The diameter, then, is the longest chord of the circle; its length is equal to twice that of the radius, and it bisects the circle into two equal *semicircles.*

The portion of the circle between the ends of any chord is called an *arc* of the circle (Figure 3-20). A chord is said to *intercept* an arc, and an arc is said to *subtend* a chord, or a *central angle* (an angle between two corresponding radii with the vertex at the center). A radius that is perpendicular to a chord bisects the chord and the arcs intercepted by it (Figure 3-20).

An *inscribed angle* is formed between two chords that meet at a point on the circle. The center of the circle may be on one of the sides (Figure 3-21a), between the sides (Figure 3-21b), or outside the inscribed angle (Figure 3-21c). In any case, *the size of the inscribed angle is equal to half of the central angle subtended by the intercepted arc.* (Figure 3-21, $\angle A\text{-}BC = 1/2 \angle O\text{-}BC$.)

A straight line which touches or meets the circle at only one point is called a *tangent* to the circle. Any tangent is perpendicular to the radius drawn to the point of tangency on the circle (Figure 3-22). Two tangents from an external point to a circle are equal in length and form equal angles with the line joining the point to the center. (Figure 3-22, $AB = AC; \angle A\text{-}BO = \angle A\text{-}OC$.)

An angle formed by a tangent line and a chord from the point of tangency is *equal to half of the angle subtended by the intercepted arc* of the chord. (Figure 3-23, $\angle A\text{-}BC = 1/2 \angle O\text{-}AC$.)

Circumference and Area   The length of the curved line that forms a circle is called the *circumference* of the circle. (Imagine that the line was cut and straightened out—the length of that straight line would be the circumference.) It has long been known that, *for any circle,* the ratio of its circumference to its diameter is a constant number. That ratio is called π (pronounced

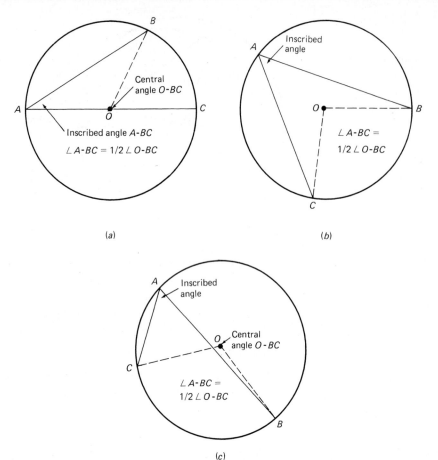

(a)

(b)

(c)

FIGURE 3-21. The size of an inscribed angle is equal to half the central angle subtended by the intercepted arc.

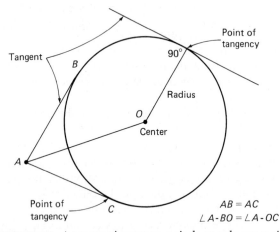

$AB = AC$
$\angle A\text{-}BO = \angle A\text{-}OC$

FIGURE 3-22. A tangent intersects a circle at only one point.

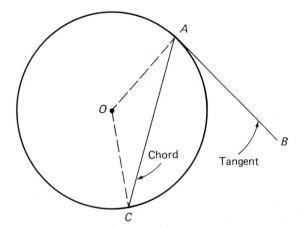

FIGURE 3-23. Angle $A\text{-}BC$, between the tangent and the chord, equals one-half central angle $O\text{-}AC$.

"pie") and is approximately equal to 3.14, a dimensionless number.

Because circumference/diameter = π, we can write

$$C = \pi D \quad \text{or} \quad C = 2\pi R \qquad (3\text{-}9)$$

where C = circumference

R = radius

D = diameter = $2R$

π = a constant ratio for all circles

The area A enclosed by a full circle is computed from either of the following formulas [note that $R^2 = (D/2)^2 = D^2/4$]:

$$A = \pi R^2 \quad \text{or} \quad \frac{\pi D^2}{4} \qquad (3\text{-}10)$$

Example 3-7

A circular concrete dance platform has a diameter of 50.0 ft. A railing is to be constructed around its edge and the top of the platform is to be painted. How long is the railing, and how many square feet of surface are to be painted?

Solution
The length of the railing is equal to the circumference of the circle, or $C = \pi (50.0) = 157$ ft. The area of the platform is computed as $A = \pi (50.0)^2/4 = 1960$ ft^2 (rounded off to three significant figures).

Length of Arc and Area of a Sector A figure formed by an arc of a circle and its subtended central angle is called a sector of the circle (Figure 3-24).

The length L of the arc is proportional to the central angle and may be computed from the following equation:

$$L = \frac{\pi R \Delta}{180} \qquad (3\text{-}11)$$

where Δ = the central angle subtended by the arc or chord.

The area A of the sector is also proportional to the central angle and may be computed as follows:

$$A = \frac{\Delta}{360} \times \pi R^2 \qquad (3\text{-}12)$$

A sector formed by a 90° central angle is a quarter of a circle and is called a *quadrant.*

A *segment* of a circle is the area enclosed by a chord and the arc intercepted by the chord (Figure 3-25). The area of a segment may be computed by subtracting the area of the triangle (formed by the two radii and the chord) from the area of the corresponding sector, as shown in Figure 3-25.

$$\text{Area of segment} = \frac{\Delta}{360}\,\pi R^2 - R^2 \sin \frac{\Delta}{2} \quad (3\text{-}13)$$

where Δ = the central angle subtended by the chord
R = the radius of the circle

Product of R and sin Δ = the altitude of the triangle

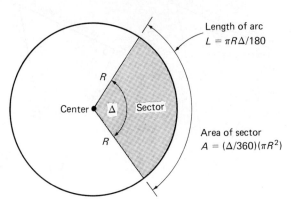

FIGURE 3-24. Determining the arc length and the sector area finds application in route surveying and boundary surveying.

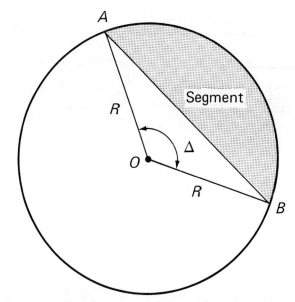

FIGURE 3-25. The area of a segment is equal to the area of the corresponding sector minus the area of triangle *AOB.*

(The term *sin*, pronounced sine, represents a trigonometric function and is defined in the next section.)

Volume

A solid figure is one that occupies three-dimensional space, the three dimensions being length, width, and height (Figure 3-26). A *rectangular solid* (such as a box or a slab of concrete) has six plane (flat) faces or sides, each of which is a rectangle. The volume V of a rectangular solid is simply the product of its three dimensions, or

$$V = LWH \qquad (3\text{-}14)$$

where L = length
W = width
H = height

A *prism* is a solid made up of several plane faces, two of which are polygons (the bases or "ends") and the remaining sides are either parallelograms or trapezoids. The volume of a prism that has identical and parallel bases is the product of its base area and its length (or height), or $V = AL$.

A *cylinder* is a solid figure with circular bases and a curved surface. Like the prism, its volume is simply the product of its base area and its height h, or $V = \pi h R^2$. A *cone* is a solid figure with a circular base, an apex or "point" opposite the base, and a curved surface. Its volume is equal to one-third the product of its base area and height, or $V = \pi h R^2/3$.

A *sphere* is a perfectly round globe or ball, formed by a curved surface every point of which is equally distant from a single point called the center. Any straight line that passes through the center and has its two ends on the surface is the diameter of the sphere. The volume is equal to $4\pi R^3/3$.

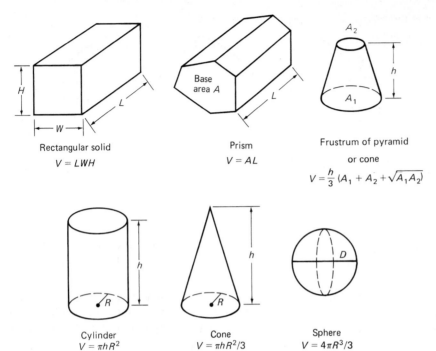

Rectangular solid
$V = LWH$

Prism
$V = AL$

Frustrum of pyramid
or cone
$V = \frac{h}{3}(A_1 + A_2 + \sqrt{A_1 A_2})$

Cylinder
$V = \pi h R^2$

Cone
$V = \pi h R^2/3$

Sphere
$V = 4\pi R^3/3$

FIGURE 3-26. Volume computation is often applied by the surveyor in the determination of earthwork (cut and fill) quantities.

3-2 TRIGONOMETRY

Trigonometry (or "trig") is one of the most important branches of mathematics for surveying. As an extension of geometry, it is the link between linear distance measurement and angular measurement.

Trigonometry is concerned with the relationships among the lengths of the sides and the sizes of the angles of a triangle. Along with basic algebra, it allows us to "solve a triangle," that is, to figure out some of the unknown sides and angles in a given triangle. (Many practical problems can be reduced to the solution of a triangle.)

Trigonometry may be applied to any shape of triangle, but the basis for defining the six trigonometric functions is the *right triangle*.

Right-Angle Trigonometry

Every right triangle has one 90° angle and two acute angles (angles less than 90°), such as *A* and *B* in the identical triangles shown in Figure 3-27. The trig functions may be defined in terms of an "adjacent side" and an "opposite side," with respect to the acute angle under consideration.

In Figure 3-27*a*, angle *B* is selected; *CB* is its adjacent side and *CA* is its opposite side. In Figure 3-27*b*, angle *A* is selected; *CB* is now the opposite side and *CA* is the adjacent side for that angle. It is important to remember that the designation of which side is "opposite" and which side is "adjacent" depends on the acute angle under consideration. The side opposite the right angle, though, is *always* called the hypotenuse.

Trig Functions From geometry, when two right triangles have an acute angle of one equal to an acute angle of the other, the triangles are similar and the lengths of their sides are proportional (see Figure 3-11). In similar triangles, the ratio of any one side divided by another side is the same, no matter how long the sides may be. Six different ratios can be written for a right triangle as follows:

$$\frac{\text{Opposite}}{\text{Hypotenuse}} \qquad \frac{\text{Hypotenuse}}{\text{Opposite}}$$

$$\frac{\text{Adjacent}}{\text{Hypotenuse}} \qquad \frac{\text{Hypotenuse}}{\text{Adjacent}}$$

$$\frac{\text{Opposite}}{\text{Adjacent}} \qquad \frac{\text{Adjacent}}{\text{Opposite}}$$

For any given angle, these ratios take on constant values. It makes no difference what the size of the triangle actually is.

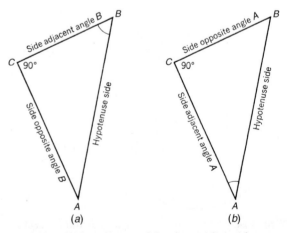

FIGURE 3-27. Nomenclature of the three sides with respect to each acute angle.

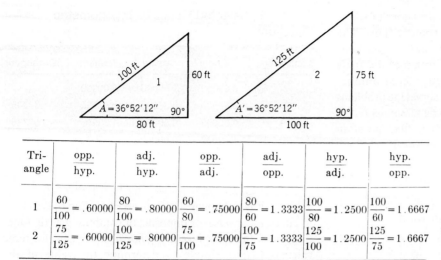

Tri-angle	opp. / hyp.	adj. / hyp.	opp. / adj.	adj. / opp.	hyp. / adj.	hyp. / opp.
1	$\frac{60}{100} = .60000$	$\frac{80}{100} = .80000$	$\frac{60}{80} = .75000$	$\frac{80}{60} = 1.3333$	$\frac{100}{80} = 1.2500$	$\frac{100}{60} = 1.6667$
2	$\frac{75}{125} = .60000$	$\frac{100}{125} = .80000$	$\frac{75}{100} = .75000$	$\frac{100}{75} = 1.3333$	$\frac{125}{100} = 1.2500$	$\frac{125}{75} = 1.6667$

FIGURE 3-28. If angles A and A' are equal, the ratios among the sides of both triangles are also equal.

Consider the example in Figure 3-28. The numerical value of each ratio is seen to be the same for each of the similar triangles. (Upon closer examination, it will be seen that this is an example of the so-called 3-4-5 right triangle.) Keep in mind that the computed ratios in this example apply only for the given angle of 36°52′12″.

Each of the trigonometric ratios, then, has a fixed value for any given angle; and for angles between 0° and 90°, once the value of any one of these ratios is known, the size of the angle is known. Because the values of these ratios depend on the size of the angle, they are called *trigonometric functions of an angle.* For convenience, they are given names. For example, the ratio of the side opposite angle A to the hypotenuse is called the *sine of A*, or simply sin A. The six different trig functions are identified in Figure 3-29.

It can be noticed from Figure 3-29 that the cotangent, cosecant, and secant functions are actually the reciprocals of the tangent, sine, and cosine functions, respectively. That is:

cotangent = 1/tangent	because $b/a = 1/(a/b)$
cosecant = 1/sine	because $c/a = 1/(a/c)$
secant = 1/cosine	because $c/b = 1/(b/c)$

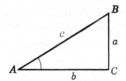

Ratios in triangle	Definition of function	Name of function	Abbreviation of name
$\frac{a}{c}$	$\frac{\text{side opposite } \angle A}{\text{hypotenuse}}$	sine A	sin A
$\frac{b}{c}$	$\frac{\text{side adjacent } \angle A}{\text{hypotenuse}}$	cosine A	cos A
$\frac{a}{b}$	$\frac{\text{side opposite } \angle A}{\text{side adjacent } \angle A}$	tangent A	tan A
$\frac{b}{a}$	$\frac{\text{side adjacent } \angle A}{\text{side opposite } \angle A}$	cotangent A	cot A or ctn A
$\frac{c}{b}$	$\frac{\text{hypotenuse}}{\text{side adjacent } \angle A}$	secant A	sec A
$\frac{c}{a}$	$\frac{\text{hypotenuse}}{\text{side opposite } \angle A}$	cosecant A	cosec A or csc A
$1 - \frac{b}{c}$	1 minus cosine $\angle A$	versine A	vers A
$\frac{c}{b} - 1$	secant $\angle A$ minus 1	exsecant A	exsec A

FIGURE 3-29. Nomenclature of trigonometric functions.

For this reason, scientific handheld calculators have keys for only sine (sin), cosine (cos), and tangent (tan). The values of the other three trig functions can easily be computed by first taking either the sin, cos, or tan of the angle and then taking the reciprocal of the displayed number (using the $1/x$ key). As it turns out, most surveying problems may be solved with only the three basic trig functions.

It should also be noted that *every trig function of an angle is equal to the cofunction of its complement.* This follows from the fact that in a right triangle with acute angles A and B, $B = 90° - A$; that is, B is the complement of A. This may be summarized as follows:

$$\sin A = \cos B \qquad \sin B = \cos A$$
$$\tan A = \cot B \qquad \tan B = \cot A$$
$$\sec A = \csc B \qquad \sec B = \csc A$$

Computing Trig Functions   The numerical value of a trigonometric function for a given angle may be determined with sufficient precision using an electronic handheld calculator. In the past, slide rules or long tables of trigonometric and logarithmic functions were needed. Now, scientific-type calculators can be used for this purpose, with angles expressed in degrees, grads, or radians. The value of a trig function for any angle can be obtained almost instantaneously.

Generally, when a calculator is first turned on, it will be in the *degree mode*; that is, it will interpret angles in units of degrees. (Some calculators can handle degrees, minutes, and seconds, while others use only degrees and decimal parts of a degree.) In the degree mode, the symbol DEG will appear on the calculator. If it is desired to enter angles in another unit, say, grads, then an appropriate key (DRG on some calculators) must be pressed to change the mode setting; the symbol GRAD will then appear on the calculator to indicate that mode.

To compute the sin 30°, for example, simply enter 30 and then press the sin key; the calculator will display 0.5, which is the value of the ratio of opposite side to hypotenuse (opp/hyp) for any right triangle. To compute the tangent of 50°45′, key in 50.75 and then press the tan key; a value of 1.2239389 will be displayed. (Some calculators will interpret 50.45 as 50°45′.) The number 1.2239389 is the ratio of opposite side/adjacent side in any right triangle with an acute angle of 50°45′. Of course, the calculator must be set in the DEG mode for these computations.

A very brief table of trig function values is presented in Table 3-1 to give a perspective of the range of values and to illustrate the cofunction and complementary angle relationships. Check some of the given values with your own calculator for practice. The symbol ∞ stands for "infinity"; this means that as an angle approaches 0° (or 90°), the value of its cotangent (or tangent) gets extremely large. Also note that the maximum value of a sine or cosine function is 1.00000, or unity.

Inverse Trig Functions   In some surveying problems, the numerical value of the trig function is known, but the

Table 3-1. Selected Values of Trigonometric Functions

Angle, deg	Sine	Cosine	Tangent	Cotangent
0	0.00000	1.00000	0.00000	∞
30	0.50000	0.86603	0.57735	1.73205
60	0.86603	0.50000	1.73205	0.57735
90	1.00000	0.00000	∞	0.00000

angle itself is unknown. The process of finding the angle is, in effect, the inverse, or opposite, of computing a trig function, hence the name *inverse trig function*. With an electronic calculator, it is simple to determine the value of the unknown angle. The following terminology is used for inverse trig functions:

Arcsin x means "an angle whose sine is equal to *x.*"

Arccos x means "an angle whose cosine is equal to *x.*"

Arctan x means "an angle whose tangent is equal to *x.*"

Other ways of writing these statements include $\sin^{-1} x$, $\cos^{-1} x$, and $\tan^{-1} x$, or invsin *x*, invcos *x*, and invtan *x*. On many calculators, an INV key is used to compute the arc or inverse trig functions.

For example, suppose we know that sin $A = 0.5$ and we need to figure out the value of angle A. We can write $A =$ arcsin 0.5, or "A is an angle whose sine is 0.5." Enter 0.5 into the calculator and press the INV key and then the sin key (or $\sin^{-1}$), the calculator will display 30° in the DEG mode (or 33.33ᵍ in the GRAD mode). Suppose that tan $B = 1.0$, what is the value of angle B? Write $B =$ arctan 1.0; enter 1.0, press the INV and sin keys and read 45° or 50ᵍ.

Solving Right Triangles   By using the previous concepts, every right triangle can be solved if two of its parts (including at least one side) are known. The following examples illustrate typical solutions of right-angle trig problems:

Example 3-8

In the right triangle shown in Figure 3-30, angle A is 35° and the length of the hypotenuse AB is 125 m. Determine the length of side BC.

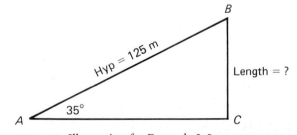

FIGURE 3-30. Illustration for Example 3-8.

Solution

In Figure 3-30, the unknown quantity is the side *opposite* the given angle; because the length of the hypotenuse is known, the ratio of opposite/hypotenuse can be used. By definition, opp/hyp is the sine of the angle and we may write

$$\sin 35° = \frac{opp}{hyp} = \frac{BC}{AB} = \frac{BC}{125}$$

Because $\sin 35° = BC/125$, multiplying both sides by 125 we get

$$BC = 125(\sin 35°) = 125(0.5735) = 71.7 \text{ m}$$

Example 3-9

Given the right triangle shown in Figure 3-31, with leg $a = 156.74$ ft and leg $b = 240.38$ ft, determine the angles A and B and the length of side c.

Solution

We are given the lengths of both the opposite and adjacent sides of angle A (or B). Because tan = opp/adj, we can write

$$\tan A = \frac{156.74}{240.38} = 0.6520509$$

From this we can write

$$A = \arctan 0.6520509 = 33.106398°$$

After converting to degrees, minutes, and seconds, we get

$$A = 33°06'23''$$

We have several options for computing angle B and side c. The simplest way to compute angle B is to use the fact that it must be complementary to A; that is, $A + B = 90°$. Therefore, $B = 90 - A$, or

$$89°59'60''$$
$$-33°06'23''$$
$$\overline{56°53'37''}$$

Note that to compute $B = 56°53'37''$ by subtracting A from 90, we wrote $90°$ as the equivalent $89°59'60''$; we "borrowed" 1° from 90° and 1' from 60' to get the 60".

Let us now *check the solution* for B using the tangent function. We can write $\tan B = 240.38/156.74 = 1.5336226$

and $B = \arctan 1.5336226 = 56.893602°$. This converts to $56°53'37''$, as computed previously.

The simplest method to compute side c is to use the Pythagorean theorem (Section 3-2). Because c is the hypotenuse of the triangle, we can write $c = \sqrt{a^2 + b^2} = \sqrt{156.74^2 + 240.38^2} = 286.97$ ft. We can check this using the cosine function because $\cos A = adj/hyp$ and, therefore, $\cos 33°06'23'' = 240.38/c$. From this, we get $c = 240.38/\cos 33°06'23'' = 240.38/0.8376577 = 286.97$ ft, as previously computed. Whenever possible, check your work with alternative computations to avoid blunders.

Example 3-10

Three right triangles are shown in Figure 3-32, each with two unknown sides. The steps for solving and checking these triangles using basic trigonometry are given.

Example 3-11

A building casts a shadow 15.0 m long on level ground, as shown in Figure 3-33. From the point on the ground at the end of the shadow, the angle between the ground and the line of sight to the top of the building is measured to be $72°30'$. How tall is the building?

Solution

The problem is to solve the right triangle formed by the ground, the building, and the edge of the shadow. We know an angle and its adjacent side and we must find an opposite side (the height of the building). We can use the tangent function and write $\tan 72°30' = opp/adj = height/15.0$. From this we get height $= (15.0)(\tan 72°30') = 15.0 \times 3.1716 = 47.6$ m.

Example 3-12

A triangular parcel of land is bounded on two sides by roads that are perpendicular. Another highway bounds the third side at an angle of 35°, as shown in Figure 3-34. We are informed that the owner recently fenced the boundary of the property with a total of 1025.5 ft of fencing, but we do not know the lengths of the individual sides. What is the area of the land in acres?

Solution

The solution to this problem requires the use of both trig and algebra. The lengths of the three sides, x, y, and z, are unknown. But we can express the perimeter of the triangle as $x + y + z$, and we can write

$$x + y + z = 1025.5 \text{ ft}$$

We can also express the area A of the triangle as

$$A = \frac{xy}{2}$$

It appears that we have two equations with four unknowns. But we can also use the trigonometric relationships to provide additional equations and then use the method of substitution to solve them.

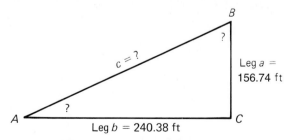

FIGURE 3-31. Illustration for Example 3-9.

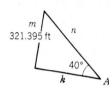

Example A	Example B	Example C
$\dfrac{f}{d} = \sin 70°$	$\dfrac{h}{g} = \tan 60°$	$\dfrac{k}{m} = \cot 40°$
$f = d \sin 70°$	$h = g \tan 60°$	$k = m \cot 40°$
$f = 80(0.93969)$	$h = 40(1.73205)$	$k = (321.395)(1.19175)$
$f = 75.175$ ft	$h = 69.282$ ft	$k = 383.02$ ft
$\dfrac{e}{d} = \cos 70°$	$\dfrac{g}{i} = \cos 60°$	$\dfrac{m}{n} = \sin 40°$
$e = d \cos 70°$	$i = \dfrac{g}{\cos 60°}$	$n = \dfrac{m}{\sin 40°}$
$e = 80(0.34202)$	$i = \dfrac{40}{0.50000}$	$n = \dfrac{321.395}{0.64279}$
$e = 27.362$ ft	$i = 80.000$ ft	$n = 500.00$ ft
Check	*Check*	*Check*
$\tan A = \dfrac{f}{e}$	$\sin A = \dfrac{h}{i}$	$\cos A = \dfrac{k}{n}$
$\tan A = \dfrac{75.175}{27.362}$	$\sin A = \dfrac{69.282}{80.000}$	$\cos A = \dfrac{383.02}{500.00}$
$\tan A = 2.74742$	$\sin A = 0.86602$	$\cos A = 0.76604$
$A = 70°$	$A = 60°$	$A = 40°$

FIGURE 3-32. Illustration for Example 3-10.

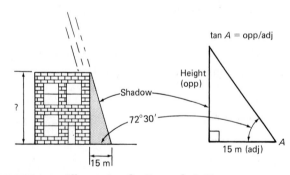

FIGURE 3-33. Illustration for Example 3-11.

From the definitions of sine and tangent, we get

$\sin 35 = y/z$. Therefore, $z = y/(\sin 35) = 1.7434y$

$\tan 35 = y/z$. Therefore, $x = y(\tan 35) = 1.4281y$

We now have the following four equations:

(1) $A = xy/2$ (2) $x + y + z = 1025.5$

(3) $z = 1.7434y$ (4) $x = 1.4281y$

Substituting Equations 3 and 4 into Equation 2, we get

$1.4281y + y + 1.7434y = 1025.5$

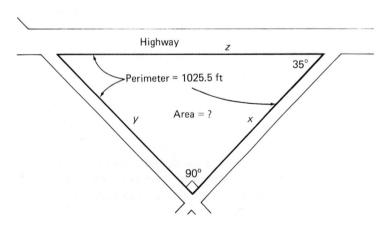

FIGURE 3-34. Illustration for Example 3-12.

Now there is only one unknown, y, in this new equation. Combining terms on the left and solving for y, we get

$$4.1716 = 1025.5$$

$$y = \frac{1025.5}{4.1716} = 245.83 \text{ ft}$$

From this and Equations 3 and 4, we get

$$z = 1.7434(245.83) = 428.59 \text{ ft}$$

$$x = 1.4281(245.83) = 351.08 \text{ ft}$$

Now we can compute the area as follows:

$$A = \frac{xy}{2} = \frac{(351.08)(245.83)}{2} = 43{,}153 \text{ ft}^2 = 0.991 \text{ ac}$$

Trig Functions of Obtuse Angles

An angle that contains more than 90° is called an *obtuse angle* (Figure 3-35). It is sometimes necessary to evaluate trigonometric functions for obtuse angles.

For our purpose in this brief review, we will only consider angles between 90° and 180°. In this range of angles ($90° < A < 180°$), we can write

$$\sin A = \sin B \quad \cos A = -\cos B \quad \tan A = -\tan B$$

where $B = 180 - A$ (B is called a reference angle).

For example,

$$\sin 120° = \sin 60° = 0.8660$$

$$\cos 140° = -\cos 40° = -0.7660$$

$$\tan 160° = -\tan 20° = -0.3640$$

Check the preceding statements with your own calculator. It is important to realize that the cosine and tangent functions are negative (are preceded by a minus sign) for any angle between 90° and 180°; your calculator will automatically show the minus sign. (A thorough explanation of the change in algebraic sign for certain trigonometric functions of obtuse angles can be found in any standard trigonometry textbook.)

Solutions of Oblique Triangles

A triangle that does not contain a right angle is called an *oblique triangle*. In practical surveying applications, it is sometimes necessary to solve problems involving oblique triangles. Two useful formulas are derived from basic

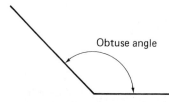

FIGURE 3-35. An obtuse angle exceeds 90°.

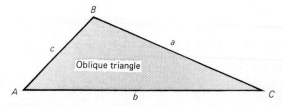

FIGURE 3-36. Nomenclature for the parts of an oblique triangle.

trigonometry and geometry for this purpose. These are called the *law of sines* and the *law of cosines*.

The conventional system for naming the parts of an oblique triangle is shown in Figure 3-36. Capital letters A, B, and C are used to designate angles (at their vertex), and the side opposite each angle is given the same letter designation, but in lowercase.

Law of Sines The law of sines states that the *sides of any triangle are proportional to the sines of the angles opposite them*. Using the nomenclature in Figure 3-36, this is expressed in the following equation:

$$\frac{a}{\sin A} = \frac{b}{\sin B} = \frac{c}{\sin C} \tag{3-15}$$

The law of sines is applied to problems in which either (a) two angles and one side of the triangle are known or (b) two sides and the angle opposite one of them is known. The following examples are presented to illustrate solutions of triangles using the law of sines:

Example 3-13
Referring to Figure 3-36 and given that $A = 60°$, $B = 40°$, and side $c = 247.8$ m, solve for sides a and b and angle C.

Solution
First solve for angle C:

$$C = 180 - A - B = 180 - 60 - 40 = 80°$$

Applying the law of sines, we can now write

$$\frac{a}{\sin 60} = \frac{247.8}{\sin 80}$$

$$a = (\sin 60)\left(\frac{247.8}{\sin 80}\right) = (0.8660)\left(\frac{247.8}{0.9848}\right) = 217.9 \text{ m}$$

Again applying the law of sines, we get

$$\frac{b}{\sin 40} = \frac{247.8}{\sin 80}$$

$$b = (\sin 40)\left(\frac{247.8}{\sin 80}\right) = (0.6428)\left(\frac{247.8}{0.9848}\right) = 161.7 \text{ m}$$

(*Note:* We cannot use the Pythagorean theorem to solve for the remaining side b because the triangle is oblique; *the Pythagorean theorem is valid only for right triangles.*)

Example 3-14

Given $A = 38°54'37''$, $a = 326.39$, and $b = 508.69$ ft, solve the triangle for angles B and C and side c.

Solution

Applying the law of sines, we get

$$\frac{b}{\sin B} = \frac{a}{\sin A}$$

$$\frac{508.69}{\sin B} = \frac{326.39}{\sin 38.9103} = 519.64 \text{ ft}$$

Multiplying both sides by sin B, we get

$$508.69 = 519.64 \,(\sin B)$$

Solving for sin B, we get

$$\sin B = \frac{508.69}{519.64} = 0.97892$$

Now applying the inverse trig function, we get

$$B = \arcsin 0.97892 = 78°.2147° = 78.12'53''$$

From this we get

$$C = 180 - A - B = 180 - (A + B) = 179°59'60''$$
$$- (38°54'37'' + 78°12'53'') = 62°52'30''$$

Again applying the law of sines, we get

$$\frac{c}{\sin C} = \frac{a}{\sin A} = 519.65 \text{ (from previous)}$$

and

$$c = (\sin 62.875°)(519.65) = 462.50 \text{ ft}$$

(When the side opposite the given angle is shorter than the other given side, as is the case in this example, there are two possible solutions to the problem. In this case, angle B can also equal $180° - 78°12'53'' = 101°47'07''$, because the sine of $101°47'07''$ also equals 0.97892. Angle C would then equal $39°18'16''$, and side c would equal 329.16 ft.)

Law of Cosines   In reference to Figure 3-36, the law of cosines is written as follows:

$$a^2 = b^2 + c^2 - 2bc(\cos A) \qquad (3\text{-}16a)$$
$$b^2 = a^2 + c^2 - 2ac(\cos B) \qquad (3\text{-}16b)$$
$$c^2 = a^2 + b^2 - 2ab(\cos C) \qquad (3\text{-}16c)$$

The law of cosines is applied to problems in which either (a) two sides and the *included* angle are known or (b) only three sides are known. (When the included angle is 90°, the foregoing equations reduce to the Pythagorean theorem because cos 90° = 0.) Any side of the triangle that appears on the left half of the equation must be the side opposite the angle used in the cosine function on the right half.

Example 3-15

Given a triangle with $a = 45.0$, $b = 67.0$, and angle $C = 145°$, solve for side c and angles A and B.

Solution

The law of sines cannot be applied here to begin with because we do not know the length of the side opposite the given angle. We must first apply the law of cosines to solve for side c, as follows:

$$c^2 = a^2 + b^2 - 2ab(\cos c)$$
$$c^2 = 45.0^2 + 67.0^2 - 2(45.0)(67.0)(\cos 145°)$$
$$c^2 = 2025 + 4489 - 2(45.0)(67.0)(-0.8192)$$
$$c^2 = 2025 + 4489 + 4940 = 11\,453.5$$
$$c = \sqrt{11,453.5} = 107.0$$

(Note that cos 145 is negative, and the product of two negative numbers is a positive number.)

From the law of sines, we can now write

$$\frac{107.0}{\sin 145} = \frac{45.0}{\sin A}$$

from which we get $A = 14°$

Finally, $B = 180 - A - C = 180 - 159 = 21°$

Example 3-16

Given a triangle with the sides $a = 49.3$ m, $b = 21.6$ m, and $c = 42.6$ m, determine the interior angles.

Solution

Applying the law of cosines to solve for angle A, we get

$$49.3^2 = 21.6^2 + 42.6^2 - 2(21.6)(42.6) \cos A$$
$$2430.49 = 466.56 + 1814.76 - 1840.32 (\cos A)$$
$$\cos A = \frac{(2430.49 - 466.56 - 1814.76)}{(-1840.32)}$$
$$\cos A = -0.08105655$$
$$A = \arccos (-0.08105655) = 94.6493°$$
$$= 94°38'57.4''$$

From the law of sines, we then get

$$B = 25°53'34.9'' \text{ and } C = 59°27'27.3''$$

Trigonometric Identities

A trigonometric identity is an equation that is true for any angle. A short list of such identities that are often useful in surveying is presented here for reference. [Note that when a trig function is squared, such as $(\sin A)^2$, it is written as $\sin^2 A$. First evaluate the trig function and then square the result; do not square the angle before taking the trig function.]

Selected Trigonometric Identities for Surveying Applications

(1) $\tan A = \dfrac{\sin A}{\cos A}$

(2) $\sin^2 A + \cos^2 A = 1$

(3) $\tan^2 A + 1 = \sec^2 A$

(4) $\sin (A + B) = (\sin A)(\cos B) + (\cos A)(\sin B)$

(5) $\sin (A - B) = (\sin A)(\cos B) - (\cos A)(\sin B)$

(6) $\cos (A + B) = (\cos A)(\cos B) - (\sin A)(\sin B)$

(7) $\cos(A - B) = (\cos A)(\cos B) + (\sin A)(\sin B)$

(8) $\tan(A + B) = \dfrac{(\tan A + \tan B)}{[1 - (\tan A)(\tan B)]}$

(9) $\tan(A - B) = \dfrac{(\tan A - \tan B)}{[1 + (\tan A)(\tan B)]}$

(10) $\sin 2A = 2(\sin A)(\cos A)$

(11) $\cos 2A = \cos^2 A - \sin^2 A$

(12) $\tan 2A = \dfrac{2\tan A}{(1 - \tan^2 A)}$

(13) $\sin\left(\dfrac{A}{2}\right) = \sqrt{\dfrac{(1 - \cos A)}{2}}$

(14) $\cos\left(\dfrac{A}{2}\right) = \dfrac{(1 + \cos A)}{2}$

(15) $\tan\left(\dfrac{A}{2}\right) = \dfrac{(1 - \cos A)}{\sin A}$

3-3 COORDINATE AND ANALYTIC GEOMETRY

One of the best ways to indicate the relative positions of survey points (such as boundary markers, control survey stations, or topographic features) is to assign a pair of coordinates to each point. *Coordinates* are numbers that represent the distances (or distance and angle) of a particular point from a fixed reference position.

In plane surveying, the *rectangular coordinate system* is most useful. The use of *polar coordinates* is also of interest to the surveyor. The increasing use of computerized land-title systems and survey data files makes the use of coordinates a necessity for most surveying applications. Also, several of the electronic total survey stations are equipped with desktop computers and software for coordinate computations in the field.

In certain surveying applications, it may be necessary to compute the coordinates of intersection points between two lines or between a line and a circle. The mathematical procedure for computations of this type is called *analytic geometry*, and it is basically a combination of algebra and geometry. It is concerned with the algebraic equations that define lines, circles, and other geometric shapes in the rectangular coordinate system.

In this section, the basic concepts of coordinate and analytic geometry are presented. This (along with the previous discussion of plane geometry and trigonometry) should help prepare the beginning student for the applied and more advanced topics covered in later chapters of the book.

Rectangular Coordinates

A rectangular coordinate system is shown in Figure 3-37. It comprises two perpendicular lines called the *x axis* (the *horizontal* line, or *abscissa* axis) and the *y axis* (the *vertical* line, or *ordinate* axis).

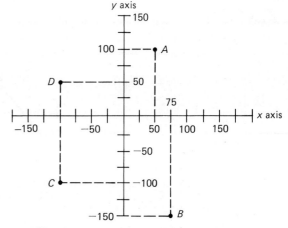

FIGURE 3-37. The rectangular, or *XY*, coordinate system.

The point of intersection of the two axes is called the *origin*. Distances measured along the *x* axis to the right of the origin are considered positive, while distances measured to the left of the origin are considered negative. (A negative distance has no physical meaning, except to indicate direction from the origin of a coordinate system.) On the *y* axis, distances above the origin are positive, while those measured below the origin are considered to be negative.

In surveying applications, as we shall see later in the text, the *y* axis usually corresponds to the north–south meridian. The north direction is represented by positive *y* values and the south by negative *y* values. Positive *x* distances are measured in an easterly direction and negative *x* distances are measured in a westerly direction.

On the *xy plane* of the rectangular coordinate system, the location of a point can be described simply by assigning it a pair of numbers (x, y). The value of *x* represents the distance of the point from the origin, measured parallel to the *x* axis (the abscissa); the value of *y* represents the distance of the point from the origin, measured parallel to the *y* axis (the ordinate).

The pair of numbers (x, y) are called the coordinates of the point. For example, in Figure 3-37, point *A* has coordinates (50, 100), point *B* has coordinates (75, −150), point *C* has coordinates (−100, −100), and point *D* has coordinates (−100, 50). The coordinates of the origin are, of course, (0, 0).

If we are given the coordinates of two different points that lie on the ends of a straight line, we can easily compute the length of the line. This simple application of coordinate geometry is most useful for solving many practical surveying problems. It is illustrated in the following example.

Example 3-17

Points *A* and *B* define the endpoints of a straight line, as shown in Figure 3-38. The coordinates of *A* and *B* are (125, 25) and (155, 65), respectively. What is the length of line *AB*?

Solution

Consider the right triangle, which has *AB* as its hypotenuse. The length of the side parallel to the *x* axis is simply the

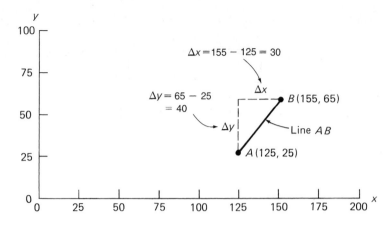

FIGURE 3-38. Illustration for Example 3-17.

difference in the x coordinates from A to B, or 155 − 125 = 30 units (feet, meters, etc.). This difference is often called Δx (pronounced "delta x"). The length of the side parallel to the y axis is the difference in the y coordinate values, or y = 65 − 25 = 40 units. Because AB is the hypotenuse of a right triangle, we can use the Pythagorean theorem to solve for its length as follows:

$$AB = \sqrt{\Delta x^2 + \Delta y^2} = \sqrt{30^2 = 40^2} = \sqrt{2500} = 50 \text{ units}$$

Polar Coordinates

In the polar coordinate system, a point may be located at a distance r from the origin and at an angle A from the horizontal or x axis. This is illustrated in Figure 3-39. The coordinates are expressed as (r, A). [Two numbers are always needed to locate a point on a plane—either (distance, distance) as with rectangular coordinates or (distance, angle) as with polar coordinates.]

It is sometimes necessary to convert from rectangular to polar, or from polar to rectangular, coordinates. Also, this type of computation will be applied (with slightly different terminology) in certain surveying problems discussed later in the text. The transformation of coordinates from one system to the other involves the application of right-angle trigonometry and the Pythagorean theorem as follows:

Rectangular to polar:

$$r = \sqrt{x^2 + y^2} \quad \text{and} \quad A = \arctan\left(\frac{y}{x}\right) \quad (3\text{-}17)$$

Polar to rectangular:

$$x = r(\cos A) \text{ and } y = r(\sin A) \quad (3\text{-}18)$$

Example 3-18

a. A point has rectangular coordinates (60, 80). Determine its corresponding polar coordinates.

b. A point has polar coordinates (130, 22.62°). Determine its corresponding rectangular coordinates.

Solution

a. Applying Equation 3-17, we get

$$r = \sqrt{60^2 + 80^2} = \sqrt{10,000} = 100$$

$$A = \arctan\left(\frac{80}{60}\right) = \arctan 1.333 = 53.13°$$

The polar coordinates are (100, 53.13°).

b. Applying Equation 3-18, we get

$$x = 130(\cos 22.62) = 130(0.9231) = 120$$

$$y = 130(\sin 22.62) = 130(0.3846) = 50$$

The rectangular coordinates are (120, 50).

The Straight Line

A straight line can be expressed algebraically in terms of the (x, y) coordinates for any point on the line. The equation of a straight line may be written as follows:

$$y = mx + b \quad (3\text{-}19)$$

where x and y are the coordinates of any point on the line
$m =$ the slope of the line (or $\Delta y / \Delta x$)
$b =$ the y intercept (where the line crosses the y axis)

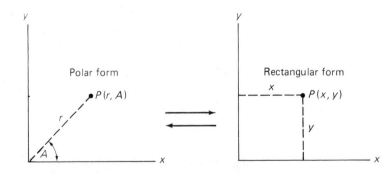

FIGURE 3-39. The location of a point may be expressed in polar or rectangular form. In polar form, a distance (r) and an angle (A) must be given.

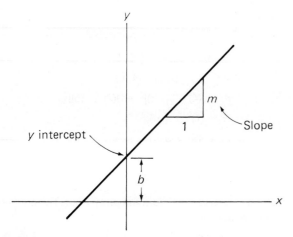

FIGURE 3-40. In the rectangular coordinate system, a straight line can be described by the equation $y = mx + b$.

The straight line on an xy plane is illustrated in Figure 3-40. [Because x is taken only to the first power ($x = x^1$), Equation 3-19 is *linear*; that is, it plots as a straight line on the xy plane.]

Example 3-19

Determine the equation of a straight line, which passes through point A with (x, y) coordinates of (20, 10), and point B, which has the coordinates (50, 40).

Solution

Each pair of coordinates on the line must satisfy Equation 3-19, $y = mx + b$, and so we can write the following set of equations:

$$40 = 50m + b \qquad (1)$$
$$10 = 20m + b \qquad (2)$$

These two simultaneous linear equations in two unknowns, m and b, can be solved as follows:
Subtract Equation 2 from Equation 1 to obtain

$$30 = 30m$$

from which $\quad m = 1$
Now substitute $m = 1$ into either Equation 1 or 2:

$$40 = 50(1) + b$$

from which $b = -10$
The equation of the line, then, which passes through the given points A and B is $y = x - 10$ (Figure 3-41); the

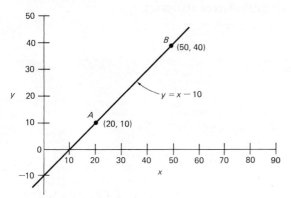

FIGURE 3-41. Illustration for Example 3-19.

coordinates of any other points on that line must satisfy this equation. For example, the coordinates of the point where the line intersects the x axis must be (10, 0) because y must be zero at that point.

Example 3-20

Line L is defined by the equation $3x - 5y = 10$ and line P is parallel to it. If line P passes through point (7, 7), what is its equation?

Solution

The equation for line L (Figure 3-42) can be rewritten in the $y = mx + b$ form by transposing terms as follows:
Subtract $3x$ from both sides

$$-5y = -3x + 10$$

Divide both sides by -5

$$y = \left(\frac{3}{5}\right)x - 2 \text{ or } y = 0.6x - 2$$

Therefore, for line L, the slope $m = 0.6$ and the y intercept $b = -2$.

Now, because line P is to be parallel to line L, it must have the same slope, or $m = 3/5 = 0.6$; also, we know one point on line P with coordinates (7, 7). Applying these data, we can write

$$7 = (0.6)(7) + b$$

from which $b = 7 - 4.2 = 2.8$
The equation of line P, then, must be $y = 0.6x + 2.8$.

Example

Line C has the equation $y = 0.5x + 2$ and line D has the equation $y = -x + 8$. Determine the coordinates of the intersection point P between lines C and D.

Solution

Because the intersection point P lies on both lines, the equations for both C and D are valid simultaneously when x

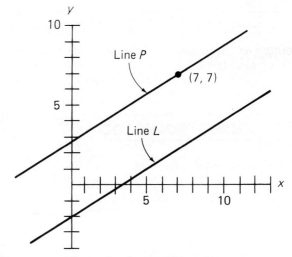

FIGURE 3-42. Illustration for Example 3-20.

and y are the coordinates of point P. Solving the equations for C and D, we get

$$2(y = 0.5x + 2) \longrightarrow 2y = x + 4$$
$$y = -x + 8 \longrightarrow \underset{3y =}{+\ (y = -x + 8)} 12$$

from which $\qquad\qquad y = 4$

and because $y = -x + 8$ (line D), we get $x = 4$.

    Therefore, the coordinates of the intersection point P are (4, 4).

The Circle

A circle is defined geometrically in terms of its center and its radius. The general form for the equation of a circle (Figure 3-43) is

$$r^2 = (x - h)^2 + (y - k)^2 \qquad (3\text{-}20)$$

where r is the radius of the circle and (h, k) are the coordinates of its center. Any point on the circle with coordinates (x, y) satisfies this equation.

Example

What is the equation of a circle that has its center at (−3, 5) and that passes through a point at (4, 2)?

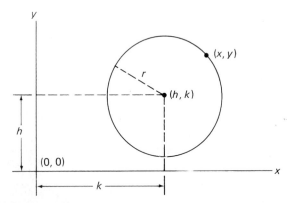

FIGURE 3-43. Any point on a circle satisfies the equation $r^2 = (x - h)^2 + (y - k)^2$

Solution

The radius of the circle may be computed as follows:

$$(h, k) = (-3, 5)$$
$$(x, y) = (4, 2)$$
$$r^2 = [(4) - (-3)]^2 + [(2) - (5)]^2$$
$$r^2 = [7]^2 + [-3]^2$$
$$r^2 = 49 + 9$$
$$r^2 = 58$$
$$r = \sqrt{58} = 7.62$$

because $h = -3$ and $k = 5$ from the given data. The equation of the circle, then, is

$$(\sqrt{58})^2 = [x - (-3)]^2 + [y - (5)]^2$$
$$58 = [x + 3]^2 + [y - 5]^2$$

Example

Determine the points of intersection of the line $y = x + 1$ and the circle $53 = (x + 3)^2 + (y - 4)^2$

Solution

We can determine the points of intersection by solving the equations of the line and the circle simultaneously as follows:

$$y = x + 1 \qquad (1)$$
$$53 = (x + 3)^2 + (y - 4)^2 \qquad (2)$$

By substitution of $x + 1$ for y, we get

$$53 = (x + 3)^2 + [(x + 1) - 4]^2$$
$$53 = (x + 3)(x + 3) + (x - 3)(x - 3)$$
$$53 = (x^2 + 6x + 9) + (x^2 - 6x + 9)$$
$$53 = 2x^2 + 18$$
$$35 = 2x^2$$
$$\frac{35}{2} = x^2$$
$$\sqrt{\frac{35}{2}} = x = \pm 4.18$$

From $y = x + 1$, we get

$$y = 4.18 + 1 = 5.18 \text{ and } y = -4.18 + 1 = -3.18$$

The two points of intersection have the coordinates (4.18, 5.18) and (−4.18, −3.18).

Practice Problems

1. Solve the following linear equations:
   a. $5x - 2 = 13$
   b. $8 - 5t = 18$
   c. $3(y - 2) = -y$
   d. $5 - (n + 2) = 5n$
   e. $3 - 6(2 - 3x) = x - 5$

2. Solve the following linear equations:
   a. $6x - 5 = 13$
   b. $11 - 7t = 17$
   c. $4(y - 3) = -2y$
   d. $8 - (2n + 12) = 6n$
   e. $5 - 7(3 - 4x) = 2x - 15$

3. Solve the following quadratic equations:

 a. $4x^2 = 100$

 b. $x^2 + 3x - 10 = 0$

 c. $3x^2 + 5x + 2 = 0$

 d. $8x^2 = 5x + 2$

 e. $5y^2 + 7y = 2$

4. Solve the following quadratic equations:

 a. $5x^2 = 125$

 b. $x^2 + x - 12 = 0$

 c. $2x^2 - 5x - 2 = 0$

 d. $3x^2 = 2x - 2$

 e. $3y^2 + 5y = 3$

5. Solve the following sets of simultaneous equations:

 a. $x - 3y = 6$
    $2x + 3y = 3$

 b. $3x - 2y = 4$
    $x + 3y = 2$

 c. $2x + y = 1$
    $5x - 2y = -11$

6. Solve the following sets of simultaneous equations:

 a. $3x - 2y = 6$
    $2x + 2y = -1$

 b. $2x - 3y = -3$
    $x + 2y = 2$

 c. $x + 2y = 1$
    $2x - 5y = -11$

7. Determine the areas of the figures shown in Figure 3-44.

8. Determine the areas of the figures shown in Figure 3-45.

9. Solve the following right triangles for the parts not given:

 a. $A = 40°10'13''$, hypotenuse = 402.36 ft

 b. $A = 62°09'15''$, hypotenuse = 338.74 m

 c. $A = 36°22'10''$, adjacent side = 360.41 ft

 d. Hypotenuse = 428.29 m, opposite side = 397.06 m

 e. Hypotenuse = 409.31 ft, adjacent side = 274.82 ft

 f. Opposite side = 375.82 m, adjacent side = 276.05 m

10. Solve the following right triangles for the parts not given:

 a. $A = 42°23'12''$, hypotenuse = 437.25 ft

 b. $A = 61°28'47''$, opposite side = 345.51 m

 c. $A = 35°46'17''$, adjacent side = 358.17 ft

 d. Hypotenuse = 432.89 m, opposite side = 398.24 m

 e. Hypotenuse = 471.65 ft, adjacent side = 270.46 ft

 f. Opposite side = 368.47 m, adjacent side = 274.61 m

11. Solve the following oblique triangles for the parts not given (capital letter = angle; lowercase = opposite side):

 a. $A = 63°29'10''$, $B = 58°42'07''$, $b = 458.24$ ft

 b. $A = 27°38'14''$, $B = 32°18'25''$, $c = 348.27$ m

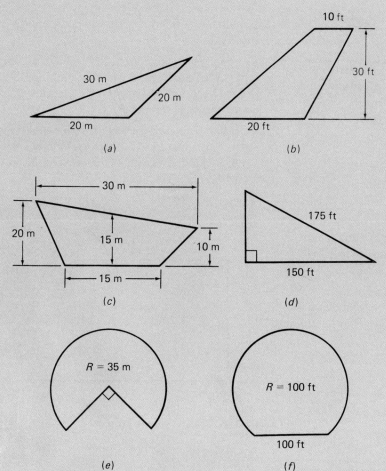

(a)

(b)

(c)

(d)

(e)

(f)

FIGURE 3-44. Illustration for Problem 7.

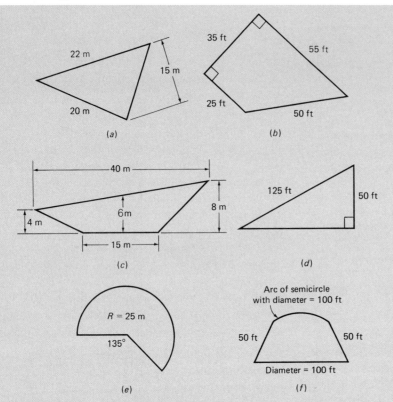

(a)

(b)

(c)

(d)

(e)

Arc of semicircle
with diameter = 100 ft

Diameter = 100 ft

(f)

FIGURE 3-45. Illustration for
Problem 8.

c. $A = 35°21'54''$, $a = 315.46$ ft, $b = 478.28$ ft
d. $A = 64°27'13''$, $a = 357.46$ m, $b = 295.87$ m
e. $A = 51°10'13''$, $b = 358.15$ ft, $c = 307.01$ ft
f. $A = 61°50'29''$, $b = 451.63$ m, $c = 197.17$ m
g. $a = 289.95$ ft, $b = 363.75$ ft, $c = 497.38$ ft

12. Solve the following oblique triangles for the parts not given (capital letter = angle; lowercase = opposite side):
    a. $A = 74°22'53''$, $B = 34°15'45''$, $a = 287.46$ ft
    b. $A = 48°17'35''$, $B = 64°26'41''$, $c = 396.41$ m
    c. $A = 25°04'16''$, $a = 228.71$ ft, $b = 517.09$ ft
    d. $A = 59°17'23''$, $a = 451.14$ m, $b = 398.36$ m
    e. $A = 55°42'35''$, $b = 426.82$ ft, $c = 411.28$ ft
    f. $A = 67°04'41''$, $b = 475.74$ m, $c = 162.27$ m
    g. $a = 305.13$ ft, $b = 485.27$ ft, $c = 572.16$ ft

13. The vertical angle from level ground to the top of a building is 40°. The angle is measured from a point that is 25 m distant from the base of the building. How tall is the building?

14. The vertical angle from level ground to the top of a building 65°. The angle is measured from a point that is 100 ft distant from the base of the building. How tall is the building?

15. A tract of land has the shape of a trapezoid, as shown in Figure 3-46. The lengths of three sides and the sizes of the two interior right angles are given. Determine the two unknown interior angles and the length of the fourth side.

16. A tract of land has the shape of a trapezoid, as shown in Figure 3-47. The lengths of three sides and the sizes of the two interior right angles are given. Determine the two unknown interior angles and the length of the fourth side.

17. A railroad embankment has the shape of a trapezoid, with a horizontal top 25 ft across, sloping sides each 15 ft in length, and a height of 8 ft. Determine the width at the base of the embankment.

18. A railroad embankment has the shape of a trapezoid with a horizontal top 10 m across, sloping sides each 4 m in length, and a height of 3 m. Determine the width at the base of the embankment.

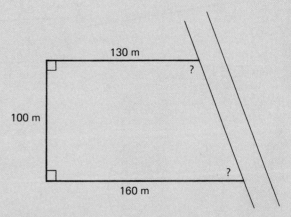

FIGURE 3-46. Illustration for Problem 15.

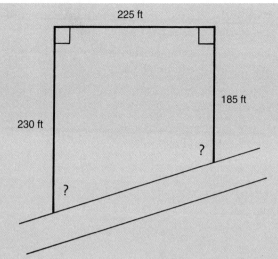

FIGURE 3-47. Illustration for Problem 16.

19. Determine the lengths of the three unknown sides of the tract of land shown in Figure 3-48.

20. Determine the lengths of the three unknown sides of the tract of land shown in Figure 3-49.

21. A triangular piece of land is bounded by 135 ft of fencing on one side, 145 ft of stone wall on another side, and 245 ft of road frontage on the third side. What are the interior angles formed by the boundary lines?

22. A triangular piece of land is bounded by 42.5 m of fencing on one side, 51.2 m of stone wall on another side, and 85.7 m of road frontage on the third side. What are the interior angles formed by the boundary lines?

23. To determine the distance between points X and Y on the opposite sides of a river, a surveyor measures a distance of 300 m between points X and Z, where Z is set on the same side of the river as X. Angle X-YZ is measured to be 85°30′ and angle Z-XY is measured to be 35°45′. Compute the distance XY.

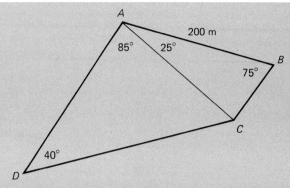

FIGURE 3-49. Illustration for Problem 20.

24. To determine the distance between points U and V on the opposite sides of a river, a surveyor measures a distance of 750 ft between points U and W, where W is set on the same side of the river as U. Angle U-VW is measured to be 75°30′, and angle W-UV is measured to be 45°15′. Compute the distance UV.

25. Two points on the opposite sides of a lake, A and B, are 355.5 and 276.2 ft, respectively, from a third point, C, on the shore. The lines joining points A and B with point C intersect at an angle of 81°15′ (angle C-AB). What is distance AB?

26. Two points on the opposite sides of a lake, D and E, are 355.5 and 276.2 ft, respectively, from a third point F on the shore. The lines joining points D and E with point F intersect at an angle of 71°45′ (angle F-DE). What is distance DE?

27. Demonstrate the validity of the following trigonometric identities (show that the left side equals the right side) for an angle $A = 30°$:

a. $\tan A = \dfrac{\sin A}{\cos A}$

b. $\sin^2 A + \cos^2 A = 1$

c. $\sin 2A = 2(\sin A)(\cos A)$

d. $\tan\left(\dfrac{A}{2}\right) = \dfrac{(1 - \cos A)}{\sin A}$

28. Demonstrate the validity of the following trigonometric identities (that the left side equals the right side) for angles $A = 10°$ and $B = 20°$:

a. $\sin(A + B) = (\sin A)(\cos B) + (\cos A)(\sin B)$

b. $\cos(A - B) = (\cos A)(\cos B) + (\sin A)(\sin B)$

c. $\tan(A + B) = \dfrac{(\tan A + \tan B)}{[1 - (\tan A)(\tan B)]}$

29. Determine the length of straight line AB, where point A has xy coordinates (15, 10) and point B has coordinates (60, 70).

30. Determine the length of straight line CD, where point C has rectangular coordinates (−20, 30) and point D has coordinates (50, −20).

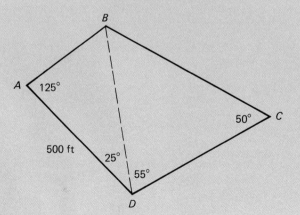

FIGURE 3-48. Illustration for Problem 19.

31. Determine the equation of a line that passes through points at $(0, 20)$ and $(20, 60)$.

32. Determine the equation of a line that passes through points $(-50, 25)$ and $(25, 25)$.

33. Determine the equation of line AB in Problem 29.

34. Determine the equation of line CD in Problem 30.

35. Line EF has the equation $y = 2x - 4$, and line GH has the equation $y = x$. Determine the coordinates of the point of intersection between EF and GH.

36. Line JK has the equation $y = -0.5x + 5$, and line LM has the equation $y = 1.5x - 5$. Determine the coordinates of the point of intersection between JK and LM.

37. What is the equation of a circle with its center at $(0, 0)$ and which passes through point $(3, 4)$?

38. What is the equation of a circle with its center at $(3, 4)$ and which passes through point $(10, 4)$?

39. Determine the intersection points between line $y = x$ and the circle of Problem 37.

40. Determine the intersection points between line $y = 10$ and the circle of Problem 38.

SURVEYING EQUIPMENT
AND FIELD METHODS

taken as the average number (most probable value) of paces, we get

$$\text{Relative accuracy} = 1 : \frac{76.9}{0.8} = 1 : 96$$

c. Measured distance = 2.6 ft/pace × 123.5 paces = 320 ft

(When pacing relatively long distances, it is easy to lose count of the number of paces. A small mechanical device called a *pedometer* can be attached to the surveyor's leg to automatically count the number of paces or strides; it may also be calibrated to display the distance paced, in meters or in feet.)

Using a Measuring Wheel

A simple *measuring wheel* mounted on a rod can be used to determine distance by pushing the rod and rolling the wheel along the line to be measured (see Figure 4-2). An attached

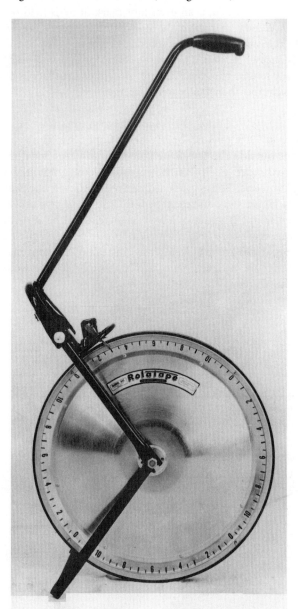

FIGURE 4-2. A typical measuring wheel used for making rough distance measurements. (*Courtesy of Sokkia Corporation*)

device called an *odometer* serves to count the number of turns, or revolutions, of the wheel. From the known circumference of the wheel and the number of revolutions, distances for reconnaissance can be determined with relative accuracies of about 1:200. This device is particularly useful for rough measurements of distance along curved lines, as well as for quick checks of route survey measurements or construction pay quantity measurements.

4-2 TAPING: EQUIPMENT AND METHODS

Measuring horizontal distances with a tape is simple in theory, but in actual practice it is not as easy as it appears at first glance. It requires skill and experience for a surveyor to be able to tape a distance with a relative accuracy between 1:3000 and 1:5000, which is a generally accepted range for most preliminary surveys, ordinary property surveys, and many types of construction layouts.

Using good-quality equipment and under normal field conditions, an experienced surveyor can readily achieve a 1:3000 accuracy without having to correct for systematic errors. Nevertheless, when handling a tape and plumb bob for the first time, many students are quite surprised at the time and effort required to achieve that degree of accuracy. It takes much practice.

Tapes and Accessories

Most of the original surveys in the United States and Canada were done using a *Gunter's chain* for measurement of horizontal distances. To this day, the term *chaining* is often used to describe the taping operation. A Gunter's chain has a length of 66 ft and is subdivided into 100 heavy wire links. It is the original unit of measurement used in the U.S. Public Land Survey. A distance like 3 ch 75 lk, for example, may still be seen on old property descriptions (3.75 ch × 66 ft/ch = 247.50 ft).

Steel Tapes   Modern steel tapes are available in a variety of lengths and cross sections; among the most commonly used are the 100-ft tape and the 30-m tape, which are 1/4 in and 6 mm wide, respectively. Both lighter as well as heavier duty tapes are also available. A steel tape is generally stored and carried on an open-reel case when not in use (see Figure 1-1*d*). Some steel tapes may have a white nylon coating for durability as well as easy-to-read graduations. (Lightweight fiberglass tapes are also available, but are generally not used for precise work.)

A surveyor's steel tape may be graduated in one of several ways. It is most important for the surveyor to be certain of the type of markings on the tape to avoid blunders. It is preferable to work with a tape that is *graduated throughout its entire length* in feet, tenths, and hundredths (0.01) of a foot, or in meters and millimeters (0.001 m). A section of a tape graduated in hundredths of a foot is shown in Figure 4-3. (The beginning student must

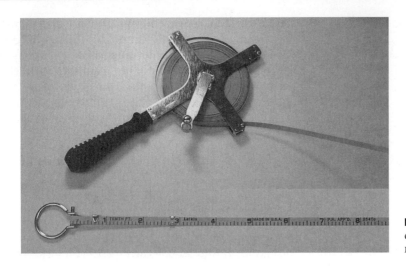

FIGURE 4-3. A steel tape in a convenient reel and typical tape markings. (See also Figure 1-1*d*.)

remember that in the United States, distances are *not* surveyed in feet, inches, and fractions of an inch; for construction, conversion from the decimal parts of a foot to inches and fractions of an inch must be made by field construction personnel, as required.)

Some tapes have the zero point at the very end of the tape or hook ring; others have the zero mark offset from the end of the tape (see Figure 4-4). Again, it is essential that the surveyor knows exactly what type of tape is being used in order to avoid blunders.

Cut Tapes   Some older or less-expensive American tapes are marked every foot, with only the first and last foot intervals graduated in tenths and hundredths of a foot. A metric tape may be marked every meter and decimeter, with only the first and last decimeters graduated in millimeters. These tapes are called *cut tapes* because a mental subtraction must be made before recording the measured distance.

For example, if an even foot mark of 57 is held over point *B* and 0.15 is read at the head of the tape (see Figure 4-5), the 0.15 must be "cut," or subtracted, from 57 ft to give the distance of 56.85 ft. This can be confusing and may lead to many serious blunders. The only benefit of a cut tape is that it is cheaper than a fully graduated tape.

Add Tapes   Some 100-ft tapes have graduations extending 0.99 ft beyond or in back of the zero mark, and thus outside the 100-ft length. A metric tape may have an extended decimeter beyond the zero, graduated in millimeters. These graduations are numbered backward (see Figure 4-6), and the tape is called an *add tape* because the decimal fraction of a foot or meter must be added to an integer value held over the opposite point. If the end graduations are mistakenly used instead of the zero mark (see Figure 4-6), a distance of 100.99 ft, or 30.1 m, would be measured.

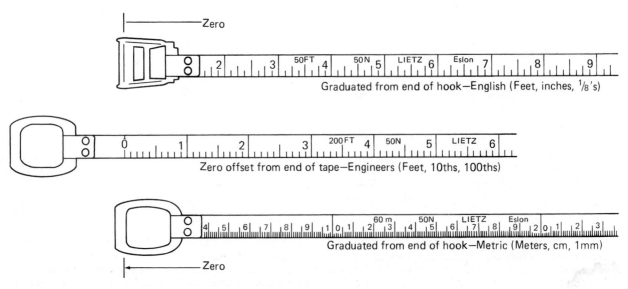

FIGURE 4-4. Some surveyors' tapes have the zero mark at the endpoint of the tape, while others have zero offset from the end. (*Courtesy of The Lietz Company*)

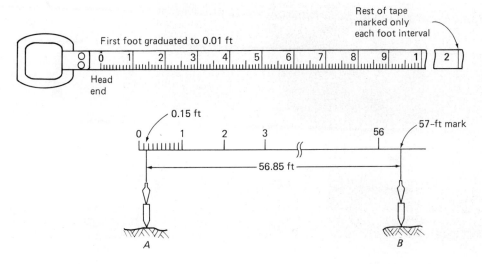

FIGURE 4-5. A cut tape.

Like the cut tape, an add tape tends to cause blunders in the work. For most surveyors, it is well worth the small extra cost of a fully graduated tape to eliminate this source of error.

Invar and Lovar Tapes For very precise measurements and for checking or standardizing the length of ordinary steel tapes, special tapes made from a nickel–steel alloy may be used. Depending on the specific alloy, they are called either *Invar* or *Lovar* tapes. These tapes are relatively insensitive to temperature changes, thus eliminating systematic errors due to expansion or contraction. But because they are relatively expensive and must be handled with great care, they are not used for ordinary surveying applications.

Accessories for Taping Accurate taping cannot be done with the tape alone. When taping horizontal distances, the tape very often must be held above the ground at one or both ends. One of the most important accessories for proper horizontal taping is the *plumb bob* (see Figure 4-7). It is a small metal weight with a sharp, replaceable point. Freely suspended from a cord, the plumb bob is used to project the horizontal position of a point on the ground up to the tape, or vice versa. This procedure, which requires much skill and practice, is described later in this section.

When taping horizontal distances, it is necessary to hold the tape as close to a horizontal position as possible. To reduce errors caused by an excessively sloped tape, some surveyors make use of a *hand level*. A horizontal line of sight can be easily obtained by looking through the level toward the surveyor at the higher end of the tape. This, along with proper judgment, gives the surveyors an idea of how high to hold their end of the tape.

Whenever possible, a spring-balance *tension handle* should be attached to the forward end of the tape to indicate

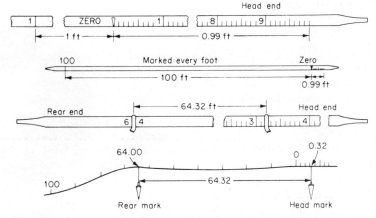

FIGURE 4-6. A 100-ft tape with graduations outside the 100-ft length. In use, the graduated end and the add mark are kept forward, with the 100-ft mark at the rear. In laying out 100-ft intervals, the 100 mark and the zero mark are used. In measuring distances less than 100 ft, for example, 64.32 ft, the head chainman stops when point *B* is reached and holds the zero mark at that point. The rear chainman finds that the previous point marked on the ground comes between the 64- and the 65-ft mark. Choosing the smaller, he or she calls "holding 64" and holds the 64-ft mark over the ground mark. The head chainman reads the value of the backward graduation, that is, 0.32 ft, at point *B*.

n easily be determined by walking
e of known distance on level ground.
taken to walk the distance is counted.
omputed as the ratio of known dis-
ber of paces.

ed along a given line that was
determine her average unit
es, recording 78, 76.5, 77,
her field book.

e.
om the given data, and
her pacing method.
rage of 123.5 paces
stance, what is the

it should be
or recording
the other
disregard
of paces

6

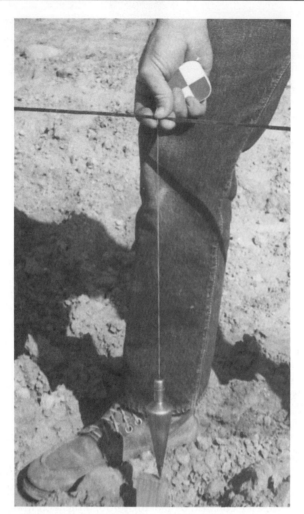

FIGURE 4-7. A plumb bob is one of the simplest yet most important accessories for accurate surveying. The vertical cord transfers a position from the steel tape to the wooden stake in the ground. (*Courtesy of The Lietz Company*)

whether or not the correct pull or tension is applied. Applying the correct tension is particularly important if a relative accuracy of better than 1:3000 is required. All beginning students should use the tension handle at least once to get a feel for the correct pull on the tape; many beginners are surprised, and a bit dismayed, at how hard they have to pull for good taping results.

For precise taping with accuracies better than 1:5000, temperature corrections must be made (in addition to applying the correct tension) to account for the possibility of tape expansion or contraction; a *tape thermometer* may be used for this purpose. It is attached to the tape near one end; the bulb should be in contact with the steel.

A tape *clamp handle* (see Figure 4-8) is used for providing a firm grip on the tape at any intermediate point, without causing damage to the tape or injury to the surveyor from the steel edge. Occasionally, however, a steel tape may be accidentally damaged in the field. *Tape repair kits* are available for splicing broken tapes; a spliced tape must first be recalibrated or standardized before being put back in use to avoid systematic errors.

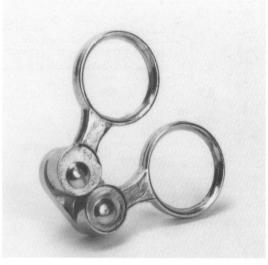

FIGURE 4-8. A tape clamp handle. (*Courtesy of The Lietz Company*)

Nonmetallic *woven tapes* made of synthetic yarn, or tapes made of *fiberglass*, may be used for measuring distances when only low relative accuracy (less than 1:3000) is required, such as in preliminary topo surveys. They are usually used in 50-ft or 15-m lengths and may be graduated on both sides, one side in U.S. Customary units and the other in metric units (see Figure 4-9).

Precautions to Avoid Damaging the Tape   Although most steel tapes used for surveying will withstand a direct tension of 80 lb (360 N) or more, it is very easy to break them by misuse. When a tape is allowed to lie on the ground, unless it is kept extended so that there is no slack, it has a tendency to form small loops like that shown in Figure 4-10. When tension is later applied, the loop becomes smaller until either it jumps out straight or the tape breaks, as shown. If a tuft of grass or any object is caught by the loop,

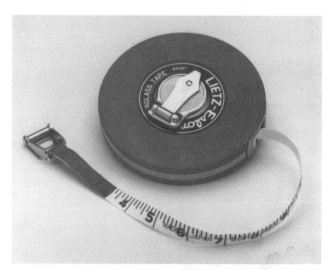

FIGURE 4-9. A nonmetallic 15-m fiberglass tape. (*Courtesy of The Lietz Company*)

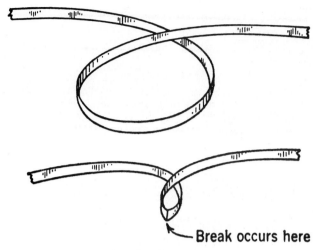

FIGURE 4-10. How a loop breaks a tape.

the tape almost always breaks or at least develops a permanent kink.

To avoid this, the tape must be handled so that no slack can occur. For measurements of less than a full tape length, the tape should be kept on the reel. It should be reeled out to the necessary length and reeled in as soon as possible. For measurements greater than the tape length, when the tape is off the reel, the tape should be kept fully extended in a straight line along the direction of measurement. It may be allowed to lie on the ground in this position, but when it is to be moved, it must be dragged from one end only. If it is necessary to raise the tape off the ground, the two surveyors must lift the tape simultaneously and keep it in tension between them.

When the end of the measurement is reached, where a less-than-tape-length measurement is required, the surveyor must not pull in the tape hand over hand. This creates a pile of tape on the ground. This is safe only on a smooth surface. Instead, he or she must do one of three things:

1. Carry the end of the tape beyond the point, lay it on the ground, and walk back.
2. Or reel in the tape the requisite amount.
3. Or take in the tape, forming figure-eight loops hanging from his or her hand.

Each length of tape must be laid in the surveyor's hand flat on the previous section and never allowed to change. Later, to extend the tape, the surveyor must lay it out carefully, as he or she walks forward, by releasing one loop at a time. This third method requires care and practice and should not be attempted until after considerable practice over a smooth floor where there is little danger.

If possible, no vehicle should be allowed to run over the tape. If the tape is across a smoothly paved street, a pneumatic tire can pass over the tape without damaging it if the tape is held flat and tightly pressed against the street surface by the two surveyors.

When a tape is wet, it should be carefully cleaned and oiled as soon as possible.

In general, it is good to remember that a tape is easily damaged, but with care and thought, damage seldom occurs.

Taping a Horizontal Distance

Taping may be used to determine the unknown distance between two fixed points on the ground, or it may be used to set marks at specified distances on a given line. The latter operation is called *setting marks for line and distance*; it requires the use of an instrument to "give line." In this section, a typical field procedure for taping an unknown horizontal distance, over level or sloping ground, will be discussed.

Clearly, at least two surveyors are needed to tape a distance—a *front*, or *head*, chainman to hold the front end of the tape and a *rear* chainman to hold the back of the tape.

In the following description, a distance is to be measured from point *A* to point *B*, each point being clearly marked on the ground by a wooden stake and tack or a concrete monument. In this text, taping is described with the zero mark of the tape kept to the rear. Some surveyors prefer to keep the tape reversed. But because it seems more logical to stretch out the tape with the numbers increasing in the direction of taping, here we assign the rear chainman the job of holding zero. (References to the position of the hands with respect to the tape and plumb-bob string refer to right-handed persons.)

In most taping operations, *the tape must be held in a horizontal position*. Ideally, if *A* and *B* are at the same elevation with no obstacles between them, the tape can be laid directly on the level ground and supported throughout its entire length (see Figure 4-11a). More often than not, a gradual slope makes it necessary to raise one end of the tape above the ground to keep it horizontal. At that end, a vertical plumb-bob string serves to line up the appropriate tape graduation with the point (see Figure 4-11b). Sometimes both ends of the tape must be raised above the ground, making it necessary for both the head and rear chainman to use plumb bobs (see Figure 4-11c).

Setting Out and Aligning the Tape   To begin, the head chainman unreels the tape by walking toward *B* with the reel, while the rear chainman holds the zero end at *A*. The zero mark of the tape must always be held exactly over point *A*, using a plumb bob when necessary, even when only a preliminary measurement is made. If not, the head chainman will waste time clearing a place for an intermediate forward mark, or may actually mark the point when the rear end of the tape is being held incorrectly.

Frequently the head chainman will raise the tape to clear obstacles and to straighten it. The rear chainman should raise the tape at the same time, but still attempt to keep the zero mark as nearly as possible over the point.

When the head chainman reaches the end of the tape, it is removed from the reel; a tension handle or a leather thong should be attached at that end. The rear chainman, sighting

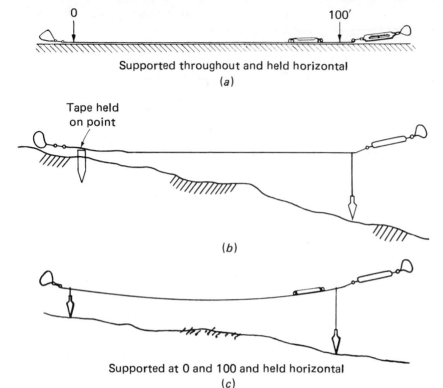

Supported throughout and held horizontal
(a)

Tape held
on point

(b)

Supported at 0 and 100 and held horizontal
(c)

FIGURE 4-11. Methods of supporting a tape.

point B, directs the head chainman by voice until the head end of the tape is on line. The direction and estimated length of tape movement may be called out as "west two-tenths, east one-tenth," etc.

Marking an Intermediate Station on Line   The head chainman pulls the tape straight and makes a rough measurement, while the rear chainman checks the alignment. The rear chainman should keep his or her eyes above the point, and the head chainman should keep on one side of the tape so that the rear chainman can see point B during this process. The head chainman prepares a place to mark the distance where the rough measurement fell. In grass, a small spot is cleared; on pavement, a yellow keel mark is made.

Next, the lengths of the plumb-bob cords are adjusted so that the bobs will swing just clear of the points (about 1/8 in. above the point) when the tape is in position. The tape should be horizontal and should be as near the ground as possible without touching intervening obstacles. With the handles of the tape in their right hands, the surveyors should face the tape (their left sides toward each other). The plumb-bob cord is held on the far side of the tape, bent over the tape, and held on the proper graduation with the thumb of the left hand (see Figure 4-12).

While holding the plumb bob in this manner, the tape is moved up and down slightly, gently tapping the point of the bob to dampen the swinging motion. The stance must be steady. Raising the tape to shoulder height should be avoided (see the following discussion on breaking tape). When the tape is waist-high, the surveyor's feet should be spread well apart along the line of the tape for good balance. When the

tape is low, one knee may be placed on the ground for extra support.

The head chainman applies the tension gradually until the spring-balance handle reads the correct tension (usually about 20 lb). If a tension handle is not used, the surveyor must estimate the proper tension. When the tension is applied, the rear plumb bob may be pulled a short distance off point A. The rear chainman must pull the tape back at once with a smooth motion. When the zero mark is stationary over the point, the rear chainman calls out "mark" or "good," and so on. The surveyor should continue to call out "mark" as long as the tape is in the correct position, and stop calling it as soon as the tape moves off the point. When the head chainman relieves the tension, the rear chainman may stop calling out.

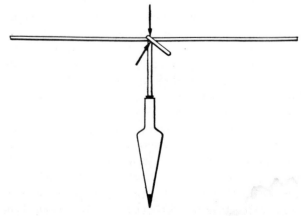

FIGURE 4-12. Holding the plumb-bob cord on the tape.

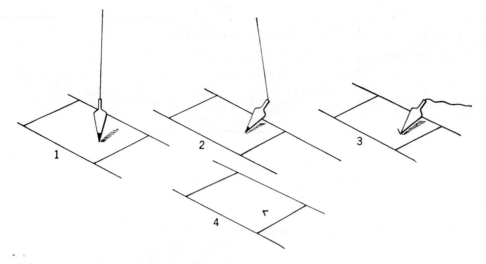

FIGURE 4-13. Steps in marking a point on a pavement.

At the forward end, when the tightly pulled tape and the plumb bob become steady, the head chainman gently lowers the tape so that the bob rests on its point. If the ground is soft, the hole made by the point is sufficient for the time being. The surveyor then releases the tape and places a tack or a nail in the hole, through a piece of colored marking tape, to make it easy for the rear chainman to find.

When working on a pavement or any other hard surface, the head chainman gently lowers the bob so that the point just touches the ground at the correct position. The surveyor then releases the tape, reaches for the bob with the right hand, and firmly marks the position of the point (see Figure 4-13). Usually, this is done by making a scratch with the point from the position it occupies; the beginning of the scratch is the mark. A second scratch is made from that mark, at right angles to the first, forming a V. The surveyor then writes the number of tape lengths, called *stations*, on the pavement with the keel. (Stationing is discussed later in this section.)

It is good practice to check the distance after it is marked, before moving up the line. The rear chainman then calls out the number of the station he or she occupies, and the head chainman calls out the number he or she has marked; an appropriate entry is made in the field book.

The head chainman moves forward toward *B*, *dragging the tape.* The rear chainman also moves forward, but does not pick up the end of the tape. When the zero mark comes up to the mark, the rear chainman calls "chain," or gives some other signal for the head chainman to stop and get in line. The procedure for measurement is then repeated.

An error in counting tape lengths is one of the chief sources of blunder in distance measurement. When taping long distances over unpaved surfaces, the rear chainman must keep a count of full tape lengths.

Completing the Measurement   Upon reaching point *B*, a distance less than one full tape length will remain to be measured. The head chainman either reels in part of the tape

or walks on past *B* carrying the head end forward. He or she then returns to *B* to make the measurement.

While plumbing as previously described, the head chainman slides the plumb-bob cord along the tape until the bob is over the mark for point *B*. Then, holding the cord in position on the tape, he or she reads the graduations silently. The rear chainman comes forward and reads the graduations out loud. If the readings agree, the value is recorded. (When the tape is used with the 100-ft mark to the rear, the head chainman holds the zero mark at *B* while the rear chainman takes the reading, and the rear chainman holds it while the head chainman moves back to check.)

To return the tape to the reel, the head chainman first removes the tension handle or thong from the 100-ft end of the tape and passes the end into the reel. The end ring is attached to the spindle so that the graduated side of the tape is up when the reel crank handle is on the right, facing the tape; with the tape in this position, it can be used conveniently to measure less-than-tape-length distances.

Breaking Tape   When the ground slope is excessive, it may be difficult or impossible to hold the full tape in a horizontal position by plumbing one end; when a surveyor tries to hold a plumb bob and tape from shoulder height, or higher, accidental errors tend to increase due to the unsteady position. Over rough terrain, then, a process called *breaking tape* should be employed (see Figure 4-14).

Breaking tape refers to the following procedure: After unreeling the tape out to its full length, the head chainman returns to a point where the tape can be held level in a comfortable and steady position. He or she then selects an integer footmark, say 60 ft, which is announced to the rear chainman. After a temporary mark is set at that distance, the rear chainman comes forward and holds the tape at that exact footmark. The measurement proceeds without moving the tape; using a clamp handle or "chain grip," the rear chainman holds the 60-ft footmark as if it were zero and the head chainman sets a new mark at the 100-ft end of the tape.

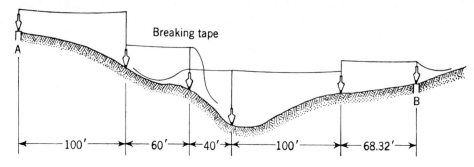

FIGURE 4-14. Breaking tape over steeply sloping ground.

The process is repeated as required until the full distance is measured. (For long distances, the use of EDM is preferable to breaking tape.)

Setting Marks for Line and Distance

When a series of marks are set on a line at measured distances, surveyors use a standard system for identifying the marks; the marks are called *stations*. The stations may be very temporary (as in the procedure described for measuring an unknown distance), or somewhat more long-lasting, but they are rarely meant to be permanent marks. Stationing is particularly important when doing profile leveling, as well as when setting marks for line and distance in a route survey, and will be discussed again in subsequent chapters.

Identifying Stations A zero position is usually established at the beginning of the survey or at the beginning of

the line to be marked out. This zero point is identified as $0 + 00$. Each point located at intervals of exactly 100 ft or 100 m from the beginning point is called a *full station* and is identified as follows: a point 100 ft from $0 + 00$ is labeled station $1 + 00$, a point 200 m from the zero point is station $2 + 00$, and so on (see Figure 4-15a).

Points located between the full stations are identified as follows: a point 350 ft from the zero point is called $3 + 50$ ("three plus fifty"), and a point 475 m from zero is called $4 + 75$. At a distance of 462.78 ft from zero, the station is called $4 + 62.78$. The $+ 50, + 75$, and $+ 62.78$ are called *pluses*. The point 462.78 is said to have a plus of 62.78 from station 4. The stationing of points in this manner is frequently carried continuously throughout an entire survey (see Figure 4-15b). Naturally, when interpreting stations, it must be known beforehand whether U.S. Customary units or metric units are being used; the symbols *ft* or *m* do not follow after the station designations.

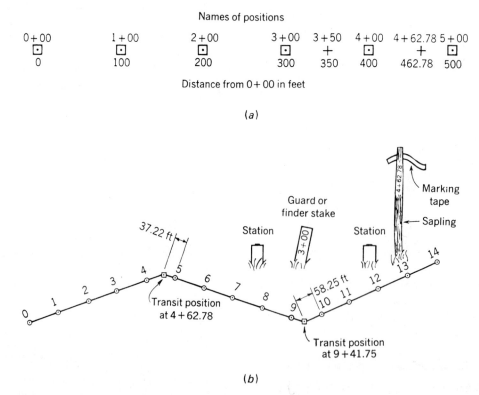

FIGURE 4-15. The positions along a measured line are called stations.

Setting marks for line and distance typically involves the use of a transit or theodolite to establish the proper direction of the line and to help keep the marks set by the chainman exactly on that line. In this section, the field procedure is described from the perspective of the taping and staking operation. The procedure for setting up an instrument over a point is described in Chapter 6.

Field Procedure Usually the measurement starts at the instrument, which is set up over the beginning point of the line and locked in the proper direction. The rear chainman holds the zero end of the tape near the instrument while the head chainman carries all the equipment forward, holding the reel so that the tape unwinds. When the proper distance is reached, the head chainman stops and the rear chainman gets in position below the instrument, with care to avoid touching the tripod legs.

The zero mark of the tape is held directly on the beginning point, if possible, while the tape is held in a horizontal position. If the tape must be raised above the point to keep it horizontal, the plumb-bob cord on the instrument is loosened until about 20 cm, or 8 in, of slack is available; the cord is then held taut by pressing it against the point with one hand (see Figure 4-16). With the other hand, the surveyor controls the tape so that the zero mark is lined up with the cord.

At the other end of the tape, the head chainman bends the plumb-bob cord over the tape at the proper graduation, holding it in position by squeezing the cord and tape together with one hand (see Figure 4-17). Tension is applied with the other hand, holding the tape at the proper height to keep it level.

When the plumb bob is steady, the head chainman calls "line for stake." The person at the instrument directs line by signal or voice, giving the direction and amount of movement. When the plumb-bob cord is brought nearly on line, the instrument person calls or signals "good for stake." At this signal, the head chainman releases the plumb bob so that it drops vertically, marking the ground slightly with its point.

Driving a Stake On unpaved ground, stations are usually marked with a wooden stake (or hub) and tack. The longest dimension of the top of the stake is kept in the direction of

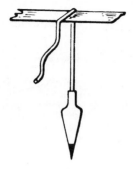

FIGURE 4-17. Plumb-bob cord bent over tape.

the measurement, and the stake is first driven at the plumb-bob mark to a depth of about 5 cm, or 2 in.

The position of the stake is then checked as follows. The head chainman calls "distance," and the rear chainman then holds zero on the mark; the tape is stretched and the distance checked. The head chainman then calls "line for stake" and holds the bob as a target for the instrument person, moving it as directed. If the position is correct, the stake is driven farther into the ground by the head chainman; the surveyor at the instrument watches it as long as it is visible. He or she will call "keep it south" or "south one-tenth," as the need arises.

It takes considerable skill to drive a stake so that the top remains in position. Usually, the surveyors will make a second check when the stake is partly driven home. The top of the stake invariably moves toward the person driving it. Slight corrections can therefore be made by driving it from the position toward which the stake should move (see Figure 4-18). When greater corrections are necessary, the ground should be pounded beside the stake, or stones can be driven into the ground beside it. Tapping the side of the stake to align it merely loosens it and sometimes breaks it.

When the stake is driven well into the ground and found to be out of position, the only recourse is to drive another stake beside it. If instead it is withdrawn, it will follow the old hole when redriven. A stake must be driven until it is firmly in position, with the top not more than several centimeters, or a few inches, above the ground surface.

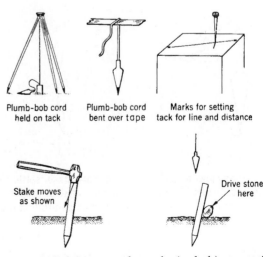

Plumb-bob cord   Plumb-bob cord   Marks for setting
held on tack   bent over tape   tack for line and distance

Stake moves
as shown

Drive stone
here

FIGURE 4-18. Driving a wooden stake (or hub) at a station.

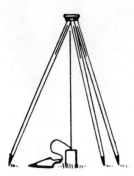

FIGURE 4-16. Holding the plumb-bob cord taut against the tack.

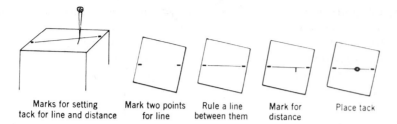

Marks for setting   Mark two points   Rule a line   Mark for   Place tack
tack for line and distance   for line   between them   distance

FIGURE 4-19. Setting a tack on a wooden hub.

Setting a Tack   A pencil is placed on top of the stake, held slanting away from the instrument or, preferably, balanced on its point. The pencil point is directed exactly on line by signals from the instrument person, and a pencil mark is made on the stake. Usually, two marks are made near the edges of the top of the stake, toward and away from the instrument, and a pencil line is ruled between them (see Figure 4-19).

If the instrument person cannot see the pencil, he or she calls "raise it," indicating to the head chainman that a plumb bob should be used instead. The plumb-bob cord should be held as close as possible to the bob without interfering with the instrument person's view (see Figure 4-20). The swing of the bob can be dampened by tapping the point against the top of the stake.

When the plumb bob is brought exactly in line by directions from the instrument person, the latter calls "good for tack"; the head chainman then gently drops the bob to the stake by slightly lowering one hand. While holding the cord and bob in this position with one hand, the surveyor reaches the bob with the other hand and marks the point by making a hole in the stake with the point of the bob.

To mark the exact distance on the stake along the pencil line, the tape is held on top of the stake along that line, tension is applied, and a tack is driven at the final mark. If this is not possible, a plumb bob is used again (see Figure 4-21). The cord is bent over the proper graduation, tension applied, and the swing damped out by moving the tape up and down so that the point of the bob taps the stake. The bob is kept over the pencil line. The exact point is marked

with the point of the bob and checked if necessary, and the tack is driven.

The station number is marked on the stake with keel, or on a guard or witness stake set near it. The station number should be checked; the head chainman calls "station," and the rear chainman calls out the number of the station where he or she is standing. Frequent checking of the work, as described in this procedure, is necessary to avoid serious blunders. Generally, it is the responsibility of the head chainman to decide when the checks are necessary because he or she actually sets the point and knows by experience whether conditions were proper for an accurate result.

When the head chainman is finished, the rear chainman drops the end of the tape and walks forward to the stake just set. In the meantime, the head chainman takes the equipment forward and drags the tape. When the zero end of the tape reaches the stake, the rear chainman calls out its station number, the head chainman stops, and the process of setting a stake is repeated. The rear chainman now handles the tape in the same manner as the head chainman, except that instead of applying tension, he or she resists it.

FIGURE 4-21. Measuring for a tack with a short hold.

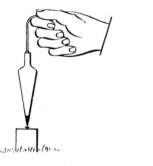

Hold as close to bob as possible and keep bob point as close as possible to stake

To mark stake, settle bob on stake at proper point; then controlling bob as shown, seize bob and make hole with point

FIGURE 4-20. Handling a plumb bob to set a tack.

Making Marks on Other Surfaces   When a wooden stake strikes an obstruction before it is driven home, the earth is cleared away and the mark is made on the obstruction.

When working on paved surfaces, wooden stakes are not set, and the process is simpler. Pencil lines or scratches on the pavement may be used for marks. In concrete, a cross can be chiseled at the mark if it must be somewhat permanent. Usually, the mark is circled with keel to make it easy to find. Also, a heavy masonry (P-K) nail or a hardened steel spike can be driven into concrete or asphalt as a mark. Often, a small piece of colored ribbon or plastic is placed on the nail to make it easy to find.

4-3 TAPING MISTAKES, ERRORS, AND CORRECTIONS

As in any kind of surveying operation, taping blunders must be eliminated, and taping errors, both random and systematic, must be minimized to achieve accurate results. In this section, some common sources of mistakes and errors are discussed, and methods to compute correction factors, which compensate for certain systematic errors, are explained and illustrated.

Taping Mistakes or Blunders

There are several opportunities for careless taping mistakes or blunders, which the surveyor must always be aware of. Awareness is the first step in prevention. The common sources of blunder include the following:

Misreading the tape, particularly reading a 6 for a 9, or vice versa. For example, the distance 49.55 might be incorrectly read as 46.55. To avoid this, the surveyor should be in position facing the graduations when reading the tape, and be in the habit of glancing at the adjacent numbers on the tape before calling out the reading.

Misrecording the reading, particularly by transposing digits. For example, the note keeper may hear the chainman call out a distance of 24.32 but erroneously write down 23.42 instead. Or the chainman may call out 40.75 as "forty (pause), seven, five," which could be interpreted and recorded as 47.5. To avoid blunders of this nature, the note keeper should always call out the recorded number, including the decimal point, for verification by the chainman.

Mistaking the endpoint of the tape. As discussed in the preceding section, tapes are manufactured and graduated in several ways. The surveyor should always be certain of which tape he or she is using on any particular job, and where the beginning or zero mark is for that tape. If the tape is not graduated throughout its length, it is particularly important that the surveyor know whether the tape is a cut tape or an add tape.

Miscounting full tape lengths, particularly when long distances are taped. Using taping pins for a tally or calling out and checking station numbers for each tape length helps to avoid this type of blunder. (Actually, the best way to avoid this mistake is to use an EDMI for measuring a long distance.)

Mistaking station markers. Taping to or from an incorrect point is a serious blunder for any surveyor, but it can happen. All survey crew members must be careful to avoid this; the identity of the points, whether they are iron bars, wooden stakes and tacks, concrete monuments, or masonry nails, should be verified before starting the taping operation.

In general, to avoid blunders it is good practice always to check every reading or mark set on line. In fact, taping the distance twice, once forward and once back, is an ideal way to avoid serious mistakes. Pacing is also very useful to detect major blunders in the work; if there is a large discrepancy between the taped distance and the paced distance, the mistake can be found and corrected before moving forward. The need to eliminate blunders in any surveying operation cannot be overemphasized.

Taping Errors

Taping errors may be systematic or random. Unavoidable random or accidental errors occur primarily when using the plumb bob; setting chaining pins, tacks, or other marks; and estimating readings to values less than the smallest tape graduation. Random errors also occur in tape tension, tape alignment, and temperature readings (when computing corrections). It is because of these errors that we say no measurement is perfect or exact. By definition, random errors cannot be completely eliminated, but they can be reduced by using good field methods and precision in the work.

When the tape is not exactly horizontal or when it is slightly off line, the measured distance will be too long (Figure 4-22). But for most ordinary surveys, this is not usually a significant problem with regard to the degree of accuracy required. In a 100-ft distance, the tape would have to be out of alignment by about 1.4 ft for the error to exceed 0.01 ft. (In a 30-m distance, the tape would have to be off line by 0.5 m for the error to exceed 0.005 m, or 5 mm.)

With moderate care, the rear chainman should be able to keep the head chainman on line well within 1.4 ft or 0.5 m by eye, using a range pole. Using an instrument to establish the line, of course, will eliminate any possibility of measurable error due to the tape being off line. And use of a hand level will help to keep the tape level.

For a taping accuracy of 1:5000, it is necessary to keep the tape level and on line within 1 ft/100 ft (or 0.30 m/30 m) and to keep plumbing or marking errors less than 0.015 ft/100 ft (or 0.05 m/30 m). This requires care and attention to the work. Also, the actual tape length must be known within ± 0.005 ft (or ±0.0015 m), the temperature must be within 7°F (4°C) of the calibration or standard temperature, and the

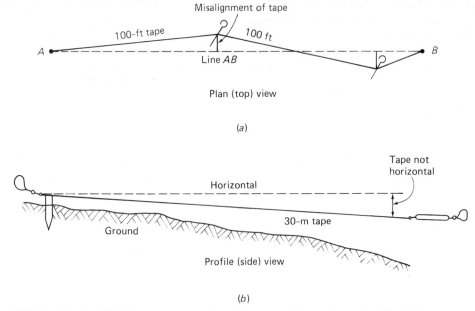

FIGURE 4-22. Accidental errors occur when the tape is (a) misaligned or (b) off-level. For good accuracy, the tape should be on line and horizontal within 1 ft/100 ft (0.3m/100m).

pull or tension on the tape must be within 5 lb (20 N) of the normal tension for the tape.

Correction of Systematic Errors

Tape manufacturers make steel tapes that are very nearly correct in length at 68°F (20°C) when supported throughout and under a tension of 10 lb (50 N). When a tape is supported at only two points, as when taping a horizontal distance over sloping ground, it always tends to sag between the points of support (see Figure 4-23). This, in effect, makes the tape too short; the apparent "length of the tape" is the straight-line distance between the supports.

Steel is an elastic material that will stretch temporarily under moderate tension (at a certain tension or pull, however, the stretch or deformation will be permanent). A medium-weight 100-ft (or 30-m) tape supported at its beginning and endpoints under a tension of 20 lb (or 100 N) is usually very nearly the same length as when it is fully supported throughout under a tension of 10 lb (or 50 N). In other words, the extra tension tends to cancel out the effect of sag.

The pull required so that systematic errors due to incorrect tension and sag cancel each other is called the *normal tension* for the tape; in practice, it should be determined for each individual working tape. For most ordinary taping surveys of about 1:5000 accuracy, it is sufficient to apply normal tension within ±5 lb (or ±20 N); a spring-balance tension handle is useful for this purpose, but many surveyors rely on a "feel" for the correct tension.

In more precise taping surveys, mathematical formulas can be used to correct for tension and sag errors when other than normal tension is applied. Generally, however, precise long-distance measurement (more than 200 ft or 60 m) is now done using electronic instruments rather than tapes. For this reason, sag and tension formulas are not presented here, but may be found in more advanced texts.

Common Tape Corrections   In most ordinary taping surveys using a properly standardized tape and normal tension, a *correction for actual tape length* and a *correction for temperature* may be applied for good relative accuracy (1:5000). Without these corrections, the relative accuracy of the work may be only average (1:3000), or worse. This is

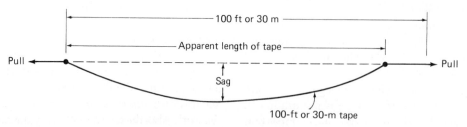

FIGURE 4-23. A steel tape always tends to sag between supports, no matter how hard it is pulled.

because the errors are systematic; that is, they are repetitive and they accumulate in proportion to the number of times the tape is used to measure a distance.

Correction for Tape Length

In use, tapes tend to change length. They wear out and thus become thinner and lighter; due to wear, they stretch more and sag less and thus become longer. Also, when a tape becomes kinked or when a broken tape is repaired by splicing, its length will change. In other words, even though the endpoints still read as zero and 100 ft or 30 m, the actual distance between those endpoints will be something other than what the graduations indicate.

Sometimes the changes in length are quite small and of little importance in many types of surveys. However, when good relative accuracy is required, the actual tape length must be known within 0.005 ft or 1.5 mm. The actual length of a working tape, then, must be compared with a *standard tape* periodically. When its actual length is known, the tape is said to be *standardized.*

Some surveying firms keep a special standard tape (Invar or Lovar) with which to compare and standardize their working tapes. Or for a fee, working tapes can be sent to the U.S. National Bureau of Standards to be standardized for any specified tension or support condition; the Bureau will return the tape with a certificate stating the tape length at 68°F (20°C), to the nearest 0.001 ft (0.0003 m).

A correction must be added (or subtracted) to a measured distance whenever its standardized length differs from its nominal or graduated length. The correction for one full tape length is

$$C_L = L_s - L \qquad (4-2)$$

where C_L = the correction per single tape length
L_s = the actual or standardized length of the tape
L = the nominal tape length (i.e., 100 ft, 30 m, etc.)

Example 4-2

A 30-m tape was standardized and found to have an actual length of only 29.985 m (between the 0 and 30.000-m tape marks). What is the required correction per tape length?

Solution

Applying Equation 4-2, we get

$$C_L = L_s - L = 29.985 - 30.000 = -0.015 \text{ m}$$

In this case, the tape is *too short*, by 15 mm. Note that the correction carries a negative sign. This is a relatively large tape length error; such a tape would probably be discarded. In one tape length, a maximum relative accuracy of only 1:30/0.015 = 1:2000 would be achieved (without applying an appropriate correction).

Use of C_L for Correct Distance

The total correction to the measured distance D depends on the number of tape lengths used to make the measurement. Thus,

$$\text{Correct distance} = D \pm C_L \ (D/L) \qquad (4-3)$$

where D/L is the number of tape lengths in the total distance.

The Sign of the Tape Length Correction

Whether to add or subtract the value of C_L may be confusing at first. In general, when *measuring an unknown distance*, the correct distance = $D + C_L$ (D/L); but when *laying out a specified distance*, the correct distance = $D - C_L$ (D/L).

It is best, however, to understand and then memorize the following set of rules:

1. When measuring an unknown distance, if the tape is too short, subtract the correction; *if the tape is too long, add the correction.*

2. When laying out a given distance, *if the tape is too short, add the correction; if the tape is too long, subtract the correction.*

Actually, it is only necessary to memorize the first rule; the other rules can easily be remembered from that, depending on the specific problem at hand. Keep in mind, however, that when Equations 4-2 and 4-3 are used directly, it is only necessary to add C_L algebraically in case 1 and subtract it in case 2.

Explanation When the tape is too short, too many tape lengths will fit into the distance. Because of this, the recorded or measured distance will be too great. (When a distance is measured, the value read on the tape graduations is recorded in the field book; that is, the value that must be corrected to find the true length of the line.)

Assume that two monuments were known to be exactly 100.000 ft apart. Suppose this distance were measured with a tape that was too short. For example, assume the tape's actual length to be 99.996 ft (see Figure 4-24).

The zero of the tape would be held at point *A*. The 100.000-ft graduation would reach to point *M*, where a mark would be made and *called* 100.000 ft. An additional distance to point B would then be measured and found to be 0.004 ft. The total distance would be recorded as 100.004 ft. To obtain the true distance, a correction of 0.004 ft would have to be *subtracted*; thus

$$\text{Correct distance} = 100.004 - 0.004 = 100.000 \text{ ft}$$

or

$$C_L = 100.000 - 100.004 = -0.004$$

and

$$\text{Correct distance} = 100.004 + (-0.004) = 100.000 \text{ ft}$$

This proves the rule that when the tape is too short, a number must be subtracted from the recorded value to obtain the true distance. It must be remembered that it is the *recorded distance* that is corrected. Following the same reasoning, it should be clear that when the tape is too long, a number must be added to the recorded value to obtain a true distance.

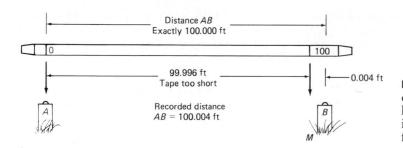

FIGURE 4-24. When measuring a distance with a tape whose actual length is *shorter* than its last marking, a correction must be *subtracted* from the recorded distance.

When a specified distance is to be laid out, the rule is reversed. Assume, for example, that exactly 30.000 m is to be laid out with a tape that has a standardized length of 29.990 m. Obviously, 0.010 m must be added to the length marked by the tape. Therefore, a tape reading of 30.010 m should be used to lay out the required distance with that particular tape. Thus, for a layout problem, when the tape is too short, add a number to obtain a correct distance.

Example 4-3

A distance between points *A and B* is measured and recorded as 567.89 ft, using a tape that has a certified standard length of 99.96 ft. What is the true distance between *A and B*? (Assume normal tension is used, and no temperature correction is required.)

Solution

Applying Equations 4-2 and 4-3, we get

$$C_L = L_s - L = 99.96 - 100.000 = -0.04 \text{ ft}$$

and

$$\text{Correct distance} = 567.89 + (-0.04)(567.89/100)$$
$$= 567.89 + (-0.04)(5.6789)$$
$$= 567.89 - 0.2272 = 567.66 \text{ ft}$$

As a check, we know that the actual distance equals the actual tape length times the number of tape lengths, or $99.96 \times 5.6789 = 567.66$ ft.

Example 4-4

It is necessary to lay out and mark a point *D* exactly 90.000 m distant from point *C* for a certain construction project. A steel tape with a standardized length of 30.006 m is used. What should be the distance measured with that tape from *C* to accurately set the mark for point *D*?

Solution

Applying Equations 4-2 and 4-3, we get

$$C_L = L_s - L = 30.006 - 30.000 = 0.006 \text{ m}$$

and

$$\text{Correct distance} = 90.000 - (0.006) \times \frac{90.000}{30}$$
$$= 90.000 - 0.018 = 89.982 \text{ m}$$

As a check, consider the opposite problem: a distance has been measured to be 89.982 m with a tape that is actually 90.006 m in length. The correct distance is 89.982 + (0.006)(89.982/30) = 90.000 m.

Correction for Temperature   As mentioned before, steel tapes are generally standardized at 68°F (20°C). But steel expands with increasing temperature and contracts with decreasing temperature. Therefore, when the tape is warmer than the standard temperature, it will be too long; when the tape is colder than the standard temperature, it will be too short. In effect, then, an additional length correction, one due to temperature differences, may have to be applied to the tape to determine a true distance.

For every 1°F change in temperature, an ordinary steel tape will change 0.0000065 ft per foot of original length. For every 1°C change in temperature, the tape will change 0.0000116 m per meter of original length. These numbers, 0.0000065 and 0.0000116, are equivalent dimensionless constants or ratios for steel, called the *coefficient of linear expansion* (note that ft/ft = m/m = 1); the first is used with °F and the second with °C.

(It is easy to lose count of the leading zeros in these numbers. It may be preferable to express them using scientific notation: we can write 0.0000065 as 6.5×10^{-6}, and 0.0000116 as 1.16×10^{-5}. The negative exponent in the first, −6, tells us to move the decimal six places to the left; the negative exponent in the second, −5, tells us to move the decimal five places to the left. Handheld scientific calculators will accept data directly in scientific notation.)

From these very small coefficients of expansion, it may seem that the effect of temperature on taped distances will be negligible. Although this may be so for certain types of surveys, it is not true where good accuracy is desired. For example, a 15°F change in temperature will change the length of a 100-ft steel tape by 0.01 ft, a measurable quantity. And without correcting for temperature, a distance of 1 mi measured in the winter at, say, 10°F, will be off by more than 3 ft when checked in the summer at 100°F. That would result in a poor relative accuracy of 1:5280/3 = 1:1760.

Air temperature readings will give the temperature of the tape when the day is hazy or cloudy, which is generally the best condition under which to use a steel tape; partly sunny conditions will cause frequent tape temperature changes and thus will increase the random errors. When the sun is shining, a tape thermometer is necessary. It should be firmly attached with the bulb in contact with the tape near the forward end; at that location, it creates little extra sag, it is easily read by the head chainman, and it is off the ground when the tape is dragged forward. The average temperature for the measurement is determined by several readings, sometimes every time the tape is used.

The correction for temperature can be applied by the formulas:

$$C_t = \beta D(T - T_s) \qquad (4\text{-}4)$$

where $\beta = 6.5 \times 10^{-6}$ (or 1.16×10^{-5} using SI metric units)

D = recorded distance, ft (or m using SI units)

T = tape temperature in °F (or °C using SI units)

T_s = standardization temperature, 68°F (or 20°C in SI units)

$$\text{Correct distance} = D \pm C_t \qquad (4\text{-}5)$$

where the rules for using either + or − are the same as described above for tape length corrections.

Example 4-5

A distance was measured with a 30-m steel tape and recorded as 96.345 m when the average tape temperature was 5°C. What is the correct distance?

Solution

Applying Equations 4-4 and 4-5, we get

$C_t = \beta D(T - T_s) = 1.16 \times 10^{-5}(96.345)(5 - 20) = -0.017$ m

Correct distance = $D + C_t$ = 96.345 + (−0.017) = 96.328 m

(In effect, "tape too short, subtract.")

Example 4-6

Point A must be laid out and marked at a horizontal distance of exactly 200.00 ft from point B, using a 100-ft steel tape. The temperature is 98°F when the work is done. What distance should be measured with the tape?

Solution

Applying Equations 4-4 and 4-5, we get

$C_t = \beta D(T - T_s) = 6.5 \times 10^{-6}(200.00)(98 - 68) = 0.04$ ft

Correct distance = $D - C_t$ = 200.00 − 0.04 = 196.96 ft

(In effect, for a layout problem, "tape too long, subtract.")

4-4 ELECTRONIC DISTANCE MEASUREMENT

Electronic distance measurement (EDM) is the measurement method of choice not only for large-scale geodetic surveys but also for ordinary plane surveys. Compared with taping, EDM offers the advantages of increased speed, accuracy, and dollar economy when routinely determining or setting relatively long horizontal distances.

After setting up the instrument, relatively long distances can be measured and displayed automatically in a matter of seconds. Except for very short distances, the excellent relative accuracy of EDM far exceeds that of most taping operations with little or no extra effort by the surveyor. And even though an EDM instrument is considerably more expensive than a tape, the size (and therefore salary cost) of a conventional surveying crew can generally be reduced from three to two persons, using EDM.

An additional advantage of EDM is that it can be used very accurately to determine inaccessible distances over lakes, rivers, swamps, busy highways, and other ground-level obstacles.

Despite these advantages, the use of EDMIs will not completely replace the steel tape. As was mentioned previously, there are many instances where it is more practical to use a steel tape than to set up an expensive instrument. The beginning surveyor must not lose sight of the need to develop and maintain good taping skills even in this age of electronic surveying.

Types of EDMIs

Many types of electronic distance-measuring devices are commercially available. They may differ in certain specific features or in precision. The general principle, however, of all these EDMIs is much the same. Briefly, they generate and project an electromagnetic beam of light waves from one end of the line being measured to the other. The beam is reflected back to the transmitting instrument (see Figure 4-25). The difference in *phase*, that is, the shift in the relative position of the electromagnetic waves, between the outgoing and the returning signals is converted electronically into the slope distance between the two stations. Several different signals of known frequency or wavelength must be transmitted by the instrument to resolve accurately the correct distance; this is all done by the EDMI automatically, within only a few seconds of time.

The physics and electronics of EDMI operation are actually quite complicated. But as with many other modern devices, the surveyor can use EDM equipment correctly and productively without having to be an expert in the scientific basis of its operation. There are, of course, many details regarding the proper setup, calibration, and handling of the instrument that the surveyor must be familiar with. Some of these will be discussed briefly in this section. But for the most part, it is necessary to study and make full use of the detailed instruction manual supplied by the manufacturer for each particular instrument.

EDMIs are classified either in terms of their type (actually wavelength) of carrier signal beam or in terms of their measuring range. With regard to carrier signal, the two basic types of EDMI used in surveying include *electro-optical* instruments and *microwave* instruments. With regard to measuring range, they are classified as either *short-range*, *medium- or intermediate-range*, and *long-range* instruments.

Modern electro-optical instruments transmit either low-power laser light or invisible infrared light. A special reflecting prism set up over the opposite station returns the transmitted signal to the EDMI, like a mirror. Most of the newer EDMIs used in ordinary boundary or construction surveys are short-range electro-optical instruments that use infrared light. These are relatively compact, light, and portable battery-operated instruments that are easy to use for a wide variety of ordinary survey work. Depending on the number of prisms used for signal reflection and on local

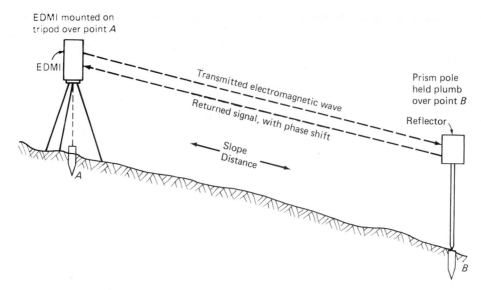

EDMI mounted on tripod over point *A*

EDMI

Transmitted electromagnetic wave

Returned signal, with phase shift

Prism pole held plumb over point *B*

Reflector

Slope Distance

A

B

FIGURE 4-25. EDM depends on the constant speed of electromagnetic waves (e.g., infrared light). The measured slope distances must be converted to corresponding horizontal distances.

weather conditions, short-range EDMIs may be used to measure distances up to about 2 mi, or 3 km. Ordinarily, however, the upper limit for most of these instruments is about 1 mi, or 1.5 km.

Microwave distance instruments are sometimes used. They require the use of a transmitter–receiver device at both ends of the line being measured. They are generally used as long-range instruments and are particularly useful for large-scale hydrographic surveys (e.g., locating offshore oil-drilling platforms) and similar applications. Microwave instruments can be used in relatively poor weather conditions, but they are much more sensitive to variations in humidity than are the electro-optical devices; appropriate corrections must be made to maintain accuracy.

Distances exceeding 40 mi can be measured with EDMIs using long radio waves, but these are not used for ordinary surveying work.

Today's instruments are available with a combined *digital electronic theodolite* and EDM device, as well as a built-in microprocessor or computer; they can automatically measure, process, and record horizontal and vertical distances, as well as station coordinates and elevations (see Figure 4-26). The angles are "read" or sensed electronically; they do not necessarily have to be read and then manually keyed into the instrument by the surveyor. This type of device is called an *electronic tacheometer instrument* (ETI) or an *electronic total station* (see Figure 4-27).

ETI data can be held in storage and then transferred to an office desktop computer or minicomputer and digital plotter; the data can be adjusted by the office computer, and the finished work can be printed out and/or shown graphically by the plotter. ETI systems offer a maximum of speed and ease for data collection and processing, and they eliminate many sources of blunder and error. Needless to say, these powerful instruments have revolutionized the practice of surveying.

Today's total stations are also available as "prismless" or robotic. That is, the instrument and all measurement functions can be operated by a single individual (further reducing salary costs).

The "prismless" instruments do not require a prism at the other end of the length to be measured. The instrument is merely focused on the object to be measured, such as a building corner, and the distance is determined.

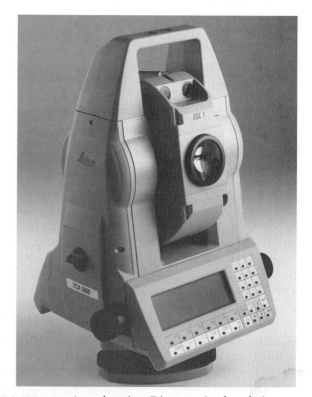

FIGURE 4-26. A total station. Distances (and angles) are displayed digitally. (*Courtesy of Leica Geosystems, Inc.*)

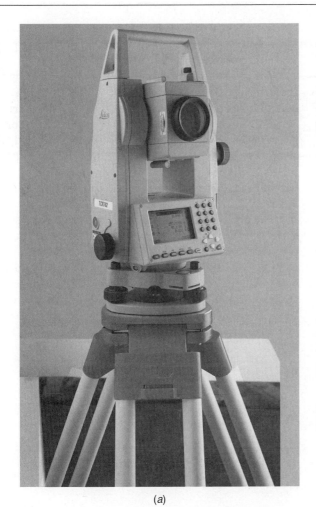

(a)

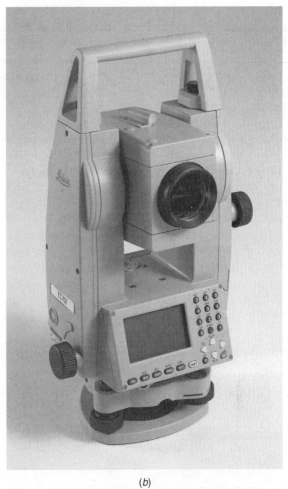

(b)

(c)

FIGURE 4-27. (*a–c*) Electronic total stations. (*Courtesy of Leica Geosystems, Inc.*)

The robotic instruments are equipped with a small motor and gear system that allows the total station to "track" a prism pole carried by the operator. The operator moves from point to point of the distance to be measured while the instrument follows along. Data are recorded at the prism pole by a data recorder through telemetry with the total station.

Reflecting Prisms   The different measurement ranges for EDMIs have been described. In general, the maximum range of an electro-optical EDMI is doubled when the number of reflecting prisms is squared. For example, if four prisms are used instead of two, the distance capability is doubled; nine prisms instead of three, and the range is tripled. Depending on the manufacturer, 12 prisms is about the upper limit of the number that can be used to reflect the light signal. (The number of prisms is not the only factor affecting range capability. The light absorption and scattering effect of fog, smoke, or dust particles can significantly reduce the measuring range of an EDMI, possibly by a factor of 3.

Direct sunlight can also reduce the range and cause inconsistent measurements; it is best to keep an electro-optical instrument pointed away from the sun.)

The prisms used to reflect electro-optical EDM signals are formed by cutting the corners off a solid glass cube. The quality of the prism depends on how flat the glass surfaces are and on the squareness of the corner. Cube-corner prisms reflect light rays back to their source in exactly the same direction they are received; this means that the prism(s) can be slightly out of alignment with the EDMI without reducing the effectiveness of the instrument (see Figure 4-28).

The prism(s) may be mounted on a tripod and set up directly over the station that marks the end of the line being measured, or it can be held vertically over that point using an adjustable-height *prism pole* with an attached bull's-eye level (see Figure 4-29). Mini or "peanut" prisms attached to the string of a plumb bob can also be used. These are good to get over the point in question with better accuracy.

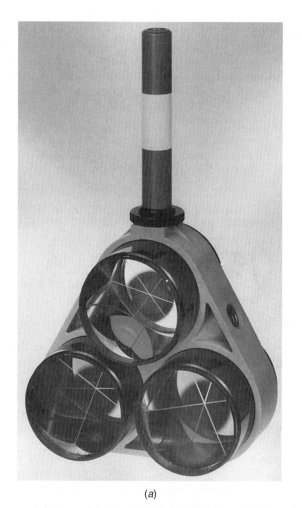

(a)

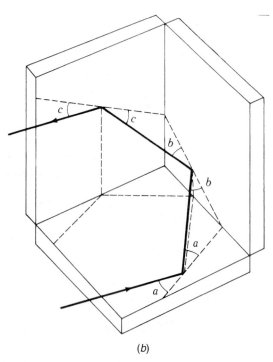

(b)

FIGURE 4-28. (*a*) A triple-prism assembly with sighting pole. (*Courtesy of Sokkia Corporation*) (*b*) The internal reflecting surfaces of a corner prism, with the path of a single beam of light coming from any direction and being reflected in a direction parallel to its original direction. (Philip Kissam, *Surveying for Civil Engineers*, 2nd edn, New York: McGraw-Hill Company, 1981. Reprinted by permission.)

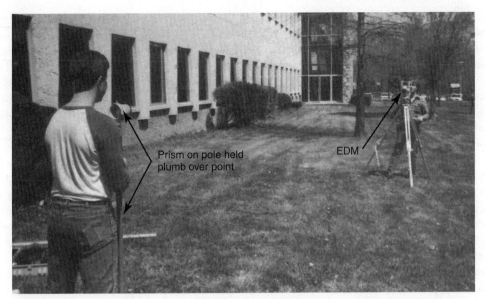

FIGURE 4-29. Instrument person pointing the line of sight at a prism pole held plumb on a point.

Accuracy of EDM   As with any survey instrument or field procedure, the surveyor must know the accuracy to be expected with the use of EDM. EDMIs must be checked and calibrated routinely. Even a carefully adjusted and precisely calibrated EDM device will have a small but constant instrumental error, as well as an error that is proportional to the distance measured. Typically, the constant error is about ±0.02 ft (or ±5 mm), and the proportional error is about 5 ppm. Accordingly, the accuracy of a typical EDMI might be listed as ±(5 mm + 5 ppm), or in U.S. units as ±(0.02 ft + 5 ppm).

When measuring very short distances, the constant error is of primary significance, while the proportional error can be neglected. For example, over a distance of 20 ft the relative accuracy of an EDMI might be only 1:20/0.02 = 1:1000, which is generally unacceptable for all but reconnaissance or preliminary topo surveys. This is why it is usually best to use a standardized steel tape, rather than an EDMI, when measuring such short distances.

The proportional part (ppm) of EDM instrumental error becomes more important when measuring long distances. Using the same EDMI as shown, with a listed error of ±(0.02 ft + 5 ppm), for measuring a distance of 6000 ft, the error of closure would be 0.02 + (5/1,000,000)(6000) = 0.02 ft + 0.03 ft = 0.05 ft, and the relative accuracy would then be 1:6000/0.05 = 1:120,000, or first-order accuracy.

The electrical center of an EDMI and the back surface of the prisms are not necessarily directly over their respective station points when the instruments are set up with optical or string plumb lines. For example, a typical prism off-center constant is 0.12 ft, or 30 mm. The reported accuracies of EDMI are based on the assumption that any off-center characteristics of the EDMI and the reflecting prisms have been compensated before measuring a line. An appropriate compensation factor can be entered into the EDMI by the manufacturer or by the surveyor in the field.

The velocity of an electromagnetic wave through air is affected by environmental factors such as atmospheric pressure, temperature, and humidity (although humidity has little effect on electro-optical devices). The operation and accuracy of an EDMI, therefore, are also affected by atmospheric conditions. Most manufacturers provide an *atmospheric correction* chart or calculator so that a suitable correction factor can be determined and keyed or dialed into the EDMI in the field at the time of measurement. That factor depends on local temperature, barometer, and humidity readings. After the correction factor is entered, any distance displayed by the EDMI will have first been automatically adjusted to account for atmospheric conditions.

EDMI Operating Procedure

The EDMI must first be set up on a tripod directly over a point that marks one end of the line being measured. A special base called a *tribrach* supports the instrument on the tripod and allows for leveling and centering operations. Once the tribrach has been centered and leveled over the survey point, other suitable instruments or accessories, such as sighting targets and reflecting prisms, can easily be interchanged with the EDMI without having to relevel and recenter over the point. The actual procedure for setting up, centering, and leveling a tripod-mounted instrument over a point is discussed in Chapter 6.

After the EDM/theodolite instrument is set up and leveled over one point and after the prism(s) is set up or held over the other point, the EDMI is turned on for a battery check. Atmospheric and off-center correction factors can be entered into the instrument at this time, if needed. The operating mode can be set with a switch to a fine, coarse, or tracking mode (for layout work), depending on the requirements of the measurement and the type of instrument used.

If an ETI is used, data such as the coordinates and elevation of the instrument station, the height of the instrument, and the height of the reflector (for horizontal and vertical distance computations) can also be entered.

The EDMI is then aimed at the prism(s) using the theodolite telescope. On some EDMIs, an audible tone indicates proper alignment with the prism(s). After alignment, the return signal level is automatically optimized and displayed. Then a measurement can be made by simply pressing the appropriate button; on some instruments, the measurement is made automatically when the return signal is optimized.

The measured distance is displayed by either liquid crystal or light-emitting diodes (LCD or LED) to the nearest 0.001 ft, or 0.001 m, in the fine mode and to the nearest 0.01 ft, or 0.01 m, in the coarse or tracking mode. The distance-measurement results are updated automatically and rapidly redisplayed about every 1–3 seconds. A meter-feet selector switch can be used at any time to change the displays from meters to feet, or vice versa.

If the instrument is an electronic total station, all the data are automatically recorded and stored electronically except for the description of the point, which must be manually entered into the data collection. The surveyor does not have to key in the data. Appropriate buttons can be pressed to display the horizontal distance between the two points.

Setting a Mark with EDM   In addition to measuring an unknown distance between two existing points, it is often necessary for the surveyors to lay out and mark the position of a new point along a specific direction and at a specific distance from some point of beginning. This procedure was described in some detail in Section 4-2, using a steel tape. EDMIs can also be used for layout work, to set stations along a route, or to set construction marks.

The so-called tracking mode of operation is particularly useful for layout work with an EDMI. A prism pole can be moved forward or back along the line of sight until the correct position is located and marked; in the tracking mode, the EDM can update and display the distance to the prism every second or so. Special tracking prism systems are also available that help the prism pole operator to stay on line, using audible tones or light signals. In some cases, voice communication between the instrument person and the prism pole operator is possible.

When using an EDMI that does not have a tracking mode, an approximate distance can first be established on line, using pacing, an initial measurement, and a tentative mark set. The distance to the tentative point is measured accurately with the EDM. Then with a steel tape or surveyor's rule held on line, the necessary correction is made to accurately adjust and move the first point to the desired distance. The adjusted point can be rechecked for line and distance with the EDMI.

Questions for Review

1. List three surveying applications where rough distance measurement is acceptable. What relative accuracy can be expected when measuring distances by pacing?

2. What is the measuring wheel particularly suited for, and with what relative accuracy?

3. What relative accuracy for distance measurement can be achieved by an experienced surveyor using good-quality taping equipment, under normal field conditions, without correcting for systematic errors?

4. What is the meaning and origin of the term *chaining*?

5. Describe three different ways in which a surveyor's steel tape may be graduated. Which is preferable? Why?

6. What is an Invar or Lovar tape?

7. What is the function of a plumb bob in measuring distance with a tape? List and briefly describe the purpose of two other taping accessories.

8. Describe the precautions that should be taken to avoid damaging a steel tape.

9. Outline the procedure for taping a horizontal distance over sloping ground, including how the tape is aligned, how intermediate stations are marked, and how the final length measurement is completed.

10. Describe what is meant by the term *breaking tape*.

11. What two mathematical relationships may be used for slope reduction? What data are required for each?

12. A point on the ground is labeled by a surveyor as "3 + 00." What is that called, and what does it tell about the point?

13. Outline the field procedure for setting marks for line and distance, including driving a stake and setting a tack.

14. Briefly describe five different types of taping blunders.

15. List five sources of random taping errors.

16. List four sources of systematic errors. Which two systematic errors can effectively cancel each other by using normal tension? Explain.

17. What two tape corrections should be applied to achieve good relative accuracy of about 1:5000?

18. Fill in the word *add* or *subtract* in the following sentences: When measuring an unknown distance, if the tape is too short, _____ a correction; when the tape is too long, _____ a correction. When laying out a given distance, if the tape is too short, _____ a correction; if the tape is too long, _____ a correction.

19. Briefly explain, by example and sketch, one of the correction rules you completed in Problem 18.

20. Briefly describe the operating principle of EDM. What are the advantages of EDM compared with taping?

21. Is taping obsolete because of EDM? Why?

22. What type of EDMI is used for most ordinary survey work?

23. What is the measuring range of a short-range EDMI?

24. What external factors affect the measuring range of an EDMI or ETI?

25. Give an example of how EDM measurement accuracy would typically be listed by the equipment manufacturer. Explain why EDM is not very accurate for short distances.

26. Outline the procedure for measuring an unknown distance with an EDMI.

27. Outline the procedure for setting a mark for line and distance with an EDMI.

Practice Problems

1. A surveyor has a unit pace of 2.8 ft/pace. (*a*) He counts 43 paces while walking from point *A* to point *B*. What is the distance between *A* and *B*? (*b*) How many paces should the same surveyor count to lay out a line approximately 300 ft long?

2. A surveyor has a unit pace of 0.9 m/pace. (*a*) She counts 37 paces while walking from point *C* to point *D*. What is the distance between *C* and *D*? (*b*) How many paces should the same surveyor count to lay out a line roughly 122 m long?

3. A surveying student walked along a 300-ft line on level ground five times and counted 122, 121, 102, 123, and 121.5 paces each time, from the beginning to the end of the line. (*a*) Determine her average unit pace, and (*b*) compute the 95 percent error and determine the relative accuracy of her pacing method.

4. A surveying student walked along a 100-m line on level ground five times and counted 116.5, 96, 119, 116, and 117.5 paces each time, from the beginning to the end of the line. (*a*) Determine his average unit pace, and (*b*) compute the 95 percent error and determine the relative accuracy of his pacing method.

5. The following distances were recorded on an old deed for a parcel of land that is to be resurveyed; convert them to their equivalent distances in feet and in meters.
   a. 7.62 ch
   b. 4 ch, 45 lk
   c. 15 ch, 23 lk

6. The following distances were recorded on an old deed for a parcel of land that is to be resurveyed; convert them to their equivalent distances in feet and in meters.
   a. 5.32 ch
   b. 8 ch, 57 lk
   c. 13 ch, 78 lk

7. A point along a road centerline is located 234.56 ft from the point of beginning. What is its station designation?

8. A point along a road centerline is located 76.543 m from the point of beginning. What is its station designation?

9. A distance between points *A* and *B* is measured and recorded as 345.67 ft, using a tape that has a certified standard length of 100.02 ft. What is the "true" distance between *A* and *B*? (Assume normal tension is used, and no temperature correction is required.)

10. A distance between points *A* and *B* is measured and recorded as 123.456 m, using a tape that has a certified standard length of 29.992 m. What is the "true" distance between *A* and *B*? (Assume normal tension is used, and no temperature correction is required.)

11. It is necessary to lay out and mark a point *D* exactly 150.00 m distant from point *C* for a construction project. A steel tape with an actual length of 30.01 m is used. What should be the distance measured from *C* to accurately set the mark for point *D*? (Assume normal tension is used, and no temperature correction is required.)

12. It is necessary to lay out and mark a point *D* exactly 250.000 ft distant from point *C* for a construction project. A steel tape with an actual length of 99.990 ft is used. What should be the distance measured from *C* to accurately set the mark for point *D*? (Assume normal tension is used, and no temperature correction is required.)

13. A distance measured with a standard steel tape was recorded as 234.56 ft when the temperature was 38°F. What is the actual distance corrected for temperature?

14. A distance measured with a standard steel tape was recorded as 65.432 m when the temperature was 28°C. What is the actual distance corrected for temperature?

15. A steel tape with a standardized length of 30.009 m is used to measure a distance on a slope, and a distance of 123.456 m is recorded. The average temperature at the time of measurement is 25°C, and the vertical distance between the endpoints of the line is 7.25 m. What is the actual horizontal distance between the two points? (Assume normal tension is used.)

16. A steel tape with a standardized length of 99.990 ft is used to measure a distance on a slope, and a distance of 223.456 ft is recorded. The average temperature at the time of measurement is 25°F, and the vertical distance between the endpoints of the line is 17.25 ft. What is the actual horizontal distance between the two points? (Assume normal tension is used.)

17. A steel tape with a standardized length of 30.009 m is used to lay out and mark a distance on level ground; the required horizontal distance is 100.000 m. The average temperature at the time of measurement is 25°C. What distance should be laid out between the two points under

those conditions so that the actual horizontal distance will be 100.000 m? (Assume normal tension is used.)

18. A steel tape with a standardized length of 99.990 ft is used to lay out and mark a distance on level ground; the required horizontal distance is 300.00 ft. The average temperature at the time of measurement is 95°F. What distance should be laid out between the two points under those conditions so that the actual horizontal distance will be 300.00 ft? (Assume normal tension is used.)

19. An old and worn 50-ft woven cloth tape is used to lay out and mark the corners of a 75.0 × 150.0 ft building. It is later found that the actual tape length was 50.15 ft. What dimensions were actually laid out for the building?

20. An old and worn 15-m woven cloth tape is used to lay out and mark the corners of a 25.00 × 50.00 m building. It is later found that the actual tape length was 15.005 m. What dimensions were actually laid out for the building?

CHAPTER FIVE

MEASURING VERTICAL DISTANCES

CHAPTER OUTLINE

The vertical direction is parallel to the direction of gravity; at any point, it is the direction of a freely suspended plumb-bob cord. The *vertical distance* of a point above or below a given reference surface is called the *elevation* of the point. The most commonly used reference surface for vertical distance is *mean sea level* (MSL). (The words *altitude* and *height* are sometimes used in place of *elevation*.) Vertical distances are measured by the surveyor to determine the elevations of points, in a process called *running levels* or, simply, *leveling*.

The importance of leveling cannot be overestimated; with few exceptions, it must always be considered in every form of design and construction.

The determination and control of elevations constitute a fundamental operation in surveying and engineering projects. Leveling provides data for determining the shape of the ground and drawing topographic maps. The elevations of new facilities such as roads, structural foundations, and pipelines can then be designed. Finally, the designed facilities are laid out and marked in the field by the construction surveyor. The surveyors' elevation marks (such as *grade stakes*) serve as reference points from which building contractors can determine the proper slope ("rate of grade") of a road, the first-floor elevation of a building, the required cutoff elevation for foundation piles, the invert elevation for a storm sewer, and so on.

The chapter covers the fundamentals of leveling, including the types and proper use of leveling equipment, leveling field procedures and field notes, benchmark and profile leveling, and other related topics. Measuring vertical distances for the specific purpose of determining and plotting ground elevation contours is discussed in Chapter 9, "Topographic Surveys and Maps."

5-1 PRINCIPLES OF LEVELING

There are several methods for measuring vertical distances and determining the elevations of points. Traditional methods include *barometric leveling, trigonometric leveling,* and *differential leveling.* Two advanced and sophisticated techniques include *inertial surveying* and *global positioning systems.*

By using special barometers (*altimeters*) to measure air pressure (which decreases with increasing elevation), the elevations of points on the Earth's surface can be determined to within ± 1 m, or ± 3 ft. This method is useful for doing a reconnaissance survey of large areas in rough country and for obtaining preliminary topographic data.

Trigonometric leveling is an indirect procedure; the vertical distances are computed from vertical angle and horizontal or slope distance data. It is also applied for topo work over rough terrain or other obstacles. (Trigonometric leveling is discussed again in Sections 5-6 and 9-3.) Inertial and global positioning methods, which depend on space-age electronic technology, are applied for certain large-scale geodetic control surveys; they are generally not used for ordinary surveying. However, reductions in equipment costs and refinements in the technology have made GPS a much more practical tool for use in solving leveling problems.

By far the most common leveling method, and the one most surveyors are concerned with, is differential leveling. It may also be called *spirit leveling* because the basic instrument used comprises a telescopic sight and a sensitive *spirit bubble vial.* The spirit bubble serves to align the telescopic sight in a horizontal direction, that is, in a direction perpendicular to the direction of gravity.

Before discussing the details of leveling equipment and specific field procedures, it is best for the beginner to become familiar with a general overview of differential spirit leveling.

Differential Leveling

Briefly, a horizontal line of sight is first established with an instrument called a *level*. The level is securely mounted on a stand called a *tripod*, and the line of sight is made horizontal. Then the surveyor looks through the telescopic sight toward a graduated *level rod*, which is held vertically at a specific location or point on the ground (called point *A*, for example, in Figure 5-1a). A reading is observed on the rod where it appears to be intercepted by the horizontal cross hair of the level; this is the vertical distance from the point on the ground up to the line of sight of the instrument.

Generally, the elevation of point *A* is already known; otherwise, it is assumed. The rod reading on a point of known elevation is termed a *backsight* (BS) reading. It is also often called a *plus sight* (+S) reading because it generally must be added to the known elevation of point *A* to determine the elevation of the line of sight. (An exception to this may occur during a tunnel survey, for example, when the rod may have to be inverted and held on the roof of the tunnel.)

For example, suppose the elevation of point *A* is 100.00 m (above MSL), and the rod reading is 1.00 m. From Figure 5-1a, it is clear that the elevation of the line of sight is 100.00 + 1.00 = 101.00 m. The elevation of the horizontal line of sight through the level is called the *height of instrument* (HI).

Suppose we must determine the elevation of point *B* (see Figure 5-1b). The *instrument person* (the surveyor operating the level) turns the telescope so that it faces

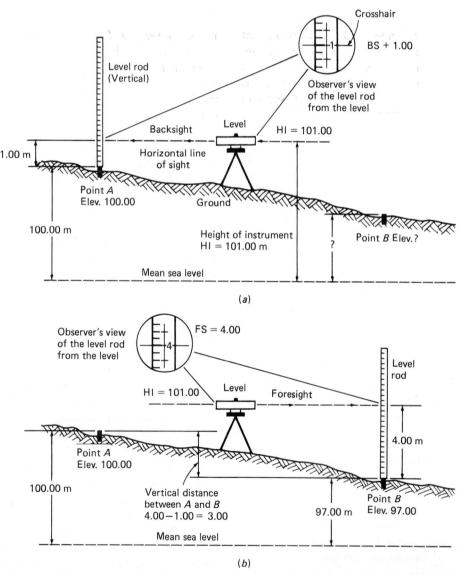

FIGURE 5-1. Differential leveling to measure vertical distance and elevation. (*a*) Step 1: Take a backsight rod reading on point *A*. (*b*) Step 2: Rotate the telescope toward point *B* and take a foresight rod reading.

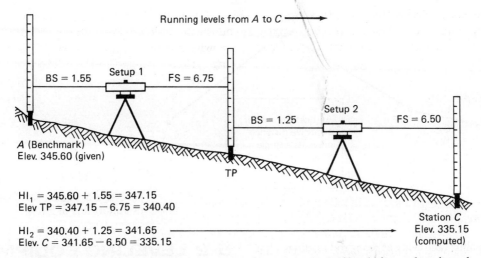

Running levels from *A* to *C* →

BS = 1.55   Setup 1   FS = 6.75

BS = 1.25   Setup 2   FS = 6.50

A (Benchmark)
Elev. 345.60 (given)

TP

Station *C*
Elev. 335.15
(computed)

$HI_1 = 345.60 + 1.55 = 347.15$
$Elev\ TP = 347.15 - 6.75 = 340.40$

$HI_2 = 340.40 + 1.25 = 341.65$
$Elev.\ C = 341.65 - 6.50 = 335.15$

FIGURE 5-2. Temporary turning points are used to carry a line of levels from a benchmark to some other station or benchmark; the process of differential leveling is repeated at each instrument setup.

point *B* and reads the rod now held vertically on that point. For example, the rod reading might be 4.00 m. A rod reading on a point of unknown elevation is called a *foresight* (FS), or a *minus sight* (–S). Because the HI was not changed by turning the level, we can simply subtract the foresight reading of 4.00 from the HI of 101.00 to obtain the elevation of point *B*, resulting here in 101.00 – 4.00 = 97.00 m.

The operation of reading a vertical rod held alternately on two nearby points is the essence of differential leveling. The difference between the two rod readings is, in effect, the vertical distance between the two points. In the preceding example, the vertical distance between *A* and *B* may be computed as either 100.00 – 97.00 = 3.00 m, or 4.00 – 1.00 = 3.00 m. Although it is the vertical distance that is actually being measured, the results are generally expressed as the elevations of points above a common reference plane or datum.

This basic cycle of differential leveling can be summarized as follows:

$$
\begin{aligned}
\text{Height of instrument} &= \text{known elevation} \\
&\quad + \text{backsight or HI} \\
&= \text{Elev}_A + \text{BS}
\end{aligned}
\tag{5-1}
$$

$$
\begin{aligned}
\text{New elevation} &= \text{height of instrument} \\
&\quad - \text{foresight or Elev}_B \\
&= \text{HI} - \text{FS}
\end{aligned}
\tag{5-2}
$$

Running Levels

Often, the elevations of several points over a relatively long distance must be determined. A process called *running levels* is used to determine the elevations of two or more widely separated points. It simply involves several cycles or repetitions of the basic differential leveling operation previously described. More specific terms for this are *benchmark*, *profile*, and *topographic leveling*.

Benchmarks and Turning Points   Suppose it is necessary to determine the elevation of point *C* relative to point *A* (see Figure 5-2). But in this case, let us assume that it is not possible to set up the level so that both points *A* and *C* are visible from one position (due to either physical obstacles or excessive distance). The line of levels can be carried forward toward *C* by establishing a convenient and temporary *turning point* (TP) somewhere between *A* and *C*. The selected TP serves merely as an intermediate reference point; it does not have to be actually set in the ground as a permanent monument.

The elevation of the turning point is computed from the first pair of BS and FS readings. The BS is on point *A*, which is the point of known elevation. A secure and permanent point of known elevation is called a *benchmark* (BM); a leveling survey should always begin with a backsight on a benchmark, such as benchmark *A* (BM_A). The BS is added to the elevation to give the HI at the first instrument position.

The elevation of the turning point is obtained by subtracting the FS from the HI. Once the elevation of the turning point is known, the level instrument can be moved to another location, one closer to *C* but still in sight of the turning point. Then another backsight is taken, this time on the turning point, to determine the new height of instrument. Finally, a foresight is taken on point *C*, and its elevation is computed.

From a diagram like Figure 5-2, beginning students sometimes get the impression that the level must be set up directly in line with the two points for BS and FS readings. This is not the case; as shown in a plan or top view in Figure 5-3, the level may be set up off line. But it is still good practice to keep the plus sight and minus sight distances about equal, for reasons that will be explained later in this chapter.

Computations for leveling simply involve successive additions and subtractions. But when running levels with

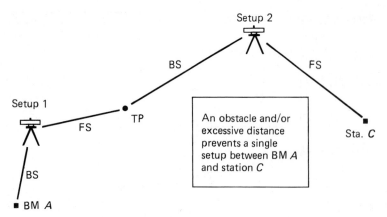

FIGURE 5-3. A plan (top) view of a short line of levels.

several turning points (and twice as many rod readings), it is necessary to keep a well-organized field book to keep track of which numbers are added or subtracted from which. The computations for the example of Figure 5-2 are set up in a typical field book format, shown in Figure 5-4. The leveling computations are simple, but it is important to record the field data in a systematic manner. Note that the FS and BS readings on the turning point are each listed on the single line labeled TP (Figure 5-4b). A more complete set of leveling field notes is presented along with a discussion of benchmark leveling in Section 5-4.

5-2 LEVELING EQUIPMENT

There are several types of surveying levels and level rods. Some are meant primarily for precise leveling work, and others are much better suited for ordinary construction layout work. The surveyor must be familiar with the basic configuration and operation of the various types of leveling equipment to be able to select and use the best instrument for a particular surveying assignment.

Compared with a total station, the level is a relatively simple instrument. It is required to give only a horizontal

Record the given elevation of A.

Read BS on A; compute HI for first setup.

(Numbers in parentheses upper left indicate order of data entry.)

Station	BS "+"	HI	FS "−"	Elevation
BM A	(2) 1.55	(3) 347.15		(1) 345.60

(a)

Read FS ON TP; compute the elevation of TP.

Read BS on TP; compute HI for second setup.

Station	BS "+"	HI	FS "−"	Elevation
BM A	1.55	347.15		345.60
TP	(6) 1.25	(7) 341.65	(4) 6.75	(5) 340.40

(b)

Read FS on C; compute elevation of station C.

Sum BS and FS columns; add to elevation of A as a check on math.

Station	BS "+"	HI	FS "−"	Elevation
BM A	1.55	347.15		345.60
TP	1.25	341.65	6.75	340.40
C			(8) 6.50	(9) 335.15
(10) Sum =	+ 2.80		−13.25	

(11) *Arithmetic check*: 345.60 + 2.80 − 13.25 = 335.15

(c)

FIGURE 5-4. Field book format for leveling notes.

line of sight in all directions of the compass, and this is easily accomplished using basic optical and mechanical components. Early surveyors, from Roman times up through the Middle Ages, used *chorobates* for leveling; these simple devices depended on the free surface of water in a trough to establish a line of sight. Modern levels still depend primarily on the surface of a liquid at rest (the spirit vial liquid) and on the force of gravity.

Single-beam or rotating low-power laser beams are being used by surveyors and construction technicians to define horizontal reference lines or reference planes at construction sites. The application of these modern laser levels and beam detectors to facilitate construction layout work is described in Chapter 11. In this section, traditional and modern optical differential leveling equipment is described.

Types of Levels

As mentioned earlier, a surveying level basically consists of a *telescope* and a sensitive *spirit bubble vial*. The spirit bubble vial can be adjusted so that, when the bubble is centered, the line of sight through the telescope is horizontal. The telescope is mounted on a vertical spindle that fits into a bearing in the *leveling head*. The leveling head has three leveling screws. The telescope can be easily rotated about its *standing axis* (or *azimuth axis*) and pointed toward any direction of the compass (see Figure 5-5).

Two types of levels are described in this section—the *automatic level* and the digital level. A simple *hand level* may be used for determining elevations when a high degree of accuracy is not required; this device is discussed in Chapter 9.

The telescopic sight and the spirit bubble vial are described here because they are common components of several types of levels and other surveying instruments.

The Telescopic Sight   The modern telescopic sight consists of the following components (see Figure 5-5):

1. A *reticle* (or reticule), which provides the *cross hairs*, near the rear of the telescope tube

2. A microscope or *eyepiece* that magnifies the cross hairs, and that must be focused on them according to the eyesight of the observer

3. An *objective lens* at the forward end of the telescope, which forms an image of the sighted target within the telescope tube

4. A *focusing lens*, which can be moved back and forth inside the scope to focus the image on the cross hairs

Because the image formed by the objective lens is inverted, the eyepieces of most instruments are designed to erect the image. Telescopes that erect the image are called *erecting telescopes*; the others are called *inverting telescopes*. When the image is focused on the cross hairs, the cross hairs become part of the image so that when the observer looks through the eyepiece, the target (such as a level rod) appears magnified (about 30 times) with the cross hairs apparently engraved on it.

To Focus a Telescopic Sight   The following three steps, illustrated in Figure 5-6, are required to focus a telescopic sight for greatest accuracy:

1. Aim the telescope at a bright, unmarked object such as the sky and regulate the eyepiece until the cross hairs are in sharp focus. Because the eye can change focus itself, there is always a short range in the movement of the eyepiece within which this condition can be satisfied.

2. Aim the telescope at the object to be viewed and, while keeping the eye focused on the cross hairs, regulate the focusing lens until the object is clear. This should occur only when the image is on the place of the cross hairs because this is the only place where the eyepiece focus is sharp. If the observer looks at the image instead of at the cross hairs while regulating the objective focus, the eye focus may change slightly so that the image is seen clearly a short distance in front of or behind the cross hairs. The cross hairs will then not be in perfect focus, but the difference may not be noticeable. When the image and the cross hairs are *simultaneously* in apparently good focus, the plane of the image and the plane of the cross hairs must be very nearly coincident.

When the image is not exactly on the plane of the cross hairs, the cross hairs will move across the image when the eye is moved left and right or up and down, just as is the case when two objects at different distances are observed with the naked eye. Under these conditions, *parallax* exists, and the direction of the sight is not fixed.

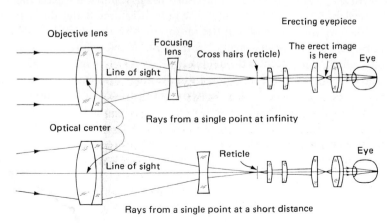

FIGURE 5-5. A modern telescopic sight with an internal focusing lens.

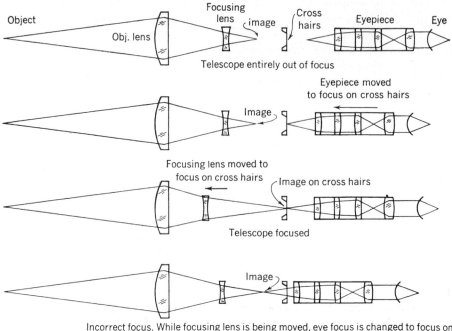

FIGURE 5-6. Principle of focusing a telescopic sight.

3. Eliminate parallax. To accomplish this, move the eye up and down or left and right. If the cross hairs appear to move with respect to the object sighted, change the focus of the objective until the apparent motion is reversed. Continue focusing back and forth, reducing the apparent motion each time until it is eliminated. It may then be necessary to adjust the eyepiece slightly to make the image and the cross hairs appear clear-cut.

Theoretically, the parallax should be eliminated by this method each time the objective focus is changed. However, when the eyepiece has been set for a particular observer after the parallax has been once eliminated, it is common practice to keep the eyepiece in this position throughout the work and to rely on focusing the objective so that both the cross hairs and the object are in sharp focus simultaneously, to eliminate parallax.

The Line of Sight   A straight line from any point on the image through the optical center of the objective lens will strike a corresponding point on the object. A straight line from the cross hairs through the optical center of the lens will strike the point on the object where the observer sees the cross hairs apparently located. Thus the *line of sight* of a telescopic sight is defined by the cross hairs and the optical center of the objective. As stated earlier, when a telescopic sight is properly focused, the eye can move slightly without changing the position of the cross hairs on the object. This differs in principle from a rifle sight, when the eye must be accurately aligned with the latter to determine where it is pointing. The telescopic sight on a level also magnifies the object about 30 diameters. The diameter of the field of view is therefore very small.

The Spirit Bubble Tube or Circle   A spirit bubble vial consists of a glass container that is partly filled with a clear, nonfreezing, very low viscosity liquid such as alcohol or ether. For some instruments, a tube-shaped vial is attached directly to the telescope and is adjusted so that when the vapor bubble is centered, the line of sight is horizontal. The inside of the vial is ground to a barrel-shaped surface that is symmetrical with respect to a longitudinal axis. The vial is mounted in a metal tube, as shown in Figure 5-7a.

Several uniform graduations at each end of the bubble are placed near, or are etched on, the glass tube so that the position of the bubble can be clearly observed. When the bubble is centered within the marked graduations, the direction of the vial, and therefore the telescopic line of sight, is horizontal (with a properly adjusted instrument). When the bubble is centered, it is said to "read zero."

The sensitivity of the spirit vial and, therefore, the precision of the instrument depends on the radius of curvature established when grinding the glass vial. In general, the larger the radius (i.e., the flatter the curvature of the glass), the more sensitive the spirit bubble and the more precise the level. But it takes more time to accurately center the bubble in a very sensitive spirit bubble tube, and this could be a disadvantage in certain types of surveys; again, it is important for the surveyor to be aware of this so that the proper instrument is selected for a particular job.

For digital levels and automatic levels, a spherically shaped spirit bubble vial is used to set the standing axis of the instrument approximately in a vertical position. These vials appear as circles when viewed from above, and the bubble is centered when it is positioned in the middle "bull's-eye" circle (see Figure 5-7b). A circular spirit vial is less sensitive than

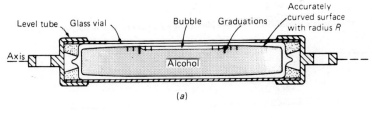

(a)

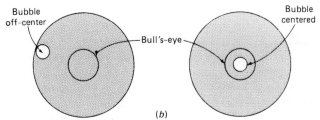

(b)

FIGURE 5-7. (*a*) Cross section of a level tube showing the mounting of the vial. The axis is horizontal when the bubble is centered. (*Courtesy of CST/Berger, Illinois.*) (*b*) Circular (bull's-eye) spirit level.

a tubular vial, but other internal optical components of the level instrument can compensate for this.

The step-by-step procedures required to center a spirit vial bubble and to level the instrument are described in Section 5-3.

The Automatic (Self-Leveling) Level   Automatic levels are used for ordinary as well as precise surveying work. They are typically accurate and easy to use, and they can be set up and leveled relatively quickly (see Figure 5-8). The use of a modern automatic level increases the productivity of a surveying crew.

These instruments do not have a tubular spirit vial attached to the telescope. Instead, the bubble in a circular spirit vial (set on a three-screw leveling head) is centered to get the instrument approximately leveled. After the bubble is centered, an internal optical compensator automatically takes over to set and maintain a truly level line of sight. No further leveling is required at that particular instrument

location; the instrument, then, may be described as being "self-leveling."

The operating principle of a pendulum-type compensator, which depends basically on the force of gravity, is illustrated in Figure 5-9. Sometimes the pendulum sticks. To make sure that it is free, after the circular level is centered, turn one of the leveling screws quickly in one direction and back while looking through the telescope. If the line of sight vibrates or suddenly shifts up and down once or twice, the pendulum is free and the level is operative. (On some automatic levels, the line of sight may even vibrate on a windy day, making it difficult to read the rod accurately.)

Digital Levels   A new generation of levels involves digital electronic technology. Digital levels have been designed to reduce human error that occurs in vertical distance measurements. These instruments are particularly useful in tunnel or mine surveys where light is limited and global positioning systems (GPS) cannot be used. They are also

(a)

(b)

FIGURE 5-8.   Automatic (self-leveling) levels. (*a, Courtesy of Leica Geosystems, Inc.; b, Courtesy of Wild Heerbrugg Instruments, Inc.*)

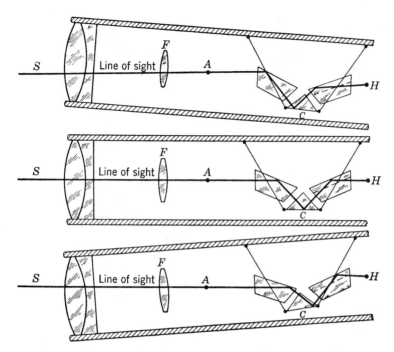

FIGURE 5-9. Schematic diagram showing the operation of an automatic level. Part *C* is a compensator that swings backward or forward as the telescope is tilted and thus keeps a level line of sight *S* on the cross hairs *H*.

becoming popular for route surveys and topographic surveys, and may be used for leveling precise networks. Using a digital level and a special bar-coded rod, instrument operators can collect and store accurate backsight, foresight, and distance data in as little as 3–4 seconds, without observation or calculation errors.

A digital level has an internal electronic "camera" called a charge-coupled device (CCD) that accurately "sees" or reads the bar-coded rod. The instrument's CCD is located at the image plane in the telescope. It converts the light–dark pattern of the bar code into a pattern of pixels and binary code, which then determines the location along the rod that is being observed, as well as the horizontal distance to the rod. This process requires the instrument operator to carefully focus the rod image before taking a measurement (i.e., pushing a button to capture the image).

Digital levels can process the data as the survey progresses, or store the data "on-board." (External data collectors may be used with some models.) The data can be downloaded through an appropriate interface connection to a desktop computer back in the office, where they can then be processed, stored, and printed in a traditional field book format. The instruments and their bar-coded rods vary among manufacturers. Therefore, a bar-coded rod from one manufacturer cannot be used with a digital level from another manufacturer. A typical instrument and rod is shown in Figure 5-10*a* and *b*.

Level Rods

There are many different types of level rods. Generally, the body of the rod is either fiberglass or made of seasoned hardwood; this acts as a rigid support for the rod face, a strip of steel graduated upward starting from zero at the bottom. The rod is held vertically by the *rod person*, on a point of known elevation for a BS or on a point of

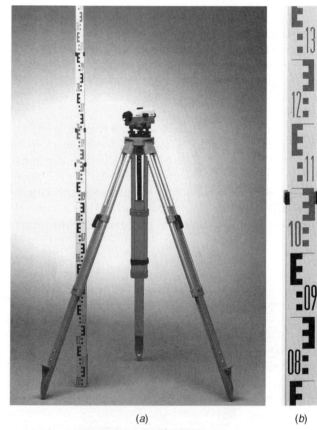

(a)   (b)

FIGURE 5-10. (*a*) Digital level with rod. (*b*) Close-up of bar-coded rod. (*Courtesy of Leica Geosystems, Inc.*)

unknown elevation for an FS. The rod is then observed with the level and read by the instrument person (or on *target rods*, by the rod person).

The rod face may be graduated in feet, tenths, and hundredths of a foot, or in meters, decimeters, and centimeters

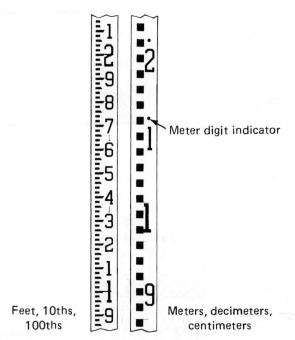

Meter digit indicator

Feet, 10ths,
100ths

Meters, decimeters,
centimeters

FIGURE 5-11. Typical level rod faces. (*Courtesy of The Lietz Company.*)

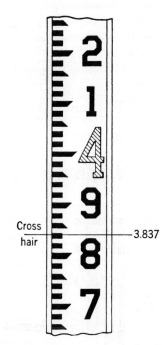

Cross
hair ———— 3.837

FIGURE 5-12. How to read a level rod.

on metric rods (see Figure 5-11). The graduations are black on a white background for high contrast and easy reading. The dividing line between the black graduations and the white face of the rod marks the exact hundredth of a foot (or centimeter on a metric rod). The whole-foot, or whole-meter, divisions are indicated with red numbers, and the tenth, or decimeter, divisions are marked with smaller black numbers. Small red foot numbers, or meter digit indicators, are also stamped on the rod face at suitable points to help avoid blunders when it is read directly by the instrument person at close range (with a small field of view).

The rod may be read directly to the nearest hundredth of a foot (0.01 ft), or to the nearest centimeter (0.01 m) for a metric rod. By estimating the position of the horizontal cross hair on the rod face, the instrument person may also be able to estimate the rod reading to the nearest thousandth of a foot (0.001 ft), or to the nearest millimeter (0.001 m). Direct reading to 0.001 ft (or 0.001 m) will be difficult however, if the line of sight is relatively long.

A surveyor must be able to read a level rod quickly, accurately, and without blunders. The reading on the rod shown in Figure 5-12 is 3.837 ft. The first digit, 3 ft, is inferred because the cross hair is somewhat below the large (red) 4-ft mark. The second digit, 8 tenths, comes from the black number just below the cross hair. (Note the little point on the black interval next to the 8; these points generally help to emphasize the tenths as well as the 0.05-ft points.) The third digit, 3 hundredths, is obtained by counting the full black and white intervals above the 8. Finally, the last digit, which represents 7 thousandths of a foot, is estimated by eye as that fraction or part of the black interval (0.01 ft thick) of the rod in which the cross hair falls. The general method for reading a metric rod is

the same as illustrated here except, of course, for the meaning of the numbers and divisions.

Level rods that can be read directly by the instrument person are sometimes called *self-reading rods*.

Types of Level Rods   Many level rods are named after cities. One of the most common is the *Philadelphia rod*, which is a combination of self-reading and target rod. It is made in two parts. The rear section can be slid upward through two brass sleeves, and when *fully extended*, the front face of the rod reads continuously from 0 at the bottom to 12 ft (or 13 ft on some models) on the top. The rod may be used in the extended position when leveling over steeply sloping terrain; this is called using *high rod*.

The top of the front face of the rod (from 6.75 ft upward to about 7.20 ft) is attached to the back section. The back face of the back section of the rod is graduated downward from about 7 to 12 or 13 ft. As the back section is slid upward, it runs under an index mark and vernier. The reading at the index indicates the height of a certain mark, usually the 7-ft mark on the front face. Thus, if the target is set at the proper mark and the back section of the rod is partly raised, the height of the target above the ground is indicated by the index on the rear face. A clamp is provided to hold the back section in place.

A stop is provided to prevent the rod from coming apart when it is extended too far. The stop is often placed so that it stops the rod when the readings are continuous from bottom to top. Sometimes it is not so placed, and sometimes it is knocked out of position by long use. The rod person should make sure that the index at the back of the rod reads exactly 12 or 13 ft (whichever applies) when he or she sets the rod in its extended position. The stop should be used only when he or she is certain that it stops the rod in the proper position.

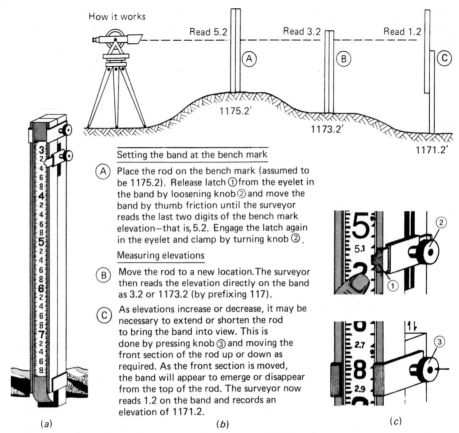

How it works

Read 5.2   Read 3.2   Read 1.2

Ⓐ   Ⓑ   Ⓒ

1175.2'

1173.2'

1171.2'

Setting the band at the bench mark

Ⓐ Place the rod on the bench mark (assumed to be 1175.2). Release latch ① from the eyelet in the band by loosening knob ② and move the band by thumb friction until the surveyor reads the last two digits of the bench mark elevation—that is, 5.2. Engage the latch again in the eyelet and clamp by turning knob ②.

Measuring elevations

Ⓑ Move the rod to a new location. The surveyor then reads the elevation directly on the band as 3.2 or 1173.2 (by prefixing 117).

Ⓒ As elevations increase or decrease, it may be necessary to extend or shorten the rod to bring the band into view. This is done by pressing knob ③ and moving the front section of the rod up or down as required. As the front section is moved, the band will appear to emerge or disappear from the top of the rod. The surveyor now reads 1.2 on the band and records an elevation of 1171.2.

(a)   (b)   (c)

FIGURE 5-13. (*a*) A direct elevation, or Lenker, rod. (*b*) How the direct elevation rod works. (*c*) Setting the band at the benchmark. (*Courtesy of Lenker Manufacturing Company.*)

Other types of level rods include the *Chicago rod*, the *San Francisco rod*, and the *Florida rod*. The Chicago rod and the San Francisco rod consist of three sliding sections; when unextended, they are somewhat more compact and portable than the Philadelphia rod. The Florida rod consists of one section, 10 ft long, graduated with alternating 0.10-ft-wide red and white stripes.

A type of rod that is sometimes used for topographic surveys or construction layout work is the *direct elevation rod* (see Figure 5-13). It is made in two sections for extension up to 10 ft. The front section carries a graduated, endless, 10-ft steel band that runs over end rollers to bring any reading into view. The back section has a clamp for holding the rod in extension and has a latch for locking the band in any required position. The numbers on the band are read downward from the top of the rod. After properly setting the band position, all rod readings will be elevations of the points on the ground where the rod is held. An advantage is that no additions or subtractions of backsight or foresight readings are necessary.

Telescoping fiberglass rods are being used more and more, due to their light weight and low cost. They are available in both metric and U.S. Customary graduations, and are manufactured in lengths up to 7 m (25 ft). Specially, "bar-coded" rods are employed with the new digital family of levels. These are identical in construction to the conventional rods except for the patterns imprinted on them (Figure 5-14).

5-3 LEVELING PROCEDURES

In the previous sections, the general principles of differential leveling were discussed, and several different types of leveling instruments and level rods were illustrated and described. In this section, the actual field procedures for setting up an instrument and handling a level rod are presented.

Setting Up and Leveling the Instrument

The level must be securely mounted on top of a three-legged wooden or aluminum stand called a *tripod* (see Figure 5-15a). Tripods have adjustable legs that make it convenient for setups even on steeply sloping ground and is more easily transported when closed. The instrument is either screwed directly onto the tripod head or attached with a fastening-screw assembly (see Figure 5-15b).

The friction of the tripod legs, at the tripod head, may be adjusted so that the legs will fall slowly of their own weight from a horizontal position. If a wide-framed tripod with metal hinges is used, the friction should be adjusted so that it is just possible to notice the friction when the legs are moved by hand.

Each leg of a tripod has a pointed metal shoe at the end. The tripod is set up with the legs well spread and pressed firmly into the ground (see Figure 5-16). If the surface is hard or paved, each tripod leg should be placed in a surface indentation or in a crack in the pavement; the log hinges may also be tightened for extra friction. The legs should be adjusted so that the head of the tripod is roughly horizontal. For leveling work, the instrument need not be set up precisely over a particular point or station; locating a good spot for the instrument will be discussed again shortly.

Remove the instrument from its case, carefully lifting it by the base, and immediately screw it firmly onto the tripod head. Remove the dust cap (if any) from the objective lens and replace it with a sunshade, if one is provided. The sunshade improves the mechanical balance of the telescope and prevents glare caused by sunlight striking the objective lens. It also improves visibility by helping to eliminate unfocused light, which tends to dim the image.

When the level is to be moved to another position, it need not be removed from the tripod (except perhaps for very expensive and precise instruments). In a clear area, hold the tripod in a vertical position.

Leveling a Three-Screw Instrument All digital and automatic levels are first approximately leveled by three leveling screws. The level position is indicated by the coincidence of a spirit bubble and the "bull's-eye" of a circular level vial. Any one of the three screws can be rotated separately. *The bubble will move toward any screw turned clockwise.*

It must always be kept in mind that turning any screw on a three-screw level slightly changes the HI. Never turn a leveling screw of a three-screw leveling head once a BS reading has been taken and an HI established. This is not a problem with four-screw levels because their main support is a fixed center bearing.

Most experienced surveyors can quickly level a three-screw instrument and circular bubble by turning the three screws simultaneously. But for beginners, it is best first to adjust any two adjacent screws so that the bubble moves to a position on an imaginary line perpendicular to a line between those two screws (see Figure 5-17). Follow the old

| (a) | (b) |

FIGURE 5-14. (*a*) Telescoping fiberglass rod. (*Courtesy of Sokkia Corporation.*) (*b*) Polymer bar-coded staff. (*Courtesy of Leica Geosystems, Inc.*)

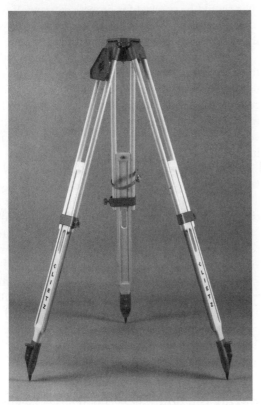

| (a) | (b) |

FIGURE 5-15. Tripod and tripod head (*a*) Adjustable-leg tripod (*b*) Tripod head adaptor. (*Courtesy of The Lietz Company.*)

FIGURE 5-16. The pointed metal shoe at the end of each tripod leg must be pressed firmly into the ground.

rule: "Thumbs in, thumbs out, the bubble follows the left thumb." Then adjust the third screw alone to bring the bubble directly under the bull's-eye.

After Setup   After any type of leveling instrument is set up and leveled, the eyepiece must be focused on the cross hairs (see Section 5-2) to suit the eyesight of the observer. Take care not to touch the instrument except when and where necessary for operating it. Never straddle the legs of the tripod, but always stand between them. Do not lean on or hold the tripod for balance when looking through the telescope. Be particularly careful not to kick or touch the tripod while walking around the instrument. *Never leave the instrument unattended*, unless it is in a protected location and can be observed at all times.

Handling the Level Rod

The task of the rod person is certainly not difficult, but proper procedures must be followed if good results are desired. The rod should be kept standing on the benchmark or turning point at all times except when actually moving or computing. It must be kept balanced in a vertical position, with the front face turned toward the instrument.

When the instrument is set up in a position that requires high rod, raise the rod *all the way* until the index on the back of it reads exactly 12 ft or 13 ft (whichever applies), and clamp it in position. If it is raised part way, the graduations are not continuous and a blunder will result. The rod

person should be watching the instrument person at all times for signals and instructions.

An experienced surveyor can readily balance the rod in a vertical position. On a windy day, or for precise work, it is best to use a *rod level*. The rod level contains a circular bull's-eye bubble vial; if it is held flush against the edge of the rod and the bubble is centered, the rod is in a vertical position. If a rod level is not available, the instrument person may ask that the rod be "waved" so that an accurate reading can be obtained; this is explained shortly under "Taking a Rod Reading."

Needless to say, the rod is a precision instrument and should be handled with care like any other piece of surveying equipment. It should not be dragged on the ground; always lower the rod to carry it. The metal base should not be banged on rocks or pavement, nor should it be allowed to get caked with mud; remember, the rod is graduated so that the very bottom is 0 ft or 0 m.

Care also needs to be taken when the rod is fully extended; it could get caught on overhead electrical wires, possibly causing serious injury to the rod person.

Taking a Rod Reading

The instrument person sights over the top of the telescope to direct it toward the rod. Then, looking through the telescope, the rod is brought into focus with the vertical cross hair on or near the rod. The clamp and tangent (slow-motion) screw may facilitate this step if the instrument is equipped with it. If an older type of level is used, the bubble tube should be checked for proper centering. If it is slightly off-center, relevel precisely with the pair of opposite screws that most nearly point toward the rod.

The instrument person carefully reads the rod, rechecks the bubble, and then records the rod reading in the field book. (With an automatic or self-leveling instrument, the constant checks of the bubble are not necessary.) The instrument person gives the rod reading to the rod person by voice or signal, naming all the digits and the decimal point in the reading.

The rod person, *while still balancing the rod vertically*, will point to the exact reading with a pencil point as a check. The instrument person will note whether or not the pencil coincides with the horizontal cross hair. If satisfied, he or she calls or signals "all right," and the rod person also records the reading. If not satisfied, the rod is read again and a corrected value obtained.

When reading to thousandths of a foot or millimeters (as for benchmark or precise leveling), there will often be a slight discrepancy between the first reading and the pencil position. The first reading is the correct one if the difference is 0.003 ft (or 1 mm) or less. If the difference is more, the reading is repeated.

Waving the Rod   To ensure that the reading is taken when the rod is vertical, the instrument person may signal

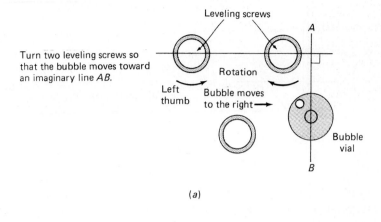

Turn two leveling screws so that the bubble moves toward an imaginary line *AB*.

(a)

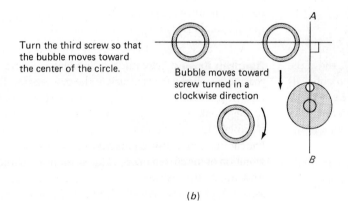

Turn the third screw so that the bubble moves toward the center of the circle.

(b)

The leveling operation is complete when the bubble is centered within the bull's-eye of the circle.

(c)

FIGURE 5-17. Leveling a three-screw instrument with a circular, or bull's-eye, level vial.

the rod person to slowly *wave the rod* back and forth in the direction of the instrument (*not sideways!*). *The correct rod reading is the lowest reading observed* when the rod is being waved (see Figure 5-18). The lowest reading always occurs when the rod just passes through the vertical position.

As much as possible, communication between instrument person and rod-person should be by voice. But on construction sites or near heavy traffic, hand signals may be necessary (unless, of course, radio communication is available). The best signal is often one that imitates the action desired; suggested hand signals follow.

Suggested Hand Signals for Leveling

1. *All right.* Hands outstretched sideways and palms forward and moved up and down together.

2. *Plumb the rod.* Hand over head, elbow straight, and palm forward and inclined in the proper direction.

3. *Wave the rod.* Both hands over head and palms forward, swung back and forth together.

4. *High rod.* Both hands extended outward to the sides, palms up, and the arms moved up to vertical together.

5. *Raise for red.* When the footmark is invisible, the instrument person reads and memorizes the tenths,

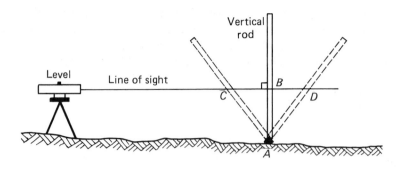

FIGURE 5-18. Waving the rod (motion greatly exaggerated). The rod reading is lowest at *B* because length *AB* is smaller than length *AD* or *AC*.

hundredths, and thousandths and then calls "raise for red" or extends one hand forward, palm up, and raises it a little. The rod person lifts the rod slowly and exactly vertically. The footmark is read when it appears.

6. *Take, or this is, a turning point.* One hand moved in a horizontal circle over the head.

7. *Kill the brass.* Same signal as "high rod." Sometimes the brass strip that is attached to the rear half of the rod at the bottom and fits around the front of the rod conceals the reading. By partly extending the rod the brass is moved upward out of the way. The rod person can always judge by the relative positions of the instrument and the rod whether "high rod" or "kill the brass" is meant.

8. *Turn the rod around.* A small horizontal circle made with the forefinger. It is given when the back or side of the rod is turned toward the instrument.

Leveling Mistakes and Errors

As with any surveying operation, blunders must be eliminated and errors minimized while running levels. *Misreading the rod* is a common blunder; it can be avoided by *always* having the rod person check the reading with pencil point, as previously described. And if the full footmark on the rod is not visible to the instrument person for any reason, he or she should always signal "raise for red" (see the preceding hand signals).

Note-keeping mistakes can be particularly troublesome. The computations of HI and turning point (TP) elevation should be done in the field as the work progresses. A simple arithmetic check at the end of the leveling run can be made to avoid addition or subtraction errors; this is illustrated in Figures 5-4 and 5-21c. For important benchmark leveling work, both the instrument person and the rod person should record data in a field book; the rod person keeps what is called the *peg* book. (Not all surveyors follow this practice, however.) The rod readings should be called out by each surveyor as they are recorded, for confirmation of correct values. Computations should be compared routinely to help avoid arithmetic mistakes.

Blunders are sometimes made by the rod person at a TP. This generally arises if a fixed, well-defined TP was not selected and marked properly to begin with. The rod person may hold the rod on one point for the foresight reading, and then inadvertently place it on a different point when the

instrument person is ready to take a backsight. To avoid this, *a TP should be clearly marked before it is used.* Another mistake with the rod occurs if it is not fully extended and clamped in the proper position for high rod readings. The rod person must also check to see that mud, snow, or ice has not accumulated at the bottom of the rod.

Random Errors   Unavoidable accidental or random errors may occur when running levels for several reasons. For example, the level rod may not be precisely vertical when the rod reading is taken. Sometimes heat waves from the ground make it difficult to read the rod, or the telescope may not be completely focused, causing parallax. On windy days, the slight vibration of the cross hair can cause small errors in the reading. And, finally, the instrument may be slightly out of level if the spirit bubble is not perfectly centered; this may occur due to slight settling of the tripod legs into the ground, or sun's heat may cause unequal expansion of instrument components.

Accidental errors can be minimized with a properly maintained and adjusted instrument if the following steps are taken:

1. Make sure the tripod legs are secure and firmly anchored before leveling the instrument. Avoid setting up on asphalt or frozen ground because the sharp legs may slowly sink; this will change the HI. It is particularly difficult to notice such movement with a self-leveling instrument.

2. Check to see that the bubble is centered before each reading; recenter it if necessary. With an automatic level, gently tap the instrument to make sure the internal prism system is not stuck or broken.

3. Do not lean on the tripod legs when reading the rod.

4. Have the rod person use a rod level or wave the rod to make sure it is held vertically.

5. Try to keep the line of sight about 0.5 m, or 1.5 ft, above the ground when positioning the instrument, particularly when leveling over pavement on a hot day.

6. Focus the eyepiece and objective lens properly before reading the rod. It is best to get in the habit of keeping both eyes open when sighting through the telescope.

7. Without actually rushing the work (which leads to blunders), take as little time as possible between BS and FS readings.

8. Do not use very long BS and FS distances.

Systematic/Instrumental Error   Leveling instruments may occasionally get out of adjustment. With the level rod, it is important that the extension mechanism is in proper working order and that the rod is of the correct length. When using a level, it is particularly important that the bubble tube axis be perpendicular to the standing axis of the instrument and that the line of sight of the telescope be parallel to the bubble tube axis. Instrumental errors are systematic because they tend to occur in the same direction (plus or minus) and with the same magnitude each time a reading is taken.

Although relatively simple methods for checking and adjusting levels can be applied by the surveyor, it is always good practice to follow field procedures that would eliminate or cancel any residual instrumental errors. For running levels, and in particular for benchmark leveling, the most important rule in this regard is to always position the instrument to *keep the BS and FS distances equal* for a single setup (see Figure 5-3). This can be done by eye or by pacing.

If the line of sight of a level is not exactly horizontal when the bubble is centered, but slopes either up or down, it will slope by the same amount for any direction of the telescope. As long as the horizontal lengths of the BS and FS are the same, from any given instrument position to the rod, the line of sight will intercept the rod held on each point with exactly the same error in height. But because one of the sights is a plus sight (+) and the other a minus sight (−), the two errors will cancel each other out in the leveling computations.

This principle is illustrated with a numerical example in Figure 5-19. In addition to canceling the instrumental error

in the level, natural errors caused by the effects of the earth's curvature and the refraction (slight bending) of the line of sight in air will also be effectively eliminated. These effects could be significant for precise leveling over long distances. In fact, even if the level rod length were grossly inaccurate (e.g., an inch of mud caked onto the bottom soleplate), the error would cancel out when computing relative vertical distances or elevations as long as the BS and FS distances between level and level rod were equal.

In some types of leveling surveys, particularly for ground profile or topographic data, several rod readings will be taken with unequal BS and FS distances. Any instrumental error in the work due to this is usually insignificant with respect to the relative accuracy needed for the project. Profile leveling and topo leveling are described later on.

Reciprocal Leveling

When it is necessary to run levels accurately over ravines, rivers, or other obstacles where the BS and FS distances must necessarily be different, a procedure called *reciprocal leveling* may be used. This provides another way to cancel or average out instrumental errors as well as the effects of refraction and the earth's curvature.

The procedure involves two instrument setups, one nearby each point (see Figure 5-20). From each instrument position, a BS on point *A* and an FS on point *B* is taken and an elevation is computed for point *B*. This will result in two different elevations for *B* due to the natural and instrumental errors. But by averaging the two elevations, the effects of the errors are canceled out and the "true" or most probable elevation is obtained.

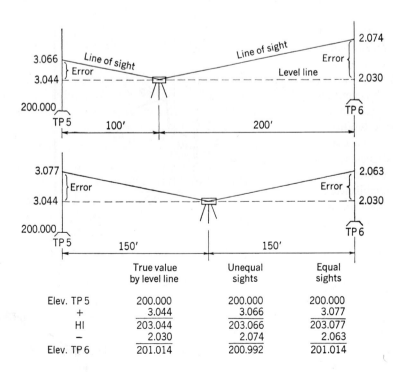

	True value by level line	Unequal sights	Equal sights
Elev. TP 5	200.000	200.000	200.000
+	3.044	3.066	3.077
HI	203.044	203.066	203.077
−	2.030	2.074	2.063
Elev. TP 6	201.014	200.992	201.014

FIGURE 5-19. When the horizontal lengths of the foresight (plus) and backsight (minus) are the same, the systematic error of adjustment of the level is canceled.

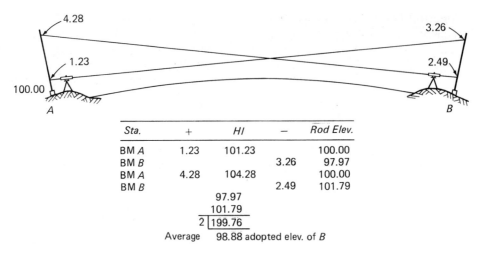

Sta.	+	HI	—	Rod Elev.
BM A	1.23	101.23		100.00
BM B			3.26	97.97
BM A	4.28	104.28		100.00
BM B			2.49	101.79
		97.97		
		101.79		
		2 ⟌ 199.76		

Average   98.88 adopted elev. of B

FIGURE 5-20. Reciprocal leveling over an obstacle such as a river.

5-4 VERTICAL CONTROL (BENCHMARK) SURVEYS

A vertical control survey establishes a series of fixed reference monuments or points whose elevations are measured with a relatively high degree of accuracy. These monuments, called *benchmarks*, can then serve as the basis for starting and checking ordinary surveys of lesser accuracy, such as for topographic mapping or construction layout. Almost any fixed and permanent object, natural or set by the surveyor, can serve as a benchmark. Generally, a benchmark should be easily recognized and found, not likely to move, and set low with respect to the surrounding ground; it should be clearly marked with an identifying number. Leveling for vertical control may be conducted in a variety of ways depending on the required accuracy.

Benchmark Leveling and Field Notes

For ordinary mapping and construction projects, the surveyor must frequently run levels from an "official" benchmark toward the project site and set new benchmarks to control elevations at that site. A system of benchmarks is always in demand from the moment any work is contemplated and throughout the life of the project. Benchmarks should be established, if possible, well before leveling is required for the original topo map. Sometimes a nail in a tree, part of a fire hydrant, or even a wooden stake may serve as a benchmark for a particular construction project. At least three benchmarks should always be established for any project so that if one is disturbed, the pair that check will be known to be correct.

Field Procedure   As previously mentioned, both the instrument person and the rod person should have a field book. The one kept by the instrument person is the *level book*; the other is the *peg book*. The work begins at a previously established benchmark in the vicinity of the project site; this may be one of the official monuments set by a federal, state, or county agency, or it may be some other point of known or

assumed elevation. In the illustration presented here, the starting point is BM 5 (see Figure 5-21).

In the field notes, both the instrument person and the rod person record BM 5 in the station ("Sta.") column: the known

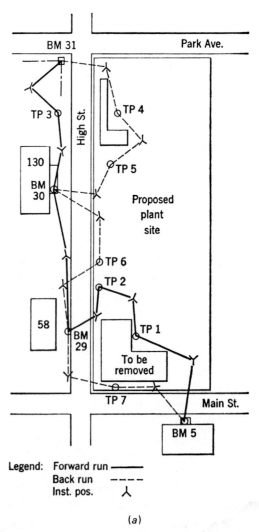

Legend: Forward run ———
Back run - - - -
Inst. pos. ⅄

(a)

FIGURE 5-21. (a) Plan of benchmark leveling.

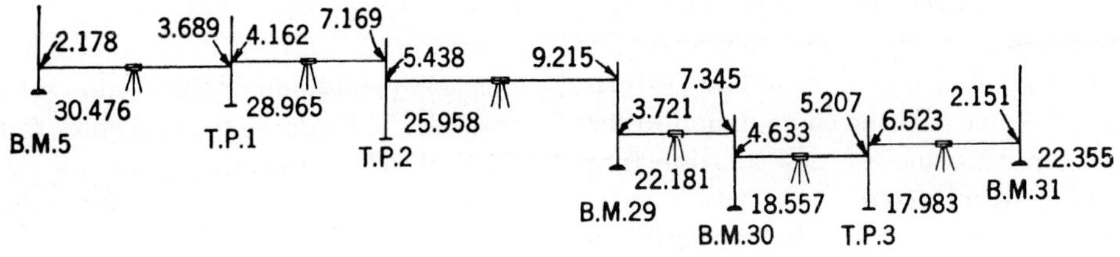

(b)

(c)

FIGURE 5-21. (*Continued*) (*b*) Side view of the benchmark leveling run in (*a*). (*c*) Form of field notes used with benchmark leveling.

elevation, 30.476, is recorded in the elevation ("Elev.") column. That represents the vertical distance of BM 5 above a specific datum, typically MSL. A description of the benchmark is recorded on the right-hand page of the field book on the same line as BM 5 (see Figure 5-21c).

The instrument is set up where BM 5 can be clearly observed, preferably not more than 150 ft (or 50 m) away. The rod person holds the rod on BM 5. The reading of the rod, 2.178, is taken using the target and vernier, checked, and recorded by both surveyors on the same line as BM 5, in the "+", or BS, column. The rod person then paces the distance to the level. An equal distance in the desired direction is paced, and a TP (TP 1) is selected to carry the line of levels forward (a turning point is a temporary benchmark). With experience, the rod person will be able to estimate a suitable distance to a TP without pacing.

The TP must have the following characteristics:

1. The rod, when held on it, will be visible from the level.

2. It must be securely fixed in the ground, preferably with a rounded top on which to rest the rod.

3. If a satisfactory object cannot be found, a metal turning pin or a wooden stake may be driven to serve as a TP. An arbitrary, unmarked point on grass or soil should never be used as a TP.

4. A TP on pavement should be marked with keel (lumber crayon) and identified with an appropriate number (such as "TP 1") immediately after it is selected.

While the rod person is engaged in selecting and marking a suitable TP, the instrument person computes the HI by adding the BS reading, 2.178, to the elevation of BM 5, 30.476, and records the result, 32.654, in the HI column *right next to the plus (BS) reading that gave it.*

The rod person then holds the rod on TP 1; the FS reading 3.689 is observed and checked. It is recorded by both surveyors in the minus (−), or FS, column *on the next line down* in the field notes, a line that is marked with TP 1 in the "Sta." column. Always remember to *record either a BS or an FS reading on the line marked with the name of the point being observed.*

The instrument person picks up the tripod and moves forward with the level. Meanwhile, the rod person computes the HI and subtracts 3.689 from it to find the elevation of TP 1, 28.965, which is recorded in the "Elevation" column on line with TP 1. The rod person should hold the rod on the turning point as soon as possible after the computation so that the instrument person can choose a new location from which the rod can be clearly observed.

A typically difficult operation for the inexperienced instrument person is to choose the proper location for the level when working on steeply sloping ground. When running levels downhill, there is a tendency to set up the level too far downhill so that the line of sight is below the foot of the rod (see Figure 5-22*a*). When working uphill, the level may be set up too far uphill, where the line of sight is above the rod, even when extended (see Figure 5-22*b*). Or even while the BS reading may be observed, the distance of the sight may be so great that the length of the following FS cannot be made equal to it. It is often advantageous to use a hand level for a quick but level line of sight from a selected instrument position to avoid this time-wasting situation.

After the instrument is set up in its new position, the BS reading of 4.162 is observed, checked, and recorded by both surveyors in the plus (+) column on line with TP 1 (remember always to record a rod reading on line with the point being observed). It may also be helpful to remember that the first reading after a new instrument setup is *always* a backsight and will be entered in the second column. The *only* time that data can be recorded in the second column is from a first reading taken after a new instrument setup. Second readings from the same instrument setup location will be foresights and will be entered in the fourth column. While the rod person then paces the new distance to the instrument, the instrument person computes and records the elevation of TP 1 and the new HI of 33.127.

When the rod person reaches the instrument after pacing the distance, both surveyors check their corresponding values for the elevation of TP 1. If there is a discrepancy, the blunder must be found before proceeding with the work. Then the process of running levels continues, repeating the steps already described.

Checking for Mistakes   When the survey is complete, an *arithmetic check* is done; this simply ensures that no mistakes in addition or subtraction were made in the "HI" and "Elev." columns of the field notes. As illustrated in Figure 5-21*c*, the check consists of summing the BS (+) and FS (−) columns and applying those sums to the starting elevation; the same result, 30.483, is obtained for the final elevation of BM 5, indicating no arithmetic error was made.

Note that in this example, the line of levels is run back to BM 5, the starting point. This is called a *closed level loop* or *level circuit*. Any leveling survey should close back either on the starting benchmark or on some other point of known elevation in order to provide a check against blunders. (The arithmetic check alone will not reveal blunders, like misreading the rod.)

In the example of Figure 5-21, there is a discrepancy of 0.007 ft between the known elevation of BM 5, 30.476, and the observed value for that point, 30.483. This difference is small enough to effectively rule out the possibility of a blunder in the work; it is due to various unavoidable random errors. As will be explained later, the order of accuracy of the leveling survey will depend on the total horizontal distance covered by the level circuit.

Error of Closure and Precise Leveling

There are about a half-million official benchmarks throughout the United States, which constitute the *National Vertical Control Network*. These benchmarks are established and maintained by U.S. federal agencies such as the *National Geodetic Survey* (NGS) and the *U.S. Geological Survey* (USGS). The elevations of these points are referenced to MSL data from 1929; that reference is called the *National Geodetic Vertical Datum of 1929* (NGVD29). An adjustment to account for natural geological changes that slowly alter the elevations to some degree has been completed; the adjusted elevations are referenced to a new MSL datum called the *North American Vertical Datum of 1988* (NAVD88).

The relative accuracy required for a vertical control or leveling survey depends on its purpose. A set of standards and specifications has been prepared by the federal government for the national control network; this also serves as a guide for

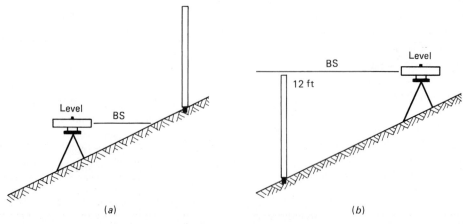

FIGURE 5-22. (*a*) Level set up too low. (*b*) Level set up too high.

surveyors in private practice. There is a hierarchy of several different orders and classes for vertical accuracy standards. These standards are expressed in terms of an *allowable error of closure*, as well as relative accuracy between points.

The allowable error of closure is a function of the length or total horizontal distance of the leveling line or circuit. The function is expressed in the following form: error = constant $\times$ $\sqrt{\text{distance}}$. The higher the order of accuracy, the smaller the constant.

The latest standards for vertical control established by the *U.S. Federal Geodetic Control Committee* are summarized in Table 5-1. They apply primarily to precise leveling work done by federal or state agencies. Benchmarks for extensive construction projects may be established at third-order accuracy, starting from an NGS or USGS second-order monument. But for most relatively small-scale local construction projects, benchmarks are often set at an even lower level of accuracy (what might be called "fourth-order"). The error of closure has units of millimeters, with the distance given in units of kilometers.

Consider, for example, a level circuit with a total length of 2000 m. At third-order accuracy, the maximum error of closure would be $12\sqrt{2} = 17$ mm. In U.S. Customary units, an error of closure equal to $0.05\sqrt{M}$ ft, where M is the distance leveled in miles, is equivalent to third-order accuracy. For a level loop 2000 ft long, for example, the maximum error of closure would be $0.05\sqrt{2000/5280} = 0.05\sqrt{0.379} = 0.03$ ft.

Average leveling work done primarily for local construction projects may have an error of closure equal to about $0.1\sqrt{M}$ ft. And the accuracy of what may be called "rough" leveling, such as for ground profile and topo mapping purposes, may be $0.5\sqrt{M}$ or less.

Precise Leveling   High-accuracy leveling is generally characterized as *precise leveling*. It requires the use of special level instruments, level rods, and field procedures.

A procedure called *three-wire leveling* has long been applied for precise work. In most instruments, the reticles are equipped with *stadia hairs* in addition to the regular cross hairs. Stadia hairs are two short cross hairs equally spaced above and below the longer central horizontal cross hair. (Their use for tacheometry and topo surveys is described in Section 9-3.) In three-wire leveling, the rod readings are taken to the nearest 0.001 ft or 0.001 m at each of the three cross hairs. The three readings are recorded and averaged to give a more precise value than would be obtained by reading only the center cross hair. Comparing the average reading with the reading of the central cross hair helps to avoid blunders, and the use of the stadia hairs also helps to keep BS and FS distances equal.

To a large extent, the use of newer high-precision instruments is replacing the time-consuming three-wire leveling procedure for precise work. A modern precise tilting level (see Figure 5-23) may be equipped with either an attached or a built-in optical micrometer. Basically, this allows the horizontal line of sight to be moved up or down parallel to itself. The optical micrometer is calibrated to give the vertical movement of the line of sight. The horizontal cross hair is moved to match the nearest lower division on the rod; the value of that division plus the reading of the micrometer scale gives a very precise rod reading. On sunny days, the level may even be shaded with an umbrella to prevent unequal expansion of parts of the instrument.

Ordinary level rods are not generally used for precise work, whether using three-wire leveling or a first-order micrometer level. Instead, a *precise level rod* is used; it is typically constructed in one solid section, with an attached graduated Invar-steel strip and with a special solid-metal foot piece called a *rod shoe*. A circular level is used to keep the rod vertical; it may also be equipped with supporting legs for added stability. The Invar scale is under constant spring tension, and a thermometer is attached to allow corrections to be made for temperature effects.

Table 5-1. Accuracy Standards for Vertical Control Surveys

Order	Maximum Allowable Error of Closure, mm	Relative Accuracy Required Between Benchmarks, mm	Applications
First			
Class I	$\pm\,3\sqrt{K}$	$\pm\,0.5\sqrt{K}$	Provides basic framework for the National Control Network and precise
Class II	$\pm\,4\sqrt{K}$	$\pm\,0.7\sqrt{K}$	control of large engineering projects and scientific studies
Second			
Class I	$\pm\,6\sqrt{K}$	$\pm\,1\sqrt{K}$	Adds to the basic framework for major
Class II	$\pm\,8\sqrt{K}$	$\pm\,1.3\sqrt{K}$	engineering projects
Third	$\pm\,12\sqrt{K}$	$\pm\,2\sqrt{K}$	Serves as vertical reference for local engineering, topo, drainage, and mapping projects

Note: Error of closure is in millimeters, while K represents the total length of the level circuit in kilometers.

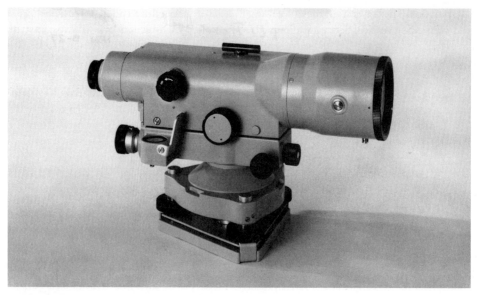

FIGURE 5-23. A precise level with parallel plate micrometer enables vertical displacement to be measured to 0.1 mm. An accuracy of ±0.2 mm in 1 km of leveling (±0.001 ft/ml) can be obtained. (*Courtesy of The Lietz Company.*)

Benchmark Monuments   Any point intended to serve as a benchmark must be properly constructed or *monumented* so that it does not move during its period of intended use. This is, of course, particularly important for points in the national control network.

Most NGS and USGS benchmark monuments comprise a 4-in-diameter bronze disk, securely embedded on top of a concrete post that extends from the ground surface to below the frost line. Some monuments use an iron rod driven about 10 ft into the ground and capped with a brass tablet.

New federal monuments are now being set on stainless steel rods that are driven into the ground and then encased in a PVC pipe sleeve. The top of the rod, which is the reference elevation point, is set about 1 ft below the ground surface; it is protected by an aluminum access cover that is stamped with the federal agency's name and the benchmark identification number. A nearby witness post and sign clearly mark the location of the point.

Adjusting Benchmark Elevations

The importance of running a line of levels back to the starting benchmark, or to some other fixed point of known elevation, was mentioned previously. There is really no way to ensure that a blunder is not made in the work without *closing the level circuit* one way or the other. It is much less expensive to find and correct a blunder in the field by closing the loop than to have to return and repeat the work at a later date (or worse, pay for the demolition, removal, and reconstruction of incorrectly placed structures).

When the line of levels or level circuit is completed, there is usually some small difference between the given fixed elevation of the benchmark and the observed elevation arrived at in the leveling notes. If the arithmetic check works out all right, then it may be assumed that the discrepancy is due to random accidental errors. It is reasonable to expect that any new intermediate benchmarks set while running the levels are also in error to some degree.

Suppose a leveling survey closes within the desired order and class of accuracy; in other words, there is an error of closure, but it is acceptable. The problem now is to distribute that total error of closure among the various intermediate benchmarks and to *adjust the circuit* so that it closes exactly (i.e., so that the observed benchmark elevation matches the given fixed elevation).

In doing this for a single level line or circuit, it may be assumed that *the elevation error at each point along the circuit or line of levels (and therefore the required correction) is directly proportional to the distance of the point from the starting benchmark*. The relationships for adjusting the leveling line or circuit, then, may be summarized as follows:

$$\text{Correction} = \text{error of closure} \times$$
$$\frac{\text{distance from starting benchmark}}{\text{total length of level run}}$$

$$\text{Error of closure} = \text{given benchmark elevation} - \text{observed benchmark elevation}$$

$$\text{Adjusted elevation} = \text{observed elevation} + \text{correction}$$

(For precise benchmark-leveling work, multiple adjoining loops would be run, and a more mathematically advanced adjustment by the *method of least squares* would be applied.)

Example 5-1

Levels are run a total distance of 12.30 km from BM 10 to BM 25 to set three other benchmarks along the route of a proposed roadway construction project (see Figure 5-24). The fixed and recorded elevations of BM 10 and BM 25 are

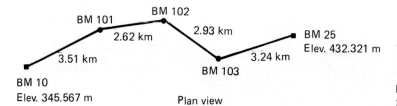

FIGURE 5-24. Illustration for Example 5-1.

Table 5-2. Adjusting (Closing) a Line of Benchmark Elevations

BM	Elevation, m	Distance, km	Correction, m	Adjusted Elevation*
BM 10	345.567	0	0	345.567[†]
BM 101	369.456	3.51	0.010	369.466
BM 102	398.435	6.13	0.017	398.452
BM 103	419.560	9.06	0.026	419.586
BM 25	432.286	12.30	0.035	432.321[†]

*Adjusted elevation = elevation + correction.
[†]Note that these are the given fixed elevations.

345.567 and 432.321 m, respectively. When closing the line of levels on BM 25, an observed elevation of 432.286 m is recorded in the field book. What is the accuracy of the survey? Adjust the benchmark elevations.

Solution
The error of closure for the line of levels is

$$432.321 \text{ m} - 432.286 \text{ m} = 0.035 \text{ m} = 35 \text{ mm}$$

Assuming that this accuracy for the work is acceptable, an adjustment to the intermediate benchmark elevations can be made as shown in Table 5-2. A typical computation, for BM 102, follows:

Distance of BM 102 from BM 10 = 3.51 + 2.62 = 6.13 km

$$\text{Correction} = 0.035 \times \frac{6.13}{12.30} = 0.017 \text{ m}$$

Adjusted elevation of BM 102 = 398.435 + 0.017 = 398.452 m

5-5 PROFILE LEVELING

Profile leveling is one of the most common applications of running levels and vertical distance measurement for the surveyor. The results are plotted in the form of a *profile*, which is a drawing that shows a vertical section or "side view" of the earth's surface. Profiles are required for the design and construction of roads, curbs, sidewalks, storm drainage systems, water supply or sewer pipelines, and many other types of public infrastructure.

Briefly, profile leveling refers to the process of determining the elevations of a series of points on the ground at mostly uniform intervals along a continuous line. The line may be straight, it may turn at sharp intersections or angle points, or it may be a series of straight lines connected by curves. For example, the line may be the centerline along the

path of a proposed storm sewer or highway. Points along the line are typically identified by stations and pluses, as described in Section 4-2 and shown in Figure 4-15; these points may be set and marked temporarily on the ground during the survey.

Field Procedure

Profile leveling is essentially the same as benchmark leveling with one basic difference. At each instrument position, where an HI is determined by a backsight rod reading on a benchmark or turning point, several additional foresight readings may be taken on as many points as desired. These additional readings are called *rod shots*, and the elevations of all those points are determined by subtracting the rod shot from the HI at that instrument location.

Generally, however, rod-shot readings are not taken as precisely as the benchmark or turning point readings, primarily because of the limit in scale and precision to which the points can actually be plotted on the profile. If benchmarks have been set and recorded to the nearest 0.001 ft (or 0.001 m), for example, then rod shots may be taken to the nearest 0.01 ft (or 0.003 m); on rough or unpaved ground, rod shots are generally taken to the nearest 0.1 ft (or 0.03 m).

The benchmark and turning point readings constitute a control survey for the work and for this reason they must be read more precisely than the rod shots; before the profile survey is complete, the line of levels should be carried back to the starting benchmark or to some other benchmark for a check against blunders.

Figure 5-25*a* illustrates the plan (or "top") view for a line of profile leveling, shown as the centerline of a street. Stations and pluses are marked (with stakes, or with keel on paved surfaces) at 50-ft intervals. Depending on the topography, the

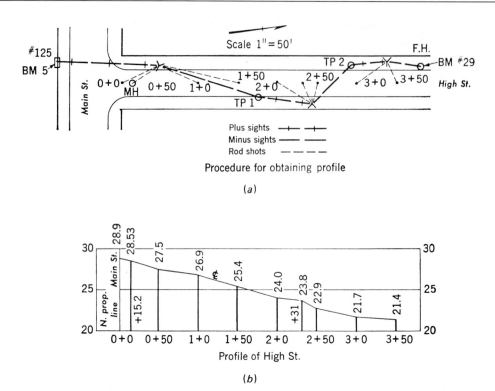

FIGURE 5-25. Profile leveling; several rod shots are taken from each instrument position.

intervals may be either longer (for uniform terrain) or shorter (for irregular terrain). A profile of the street would be required, for example, to design and construct a new subbase and pavement for the road. The profile view is usually shown

directly under the plan view (see Figure 5-25*b*); drawing the profile is discussed shortly.

The field notes for this profile-leveling example are shown in Figure 5-26. It will be seen that the form is similar

Sta.	+	HI	−	Rod	Elev.	
PROFILE-₵ HIGH ST., MAIN TO PARK						
B.M.5	2.587	33.063			30.476	Precise B.M. Disk Set in Top Step of Entrance #125 Main St.
0+0				4.2	28.9	North Prop. Line Main St. Produced
0+15.2				4.53	28.53	Top of San. Sewer Manhole Frame
0+50				5.6	27.5	
1+0				6.2	26.9	
1+50				7.7	25.4	
T.P.1	3.655	32.936	3.782		29.281	
2+0				8.9	24.0	
2+31				9.1	23.8	Break in Gd.
2+50				10.0	22.9	
T.P.2	6.006	32.581	6.361		26.575	
3+0				10.9	21.7	
3+50				11.2	21.4	
B.M.29			10.377		22.204	"R" in Corey F. H. Opp. #58 High St.
	12.248		20.520			Adj. Elev. = 22.185

Ch. & Recorder Roberts — Date

π   Smith — Clear Hot Sun

Rod Jones — 85°F.

Berger 12978

Arith. Ck.   30.476
+ 12.248
42.724
− 20.520
22.204

Error +.019

FIGURE 5-26. Example of profile-leveling field notes.

to that for benchmark leveling, with an additional "Rod" column to record the rod shots. Although rod shots are treated as foresights in the leveling computation for elevations, they are not recorded in the FS, or "+," column. They are, in effect, isolated readings that are not used to carry elevations forward in the direction of the work.

The level is set up near station 0 + 0, and a backsight reading of 2.587 is taken on BM 5. This is added to the benchmark elevation 30.476 to obtain the HI of 33.063. Then the rod is held on station 0 + 0, and a rod-shot reading of 4.2 is recorded in the "Rod" column. (In this survey, the existing road surface can be assumed to be poorly paved and irregular, and so the rod shots need only be read to the nearest tenth of a foot; this helps to speed up the field work.)

The rod shot is then subtracted (like a foresight) from the HI to obtain the ground elevation at station 0 + 0 as 28.9 (again, it is rounded off to the nearest tenth). From this same setup of the level, rod shots are taken until the view is obstructed, or a sight distance over about 150 ft is required. This includes shots on station and half-station points as well as the top of the manhole frame at station 0 + 15.2.

At this time, a turning point is established so that the level can be moved forward. In this example, TP 1 is shown to be marked (with keel) on a curb. The rod is held on TP 1, and a foresight of 3.782 is read, recorded in the FS, or "−," column, and subtracted from the HI elevation of 33.063. This gives an elevation of 29.281 for TP 1. The instrument is now moved to its second location near station 2 + 50 on the other side of the street. (Note that the instrument does not have to be set up on the profile centerline itself.) Before moving the instrument to a new location, reshoot the backsight for that setup to confirm the backsight reading. If there is a discrepancy, disregard all data collected at that instrument setup. That portion of the survey will have to be redone.

Now that the instrument has been moved, *a new HI must be determined before any additional rod shots can be taken.* One of the most common blunders for beginning students is to forget to determine the new HI. In this example, a backsight of 3.655 is taken on TP 1 and added to the elevation of TP 1 to give the new HI of 32.936. The work then proceeds as before. It ends with a foresight on a fixed benchmark so that a check may be obtained. In this example, the error of closure of 0.019 ft is typical of what may be called fourth-order or average accuracy for profile leveling. (Check this out yourself, assuming a total level run distance of, say, 400 ft.)

As previously seen, the elevation at each station is computed by subtracting the rod shot from the *proper* HI. It is therefore essential that all the rod shots from one HI be recorded before the foresight reading to the next TP. Also, the foresight to that TP should be taken after all the rod shots so that if the field check does not indicate a blunder, it is an immediate indication that the level was not disturbed at any HI. These two considerations dictate the order of procedure for profile leveling; that is, *all the rod shots shall be taken at any HI before the foresight to the next TP is taken.* Other than that, all the rules for benchmark leveling apply.

Under no circumstances should leveling of any type be performed without starting on, or setting, at least one benchmark. If an official benchmark of known elevation is not available, a secure point should be set and given an arbitrary elevation. The benchmarks established on the original profile are later used as starting points for the leveling necessary to mark the proper elevations for construction.

If a benchmark does not exist at the end of the work, it is necessary to carry the levels back to the original benchmark to obtain a field check. Often, it is advisable to establish several benchmarks on the forward run. This can be accomplished by merely recording the location and description of TPs. These are useful for giving grades for construction. On the way back for closure, they should be used as TPs again so that any blunders can be isolated.

Plotting the Profile

The profile drawing is basically a graph of elevations, plotted on the vertical axis, as a function of stations plotted on the horizontal axis. A gridded sheet called *profile paper* is usually used to plot the profile data from the field book. Profile paper generally has light blue, green, or orange lines uniformly spaced to represent the required distances and elevations on the horizontal and vertical scales. When both plan and profile views are to be shown, special sheets, half plain on top and gridded profile on the bottom, are used. All profile drawings must have a proper title block, and both axes must be fully labeled with stations and elevations.

The vertical or elevation scale is typically exaggerated; that is, it is "stretched" in comparison to the horizontal scale. For example, if the horizontal scale is set at 1 in = 100 ft, the vertical scale might be 10 times as large, or 1 in = 10 ft.

The profile must always be plotted exactly to scale, and the vertical scale may occasionally be as much as 20 times as large as the horizontal scale. This causes a distortion, making the slope of the ground appear much steeper on paper than it actually is in the field. But it serves to make the general shape of the ground, and the relative elevations, easier to read and interpret; it also facilitates the design process.

The horizontal line at the bottom of the profile does not necessarily have to start at zero elevation. That line, which is the origin for the vertical scale, is usually assigned the highest elevation, in round numbers, that is still lower than the lowest point in the profile. The shape of the profile would not change; it would simply be positioned higher on the profile paper.

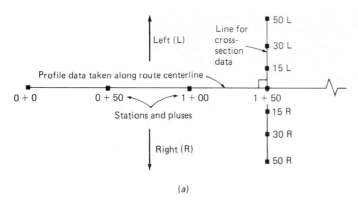

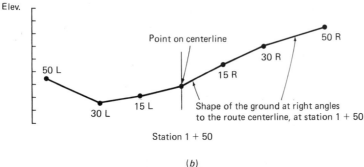

FIGURE 5-27. (*a*) Top view showing the route centerline and the line for cross-section leveling at station 1 + 50. (*b*) The cross section, showing ground elevations at points left and right of the centerline.

A technician can also perform the profile plotting using one of the many CAD programs currently available. The data are inputted using *x*, *y*, and *z* coordinates, thereby providing the three-dimensional data that are needed for the computer to plot the profile.

Cross-Section Leveling

The term *cross section* generally refers to a relatively short view of the ground that is drawn perpendicular to the route centerline of a highway or other linear type of project (see Figure 5-27). Cross-section drawings are particularly important for estimating the earthwork volumes needed to construct a roadway; they show the existing ground elevations, the proposed cut or fill side slopes, and the grade elevation for the road base. Earthwork sections and computations are discussed in more detail in Chapter 10.

There is really no difference in procedure between profile and cross-section leveling except for the form of the field notes. Cross-section rod shots are usually taken during the route profile survey from the same instrument positions used to take rod shots along the centerline. Cross-section data are obtained at the same locations along the route that are used for the profile rod-shot stations.

For a given route profile, there are many cross sections; a mile-long route, for example, would have more than 100 cross sections, 1 every 50 ft. The cross-section rod shots are taken at specified lateral distances from the route centerline stations, such as 15, 30, and perhaps 50 ft, to the left and right. Cross-section rod shots would also be taken at sudden changes in the ground slope on the line at right angles to the route.

Some surveyors use the left-hand page of the field book for centerline profile notes and the right-hand page for cross-section notes. Others record both profile and cross-section data on the same page, as illustrated in Figure 5-28; the "#L" or "#R" indicates the distance to the left or right of the centerline that the rod shot was taken. If the cross-section rod shot is taken at the edge of an existing pavement (EP), or at some other identifiable point, it should be so noted in the field book to facilitate drafting of the section.

5-6 TRIGONOMETRIC LEVELING

The difference in elevation between two points may be obtained indirectly by measuring a vertical or zenith angle and the horizontal or slope distance between the points. This is called *trigonometric leveling* because the vertical distance is computed using right-angle trigonometric formulas (see Figure 5-29). The use of *electronic distance measurement* (EDM) is making trigonometric leveling an increasingly

		Profile &					Ch. & Recorder – Roberts	7/15/85
		Cross sections – new road					A Smith	Clear
Sta	BS	HI	FS	Rod	Elev		Rod Jones	80° F
BM6	3.53	93.77			90.24		Precise BM disc set in	Level
0 + 0							top step # 234 Maple Ave	Berger # 12978
50 L				4.2	89.6		ROW	
30 L				6.7	87.1		Bottom of swale	
15 L				5.6	88.2			
₵				5.2	88.6			
15 R				4.1	89.7			
30 R				3.4	90.4			
50 R				2.6	91.2		ROW	
0+50								
50 L				4.4	89.4		ROW	
30 L				6.9	86.9		Bottom of swale	
15 L				5.8	88.0			
₵				5.5	88.3			
15 R				4.3	89.5			
30 R				3.7	90.1			
50 R				2.8	91.0		ROW	
1+00								
50 L				4.7	89.1		ROW	
30 L				7.3	86.5		Bottom of swale	
15 L				6.1	87.7			
₵				5.7	88.1			
15 R				4.5	89.3			
23 R				4.0	89.8		Change in slope	
50 R				3.1	90.7		ROW	

FIGURE 5-28. Cross-section field notes.

popular procedure among surveyors because it greatly increases both the accuracy and speed with which the required horizontal or slope distances can be determined.

Trigonometric leveling is particularly useful for topographic work, and this application is discussed in more detail in Chapter 9. The measurement of a vertical or zenith angle is discussed in Section 5-1. For very precise trigonometric leveling work with EDM, angles should be measured to within ±6 in of arc (see Section 2-1) with a theodolite; when the line of sight exceeds about 1000 ft (300 m), corrections must be made to account for the refraction of light and the curvature of the earth. In some cases, *reciprocal vertical-angle measurements* are made at each point to minimize the effects of refraction and curvature.

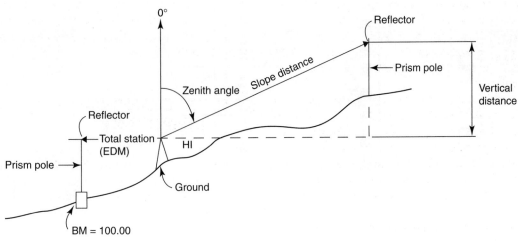

FIGURE 5-29. Trigonometric leveling.

Questions for Review

1. What does the term *elevation* mean?

2. What is the purpose of running levels?

3. List four different methods of leveling.

4. Briefly outline the process of differential leveling.

5. Define the following terms: *backsight, foresight, height of instrument, benchmark,* and *turning point.*

6. Briefly describe the basic components and operation of the telescopic sight of a leveling instrument. What is *parallax?* What is the *line of sight?*

7. Briefly describe the configuration and use of a spirit vial.

8. How does an automatic level differ from a tilting level?

9. What is a *coincidence bubble?*

10. What is meant by *automatic level?* How does it work?

11. Briefly describe the configuration and use of a level rod.

12. Briefly describe the use of a direct elevation rod.

13. Outline the procedure for setting up a level.

14. What are some important factors regarding the use of a level rod?

15. Briefly describe the procedure for taking a rod reading.

16. What is the purpose of *waving the rod?* Which rod reading should be recorded—the highest or lowest?

17. Briefly describe three hand signals used by surveyors.

18. What are three possible sources of leveling blunders? How can they be avoided?

19. List five sources of random errors in leveling.

20. List six rules for leveling that can minimize random errors.

21. What is the purpose of equalizing BS and FS distances?

22. Describe the purpose and procedure of reciprocal leveling.

23. What is meant by *benchmark leveling?*

24. List three important characteristics of a turning point.

25. What is meant by *level circuit* and *arithmetic check?*

26. What is the purpose of a vertical control survey? Briefly describe the orders of accuracy established for vertical control standards.

27. What do MSL, NGS, USGS, NGVD29, and NAVD88 stand for?

28. What are some distinctive aspects of precise leveling?

29. What is the basic assumption for adjusting a level circuit?

30. What is a profile? What is it used for?

31. Briefly describe the process of profile leveling. How does it differ from benchmark leveling?

32. Should rod shots be taken with greater precision than other rod readings? Why?

33. Why is the vertical scale of a profile exaggerated? How is the starting value of the profile's vertical axis selected?

34. What is a cross section? How are the data for it obtained?

Practice Problems

1. What are the rod readings at the horizontal lines in Figure 5-30?

2. What are the rod readings at the horizontal lines in Figure 5-31?

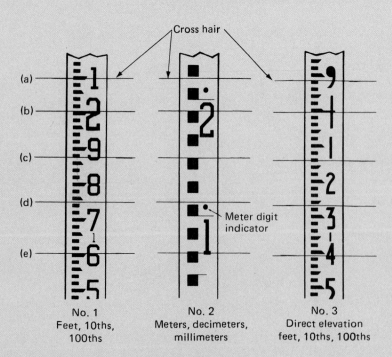

No. 1
Feet, 10ths,
100ths

No. 2
Meters, decimeters,
millimeters

No. 3
Direct elevation
feet, 10ths, 100ths

FIGURE 5-30. Illustration for Problem 1.

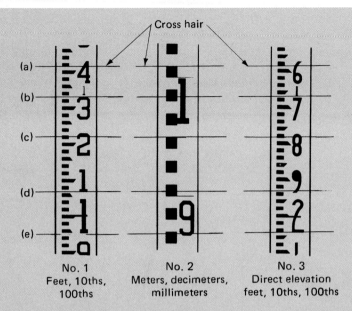

No. 1
Feet, 10ths,
100ths

No. 2
Meters, decimeters,
millimeters

No. 3
Direct elevation
feet, 10ths, 100ths

FIGURE 5-31. Illustration for Problem 2.

3. Complete the benchmark-leveling field notes shown in Figure 5-32 by computing and recording the HI and elevation for each TP and benchmark. Do the arithmetic check.

4. Complete the benchmark-leveling field notes shown in Figure 5-33 by computing and recording the HI and elevation for each TP and benchmark. Do the arithmetic check.

Sta.	BS	HI	FS	Elev.
BM 1	2.25			500.00
TP 1	1.89		4.56	
TP 2	2.55		5.68	
TP 3	2.75		3.45	
BM 2			3.08	
Sum =				

(a)

Sta.	BS	HI	FS	Elev.
BM 1	0.335			150.000
TP 1	0.468		1.223	
TP 2	0.680		1.765	
TP 3	0.963		2.468	
TP 4	1.369		1.234	
BM 2			0.852	
Sum =				

(b)

FIGURE 5-32. Illustration for Problem 3.

Sta.	BS	HI	FS	Elev.
BM 10	3.45			753.20
TP 1	4.68		2.36	
TP 2	6.85		1.23	
TP 3	9.63		1.79	
BM 20			2.46	
Sum =				

(a)

Sta.	BS	HI	FS	Elev.
BM 10	1.567			200.00
TP 1	1.345		3.579	
TP 2	1.136		2.760	
TP 3	0.987		2.575	
TP 4	0.876		2.055	
BM 20			1.579	
Sum =				

(b)

FIGURE 5-33. Illustration for Problem 4.

5. Repeat Problem 3 on the premise that all benchmarks and TPs are located on the crown (ceiling) of a tunnel and the level rod was held in an inverted position on those points.

6. Repeat Problem 4 on the premise that all benchmarks and TPs are located on the crown (ceiling) of a tunnel and the level rod was held in an inverted position on those points.

7. Plan-view sketches of benchmark leveling runs are shown in Figure 5-34. Along each line representing a sight is the value of the rod reading for that sight. The numbering of the TPs shows the direction of the level run. Place the data in the form of field notes. Include the arithmetic check. Assuming that the average length of each BS and FS is 125 ft, determine the accuracy of the survey.

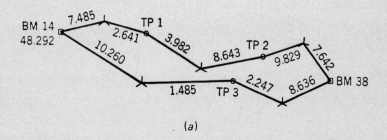

(a)

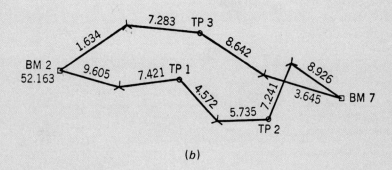

(b)

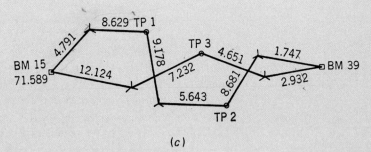

(c)

FIGURE 5-34. Illustration for Problem 7.

8. Plan-view sketches of benchmark leveling runs are shown in Figure 5-35. Along each line representing a sight is the value of the rod reading for that sight. The numbering of the TPs shows the direction of the level run. Place the data in the form of field notes. Include the arithmetic check. Assuming that the average length of each BS and FS is 40 m, determine the accuracy of the survey.

9. Listed below are rod readings in the order in which they were taken in benchmark leveling. The elevation of the starting benchmark is given at the head of each column; the last reading is taken on the starting benchmark as a check. Give the complete form of field notes, including the arithmetic check. If the average BS and FS distance is 150 ft, what is the accuracy for each level run?

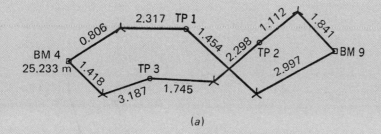

(a)

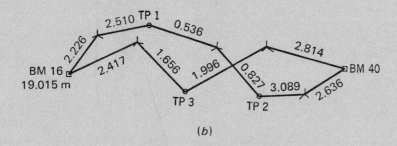

(b)

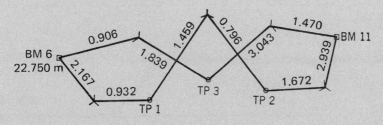

(c)

FIGURE 5-35. Illustration
for Problem 8.

benchmark as a check. Give the complete form of field notes, including the arithmetic check. If the average BS and FS distance is 50 m, what is the accuracy for each level run?

(a)	(b)	(c)
74.36	**67.428**	**59.27**
6.48	8.562	11.36
5.72	4.077	5.32
1.06	9.714	1.87
2.38	2.394	10.24
8.67	4.758	2.65
9.22	11.645	6.23
0.27	2.625	4.68
8.13	6.755	5.27
6.42	8.481	8.41
1.75	9.262	7.59
5.23		10.36
0.90		4.71

(a)	(b)	(c)
12.000	**26.34**	**27.934**
2.300	2.58	0.528
1.110	2.93	2.827
2.088	2.25	1.290
1.652	1.99	2.508
2.506	1.63	1.684
1.833	2.52	1.408
3.257	2.81	2.762
2.666	3.14	1.904
0.497	1.94	2.549
3.384	2.26	0.170
	2.81	
	1.18	

10. Following are rod readings in the order in which they were taken in benchmark leveling. The elevation of the starting benchmark is given at the head of each column; the last reading is taken on the starting

11. The following sets of field note data were taken in the order given during profile leveling. Place each set of data in standard field book form. On graph paper, draw the profile to the following scales: horizontal 1 in = 100 ft; vertical 1 in = 10 ft.

Elev.	Point	Rod Reading	Point	Rod Reading	Point	Rod Reading
(a) BM 20	BM 20	3.516	TP 1	4.280	7 + 0	8.3
50.312	0 + 00	2.0	4 + 0	3.9	8 + 0	9.9
	1 + 00	7.3	5 + 0	1.4	9 + 0	9.7
BM 21	2 + 00	11.1	TP 2	1.201	BM 21	9.989
43.047	3 + 00	10.4	TP 2	3.016		
	TP 1	6.872	6 + 0	4.2		
(b) BM 14	BM 14	4.674	TP 1	8.149	7 + 0	9.6
35.792	0 + 00	7.1	4 + 0	4.0	8 + 0	6.6
	1 + 00	10.7	5 + 0	2.7	9 + 0	5.8
BM 15	2 + 00	12.3	TP 2	9.614	BM 15	7.167
34.680	3 + 00	7.8	TP 2	9.677		
	TP 1	6.842	6 + 0	6.8		

12. The following sets of field note data were taken in the order given during profile leveling. Place each set of data in standard field book form. On graph paper, draw the profile to the following scales: horizontal 1:1000; vertical 1:100 (units are meters).

Elev.	Point	Rod Reading	Point	Rod Reading	Point	Rod Reading
(a) BM 27	BM 27	2.860	TP 1	0.390	2 + 40	1.61
			1 + 20	0.20		
19.750	0 + 00	3.29	1 + 50	0.06	2 + 70	0.94
	0 + 30	1.92	1 + 80	1.83	3 + 00	0.52
BM 48	0 + 60	0.67	2 + 10	2.80	BM 48	0.951
19.270	0 + 90	0.37	TP 2	1.990		
	TP 1	1.680	TP 2	0.887		
(b) BM 16	BM 16	1.715	TP 1	1.144	2 + 40	1.83
			1 + 20	4.15		
19.885	0 + 00	3.90	1 + 50	3.90	2 + 70	1.65
	0 + 30	2.47	1 + 80	3.23	3 + 00	3.54
BM 17	0 + 60	1.43	TP 2	2.475	BM 17	1.591
19.365	0 + 90	2.56	TP 2	1.914		
	TP 1	1.230	2 + 10	1.98		

13. Levels were run from BM 100 to BM 100A. An elevation of 1234.567 ft was observed at BM 100A. It was later discovered that the level rod was 0.025 ft too short. If there were 14 TPs in the level run, what is the correct elevation of BM 100A? Assume that each pair of BS and FS distances was equal.

14. Levels were run from BM 10 to BM 10A. An elevation of 376.296 m was observed at BM 10A. It was later discovered that the level rod was 5 mm too short. If there were 14 TPs in the level run, what is the correct elevation of BM 10A? Assume that each pair of BS and FS distances was equal.

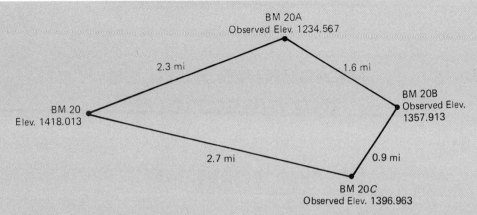

FIGURE 5-36. Illustration for Problem 15.

15. A level circuit is run a total distance of 7.5 mi from BM 20 to set three other benchmarks in the vicinity of a construction project (see Figure 5-36). The given elevation of BM 20 is 1418.013 ft. When closing the level loop, its elevation is observed to be 1417.890 ft. What is the accuracy of the survey? Adjust the benchmark elevations.

16. A level circuit is run a total distance of 10 km from BM 30 to set three other benchmarks in the vicinity of a construction project (see Figure 5-37). The given elevation of BM 30 is 456.78 m. When closing the level loop, its elevation is observed to be 456.82 m. What is the accuracy of the survey? Adjust the benchmark elevations.

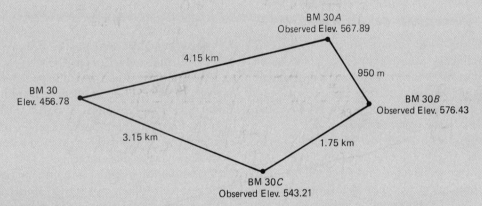

FIGURE 5-37. Illustration for Problem 16.

MEASURING ANGLES AND DIRECTIONS

CHAPTER OUTLINE

One of the basic purposes of surveying is to determine the relative positions of points on or near the earth's surface. Assigning coordinates to a given point is a useful and common way to indicate its position. *Angles*, as well as linear distances, are usually measured to compute the coordinates of any particular point.

Angles are measured between two intersecting lines in either a horizontal plane or a vertical plane (see Figure 1-8). They are usually expressed in terms of degrees, minutes, and seconds of arc, although other types of units may also be used (see Section 2-1). The horizontal angle between a given line and a specified reference line is called the *direction* of the line. The reference line is called *meridian*. In addition to serving for the computation of coordinates, angles are measured so that the directions of lines (such as property boundaries) can be established.

The relative positions of points on the ground are generally determined by a horizontal control survey, such as a *traverse* network. Horizontal control surveys are discussed in detail in Chapter 7. Briefly, a traverse survey consists of the measurement of a series of horizontal lengths, called *courses*, and the horizontal angles between these courses.

The final results of a horizontal control survey are generally expressed by *rectangular coordinates* (see Section 3-3). One of the courses or sides is assigned a direction, usually with respect to the north-south meridian, by measurement or assumption. Then the directions of the other lines are computed from the measured angles. The direction of north thus fixes the orientation of the coordinate system with respect to the survey courses (see Figure 6-1).

Vertical angles are frequently measured for slope distance reduction and trigonometric leveling. (The elevation of a point as determined from differential or trigonometric leveling is, in effect, its third or *z* coordinate in a three-dimensional *x, y, z* coordinate system.) Angles may be measured *indirectly* using measured lengths or distances and trigonometry, or they may be measured *directly* using appropriate surveying field instruments.

Measurement of both horizontal and vertical angles is a most essential skill for any surveyor. Generally, the surveyor will use either a total station or an instrument called a *theodolite* for direct angular measurement. The magnetic *compass needle* and *transit* were used extensively in the past to determine magnetic north and to measure directions and angles; transits may still be used on some construction sites and the compass may still be used for making reconnaissance surveys, doing rough mapping, and retracing old boundaries. In Appendix A, the configuration and field use of the compass and transit will be discussed. In this chapter, the total station and theodolite are described in detail.

The chapter begins with a discussion of vertical angles. In the second section, we examine the various ways in which horizontal angles and the directions of lines are defined and computed. Following the next three sections on magnetic declination, the theodolite, and the total station, a discussion of accuracy, errors, and mistakes in angular measurement is presented. The focus in this chapter is on measuring angles; the layout of a given angle, along with other miscellaneous field procedures with the total station or theodolite, is presented in Chapter 11.

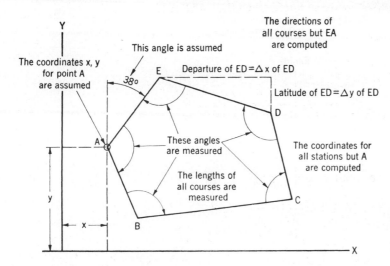

FIGURE 6-1. Method of establishing a coordinate system: First, the coordinates of station *A* and the direction of line *EA* are assumed. Latitudes and departures are added to the ordinates and abcissas, respectively, of the stations, to obtain their coordinates.

6-1 VERTICAL ANGLES

A *vertical angle* between two lines of sight is measured in a plane that is vertical at the point of observation. Sometimes the two points sighted do not lie in the same plane (see Figure 1-8): the total vertical angle measured from *A* to *B* is the sum of V_1 and V_2, each of which, though, does lie in a vertical plane. Angle V_1 is measured upward from a horizontal reference line and is considered a positive, or plus (+), angle; it may also be called an *angle of elevation*. Angle V_2 is measured downward from the horizon and is considered to be a negative, or minus (−), angle; it may also be called an *angle of depression* (see Figure 6-2). It is very important to identify the type of vertical angle (i.e., plus or minus) in the field notes.

In modern surveying instruments, the upward vertical direction is usually used as a reference for measuring vertical angles, instead of the horizon. That direction is called the *zenith direction*, and an angle measured with respect to

it is called a *zenith angle* or a *zenith distance*. It may sometimes be necessary to convert plus or minus vertical angles to zenith angles, and vice versa. For example, a vertical angle of 8°45′ is equivalent to a zenith angle of 89°60′ − 8°45′ = 81°15′. A vertical angle of −15° is equivalent to a zenith angle of 90° + 15° = 105°. And a zenith angle of 95°25′ is equivalent to an angle of depression of 5°25′ (see Figure 6-3).

6-2 HORIZONTAL ANGLES AND DIRECTIONS

A horizontal angle may be described in one of several different ways depending on how it is measured. The type of angle must be clearly noted in the field book to avoid confusion and a possible blunder in data reduction. An *interior angle* is measured on the inside of a closed polygon: an *exterior angle*

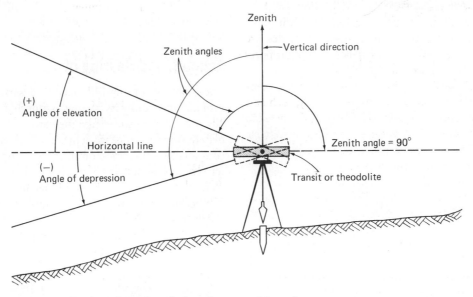

FIGURE 6-2. Designation of vertical angles or zenith angles.

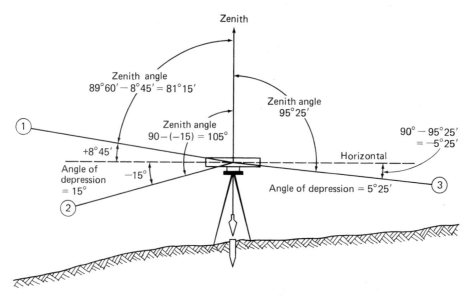

Zenith angle = 90° − vertical angle
Vertical angle = 90° − zenith angle

FIGURE 6-3. Relationship between zenith angle and vertical angle.

is measured outside of the closed polygon (see Figure 6-4). At any point, the sum of the interior and exterior angles must equal 360°. [The sum of all interior angles in a closed polygon is equal to $(180°)(n − 2)$, where n is the number of sides (see Section 3-3); the sum of the exterior angles must equal $(180°)(n + 2)$.]

An angle *turned* (measured) in a clockwise direction, from the "rear" to the "forward" point or station, is called an *angle to the right*. Stations are commonly labeled consecutively in the direction of the survey with numbers or letters. For example, point 6 or *F* would be a rear station with respect to point 7 or *G*, the forward station.

Pointing the instrument toward the rear station may be called the *backsight* and toward the forward station, the *foresight*; this terminology is similar to that used for leveling.

An angle turned counterclockwise from the rear to the forward station is called an *angle to the left*. To avoid blunders, it is best to adopt a consistent procedure for turning angles; usually work proceeds in a counterclockwise direction around a closed polygon or traverse, and interior angles to the right are measured.

A horizontal angle between the extension of a back or preceding line and the succeeding or next line forward is called a *deflection angle* (see Figure 6-5). Deflection angles are always less than 180°; they must be clearly identified as being turned either to the left (counterclockwise) or to the right (clockwise), using the letters L or R, respectively. Deflection angles are commonly measured during open traverse or route surveys, such as for a highway. They are easily visualized and plotted on a drawing, and their use simplifies the computation of direction for succeeding lines.

Azimuth and Bearing of a Line

The direction of any line may be described either by its *azimuth* angle or by its *bearing*. Azimuth directions are usually preferred by surveyors; they are purely numerical and help to simplify office work by allowing a simple routine for computations. Bearings, on the other hand, require two letter symbols as well as a numerical value, and each bearing computation requires an individual analysis with a sketch. But because they are easy to visualize, bearings are almost always used to indicate the direction of boundary lines in legal land descriptions (deeds) and on most official survey plats or subdivision maps.

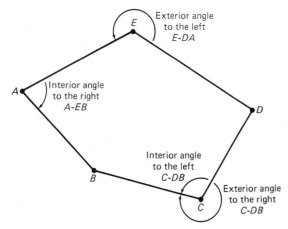

FIGURE 6-4. A horizontal angle may be classified as an interior angle, an exterior angle, an angle to the left, or an angle to the right.

Azimuths   The azimuth of a line is the *clockwise* horizontal angle between the line and a given reference direction or

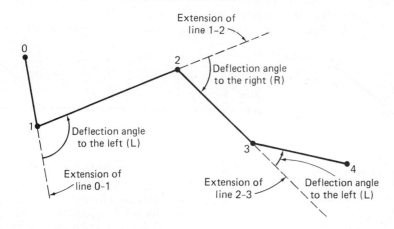

FIGURE 6-5. A deflection angle *must* be designated as being either an angle to the left (L) or an angle to the right (R).

meridian. Usually, north is the reference direction; south is sometimes used as a reference for geodetic surveys that cover large areas. An azimuth angle should be identified as being measured from the north (Azim_N) or from the south (Azim_S); north is generally assumed if no specific identification is given. Any azimuth angle will have a positive value between 0 and 360° (see Figure 6-6). Line *AB*, for example, has an azimuth of 125°.

Bearings   A bearing of a line is the angle from the north (N) *or* the south (S) end of the meridian, *whichever is nearest*, to the line; it has the added designation of east (E) or west (W), whichever applies. The directions *due east* and *due west* are, of course, perpendicular to the north–south meridian. A line may fall in one of four *quadrants:* northeast (NE), southeast (SE), southwest (SW), or northwest (NW), as shown in Figure 6-7.

A bearing may be measured either in a clockwise or in a counterclockwise direction, depending on which quadrant the line is in. A bearing angle is *always* an acute angle, that is, less than 90°. It must *always* be accompanied by the two letters that indicate the quadrant of the line. For example, a line may have a bearing of N 42°30′ W; this is read as "north 42 degrees 30 minutes west," or "northwest 42 degrees

30 minutes." It is important to remember that the numerical value of a bearing never exceeds 90°.

It is often necessary to convert directions from azimuths to bearings, or vice versa. Although a systematic set of rules can be used for this, it is usually best to first make a sketch of the line and its meridian. In the NE quadrant, the numerical values of bearing and Azim_N are always identical. In the other quadrants, the conversion involves either a simple addition or subtraction with 180° or 360°, whichever applies, as shown in Figure 6-8.

Directions   Every line actually has two directions, a *forward direction* and a *back direction*. The difference depends, in effect, on which way the line is being observed. Generally, the forward direction is taken in the same sense with which the field work was carried out. For example, the forward direction of line *AB* can be taken as the direction the surveyor faces when occupying point *A* and sighting toward point *B* (see Figure 6-9). The back direction of that line, then, would be that which is observed when standing on *B* and looking toward *A*. Calling the line "*AB*" implies its forward direction; calling the line "*BA*" implies its back direction. For connected lines, it is necessary to be consistent in designating forward or back direction. For example, line

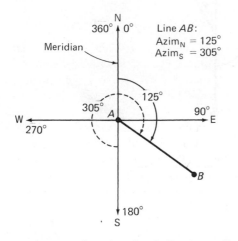

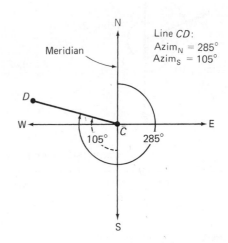

FIGURE 6-6. The azimuth of a line is usually referenced to the north end of the meridian. That is, Azim_N differs from Azim_S by 180°.

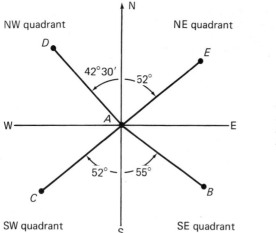

Line	Bearing
AB	S 55° E
AC	S 52° W
AD	N 42° 30′ W
AE	N 52° E

FIGURE 6-7. The bearing of a line is measured from the north or from the south (whichever is closer), in a clockwise or counterclockwise direction (whichever applies).

Equivalent Azimuths and Bearings

	Azimuth$_N$		Azimuth$_S$		Bearing
(a)	120°	=	300°	=	S60° E
(b)	200°	=	20°	=	S20° W
(c)	290°	=	110°	=	N70° W
(d)	30°	=	210°	=	N30° E

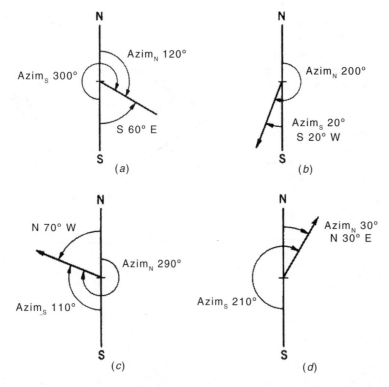

Conversion Computations

Bearing to Azimuth(N)		Azimuth(N) to Bearing Angle	
(a)	180° − 60° = 120°	(a)	180° − 120° = 60°
(b)	180° + 20° = 200°	(b)	200° − 180° = 20°
(c)	360° − 70° = 290°	(c)	360° − 290° = 70°
(d)	30° = 30°	(d)	30° = 30°

FIGURE 6-8. Conversion between azimuth and bearing is best done by examining a simple sketch of the line and meridian.

Azimuth $AB = 100°$ Back azimuth $AB = BA = 280°$
Bearing $AB - S80°E$ Back bearing $AB = BA = N80°W$
Azimuth $BC = 70°$ Back azimuth $BC = CB = 250°$
Bearing $BC = N70°E$ Back bearing $BC = CB = S70°W$

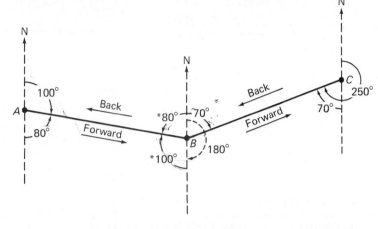

*Recall that alternate-interior angles between parallel lines are equal

FIGURE 6-9. A line can be designated by either its forward direction or its back direction; back direction is useful for computing the azimuth of an adjoining line.

BC in Figure 6-9 should be considered a forward direction so that it is consistent with the direction of AB.

The *back azimuth* of a line is determined simply by adding (or subtracting) 180° to the forward azimuth; when the forward azimuth is more than 180°, 180° is subtracted so that the numerical value of the back azimuth does not exceed 360°. To determine the *back bearing* of a line, though, it is only necessary to reverse the letters; the numerical value does not change. For example, the back bearing of N 47°10′ E is simply S 47°10′ W.

Computing Angles, Azimuths, and Bearings

Many types of surveying problems involve the computation of the azimuths or bearings of adjoining lines, given a starting direction and a series of measured angles. These computations are particularly important for traverse surveys, as demonstrated in Chapter 7. Another common type of problem involves the computation of an angle at the intersection of two lines of known direction.

For problems involving angles and bearings, it is always best to *start with a neat, clearly labeled sketch* of the lines. Although azimuth computations can be systematized with a formula or rule, it is also advisable to use a sketch as an aid in their computation. The following examples serve to illustrate a basic visual approach to solving problems with angles, azimuths, and bearings. At each point, the sketch includes a reference meridian line representing the direction of due north–due south. Later, in Section 6-3, a distinction will be made between directions referenced to a "true" meridian and those referenced to a magnetic meridian.

Example 6-1

The azimuth of side 1–2 is given for the three-sided traverse shown in Figure 6-10. The three interior angles are also given. Determine the azimuth direction for sides 2–3 and 3–1.

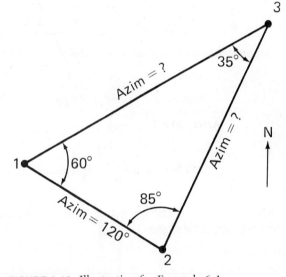

FIGURE 6-10. Illustration for Example 6-1.

Solution

First, verify that the sum of the interior angles equals $(n - 2)$ 180°. If not, adjust the angles accordingly. Next, make a sketch of station 2, which includes lines 1–2 and 2–3, with lightly drawn or dashed meridian lines through points 1 and 2; show the given angles in the proper location on the sketch (see Figure 6-11a). The azimuth of line 2–1 (back azimuth of 1–2) is simply 120° + 180° = 300°. The azimuth of 2–3 is then determined by adding the interior angle (and subtracting 360°) as shown.

The procedure is repeated at station 3 to determine the azimuth of line 3–1 (see Figure 6-11b). As a check, station 1 is sketched, and the original azimuth of 120° is then observed. In general, for the computation of a line's azimuth in a closed traverse, *proceed in a counterclockwise direction around the loop, adding the clockwise interior angle to the back azimuth*

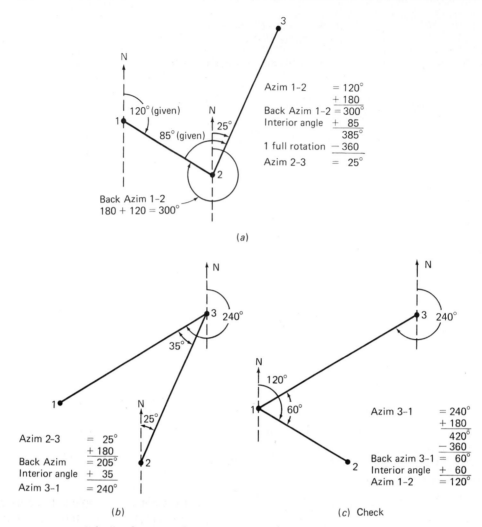

Azim 1–2   = 120°
             + 180
Back Azim 1–2 = 300°
Interior angle + 85
                385°
1 full rotation − 360
Azim 2–3   = 25°

(a)

Azim 2–3   = 25°
           + 180
Back Azim   = 205°
Interior angle + 35
Azim 3–1   = 240°

(b)

Azim 3–1 = 240°
         + 180
           420°
         − 360
Back azim 3–1 = 60°
Interior angle + 60
Azim 1–2   = 120°

(c) Check

FIGURE 6-11. Solution for Example 6-1.

of the preceding line. (Subtract 360° if necessary, to avoid angles exceeding a full rotation.)

Example 6-2

In the traverse shown in Figure 6-12, the bearing of side *CA* and angles *A* and *B* are given. Determine the bearings of side *AB* and side *BC*. Check by recomputing the bearing of *CA*.

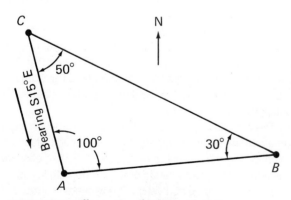

FIGURE 6-12. Illustration for Example 6-2.

Solution

Start with a sketch of sides *CA* and *AB* at station *A*, as shown in Figure 6-13*a*. Examine and analyze the sketch to determine the required bearing of *AB* as shown. Repeat the procedure for *BC*, as shown in Figure 6-13*b*.

There is no systematic rule for computing bearings; each sketch must be evaluated as a *separate* problem. It may often be helpful to first identify the unknown bearing angle with an asterisk (*) or some other symbol; then study the sketch and the given angles to determine a sequence of additions and/or subtractions that will result in the bearing angle value. Finally, assign the appropriate letters—NE, NW, SE, or SW—depending on which quadrant the line is in.

Example 6-3

The bearings of two adjoining lines, *EF* and *FG*, are N 46°30′ E and S 14°45′ E, respectively. Determine the deflection angle formed at the point of intersection, station *F*.

Solution

Make a sketch of the two lines, as shown in Figure 6-14. The angle between *FE* and the south end of the meridian

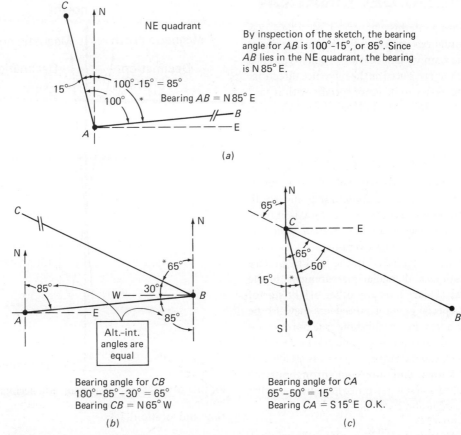

FIGURE 6-13. Solution for Example 6-2; the symbol (*) marks the bearing angle being solved for.

is 46°30′. (This follows from the fact that either alternate interior angles are equal or the back bearing of *EF* has the same numerical value as its forward bearing.) The angle between line *FG* and the south end of the meridian line is the bearing angle of *FG*, or 14°45′. By inspection, the value of the deflection angle is the difference between a straight angle (180°) and the sum of the two bearing angles, or 118°45′. Because *FG* deflects in a clockwise direction from *EF* extended, the deflection angle should be designated as 118°45′ *R*.

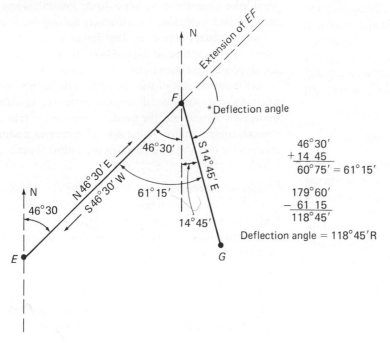

FIGURE 6-14. Illustration for Example 6-3.

6-3 MAGNETIC DECLINATION

At the very beginning of this chapter, a meridian was defined as a horizontal reference line for measuring direction. In the example azimuth and bearing problems given, a "north–south" meridian was used as the reference direction. At this time, it is necessary to be more specific with regard to reference meridians. In particular, we must distinguish between a true meridian and a magnetic meridian.

True Meridian

A *true meridian* at a point is an imaginary line that passes through that point and the geographic north and south poles of the earth; the poles, of course, lie on the axis of rotation of the earth. At any given point, the *direction of the true meridian is fixed;* it does not change over time.

True north may be established in the field by precise instrument observations and angular measurements of the sun, the North Star (Polaris), or any other bright star of known position. A special *gyroscope theodolite* may also be used to obtain true north. But establishing true north is not a routine task for most surveyors in private practice. For this reason, the National Geodetic Survey (NGS) has established reference lines of known true direction throughout the United States. It is always best to reference new surveys to the true meridian, if possible and convenient.

Magnetic Meridian

A *magnetic meridian* is the direction taken by a pivoted, freely swinging magnetic needle, suspended in a device called a *compass.* The compass needle aligns itself with the horizontal component of the earth's magnetic field.

The magnetic field of the earth can be approximately described as the field that would result if a huge bar magnet were embedded within the earth, with one end located far below the surface in the Hudson Bay region and the other end in a corresponding position in the southern hemisphere. The lines of magnetic force follow somewhat irregular paths, running from the south magnetic pole to the north magnetic pole. They are approximately parallel with the earth's surface at the equator and dip downward toward each of the poles.

Magnetic Declination

The earth's magnetic poles are not at the same location as the true geographic poles; they are separated by a significant distance. In addition, the field slowly changes in general direction over time, and it is slightly affected by the position of the sun and changes in radiation from the sun. Consequently, *the magnetic meridian is not necessarily parallel to the true meridian.* A magnetic needle will therefore point exactly true north only by chance.

At any given time, at any point on the earth's surface, the true geographic bearing of a freely suspended magnetic needle is called the *magnetic declination* or, simply, the

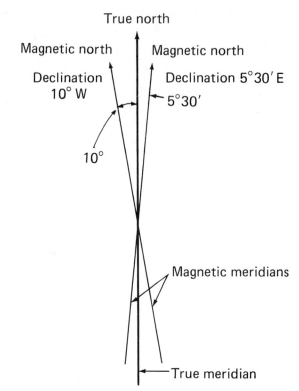

FIGURE 6-15. Examples of magnetic declination, the angle between true north and magnetic north (that varies with time and location).

declination. In other words, the declination is an angle east or west of the true meridian. For example, when the needle points 10° west of true north (N 10° W), the declination is said to be 10° west (10° W). If the needle points N 5°30′ E, its declination is 5°30′ E (see Figure 6-15).

The magnetic declination varies with location on the earth's surface. The USGS periodically publishes an *isogonic chart,* which shows lines of equal declination. These charts provide a means of determining the declination at any point in the United States. The solid lines are the *isogonic lines,* that is, lines of equal declination. The line of zero declination is called the *agonic* line; at locations on that line, a magnetic needle points true north.

At locations east of the agonic line, the compass needle will point west of true north (i.e., have a westerly declination); west of the agonic line, the needle points east of true north. Overall, there is more than a 40° difference in declination between the east and west coasts of the United States.

Changes in Declination   At a given location, the magnetic declination changes with time. Changes in the earth's magnetic field cause the following four types of *variations* in declination: secular variation, annual variation, diurnal variation, and irregular variation.

Secular Variation   The secular variation is a long-term change in declination, with a cycle of approximately 300 years. Its cause is not well understood and there is no precise law or formula to predict it exactly. But average observations over periods of time at different locations on the earth allow approximate predictions of its value and direction using tables and charts. In the United States, the maximum rate of secular variation is about 7.5 minutes of arc per year. This amounts to several degrees over the years, and over the 300-year cycle, the declination at a given location may vary as much as 35° from east to west. Because of its large magnitude, secular variation is of particular significance to the surveyor.

The lines on an isogonic chart are the lines of equal annual change in declination. They give the yearly rate and direction of movement of the north end of a compass needle. These data, along with the isogonic lines of the chart, provide the surveyor a means for estimating the declination *at any time* as well as at any point in the United States. This may be necessary when surveying land described in old deeds.

Other Variations   The annual variation is a magnetic meridian swing of at most 1 minute (01′) of arc, back and forth, during the year. The diurnal or daily variation is a swing of approximately 4–10 minutes of arc, depending on the locality. At night the needle is quiescent in its mean position. It swings east 2–5 minutes in the morning and west 2–5 minutes in the afternoon. During some of the magnetic disturbances associated with sunspots, there may also be significant irregular variations of declination.

Generally, the annual and daily variations are too small to be detected in the field with a magnetic compass. Overall, the secular variation is the most important type of variation for the purposes of surveying and it must be accounted for with appropriate adjustments to past records of direction.

Adjustments for Declination

It is sometimes necessary to convert magnetic bearings or azimuths to true directions or to convert past magnetic directions to magnetic directions at the present or some other point in time. This may be the case when using a magnetic compass to obtain an estimate for the direction of a line, or when resurveying a tract of land that was originally surveyed using compass directions. An isogonic chart may be used to obtain data regarding past and present declinations. As demonstrated in the following examples, a large and clear sketch is essential for solving these problems without blunder.

Example 6-4

The magnetic bearing of a boundary line for a tract of land was recorded as S 55°30′ W in a deed dated 1905. It is determined that the magnetic declination at that time and location was 3°45′ W. Determine the true bearing of that line.

Solution

The first step is to make a clear sketch of the given data. A heavy solid line drawn parallel to the side of the paper is used to indicate true north; a dashed or lighter line with a half-headed arrow may be used to indicate the direction of magnetic north (see Figure 6-16). In this example, magnetic north is sketched to the left of true north because of the westerly declination; the declination angle of 3°45′ is shown (not to scale).

The boundary line, labeled *AB*, is shown in the SW quadrant; the *magnetic bearing angle* of 55°30′ is sketched

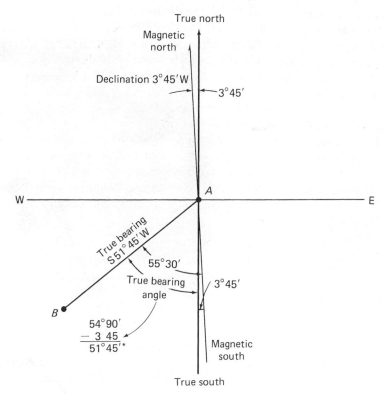

FIGURE 6-16. Illustration for Example 6-4.

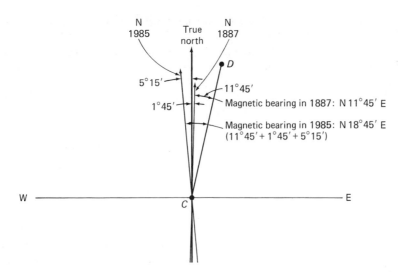

FIGURE 6-17. Illustration for Example 6-5.

from the south end of the *magnetic meridian*, as shown in Figure 6-16. The true bearing angle is that measured from the true meridian; an asterisk (*) labels that angle. It is clear from the sketch that, in this particular problem, the declination angle must be subtracted from the magnetic bearing to arrive at the true bearing angle: 55°30′ − 3°45′ = 51°45′. The true bearing of line *AB,* then, is S 51°45′ W.

Example 6-5

The magnetic bearing of line *CD* was recorded as N 11°45′ E in 1887, at which time the declination was 1°45′ E. In 1985 the declination was 5°15′ W. What reading of a compass in 1985 would be used to retrace the line?

Solution

The problem is sketched in Figure 6-17. From the sketch, it is seen that the necessary computation for the 1985 magnetic bearing is 11°45′ + 1°45′ + 5°15′ = 18°45′. The 1985 magnetic bearing of line *CD*, then, is N 18°45′ E.

6-4 THE THEODOLITE

A fundamental weakness of the American engineer's transit was the difficulty in reading the graduated circles precisely with the verniers. As a result, many repetitions are required to accurately measure or stake out an angle.

European manufacturers have, for many decades, been producing precision instruments, called *theodolites*, for angular measurement. These compact instruments have internal optical devices that make it possible to read the circles much more precisely than is possible with American instruments. And they can be read more quickly with less chance for blunder. The precision varies from ±0.1 second of arc read directly on some of the finer instruments to 0.1 minute (6 seconds) read by estimation on others. Very high accuracies can usually be achieved with any theodolite in considerably less time than is required by the method of repetition used with the American-style transit. It is basically for this reason that theodolites came into general use in the United States and Canada.

General Features of a Theodolite

Theodolites differ from the transit in several ways (Figures 6-18 and 6-19). In *overall appearance*, they are noticeably lighter in weight and more compact than an engineer's transit. They generally do not have a built-in compass box on the alidade plate. The telescopes are shorter and are not usually equipped with spirit bubble tubes. There is no circle or vernier window seen on the alidade, but there is a small reading microscope eyepiece attached next to the telescope through which the enclosed

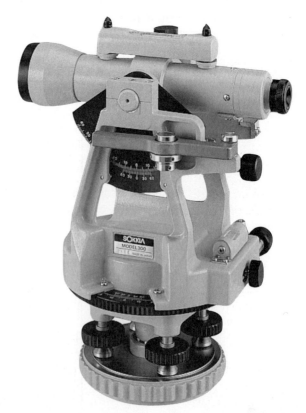

FIGURE 6-18. Example of a theodolite. (*Courtesy of Sokkia Corporation.*)

After the theodolite is leveled, the optical plummet shows the position of the standing axis with respect to the tack or some other mark on the survey station. Because the device does not swing, it is totally unaffected by wind. After the theodolite has been placed in position with the ordinary plumb bob and has been leveled, the position is checked and precisely adjusted with the optical plummet. Some experienced surveyors prefer to set up the theodolite with the optical plummet alone; this procedure is described in the next section.

A theodolite alidade generally fits into the leveling head with a smooth steel cylinder and rotates freely about the azimuth axis on precision ball bearings (see Figure 6-21). The horizontal and vertical circles are constructed of glass; they are precisely graduated with very thin, sharply defined lines etched on their surfaces. An optical system, including a microscope with prisms and/or mirrors, allows the circles to be read quickly and accurately.

Repeating and Direction Instruments Many different models of theodolites are available. Two general types are the *repeating theodolite* and the *direction theodolite*. Generally, the directional type is more precise than the repeating type. The repeating theodolite, like the transit, has two independent upper and lower motions with corresponding clamps and tangent screws. Some repeating instruments, though have only one clamp and tangent screw, are equipped with a lever that can switch clamp and tangent operation from one motion to the other. Angles are turned, essentially, as they are with the transit.

The direction theodolite has only an upper motion, with a single clamp and tangent screw that connects the alidade to the leveling head. A little friction between the circle and the leveling head keeps the circle from turning, while the alidade can turn freely on the bearings. In some directional instruments, the circle can be rotated and oriented with respect to the leveling head using a special finger-operated wheel. Ordinarily, though, the circle is not set exactly to zero when turning or measuring an angle.

With directional theodolites, angles cannot be measured by the repetition method. A horizontal angle is usually measured as the difference between an initial and the final direction of the alidade and the two corresponding readings of the circle. This procedure is explained in a subsequent section. The internal optics are designed so that each reading represents an average of two values on opposite sides of the circle, compensating for any eccentricity errors. (This is equivalent to averaging the readings of the A and B verniers on the engineer's transit.)

Setting Up and Leveling a Theodolite

The theodolite should be carefully removed from its case, lifting it by taking hold of the attached carrying handle or by grasping the standards. It must be securely mounted on the

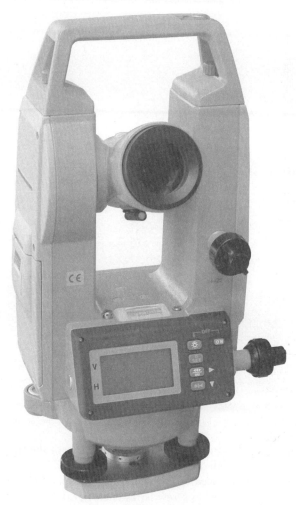

FIGURE 6-19. Another example of a theodolite. (*Courtesy of Sokkia Corporation.*)

graduated circle is read. Theodolites are also generally characterized by an enclosed, dustproof, and moisture-proof form of construction with a light-colored finish to minimize the temperature effects of direct sunlight.

A theodolite is typically mounted on a *three-screw leveling head* instead of on a four-screw leveling head, which is used for the American transit. A circular bull's-eye bubble vial is used for rough leveling; a more sensitive plate bubble tube is mounted on the alidade for precise leveling. The base of the instrument is called a tribrach. It is designed with a release mechanism so that the theodolite can be easily removed from the tripod and exchanged with an electronic distance measuring instrument (EDMI), a target, or a reflector without disturbing the leveled and centered position of the base over the survey station (see Figure 6-20). This is called *forced centering*.

Another characteristic feature of the theodolite is the *optical plummet*. This is a small telescopic sight mounted in a vertical hole through the spindle and adjusted to coincide with the azimuth or standing axis of the alidade. It is viewed during instrument setup through a horizontal eyepiece located at the side of the alidade or on the base of the instrument.

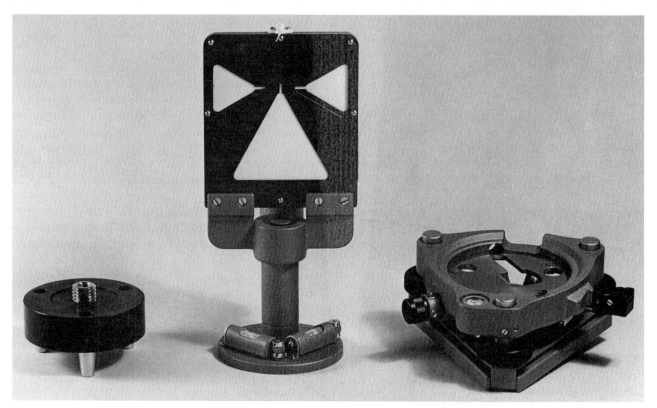

FIGURE 6-20. Traverse set: adapter, sighting target, and tribrach.

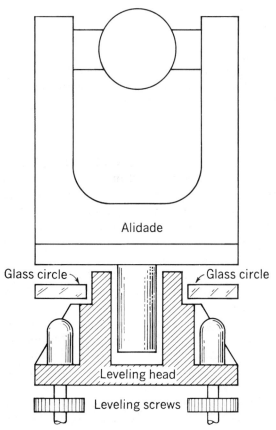

FIGURE 6-21. Schematic drawing showing the arrangement of the vertical axis of a theodolite. The bearings have been opened up for clarity.

tripod (see Figure 6-22*a*). Attached underneath the tripod head is a threaded *centering screw* with a knurled handle; the instrument is placed on the center of the tripod head, and the tripod centering screw is fastened tightly to its base. When the screw is loosened slightly, the theodolite can be shifted laterally on the tripod head for precise positioning over the survey point.

If a plumb bob is used, the theodolite can be set up over the station in a manner similar to that for an engineer's transit (see Appendix A). After the instrument is leveled, the optical plummet is used to check the position of the instrument (see Figure 6-22*b*). First, the optical plummet eyepiece is focused. Then, if its cross hairs or bull's-eye circle is not exactly centered over the point, the centering screw is loosened. While the point is viewed through the optical plummet, the instrument is shifted until it is exactly in position. This should be accomplished without rotating the leveling head in azimuth because this throws the instrument out of level.

When exactly over the point, *the tripod centering screw must be tightened* to securely fasten the instrument on the tripod. If releveling is then necessary, the optical plummet should again be used to check centering. This centering and leveling process is repeated until both are satisfactory. It is important to remember that *the optical plummet is accurate only when the instrument is level.*

When the work at a particular survey station is completed, some surveyors prefer to remove the theodolite from the tripod and carry it to the next station in its case. They usually set the tripod over the point before mounting the

(a)

(b)

FIGURE 6-22. (*a*) Carefully place instrument on tripod using handle. (*b*) Adjust position using optical plummet.

instrument. A plumb bob is first used to center the tripod over the point, with its head kept level by eye. Then the instrument is lifted from its case and securely fastened to the tripod. The plumb bob is removed from the tripod and the leveling and centering process proceeds using the optical plummet.

Leveling the Instrument   The theodolite is first leveled roughly with the three leveling screws by centering the bubble in the circular bull's-eye spirit vial (see Figure 6-23). Then the alidade is turned so that the tubular spirit vial on the top plate is parallel to an imaginary line running through the centers of any pair of leveling screws (see Figure 6-23). The bubble in the tube is centered by adjusting those two screws ("thumbs-in, thumbs-out, the bubble follows the left thumb"). Next, the alidade is rotated 90° and the bubble is centered in the tube with the one screw that was not used before. (The bubble moves toward the screw when it is turned clockwise, and vice versa.) This process with the plate level vial is repeated for additional 90° revolutions of the instrument until the bubble remains centered in all positions.

Setting up and Leveling a Theodolite or Total Station without a Plumb Bob   When the theodolite is mounted on an adjustable-leg tripod, it is possible to set up rapidly over a point without using an ordinary plumb bob at all. One method relies only on the optical plummet. First, the instrument is placed over the point by eye, with the footplate kept approximately level (see Figure 6-24*a*). When looking through the optical plummet, the instrument may be several centimeters or about 0.1 ft off the point at this time (see Figure 6-24*b*).

The optical plummet is then centered over the point by adjusting the three leveling screws. But the circular vial bubble will still be off-center. That bubble is now centered by adjusting the lengths of the tripod legs (the bubble will move away from a shortened leg and toward a lengthened leg). Finally, the instrument is leveled precisely using the tubular plate level vial, as described previously (see Figure 6-24*c*).

Another method for setting up without a plumb bob involves the use of a special *telescopic centering rod*, which

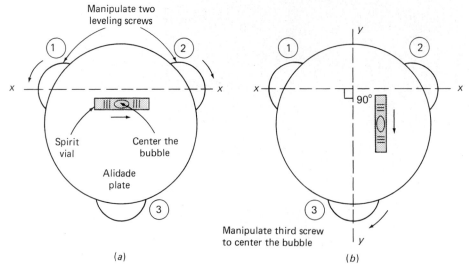

FIGURE 6-23. The plate spirit bubble tube is used for precise leveling of the instrument. (*a*) Align the tube with axis *x–x* running through any pair of screws, say, 1 and 2, and then center the bubble. (*b*) Rotate the alidade 90° and center the bubble with the remaining screw, 3.

can be attached directly to the leveling head. The rod is clamped against the lower surface of the tripod head and is attached above to a supporting plate. The tripod is set over the station with the rod clamp loose, and the lower end of the rod is placed directly on the survey point. A

circular bubble on the rod is centered by adjusting the tripod legs; when the bubble is accurately centered, the tripod plate is horizontal. The theodolite is then fastened to the plate and leveled precisely with the tubular plate bubble vial.

FIGURE 6-24. Setting up the instrument without a plumb bob.

(c)

FIGURE 6-24. (*Continued*)

6-5 ELECTRONIC INSTRUMENTS

The use of electronic surveying instruments is discussed in Section 4-4, with particular reference to the application of EDMIs. As mentioned in that section, EDMIs are generally used in conjunction with theodolites; vertical angles must be measured so that the slope distances obtained by the EDMI can be reduced to horizontal distances. The EDM devices may be mounted on optical theodolites and the angles read through the microscope eyepiece on the micrometer scale.

Electronic instruments are also available exclusively for angular measurement. These are called *electronic digital theodolites.* Some models closely resemble conventional optical theodolites, except that the reading microscope eyepiece is noticeably absent (see Figure 6-25). Instead, horizontal or vertical angles are displayed digitally in an external liquid crystal display (LCD) window, much like the display of numbers on a hand-held calculator.

On the instrument shown in Figure 6-25a, angles are displayed to the nearest 20 seconds; on some displays, decimal points are used to separate degrees, minutes, and seconds. For example, a display of the number 350.30.20 would stand for an angle of 350°30'20". Letter symbols for horizontal angles (H) vertical angles (V), and left (L) or right (R) angles are also displayed in the LCD window to indicate the type of angle. A battery voltage indicator is displayed for a check on battery power.

An electronic theodolite is centered and leveled over a survey point in the same manner as an ordinary theodolite. Focusing and sighting on a station are also done in the same manner as previously described. The telescope is aimed at the backsight station of the angle and the upper- and lower-motion clamps are tightened.

Zero is set by simply depressing the "set 0" button; the number 00.00.00 is then displayed. Then the foresight is taken by turning the angle to the right with the upper motion and its tangent screw. The value of the angle is displayed (see Figure 6-25b). If the angle is to be measured in a counterclockwise direction, an appropriate button is depressed once and L for "left" is displayed.

Some electronic theodolites are repeating-type instruments; horizontal angles can be accumulated in the display window up to 2000°. The procedure is basically the same as described for the engineer's transit. The average angle may be computed by dividing the digital display value by the number of repetitions. On some models, repeated angles are stored and processed by a microprocessor and the average angle is displayed.

Most modern instruments do not have a "set 0" button for vertical angles. These instruments are indexed after setup by rotating the scope in a vertical plane so that the horizon can be determined automatically. Once the horizon has been determined, the vertical readings are properly indexed and vertical reference will not be changed over the series of shots. The "set 0" function for these instruments is only for horizontal angles.

The glass measuring circle in an electronic theodolite is coated with a metallic film that forms a coded pattern of dark and bright spaces. A beam of light is directed toward the circle; the amount of light passing through varies with the circle's position because of the interfering pattern of the metallic film coating. A set of several photodiodes on the opposite side of the circle detects and converts the varying intensity of light into small electric currents. A special microprocessor decodes and converts the photocurrents into angles for digital LCD (or LED) display.

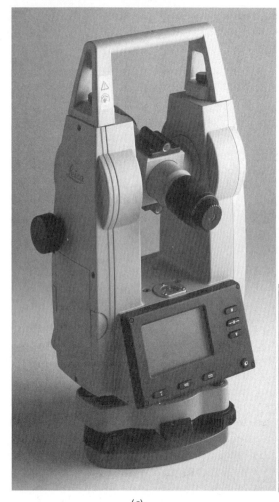

(a)

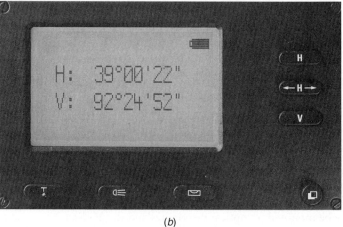

(b)

FIGURE 6-25. (a) An electronic digital theodolite. (b) Digital display of horizontal angle = 39°00′22″ and vertical angle = 92°24′52″. (*Courtesy of Leica Geosystems, Inc.*)

An electronic theodolite that displays measured angles to the nearest 3 seconds is shown in Figure 6-26. The data can be transmitted automatically to an attached recording instrument for storage; the recording device can later be connected to an office computer for data reduction. By combining a theodolite with an EDMI, the theodolite can be converted to a *recording electronic tacheometer* or *total station* (see Figure 6-26). The instrument shown in Figure 6-26 is accurate to 0.6 second of arc.

A special electronic transducer can sense horizontal and vertical angles to within ±6 seconds, thus eliminating the need for a theodolite with optical scales. The infrared EDM beam has a range of 3000 m. An alphanumeric dot-matrix readout allows the instrument to "talk" to the operator by displaying questions and messages during operation. An electronic data collection module can be interfaced with several types of computer systems.

The total station with its on-board computer software and data storage capabilities has brought the office into the field. Survey crews can now download entire design projects into the total station and, using radial stakeout techniques

(discussed in Section 11.5), can perform an extensive amount of layout. The total station, for the most part, is the only instrument the average land surveyor uses today.

6-6 MEASURING HORIZONTAL AND VERTICAL ANGLES

Measuring a Horizontal Angle

The procedure described here is to measure an unknown horizontal angle between two lines or courses by turning the angle once. As will be explained in the next section, it is usually best to measure an angle by repetition, that is, by turning it two or more times. (A somewhat different field procedure, for turning and laying out or marking a given angle, is described in Section 11-1.)

The basic steps for measuring a horizontal angle are summarized briefly as follows:

1. Set up and level the instrument directly over the point where the angle is to be measured; that point is the angle's vertex.

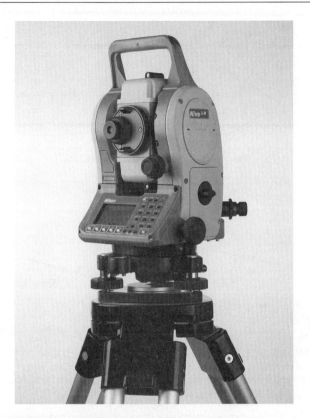

FIGURE 6-26. An electronic total station with on-board data storage capabilities. (*Courtesy of Trimble Navigation.*)

2. Backsight: Aim at the point that marks the left-hand side of the angle and lock the motion.

3. Set zero on the instrument.

4. Foresight: Free the motion and aim at the point that marks the right-hand side of the angle.

5. Read the angle.

Step 1: **Take the Backsight** Looking over the telescope, aim approximately at the initial point of the angle. If the point is not directly visible (usually it is not), a pencil or plumb-bob cord must be held over the point as a target for the instrument person (see Figure 6-27).

When the target is brought into the field of view, tighten the *motion clamp.* Move the telescope up or down until the horizontal cross hair is near the target; then bring the *vertical cross hair* directly on the target. Set zero by depressing the "set 0" button on the keyboard.

Step 2: **Take the Foresight** Aim at the second point, using the *motion.* This is done by first unlocking the motion and then rotating the alidade; the alidade may be turned either clockwise or counterclockwise to aim at the second point.

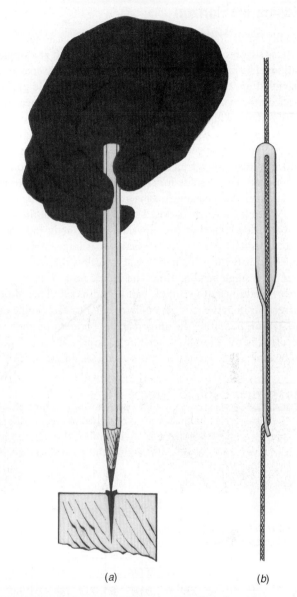

(a)   (b)

FIGURE 6-27. Targets for observation: (*a*) Balancing a pencil for a target. (*b*) Target painted white and red attached to plumb-bob cord.

When the point or target is in the field of view, the motion is tightened and the screw is used for fine adjustment of the line of sight.

Read the digital readout and record the data in the field book.

Field Records   There are several different ways in which horizontal angles can be recorded in a field book, depending on the type of survey, the precision used, and the preference of the surveyor. Electronic field books called data collectors are employed with modern theodolites and total station instruments. These are connected to office computers using an RS-232 interface, and the data are produced using an array of different software packages that are commercially available.

Closing the Horizon

Usually in triangulation networks, and occasionally in traverse surveys, more than one angle is measured at a single station. (Horizontal control surveys, including traverse and triangulation, are discussed in Chapter 7.) A quick and useful check on the work can be obtained at that station by measuring the unused angle that completes the circle or, in other words, that *closes the horizon* (see Figure 6-28a). Sometimes this procedure is applied to traverse angles where only one angle is measured (see Figure 6-28b). Closing the horizon is also a good field exercise for students who are first learning how to turn and read angles using a transit or theodolite.

When the horizon is closed and all the angles at the station are added together, the sum should be exactly 360°, but there is usually some error. If the error is large, a blunder has been made; if it is small (equal to or less than the least count of a single reading times the square root of the number of readings), the angles can be adjusted. The same correction increment is generally applied to each angle at the station (including the unused angle) because the chance for error is the same for each angle, despite its size. This procedure is called a *station adjustment* (see Figure 6-29).

Measuring Vertical Angles

The vertical circle of a theodolite is designed to give readings of *zenith angles* (see Section 6-1). With the telescope pointing vertically, toward the zenith, the scale would read

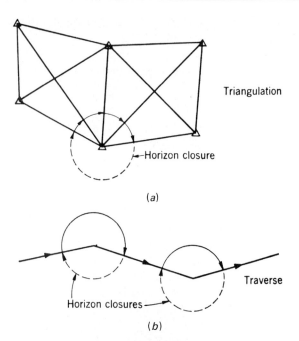

Triangulation

Horizon closure

(a)

Traverse

Horizon closures

(b)

FIGURE 6-28. Horizon closures. Only the angles shown by full lines are required. The angles shown by dotted lines close the horizon so that station adjustments can be made.

exactly zero. When the line of sight is horizontal, the reading will be 90°00′00″ (or 270°00′00″ with the scope reversed). To obtain a plus or minus vertical angle, that is, an angle of elevation or depression, simply subtract the zenith angle

Pointing		0 ′		STATION A ″ A	″ B	Aver.	Angles		
B	OD	0 0		00	15	7.5			
C	1D	74 13		45			74	13	37.5
C	3DR	85 22		15	30	22.5	85	22	15
							14	13	42.5
							74	13	42.5
C	OD	0 0		00	30	45			
D	1D	158 48		00			158	48	15
D	3DR	232 49		30	15	22.5	232	49	37.5
							36	48	16.2
							158	48	16.2
D	OD	0 0		00	45	52.5			
B	1D	126 57		45			126	57	52.5
B	3DR	41 47		00	45	52.5	41	47	00
							6	57	50
							126	57	50

Obs. J. Smith		Date		
Record H.Jones		Clear 60°F.		
	Sta. Adj.			
			Adj. Angles	
A-BC =				
74	13	42.5	+3.8	74° 13′ 46.3″
A-CD =				
158	48	16.2	+3.8	158° 48′ 20.0″
A-DB =				
126	57	50	+3.7	126° 57′ 53.7″
358	118	108.7	+11.3	358° 118′ 120.0″

FIGURE 6-29. Field notes for a horizon closure and station adjustment.

from 90°, or subtract 270° from the zenith angle, whichever applies. For example:

Zenith Angle	Vertical Angle
$90° - 92°10'06''$	$= -2°10'16''$
$90° - 87°32'17''$	$= +2°27'43''$
$264°18'20'' - 270°$	$= -5°41'40''$
$281°17'46'' - 270°$	$= +11°17'46''$

It is not necessary to apply an index correction to the observed angles. Most modern theodolites have an *automatic index system*, which ensures that all vertical circle readings are referenced to the direction of gravity. This is accomplished with either a built-in suspended prism apparatus or a liquid compensator device, which reflects and bends light in the optical path of the circle and its reading scale. The optics are designed so that if the azimuth axis of the instrument is not exactly vertical, the light rays are bent an equal amount to compensate.

For accurate work, it is best to measure a vertical angle at least twice, once direct and once reversed. The average of the vertical angle readings is used to cancel instrumental error. For example, assume that the two zenith angle readings are $85°26'10''$ and $274°33'58''$. The average is determined as follows:

$$89°59'60''$$
Subtract reading $= -85°26'10''$
Vertical angle $= + 4°33'50''$

$$\text{Reading} = 274°33'58''$$
$$-270°$$
$$\text{Vertical angle} = + 4°33'58''$$

$$\text{Average vertical angle} = + 4°33'54''$$

Some older theodolites make use of an *index level* instead of an automatic index. This basically is a sensitive spirit vial attached to the vertical circle; split-bubble coincidence is obtained by viewing the vial through an internal prism system. When the split bubble is aligned (the bubble centered), the zero reading displayed on the circle corresponds with true zenith.

6-7 ACCURACY, MISTAKES, AND ERRORS

In most surveys, both angles and distances are measured. It is good practice for the surveyor to balance the accuracy of the angular and linear measurements. It makes little sense, for example, to repeat and measure angles to the nearest second of arc when distances are being measured with a relative accuracy of only 1/500 (e.g., for stadia surveys). The extra effort and time spent in repeating the angles would be wasted. Of course, if a total station is being used, and no extra effort is required to read the angle precisely, the surveyor would do so.

Angle–Distance Relationships

The location of a point can be defined with reference to a horizontal angle from a given line and the linear distance from the vertex of the angle (see Figure 6-30). Because no measurement is perfect, there will be some error in both the angle and distance determined for the point. The accuracy of the linear measurement is expressed as the ratio C/D, where C is the error and D is the distance measured (see Section 2-4). The angular and linear measurements may be considered to be "balanced" or consistent when the "true" location of the point is in the center of an approximate square with the side dimension of $2C$.

From Figure 6-30b, it can be seen that, for relatively long lengths and small errors, we can apply a trigonometric

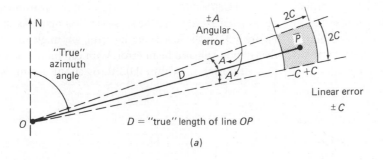

(a)

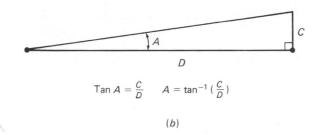

$$\text{Tan } A = \frac{C}{D} \qquad A = \tan^{-1}\left(\frac{C}{D}\right)$$

(b)

FIGURE 6-30. Linear and angular measurements are balanced when point P is located in the center of the shaded "square." The tangent function relates the relative accuracies.

relationship to the linear accuracy *C/D* and the corresponding angular error *A*. In effect, we can say that tan *A* = *C/D*. From this we can compute either the angle that corresponds to a given linear accuracy ratio or the ratio that corresponds to a given angle. For example, if the accuracy ratio is 1/1000, the corresponding angular error is *A* = invtan 0.001 = 0.0573° = 03'26". If the angular error is 1 minute, then the matching linear accuracy is *C/D* = $\tan(\frac{1}{60})° = 0.00029$ or 1/3440. Several angular errors are listed in Table 6-1, along with their corresponding or "balanced" linear accuracy ratios.

Angular Error	Accuracy Ratio
5 minutes	1/688
1 minute	1/3440
30 seconds	1/6880
20 seconds	1/10,300
10 seconds	1/20,600
5 seconds	1/41,200
1 second	1/206,000

It can be seen from Table 6-3 that to achieve the accuracy required for topographic mapping surveys, usually about 1/500, it is sufficient to measure angles to the nearest 5 minutes.

Accurate target sighting and instrument centering over a point are important. For a particular angular error, the error in position increases with the line of sight distance; conversely, for a fixed error in position (or sighting), the angular error decreases with sight distance. The longer the sight distance, the better the relative accuracy of the work.

Systematic and Accidental Errors

A surveyor must be aware of the common sources of error so that precautions can be taken to minimize them. These errors may arise from imperfections in the instrument; from natural causes; or from human limitations in setting up and leveling the instrument, sighting targets, and reading scales. Several typical errors are listed and briefly described as follows:

Instrumental Errors   In a new and properly adjusted instrument, certain geometric relationships among the principal axes and components of the instrument must hold true. With frequent field use (or abuse), some surveying instruments will occasionally get out of adjustment. And even in the finest instrument, there will be a few inherent imperfections due to the manufacturing process. Whatever the cause, measuring angles with an instrument that is out of adjustment will almost always give inaccurate results.

Many instrumental errors are *systematic error*; they will occur in the same direction or sense (plus or minus) and with the same magnitude for each measurement. Systematic instrumental errors can be eliminated by adjusting the instrument or by following certain field procedures that cause them to cancel out (e.g., reading both verniers, plunging the scope, and repeating the angle). Several types of instrument adjustments can be made by the surveyor in the field, particularly on the engineer's transit and level. Adjustments can also be made on theodolites and total stations, but it is usually best to send precise and expensive instruments to an expert for proper repair and maintenance. Some common instrumental errors include the following:

1. Line of sight not perpendicular to the horizontal axis
2. Horizontal axis not perpendicular to the vertical axis
3. Telescope bubble axis not parallel to the line of sight
4. Plate bubble axis not perpendicular to the vertical axis
5. Eccentricity of markings on the graduated circles
6. Optical plummet not aligned with the vertical axis
7. Vertical cross hair not perpendicular to the horizontal axis

Personal Errors   Personal errors include random or accidental errors due to the limit on how accurately a surveyor can set up and level an instrument, sight a target, and observe a scale.

Error in Centering   The vertical axis of the instrument must be centered exactly over the survey station mark. As shown in Figure 6-31, if there is centering error, any angle measured at that station will also be in error. With careful use of a plumb bob, centering to within 0.02 ft, or about 6 mm, is easily

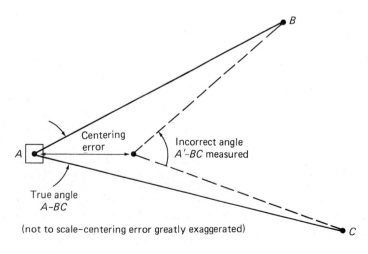

(not to scale–centering error greatly exaggerated)

FIGURE 6-31. One type of accidental error in which the instrument is off-center, over *A'* instead of exactly over station *A*.

obtained. With an optical plummet or centering rod, positioning over a point to within 0.003 ft, or about 1 mm, is possible. The longer the line of sight, the less the effect of centering error.

Error in Sighting   When turning an angle, the vertical cross hair must be directly on the survey point for a proper line of sight. The effect of error in sighting is similar to that of inaccurate centering over the point.

When the point cannot be viewed directly through the telescope, it is necessary for a *signal person* to hold a pencil point or to suspend a plumb-bob cord over the point, which may introduce some error. The use of a suitable red-and-white target on the cord helps to minimize the error. Sometimes vertical chaining pins or range poles are used as targets; it is important to sight with the central portion of the cross hair onto the lower part of the pin or rod to minimize error due to incorrect plumbing.

In general, for angular measurements, the effect of a sighting error can be minimized by keeping sight distances *as long as possible*.

Error in Focusing   The eyepiece and objective lens of the telescope must be properly focused to eliminate *parallax error* (see Section 5-2).

Error in Leveling   The plate bubble(s) on the alidade must be centered in the vial tube to obtain accurate angles; the plate must be perfectly horizontal. The effect of inaccurate bubble centering is most significant when steeply inclined lines of sight are observed. The bubble(s) should be checked frequently during the survey. Level adjustments may be made by recentering the bubble before the backsight or after the foresight, but never in between the two.

Natural Errors   Random errors not due to instrumental or personal causes are often characterized as natural errors. They are usually small. One such error that can significantly affect the results, though, is *setting of the tripod* on soft ground. The use of wooden stakes in boggy or thawing ground, or a small wooden platform when working on asphalt pavement, to provide support for the tripod legs, can help to eliminate this type of problem.

Other sources of natural errors in transit and theodolite work include vibration due to *wind* and unequal expansion of parts due to *temperature* effects. They can be minimized by properly shielding the instrument. Also, unequal bending or *refraction* of light causes the observed target to shimmer; this effect is commonly attributed to "heat waves." It can be minimized or avoided by keeping the line of sight as high above the (hot) ground as possible.

Typical Mistakes

As described in Section 2-3, a gross mistake or blunder is due to the personal carelessness and inattentiveness of the surveyor; it is not accidental in the same sense as previously described for personal errors. Personal errors can never be completely eliminated, although they can be minimized.

But blunders, or "busts," as they sometimes are called in the field, *can and must be eliminated*. Common blunders made in transit or theodolite work are listed as follows. Usually, measuring all angles by repetition (at least doubling), and closing the horizon, provides the best insurance against blunders.

Using the wrong clamp and/or tangent screw.

This is perhaps the most common mistake made by surveying students. A good way to avoid it is always to keep a mental picture of the alidade and the horizontal circle when turning the angle. Doubling the angle will generally reveal any gross mistakes, but then the work has to be redone until the angles check.

Forgetting to level the plate with the spirit bubble tube.

This is a possible mistake with the theodolite, which is first leveled roughly with the circular bull's-eye spirit vial.

Reading the wrong circle.

This is also a possibility with a theodolite when viewing through the reading microscope eyepiece.

Additional blunders include the following:

Calling out or recording an incorrect value.

Forgetting to record a vertical angle as plus or minus.

Setting up over, or sighting on, the wrong survey point.

Care of Instruments

Complete directions for instrument care are beyond the scope of this text. The following rules, plus a recognition of the delicacy of the instrument, will usually prevent damage. The most important rule is to prevent falls. A fall will always result in the need for extensive repairs or will destroy the instrument entirely. The rules apply to all tripod-mounted instruments.

1. *Handle the instrument by the base* when not on the tripod. This prevents deflecting the more delicate parts.

2. *Never stand the tripod on a smooth surface.* The legs may slip outward.

3. *Always stand the tripod up carefully.* The legs must be wide and firm even when the setup is not to be used for observations. The wind or a slight touch may knock it over.

4. *Never leave the instrument unattended* unless special precautions are made for its protection.

5. *Never subject the instrument to vibration*, which ruins the adjustments. Most instrument cases have large rubber feet, which absorb vibration if the rest of the case is free from contacts.

6. *Never force the instrument.* If the telescope or alidade does not turn easily, do not continue to use the instrument. Such use might damage a bearing.

7. *Keep the instrument in its case when not in use.* This usually guarantees protection.

8. *Place it in the case so that the only contact is with the base.* Some manufacturers suggest keeping all three motion clamps tight. This reduces chances for vibration. However, others suggest keeping the motor screws loose to prevent stripping the threads.

9. *Keep the instrument free from dust and rapid temperature changes.* Dust ruins the finish and the bearings. Temperature ranges introduce moisture into the telescope tube. The moisture will fog the telescope, and the telescope must be dismantled to remove it.

10. *If the instrument is wet, let it dry.* Do not dry it; this ruins the finish and smears the glass and graduations.

11. *Disassemble instruments and store them properly.* Precise theodolites and total stations are generally disassembled from the tripod and moved in their protective case; they are *not* carried to the next station attached to the tripod.

Questions for Review

1. Define *zenith angle*. What is the distinction between a plus and a minus vertical angle?

2. What is meant by *angle to the right?* What is a deflection angle?

3. Explain the difference between the azimuth and the bearing of a line. What is a back direction?

4. Explain the difference between a true meridian and a magnetic meridian. What is meant by *declination?*

5. Outline the basic differences in construction and operation between an engineer's transit and a theodolite.

6. List six important geometric relationships among the components of a transit or theodolite.

7. Outline the basic steps in the procedure for measuring a horizontal angle with an instrument.

8. What is meant by *closing the horizon?*
   Outline a procedure for precise measurement of vertical angles, using a transit. Also, outline a procedure for leveling the transit precisely.

9. Define *tribrach*, *forced centering*, and *optical plummet*.

10. Briefly describe how to level and center a theodolite.

11. What is the basic difference between an optical theodolite and an electronic digital theodolite? Briefly describe how an angle is measured with an electronic theodolite.

12. What is a total station? What does EDMI stand for?

13. What is meant by saying that both angular and linear measurements are "balanced"? Should they be? Why?

14. Does the effect of error in a measured angle increase or decrease with increasing length of sight distance?

15. When measuring angles, is it best to keep the line-of-sight distances as short as possible? Explain.

16. List six possible instrumental errors that may occur during surveys with a transit or theodolite.

17. List and briefly discuss four personal errors that may occur when working with a transit or theodolite.

18. List four natural errors that affect angle measurement.

19. List six typical blunders that can occur with a transit or theodolite.

Practice Problems

1. Express the following vertical angles as zenith distances:
   a. 20°10′
   b. −6°20′
   c. 60°40′
   d. −7°10′

2. Express the following vertical angles as zenith distances:
   a. −10°40′
   b. 40°30′
   c. 0°10′
   d. −4°50′

3. Express the following zenith distances as vertical angles:
   a. 82°45′15″
   b. 88°05′55″
   c. 102°40′30″

4. Express the following zenith distances as vertical angles:
   a. 92°35′25″
   b. 108°15′45″
   c. 72°32′48″

5. Express the following directions by two other means; set up and fill in a table with three columns, one for bearing, one for azimuth$_N$ (Azim$_N$), and one for azimuth$_S$ (Azim$_S$):
   a. N 20°10′ E
   b. Azim$_N$ 130°30′
   c. Azim$_S$ 320°20′
   d. N 10°30′ W
   e. Azim$_S$ 90°50′
   f. S 20°30′ E
   g. Azim$_N$ 30°10′
   h. Azim$_S$ 40°20′
   i. Azim$_N$ 310°50′
   j. Azim$_S$ 210°20′
   k. S 40°10′ W
   l. Azim$_N$ 250°40′

6. Express the following directions by two other means; set up and fill in a table with three columns, one for bearing, one for azimuth$_N$ (Azim$_N$), and one for azimuth$_S$ (Azim$_S$):
   a. N 30°40′ E
   b. Azim$_S$ 120°10′
   c. Azim$_N$ 350°40′

d. N 40°20′ W

e. Azim$_N$ 10°30′

f. S 0°30′ E

g. Azim$_N$ 90°20′

h. Azim$_N$ 250°00′

i. S 20°40′ W

j. Azim$_N$ 150°30′

k. Azim$_S$ 160°10′

l. Azim$_N$ 130°30′

7. Determine the back directions for the values given in Problem 5.

8. Determine the back directions for the values given in Problem 6.

9. From a single position O, vertical angles A and B were measured to the tops of two flagpoles A′ and B′ (see Figure 6-32). The distances from O to the flagpoles were found to be a and b, as shown. Find the difference in elevation between the tops of the two flagpoles, to the nearest 0.01 ft, according to the following data. If A′ is above B′, call the difference plus, and vice versa.

	(1)	(2)	(3)
A	20°	10°	16°
B	10°	15°	−6°
a	100′	200′	300′
b	200′	100′	200′

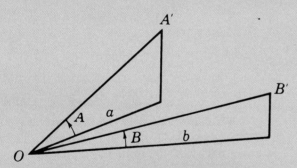

FIGURE 6-32. Illustration for Problems 9 and 10.

10. From a single position O, vertical angles A and B were measured to the tops of two flagpoles A′ and B′ (see Figure 6-32). The distances from O to the flagpoles were found to be a and b, as shown. Find the difference in elevation between the tops of the two flagpoles, to the nearest 0.01 ft, according to the following data. If A′ is above B′, call the difference plus, and vice versa.

	(1)	(2)	(3)
A	18°	−4°	−6°
B	−4°	−2°	−7°
A	100′	200′	200′
B	300′	100′	100′

11. Determine the unknown azimuths for the traverse courses shown in Figure 6-33.

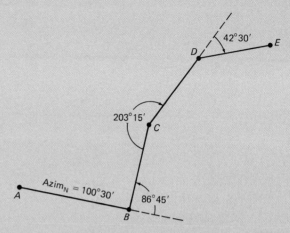

FIGURE 6-33. Illustration for Problem 11.

12. Determine the unknown azimuths for the traverse courses shown in Figure 6-34.

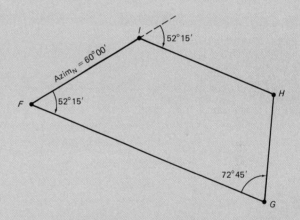

FIGURE 6-34. Illustration for Problem 12.

13. Determine the unknown bearings for the traverse courses shown in Figure 6-35.

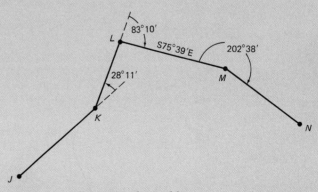

FIGURE 6-35. Illustration for Problem 13.

14. Determine the unknown bearings for the traverse courses shown in Figure 6-36.

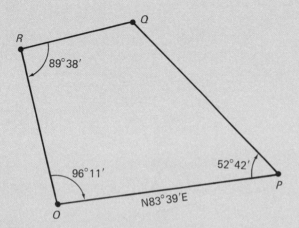

FIGURE 6-36. Illustration for Problem 14.

15. Determine the unknown interior and deflection angles for the traverses shown in Figure 6-37.

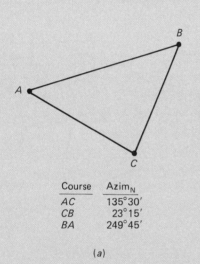

Course	Azim$_N$
AC	135°30′
CB	23°15′
BA	249°45′

(a)

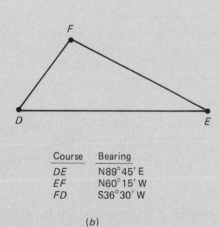

Course	Bearing
DE	N89°45′ E
EF	N60°15′ W
FD	S36°30′ W

(b)

FIGURE 6-37. Illustration for Problem 15.

16. Determine the unknown interior and deflection angles for the traverses shown in Figure 6-38.

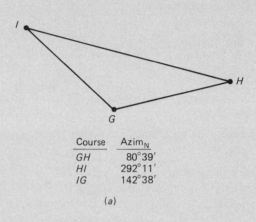

Course	Azim$_N$
GH	80°39′
HI	292°11′
IG	142°38′

(a)

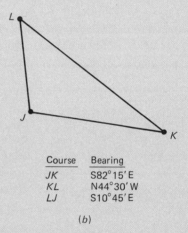

Course	Bearing
JK	S82°15′ E
KL	N44°30′ W
LJ	S10°45′ E

(b)

FIGURE 6-38. Illustration for Problem 16.

17. The magnetic bearing of a boundary line was recorded as N 35°00′ W in a deed dated 1903. At that time and place, the magnetic declination was known to be 3°15′ W. Determine the true azimuth and bearing for the line.

18. The magnetic bearing of a boundary line was recorded as S 55°30′ E in a deed dated 1913. At that time and place, the magnetic declination was known to be 5°45′ E. Determine the true azimuth and bearing for the line.

19. The magnetic bearing of a boundary line was recorded as S 76°30′ W in 1897, at which time the declination was 2°45′ W. It is desired to retrace the line with a compass today, when the declination is 5°35′ E. What reading of the compass should be used to retrace the line? What is the true azimuth of the line?

20. The magnetic bearing of a boundary line was recorded as N 86°00′ W in 1918, at which time the declination was 3°45′ E. It is desired to retrace the line with a compass today, when the declination is 6°35′ E.

What reading of the compass should be used to retrace the line? What is the true azimuth of the line?

21. A six-sided closed traverse was surveyed over the stations *ABCDEF*. At each station, the back bearing of the previous course and the forward bearing of the next course were observed, on a compass, with the following results. Compute the forward bearings for all six courses, corrected for local attraction.

Compass Sta.	Point Sighted	Bearing
A	F	N 10°15′ W
A	B	S 72°00′ E
B	A	N 73°00′ W
B	C	N 64°30′ E
C	B	S 62°45′ W
C	D	N 3°00′ W
D	C	S 1°30′ E
D	E	S 81°15′ W
E	D	N 82°00′ E
E	F	N 77°45′ W
F	E	S 77°15′ E
F	A	S 10°15′ E

Suggestion: Draw a sketch of the traverse and, at each station, indicate the direction of the magnetic meridian and the relative direction of the compass needle as affected by local attraction.

22. Similar to Problem 21 but a five-sided traverse:

Compass Sta.	Point Sighted	Bearing
A	E	S 88°30′ E
A	B	S 22°15′ E
B	A	N 22°45′ W
B	C	S 40°15′ E
C	B	N 40°15′ W
C	D	N 51°45′ E
D	C	S 50°15′ W
D	E	N 31°45′ W
E	D	S 32°15′ E
E	A	S 89°00′ W

23. What angular error corresponds to a relative accuracy of
   a. 1/200
   b. 1:5000

24. What angular error corresponds to a relative accuracy of
   a. 1/3000
   b. 1:6000

SURVEYING APPLICATIONS

HORIZONTAL CONTROL
SURVEYS

One of the first steps in a typical mapping, land development, or construction project is to establish a network of both vertical and horizontal *control points* on or near the ground in the vicinity of the project. The relative positions of all the points are accurately determined in a *control survey.* The control points serve as fixed reference positions from which other surveying measurements are made later on to design and build the project. *Vertical control* (benchmark) surveys are discussed in Section 5-4; the basics of *horizontal control* surveys are covered in this chapter.

More than 250,000 horizontal control monuments have been established throughout the United States by the National Geodetic Survey (NGS) and other agencies. These survey stations form the National Spatial Reference System (NSRS).

The framework of national and local control survey points can provide a common datum or reference for almost all mapping, design, and construction operations. Topographic features may be tied into the control network by angle and/or distance measurements. The same control points may then be reused as reference positions for layout measurements during construction.

A horizontal control network may be established by one or a combination of the following methods: traversing, triangulation, and trilateration. Other methods make use of photogrammetry, or of *global positioning systems* (GPS).

A *traverse survey* involves a connected sequence of lines whose lengths and directions are measured. It is perhaps the most common type of control survey performed by surveyors in private practice or employed by local governmental agencies. *Triangulation* involves a system of joined or overlapping triangles in which the lengths of two sides (called *baselines*) are measured; the other sides are then computed from the angles measured at the triangle vertices. *Trilateration* also involves a system of triangles, but only the lengths are measured.

In years past, triangulation provided the best method for establishing precise horizontal control over large areas (see Figure 7-1). This was because precise angular measurement was more feasible than precise distance measurement by taping; only two baseline distances need be taped in a triangulation survey. But now, with the use of electronic distance measuring (EDM) devices, precise traverse surveys are much more practical.

New control surveys now generally make use of a combination of GPS technology and total surveys to perform precise traversing. Coordinate geometry also plays an important role in surveying computations related to defining the relative positions of the control survey points; computer programs now used both in the office and in the field are based on the use of coordinate geometry computations.

The primary focus of this chapter is on traverse surveys and computations. The basics of triangulation surveys and trilateration computations are also discussed, and typical coordinate geometry applications are presented. Finally, the application of sophisticated aerospace technologies such as global positioning systems to large-scale or geodetic control surveys is discussed at the end of the chapter. (The relationship between aerial photogrammetry and horizontal control is covered in Chapter 9.)

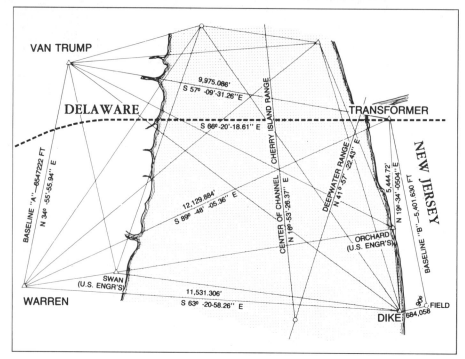

FIGURE 7-1. The triangulation control network used for the design and construction of the Delaware Memorial Bridge. (*Courtesy of Professional Surveyor Magazine.*)

7-1 TRAVERSES

A *traverse* consists of an interconnected series of lines called *courses*, running between a series of points on the ground called *traverse stations*. A traverse survey is performed to measure both the distances between the stations and the angles between the courses. As discussed previously, the traverse stations can serve as control points. From those points, many less precise measurements can be made to features that are to be located for mapping, without accumulating accidental errors. When plans for construction are then drawn, the traverse stations can again be used as beginning points from which to lay out the work.

Traverses have generally been used for local horizontal control over relatively small areas, or over areas where many obstacles interfere with sight lines. They may now be used for precise control over relatively large areas, due to the advantage of EDM. In addition to application as a control survey method, traversing may be applied to land or property surveys. Unobstructed boundary lines form the traverse courses, and the property corners are the traverse stations.

Types of Traverses

Traverses are classified as being either *open* or *closed*. An open traverse neither forms a closed geometric figure nor does it end at a point of known position. It cannot be checked, then, for error of closure and relative accuracy. Open traverses are not recommended, but they are sometimes used out of necessity. All open traverse measurements *must* be repeated to avoid blunders.

There are two types of closed traverses—*loop* traverses and *connecting* traverses. A loop traverse starts and ends at the same point, forming a closed geometric figure called a *polygon* (see Figures 6-1 and 7-6). (The boundary lines of a tract of land, for example, form a loop traverse.)

A connecting traverse looks like an open traverse, except that it begins and ends at points (or lines) of known position (and direction) at each end of the traverse (see Figure 7-13). A connecting traverse, then, is "closed" in the sense that it can be checked mathematically for the error of closure and the relative accuracy of the survey. Connecting traverses are generally used for horizontal control in route surveys.

Field Work

The positions of control traverse stations are chosen so that they are as close as possible to the features or objects to be located, without unduly increasing the work of measuring the traverse. Establishing too many points will increase the time and cost of the survey, but too few points may not provide sufficient control for the project; the judgment of an experienced surveyor is necessary when establishing traverse stations.

The control traverse stations are usually marked by wooden stakes with tacks, or by concrete monuments set nearly flush with the ground, with a precise point marked on the top by a chiseled cross, a drill hole, or a special bronze tablet.

Witnessing a Point   It is frequently necessary to *witness* or *reference* a control point. This serves as an aid to finding the point when it is covered with snow, leaves, or soil, or as a means to replace it if the point is accidentally disturbed (as often happens during construction activities). The supplementary points used for this purpose are called *witness marks*, *witnesses*, or *ties*.

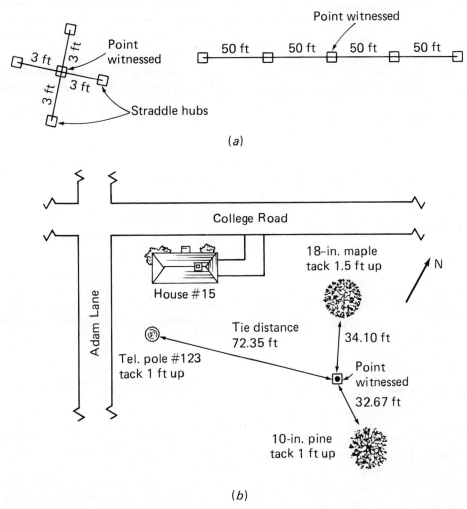

FIGURE 7-2. Two methods for referencing, or witnessing, a point: (*a*) straddle hubs and (*b*) ties to existing fixed marks.

Two methods may be used to witness a point. In one method, wooden stakes (sometimes called *straddle hubs*) may be set near the point, so that the intersection of two strings stretched between opposite pairs of hubs will mark the position of the station (see Figure 7-2a). In the second method, a control station may be tied in, by distance measurement, to nearby existing points that can serve as witnesses (see Figure 7-2b). The station can then be relocated by the intersection of arcs swung at the measured distances from the witness marks.

For proper witnessing of a station, the following factors should be noted:

1. At least three witnesses should be used.

2. Witnesses should be permanent and readily visible points, situated somewhat above the ground surface.

3. Witnesses should not be more than 100 ft (or 30 m) from the control station.

4. The ties should be roughly at right angles to each other.

5. Ties to trees (or poles) should be made to tacks or nails marked with colored ribbon.

6. Distances of ties should be measured with an appropriate degree of accuracy, depending on the purpose of the survey.

7. A neat and legible sketch should be made in the field book, showing recognizable landmarks as well as the witnesses; a brief written description of the control station location should accompany the sketch.

Measurements   The angle and distance measurements are made as described in Part 2 of the text. Steel tape and transit have been, for the most part, replaced by the use of the total station.

For a closed traverse, the length of each course is recorded as a separate distance; the courses are identified by the station labels (e.g., course *BC* or course 2-3). For an open or connecting traverse, particularly that used for a route survey, distances are often carried along the traverse courses continuously from beginning to end, and expressed in terms of *stations* (see Section 4-2).

For purposes of consistency, it is necessary to assume the forward and the back direction for any traverse. The direction or order in which the courses are measured is usually taken as the forward direction. Loop traverses should generally be traversed or measured in a counterclockwise direction around the loop (see Figure 7-3).

The *field angles* of a traverse should be measured clockwise (to the right), from the back direction of the preceding

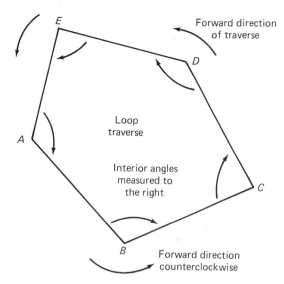

FIGURE 7-3. Loop traverses are best surveyed in a counterclockwise direction, with interior angles "turned" to the right.

course to the forward direction of the next course. This is the most rapid field method and the least likely to introduce blunders. For a loop traverse, these should be the *interior angles*. If for some reason an exterior angle is measured, it should be clearly noted in the field record.

Some surveyors prefer to measure the *deflection angles*, particularly for open or connecting traverses (see Figure 7-4). A deflection angle is the angle between the forward prolongation of the preceding course and the forward direction of the next course (see Section 6-2). It can also be defined as the change of direction of the traverse at a station. Unless the directions of the deflection angles are properly recorded as angle left (L) or angle right (R), a blunder will result. To determine the deflection angle, simply measure the clockwise field angle at the station (as described in the preceding paragraph) and subtract 180°. If the difference is positive (+), it is a right deflection angle; if the difference is negative (−), it is a left deflection angle.

For measuring deflection angles directly with a vernier transit, the following steps are followed by many surveyors:

1. Set the vernier scale to zero.
2. Backsight with the telescope reversed (lower motion).
3. Foresight with the telescope direct (upper motion).

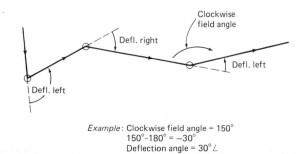

Example: Clockwise field angle = 150°
150°−180° = −30°
Deflection angle = 30° ∠

FIGURE 7-4. Deflection angles must be identified as being turned either clockwise, that is, to the right (R), or counterclockwise, to the left (L).

4. Record the clockwise or counterclockwise angle, whichever is less than 180°. If clockwise, it is a right deflection; if counterclockwise, it is a left deflection.

The preceding procedure introduces a systematic error of the instrument. Repeat the angle to cancel the error, as follows:

1. Leave the vernier as it is after step 4; backsight with the telescope direct (lower motion).
2. Foresight with the telescope reversed (upper motion).
3. Read the angle as in step 4, and take the average of the two readings.

Data Reduction

The relative positions of control traverse stations are usually described mathematically by the *rectangular coordinates* of the stations. The process of converting all the distance and angle measurements into coordinates is called *data reduction*. Although computer programs are available to automatically reduce the raw field data, it is necessary that the surveyor has a good understanding of all the computational steps involved in the process. In fact, it would be difficult, if not impossible, to read and interpret the software documentation and to use the programs intelligently without this basic knowledge and understanding.

Error of Closure   Because no measurement is perfect, it is most unlikely that the raw traverse data will "close" exactly. This means, for example, that the given or assumed coordinates of the starting point in a loop traverse will not be precisely the same as the position or coordinates of that point as computed from the raw field data (see Figure 7-5).

If the discrepancy or error of closure exceeds some specified or acceptable limit, the field measurements will have to

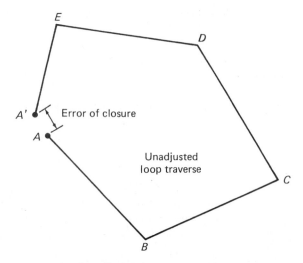

A : Coordinates given or assumed
A': Coordinates computed from field data

FIGURE 7-5. Error of closure in a loop traverse. Starting at station A and following the measured distances and angles around the traverse, you would be unlikely to wind up exactly on point A again.

be repeated. But if the error of closure (or relative accuracy) is acceptable, it is then necessary to *adjust the traverse* so that it closes perfectly, with complete geometric consistency. For example, in Figure 7-5, the field data would be adjusted so that the traverse "closes" and position $A' = $ position A. This process of adjusting or *closing the traverse* ensures that the station coordinates will be as accurate as possible. Traverse adjustment is also important for land or boundary surveys because legal descriptions of property must have no geometric inconsistencies.

7-2 TRAVERSE CLOSURE COMPUTATIONS

The computations for adjusting and closing a traverse can be summarized in six basic steps, as follows:

1. Compute the angular error and adjust the angles.
2. Compute course bearings or azimuths.
3. Compute course latitudes and departures.
4. Determine the error of closure and accuracy; if unacceptable, then redo traverse or parts of traverse. If acceptable, move to step 5.
5. Adjust course latitudes and departures.
6. Compute station coordinates.

In addition to these steps, a boundary traverse would include computation of the enclosed area, as well as computation of the final bearings and lengths of the courses that result from the adjustment of the traverse (in the preceding step 5). The area, as well as the final boundary lengths and directions, is needed for a legal property description.

In this section, the six basic steps of traverse computations are illustrated and discussed for a loop traverse, as well as for a connecting traverse. Area determination and related traverse computations are presented in subsequent sections.

A Loop Traverse

Figure 7-6 illustrates a sketch of a loop traverse, along with the raw, or unadjusted, field data. A sketch of a traverse should always be drawn as a guide to computation, showing the names of each of the traverse stations. If it is plotted to scale, it can serve as a visual check against major blunders in the survey.

The step-by-step procedure for the computation and closure of the traverse shown in Figure 7-6 is listed and described as follows:

1. **Compute the angular error and adjust the angles.**

   The sum of the interior angles in any loop traverse *must* equal $(n - 2)(180°)$ for geometric consistency; n is the number of angles (or sides) in the traverse. For the given five-sided traverse, the sum of angles should be exactly $(5 - 2)(180°) = 3(180°) = 540°$.

   The sum of the unadjusted field angles for the given traverse is actually $540°02'30''$ and the error per angle is 30 seconds. This is easily determined as follows:

Station	Field Angles		
A	64°	53'	30''
B	206	35	15
C	64	21	15
D	107	33	45
E	96	38	45
	Sum = 537°	180'	150'' = 540°02'30''

$$\text{Total angular error} = 540°02'30'' - 540°00'00''$$
$$= 00°02'30''$$

and therefore,

$$\text{Error per angle} = \frac{2'30''}{5} = \frac{150''}{5} = 30'' \text{ per angle}$$

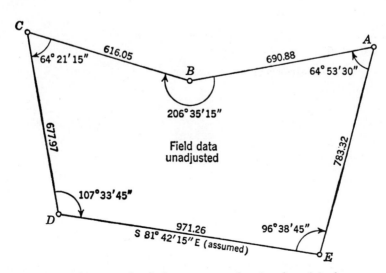

FIGURE 7-6. An example of a loop traverse showing the original (unadjusted) field data.

For average work with a 1-minute vernier transit, an error of 1 minute per angle, or less, would generally be allowed; we can assume, then, that the angular measurement for this traverse is acceptable. (For precise work with a transit, the total error should generally not exceed $\pm\, 30'' \sqrt{n}$, where n is the number of angles.)

The angles of the traverse may be adjusted by applying the same correction to each angle; the correction is the error per angle, with the opposite sign. This procedure assumes that the chance for error was the same for each measurement. Because the sum exceeds 540° and the error is positive, a negative correction of 30 seconds should be used here, as follows:

Station	Field Angles	Correction	Adjusted Angles
A	64°53′30″	−30°	64°53′00″
B	206°35′15″	−30°	206°34′45″
C	64°21′15″	−30°	64°20′45″
D	107°33′45″	−30°	107°33′5″
E	96°38′45″	−30°	96°38′15″
		Sum = 540° 00′ 00″	(Check)

In some cases, a larger correction may be applied to particular angles if the chances for error were greater due to poor observing conditions (or short sight lines) at those stations. Generally, the applied corrections should not be less than the least angular values that can be measured with the instrument. They may be rounded off for ease of computation. In any case, the sum of the adjusted angles should always check out to be $(n-2)(180°)$, for geometric consistency.

2. Compute course bearings or azimuths.

The direction of one side of the traverse must be known or assumed; this is called the *base bearing* (or *base azimuth*). In this example problem, the bearing of *DE* is assumed to be S 81°42′15″ E. Using the *adjusted angles* from the preceding step 1, the bearings of the other courses are determined, as shown in Figure 7-7. (The procedure for computing bearings is also explained in Section 6-2.)

3. Compute course latitudes and departures.

The *latitude* of a traverse course is simply the *Y* component of the line in a rectangular *XY* coordinate system (see Figure 7-8a). In surveying, the *Y* axis is usually taken as the *north–south* meridian axis. A latitude, then, may also be defined as the projection of a traverse course

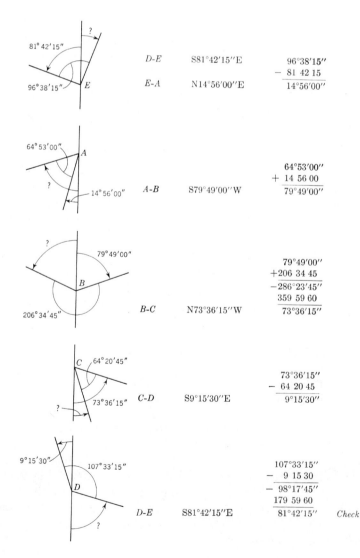

D-E	S81°42′15″E	96°38′15″
		− 81 42 15
E-A	N14°56′00″E	14°56′00″

		64°53′00″
		+ 14 56 00
A-B	S79°49′00″W	79°49′00″

		79°49′00″
		+206 34 45
		−286°23′45″
		359 59 60
B-C	N73°36′15″W	73°36′15″

		73°36′15″
		− 64 20 45
C-D	S9°15′30″E	9°15′30″

		107°33′15″
		− 9 15 30
		− 98°17′45″
		179 59 60
D-E	S81°42′15″E	81°42′15″ *Check*

FIGURE 7-7. Bearing computations for the traverse shown in Figure 7-6, using adjusted interior angles.

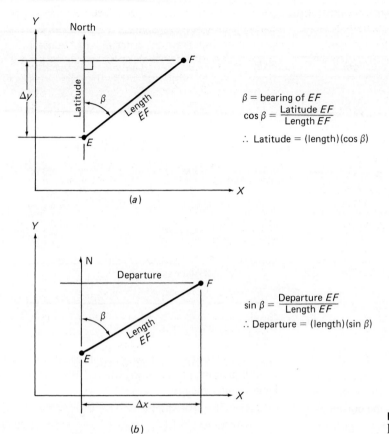

FIGURE 7-8. Definition of the latitude and departure of a line.

onto the north–south axis of the survey. From basic right-angle trigonometry, it is computed as the product of the course length L and the cosine of the bearing angle β:

$$\text{Latitude} = \Delta y = L \cos (\beta) \qquad (7\text{-}1)$$

The *departure* of a traverse course is simply the X component of the line in a rectangular XY coordinate system (see Figure 7-8b). The X axis is usually the same as the *east–west* axis of the survey. A departure, then, may also be defined as the projection of a traverse course onto the east–west axis. From right-angle trigonometry, it is computed as the product of the course length L and the sine of the bearing angle β:

$$\text{Dep} = \Delta x = L \sin (\beta) \qquad (7\text{-}2)$$

Sign Convention   If the traverse course has a northerly (N) bearing, its latitude will have a positive sign (+); a positive latitude is sometimes called the *northing* of the line (see Figure 7-9). If the course has a southerly (S) bearing, its latitude will carry a negative (−) sign; it may also be called the *southing* of the line.

If a line has an easterly (E) bearing, its departure will have a positive sign; a positive departure may be called the *easting* of the line (see Figure 7-9). If the line has a westerly (W) bearing, its departure will be negative; it may be called the *westing* of the line.

When computing a traverse using bearing angles, it is necessary to "manually" apply the appropriate algebraic signs to the latitudes and departures. A line with a SE

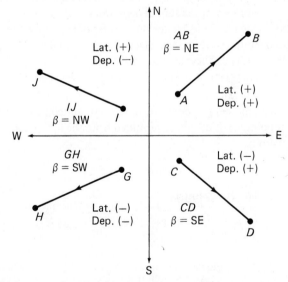

FIGURE 7-9. Algebraic sign convention for latitude and departure.

bearing, for example, would be assigned a negative latitude $(-\Delta y)$ and a positive departure $(+\Delta x)$.

The computations of latitudes and departures for the traverse shown in Figure 7-6 are summarized in Table 7-1. Note the format of this table—the data for each course are listed on the lines between the station names. The values of the trig functions are rounded to four decimal places for display only.

Table 7-1. Computations for Latitude and Departure

Station	Bearing, β	Length, L	cos β Cosine	sin β Sine	L cos β Latitude	L sin β Departure
A						
	S 79°49'00" W	690.88	0.1768	0.9842	−122.15	−679.99
B						
	N 73°36'15" W	616.05	0.2823	0.9593	+173.89	−591.00
C						
	S 9°15'30" E	677.97	0.9870	0.1609	−669.14	+109.08
D						
	S 81°42'15" E	971.26	0.1443	0.9895	−140.14	+961.10
E						
	N 14°56'00" E	783.32	0.9662	0.2577	+756.86	+201.86
A						

Perimeter $(P) = 3739.48$　　　　Sum of latitudes = $\Sigma\Delta y = -0.68$

Sum of departures = $\Sigma\Delta x = +1.0$

4. Determine the error of closure and accuracy.

Because a loop traverse begins and ends at the same point, the sum of the latitudes and the sum of the departures should both be equal to zero. In other words, the northings should be equal to the southings (but opposite in sign), and likewise, the eastings should equal the westings. But because the field measurements are not perfect, it is unlikely that the sum of latitudes, or the sum of departures, will be exactly zero. As seen in Table 7-1, for the traverse of Figure 7-6 the sum of latitudes $\Sigma\Delta y = -0.68$ ft, and the sum of departures $\Sigma\Delta x = +1.05$ ft. These are the y and x components, respectively, of the error of closure of the traverse (see Figure 7-10).

The total *error of closure* E_c is the horizontal distance between the starting point, A, and the computed position of that point, A'. It may be determined from the following equation:

$$E_c = \sqrt{(\Sigma\Delta y)^2 + (\Sigma\Delta x)^2} \qquad (7\text{-}3)$$

For this example,

$$E_c = \sqrt{(-0.68)^2 + (1.05)^2} = 1.25 \text{ ft}$$

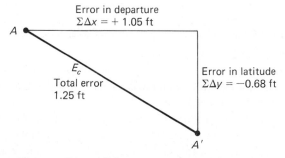

FIGURE 7-10. Error of closure is computed from the error in departure and error in latitude, using the Pythagorean theorem.

The relative accuracy of the traverse is computed from Equation 2-3 as follows, where P is the total traverse length or perimeter:

$$\text{Accuracy} = 1{:}\left(\frac{P}{E_c}\right) = 1{:}\left(\frac{3739.48}{1.25}\right) = 1.2990$$

For average land surveying with a vernier transit, an accuracy of about 1:3000 is typical. An accuracy of at least 1:5000 would be required for third-order control traverse surveys. For this example, we will consider that the accuracy is acceptable, and now proceed to adjust the latitudes and departures so that the traverse will close exactly.

5. Adjust course latitudes and departures.

There are several methods of traverse adjustment. The simplest are "approximate" procedures called the *compass* (or *Bowditch*) *rule* and the *transit rule*. With the advent of numerous software packages, a method called *least squares adjustment* can easily be applied. The *least squares* method is most accurate. This allows the surveyor to "weigh" the control points. In other words, the surveyor can apply or apportion more, or less, correction to their location, depending on the certainty of the specific measurements. (The mathematics of least squares adjustment is beyond the scope of this book. The various software suppliers provide theory and application instruction with their software.)

The Compass Rule　In this method, corrections are applied to the latitudes and departures in proportion to the lengths of each of the courses. It is assumed that angles and distances have been measured with equal precision (e.g., with transit and steel tape). Application of the compass rule changes both the latitudes and departures in such a way that

Table 7-2. Compass Rule Corrections to Latitude and Departure

Station	Unadjusted Latitude	Unadjusted Departure	Corrections Latitude	Corrections Departure	Adjusted Latitude	Adjusted Departure
A						
	−122.15	−679.99	0.13	−0.19	−122.02	−680.18
B						
	+173.89	−591.00	0.11	−0.17	+174.00	−591.17
C						
	−669.14	+109.08	0.12	−0.19	−669.02	+108.89
D						
	−140.14	+961.10	0.18	−0.27	−139.96	+960.83
E						
	+756.86	+201.86	0.14	−0.22	+757.00	+201.63
A						
	Σ = −0.68	+1.05	0.68	−1.05	0.0	0.0
			Check		*Check*	

both the bearings and lengths of the courses are slightly changed. A formula for this rule may be written as follows:

$$\text{Correction} = \frac{-\Sigma \Delta y}{P} \times L \quad \text{or} \quad \frac{-\Sigma \Delta x}{P} \times L \quad (7\text{-}4)$$

where $\Sigma \Delta y$ and $\Sigma \Delta x$ = the error in latitude or in departure

P = the total length or perimeter of the traverse

L = the length of a particular course

For example, the correction to the latitude of course AB is $-(-0.68)/3739 \times 691 = +0.13$. Note that *the corrections will have the opposite sign as that of the errors.* The correction to the departure of course BC, for example, is computed as $-1.05/3739 \times 616 = -0.17$. The compass rule corrections of latitudes and departures, for the traverse in Figure 7-6, are summarized in Table 7-2.

The Transit Rule   In this method, corrections are applied to the latitudes in proportion to the lengths of the latitudes and to the departures in proportion to the lengths of the departures. This rule is best used for traverse surveys in which the angles have been measured with greater precision than the distances. It changes the latitudes and departures in such a way that the lengths of the courses are changed slightly, but the bearings remain almost the same.

A formula for the transit rule can be written as follows:

$$\text{Correction} = \frac{-\Sigma \Delta y}{\Sigma |\text{Lat}|} \times CL \quad \text{or} \quad \frac{-\Sigma \Delta x}{\Sigma |\text{Dep}|} \times CD \quad (7\text{-}5)$$

where $\Sigma \Delta y$ and $\Sigma \Delta x$ = the error in latitude or in departure

Σ Lat and Σ Dep = the sum of latitudes and the sum of departures, without regard to sign (absolute values)

CL and CD = the length of the particular course latitude or departure

For example, the correction to the latitude of course AB is $(-0.68)/1862 \times 122 = +0.04$. Again, note that *the corrections must have the opposite sign as that of the errors.* The correction to the departure of course BC, for example, is computed as $-1.05/2543 \times 591 = -0.24$. The transit rule corrections of both latitudes and departures are summarized in Table 7-3.

The sums of the corrections must be equal to their respective errors, with the signs changed. And the sums of the adjusted latitudes and departures, for both the compass rule and the transit rule, must be equal to zero for exact closure of the traverse. This serves as a check on the computations. Be careful to add the corrections algebraically. For example, for course AB, the (transit) adjusted latitude = $-122.15 + (+0.04) = -122.1$; the (transit) adjusted departure = $-679.99 + (-0.28) = -680.27$.

Because of rounding off the computed corrections, it is sometimes necessary to change (fudge) one or two corrections slightly so that the traverse will close exactly. Usually, the changes are applied to the largest values. It can be seen (from Tables 7-2 and 7-3) that this was done to the compass rule correction for the departure of course EA, to the transit rule correction for the latitude of course EA, and to the transit rule correction for the departure of course DE.

An adjustment method that is mathematically more correct or rigorous than either the compass or transit rules is the *method of least squares.* It is based on statistical theory and results in the most probable positions for the stations. Although it is a complicated and lengthy procedure when done manually, it is now being applied by surveyors with increasing frequency when canned computer programs are used to adjust and close the traverse.

6.   **Compute station coordinates.**

The relative positions of control stations are best defined by their *rectangular* or *XY coordinates.* In most surveying applications, the Y, or *north* (N) coordinate precedes the X, or *east* (E), coordinate. For many computer or

Table 7-3. Transit Rule Corrections to Latitude and Departure

Station	Unadjusted		Corrections		Adjusted	
	Latitude	Departure	Latitude	Departure	Latitude	Departure
A						
	−122.15	−679.99	+0.04	−0.28	−122.11	−680.27
B						
	+173.89	−591.00	+0.06	−0.24	+173.95	−591.24
C						
	−669.14	+109.08	+0.24	−0.04	−668.90	+109.04
D						
	−140.14	+961.10	+0.05	−0.41	−140.09	+960.69
E						
	+756.86	+201.86	+0.29	−0.08	+757.15	+201.78
A						
	Σ = −0.68	+1.05	+0.68	−1.05	0.0	0.0
				Check		Check
	Absolute Σ|Lat| = 1862	Absolute Σ|Dep| = 2543				

programmable calculator solutions, for example, the N coordinate (also called the *northing*) must be entered before the E coordinate (also called the *easting*) of a station; the order of coordinate data is (N, E), or (Y, X).

Usually, an arbitrary position is assigned to one of the stations, in a manner that assures that all station coordinates will be positive (+) (i.e., in the northeast quadrant). Sometimes, only an X coordinate will be assigned to the point closest to due west, and its corresponding Y coordinate

will be calculated. Also, only a Y coordinate to the point closest to due south, and its corresponding X coordinate will be calculated. All points will have two values (X, Y) to accomplish the task of assuring positive values. In the traverse adjusted earlier, the point closest to due south, station E, is given a Y, or north, coordinate of 100.00 ft; and the point closest to due west, station C, is given an X, or east, coordinate of 100.00 ft (see Figure 7-11). Explanation of the method for computing the other station coordinates follows.

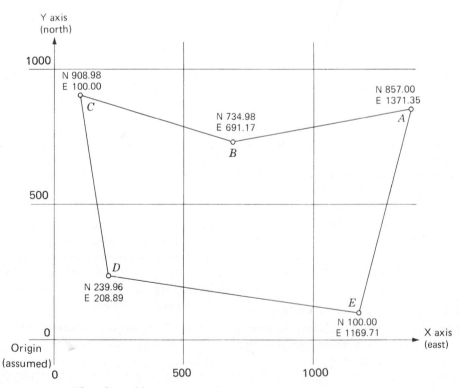

FIGURE 7-11. The adjusted loop traverse plotted by coordinates.

Coordinates of a point may be computed by successive algebraic addition of the adjusted latitudes and departures to the assumed N and E coordinates, respectively. In equation form, this is written as

$$N_2 = N_1 + Lat_{1-2} \qquad (7\text{-}6a)$$

$$E_2 = E_1 + Dep_{1-2} \qquad (7\text{-}6b)$$

where N_2 and E_2 = the Y and X coordinates of station 2

N_1 and E_1 = the Y and X coordinates of station 1

Lat_{1-2} = the latitude of course 1–2

Dep_{1-2} = the departure of course 1–2

An example is shown in Figure 7-12, and the computation of coordinates for the traverse shown in Figures 7-6 and 7-11 (using the compass rule adjustments) is summarized in Table 7-4. An arithmetic check is obtained when the computation is carried around to the starting point, which should have the same coordinates as before. In Table 7-4, the coordinate values are written in *italics* on the same line as the station names. Usually, in practice, all the computations included in Tables 7-1–7-4 are combined into one larger table.

A Connecting Traverse

Figure 7-13 illustrates a connecting (or *link*) traverse. It begins at the known position of control station Dog. The fixed coordinates of another nearby control station, Cat, are also known. From those coordinates, it is possible to compute the length and direction of line Dog–Cat, through a process called *inversing* (which is explained in the next section). The traverse

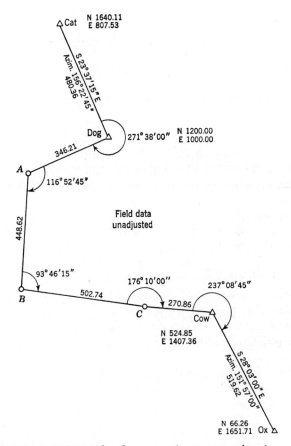

FIGURE 7-13. Example of a connecting traverse showing original (unadjusted) field data.

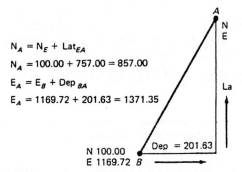

$N_A = N_E + Lat_{EA}$

$N_A = 100.00 + 757.00 = 857.00$

$E_A = E_B + Dep_{BA}$

$E_A = 1169.72 + 201.63 = 1371.35$

FIGURE 7-12. Typical computation of coordinates for Figure 7-11.

Table 7-4. Computation of Station Coordinates

Station	N Coordinate* Latitude	E Coordinate* Departure	
A	857.00	1371.35	
	−122.02	−680.18	(Course lat. and dep.)
B	734.98	691.17	
	+174.00	−591.17	
C	908.98	100.00	Start/return here for dep. check
	−669.02	+108.89	
D	239.96	208.89	
	−139.96	+960.83	
E	100.00	1169.72	Start/return here for lat. check
	+757.00	+201.63	
A	857.00	1371.35	

*Compass-adjusted coordinates.

closes on the known position of station Cow, and the known length and direction of line Cow–Ox. Clockwise field angles are measured at Dog and at Cow and at each traverse station, *A*, *B*, and *C*. The length of each new course is also measured.

The step-by-step procedure for the computation and closure of the connecting traverse is described as follows:

1. Compute the angular error and adjust the angles.

Starting with the known direction of course Cat–Dog, the directions of the new courses may be computed by applying the field angles successively (see Table 7-5). Either bearings or azimuths may be used. A computation by azimuth using deflection angles is also shown. The deflection angle is taken as the difference between the field angle and 180°. By either of the three methods shown, the clockwise angular error is +1°30″, or +18 seconds per angle (90″/5 = 18″). If it is assumed that an error of 30 seconds per angle would be allowed, then the angular measurement for this traverse is acceptable.

To adjust the field angles, it is assumed that the chance for error at each station is the same; a correction of −18 seconds, then, is applied to each field angle as follows:

Adjust Angles Give the same correction to each angle; the chance for error is the same.

Dog	271°38′00″ − 18″ = 271°37′42″
A	116°52′45″ − 18″ = 116°52′27″
B	93°46′15″ − 18″ = 93°45′57″
C	176°10′00″ − 18″ = 176°09′42″
Cow	237°08′45″ − 18″ = 237°08′27″

2. Compute course bearings or azimuths.

The bearings and azimuths are recomputed using the adjusted angles, as shown in Table 7-6.

Table 7-6. Computation of Directions

By Bearings		By Azimuths
S 23°37′15″ E	Cat–Dog	156°22′45″
+271°37′42″		+271°37′42″
248°00′27″		428°00′27″
−180°		−180°
S 68°00′27″ W	Dog–A	248°00′27″
+116°52′27″		+116°52′27″
184°52′54″		364°52′54″
−180°		−180°
S 4°52′54″ W	A–B	184°52′54″
+ 93°45′57″		+ 93°45′57″
98°38′51″		278°38′51″
−179°59′60″		−180°
S 81°21′09″ E	B–C	98°38′51″
+176°09′42″		+176°09′42″
94°48′33″		274°48′33″
−179°59′60″		−180°
S 85°11′27″ E	C–Cow	94°48′33″
+237°08′27″		+237°08′27″
151°57′00″		331°57′00″
−179°60′00″		−180°
S 28°03′00″ E	Cow–Ox	151°57′00″
S 28°03′00″ E	Cow–Ox fixed	151°57′00″
0	Check	0

Table 7-5. Computation of Angular Error

By Bearings with Angles		By Azimuths with Angles	By Azimuths with Deflection Angles
S 23°37′15″ E	Cat–Dog	156°22′45″	156°22′45″
+271°38′00″		+271°38′00″	+ 91°38′00″
248°00′45″		428°00′45″	
−180°		−180°	
S 68°00′45″ W	Dog–A	248°00′45″	248°00′45″
+116°52′45″		+116°52′45″	− 63°07′15″
184°53′30″		364°53′30″	
−180°		−180°	
S 4°53′30″ W	A–B	184°53′30″	184°53′30″
+ 93°46′15″		+ 93°46′15″	− 86°13′45″
98°39′45″		278°39′45″	
−179°59′60″		−180°	
S 81°20′15″ E	B–C	98°39′45″	98°39′45″
+176°10′00″		+176°10′00″	− 3°50′00″
94°49′45″		274°49′45″	
−179°59′60″		−180°	
S 85°10′15″ E	C–Cow	94°49′45″	94°49′45″
+237°08′45″		+237°08′45″	+ 57°08′45″
151°58′30″		331°58′30″	
−179°59′60″		−180°	
S 28°01′30″ E	Cow–Ox	151°58′30″	151°58′30″
−S 28°03′00″ E	Cow–Ox fixed	151°57′00″	−151°57′00″
+ 1′30″	Error	+ 1′30″	+ 1′30″

Table 7-7. Computation of Coordinates

Station	Lengths	cos sin	Latitude (Unadjusted)	Departure (Unadjusted)	Latitude (Corrections)	Departure (Corrections)	Latitude (Adjusted Coordinates)	Departure (Adjusted Coordinates)
Dog	S 68°00'27" W	0.37449					1200.00	1000.00
A	346.21	0.92723	−129.65	−321.02	−0.04	−0.08	−129.69	−321.10
A	S 4°52'54" W	0.99637					1070.31	678.90
B	448.62	0.08510	−446.99	−38.18	−0.06	−0.11	−447.05	−38.29
B	S 81°21'09" E	0.15036					623.26	640.61
C	502.74	0.98864	−75.59	+497.03	−0.07	−0.12	−75.66	+496.91
C	S 85°11'27" E	0.08384					547.60	1137.52
Cow	270.86	0.99648	−22.71	+269.91	−0.04	−0.07	−22.75	+269.84
						Cow	524.85	1407.36
Sums	1568.43		−674.94	+407.74				
	Coord. Diff.		−675.15	+407.36				
	Error		+0.21	+0.38				

3. **Compute course latitudes and departures.**

Latitudes and departures are computed using Equations 7-1 and 7-2 for courses Dog–*A*, *AB*, *BC*, and *C*–Cow. The results are listed in Table 7-7. The sum of the computed latitudes is −674.94, and the sum of the computed departures is +407.74.

4. **Determine the error of closure and accuracy.**

The difference between the N coordinate of station Cow and the N coordinate of station Dog is 524.85 − 1200.00 = −675.15. In other words, station Cow is exactly 675.15 ft south of station Dog, according to the known positions of those points. But the sum of computed latitudes is only −674.94. This means that the N, or *Y*, component of the error of closure is +0.21. Likewise, the error in departure is determined to be +0.38.

Applying Equation 7-3, the total error $E_c = \sqrt{(0.21^2 + 0.38^2)} = 0.43$ ft. The total traverse length is 1568.43 ft. The accuracy of the survey, then, is computed to be 1:(1568.43/0.43) = 1:3650.

5. **Adjust course latitudes and departures.**

In this example, the corrections for latitude and departure are computed using the compass rule (Equation 7-4),

as shown in Table 7-8. The corrections are applied for each course, as shown in Table 7-7.

6. **Compute station coordinates.**

Beginning with the fixed coordinates of station Dog at the start of the traverse (N 1200.00/E 1000.00), the coordinates of each station are computed by successive algebraic addition of latitudes and departures (using Equation 7-6). This is shown in the two columns on the right of Table 7-7. An arithmetic check is obtained when the computed coordinates of Cow agree with its fixed coordinates. The plotted traverse is shown in Figure 7-14.

Plotting the Traverse   In plotting traverses, a protractor may be used to lay out the angles, and an engineer's scale may be used to lay out the course lengths or drawn using CAD software. If the station coordinates have been computed, much greater accuracy may be obtained when the stations are plotted by coordinates. After the stations are plotted, they are identified by name or letter, and the coordinates are printed nearby; connecting lines should be drawn to represent the traverse courses. The plotted traverse should then be checked by scaling the lengths of the courses and by measuring the traverse angles with a protractor. (The results should be compared with the original field notes.)

Table 7-8. Computation of Corrections by Compass Rule

Course	Correction to Latitudes	Correction to Departures
Dog–A	$\dfrac{-0.21}{1568} \times 346 = -0.04$	$\dfrac{-0.38}{1568} \times 346 = -0.08$
A–B	$\dfrac{-0.21}{1568} \times 449 = -0.06$	$\dfrac{-0.38}{1568} \times 449 = -0.11$
B–C	$\dfrac{-0.21}{1568} \times 503 = -0.07$	$\dfrac{-0.38}{1568} \times 503 = -0.12$
C–Cow	$\dfrac{-0.21}{1568} \times 271 = -0.04$	$\dfrac{-0.38}{1568} \times 271 = -0.07$
Sums	−0.21	−0.38

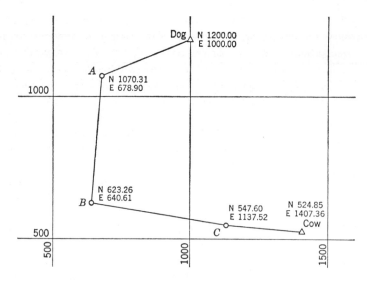

FIGURE 7-14. Adjusted connecting traverse plotted by coordinates.

Mapping Natural and/or constructed topographic features are generally located by field measurements from the traverse stations or from points set at known distances along the traverse courses. The measurements may consist of any convenient combination of angles and distances; any two of these measurements will locate a point. The topics of mapping and plotting traverses are covered in detail in Chapter 9.

Inverse Computations

It is generally necessary to compute the new directions and lengths of the traverse courses that result from the adjustment of the traverse. The process is called *inversing*. This can be done using either the corrected latitudes and departures or the station coordinates. Inversing may also be used in connection with side-shot computations, as will be explained in the next section. In either case, the formulas that are used for inversing are derived from right-angle trigonometry and the Pythagorean theorem. They are as follows:

Inversing from corrected latitude and departure

$$\beta = \tan^{-1}\frac{|\text{Dep}|}{|\text{Lat}|} \qquad (7\text{-}7a)$$

$$L = \frac{|\text{Lat}|}{\cos B} = \frac{|\text{Dep}|}{\sin B} = \sqrt{\text{Lat}^2 + \text{Dep}^2} \qquad (7\text{-}7b)$$

where β = new bearing angle

Dep = corrected departure

Lat = corrected latitude

L = new course length

Recall that θ^{-1} is the inverse or arctangent function. Also, the symbol "| |" stands for absolute (or positive) value. To compute L, use the formula containing Lat when Lat is larger than Dep, and vice versa. If either Lat or Dep is not available, compute it from the final station coordinates, or use the following formulas directly:

Inversing from coordinates (station S to station T)

$$\beta = \tan^{-1}\frac{|E_T - E_S|}{|N_T - N_S|} \qquad (7\text{-}8a)$$

$$L = \sqrt{(E_T - E_S)^2 + (N_T - N_S)^2} \qquad (7\text{-}8b)$$

where E_S and E_T = the eastings (X coordinates) of station S and station T, respectively

N_S and N_T = the northings (Y coordinates) of station S and station T, respectively

It can be seen that Equations 7-7 and 7-8 are, in effect, the same: the latitude of a course is equivalent to the difference in the Y coordinates of the stations, ΔY, and the departure is equivalent to the difference in the X coordinates, ΔX (see Figure 7-15).

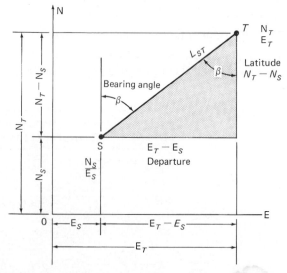

FIGURE 7-15. Geometry for the process of inversing between two points.

Example 7-1

Compute the adjusted bearing and length for course *AB* of the loop traverse shown in Figure 7-11, using its adjusted latitude and departure.

Solution

The adjusted latitude and departure for *AB* are (see Table 7-2)

$$\text{Lat} = -122.02$$

$$\text{Dep} = -680.17$$

From Equation 7-7a, we get a new bearing angle as follows:

$$\beta = \theta^{-1}\left(\frac{680.18}{122.02}\right) = 79.83° = 79°49'47''$$

Because both Lat and Dep are negative, the course is in the SW quadrant and the corrected bearing of *AB* is S 79°49'47'' W (as compared with S 79°49'00'' W in Table 7-1).
From Equation 7-7b, we get a new length as follows:

$$L = \sqrt{122.02^2 + 680.18^2} = 691.04 \text{ ft}$$

(as compared with the measured length of 690.88 ft).
Alternatively, $L = 680.18/\sin 79.83° = 691.04$ ft.

Example 7-2

Compute the adjusted bearing and length for course *BC* of the loop traverse shown in Figure 7-11, using the computed coordinates of stations *B* and *C*.

Solution

The coordinates for *B* and *C* are (see Figures 7-11 and 7-16)

Station *B*: N 734.98   E 691.17
Station *C*: N 908.98   E 100.00

Using Equation 7-8a, we get the new bearing angle as follows:

$$\beta = \tan^{-1}\frac{|100.00 - 691.17|}{|908.98 - 734.98|}$$

$$= \tan^{-1}(+3.3975287) = 73.599° = 73°35'57''$$

It can be seen from Figures 7-11 and 7-16 that course *BC* is in the NW quadrant and the bearing of *BC*, then, is N 73°35'57'' W (as compared with N 73°36'15'' W in Table 7-1).
From Equation 7-8b, we get a new length of *BC* as follows:

$$L = \sqrt{(100.00 - 691.17)^2 + (908.98 - 734.98)^2} = 616.25 \text{ ft}$$

(as compared with its measured length of 616.05 ft).

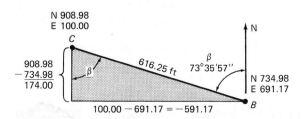

FIGURE 7-16. Illustration for Example 7-2.

Computer Software   Desktop computers and handheld programmable calculators are being used by surveyors for data reduction. Software (canned programs) that performs all common surveying computations, particularly traverse and other horizontal control applications, is readily available at reasonable cost. It would be very difficult for a modern-day surveyor to perform computations by hand (i.e., by using all the formulas directly and making tables as we did in the preceding examples) and still remain competitive in the surveying business.

Computers and calculators are discussed briefly in Section 2-2 and illustrated in Figure 1-2. As previously mentioned, computers are only computational tools. They are helpful only when used by someone who thoroughly understands the underlying concepts and principles of the problems being solved. And the fact that all surveying students *must* first solve problems by hand to understand and develop a feel for them cannot be overemphasized.

Because there are so many types of computer systems as well as surveying software packages, it is impossible to cover them all in an introductory textbook. However, if the student first learns the basics, he or she should be able to read, interpret, and apply the system documentation for most of the hardware and surveying software packages on the market today.

7-3 TRAVERSE AREA COMPUTATIONS

When the courses or sides of a loop traverse represent boundary lines, it is usually necessary to compute the enclosed land area for the deed description or plotted survey plat. Traditionally, the area is expressed in terms of square feet (ft^2), or acres (ac) for relatively large parcels; in SI metric units, area is expressed in terms of square meters (m^2), or hectares (ha). (Refer to Section 2-1 or Appendix B for conversion factors.)

When the tract of land is formed by straight lines only, it is possible to divide up the tract into adjacent triangles, rectangles, and trapezoids and to compute the sum of the areas of all those regular geometric figures. Most surveyors, however, prefer to use the *coordinate method* to determine the enclosed area of a traverse. This method is illustrated in this section. Computational procedures for determining areas enclosed by curved or irregular boundaries are also presented here.

Area by Coordinates

When the rectangular coordinates of each traverse station are known, the *coordinate method* may be used to compute the enclosed area. This method also finds application in cross-section area calculations for route surveys, as discussed in Section 11-2.

A formula for the coordinate method can be derived, but for the purposes of this text, a convenient computational procedure will be outlined and illustrated here instead. The areas of trapezoids are, in effect, being summed with appropriate algebraic signs. The result of the computation is double the area, which must be divided by 2.

The first step is to list the N and E (or Y and X) coordinates of all the stations in a systematic manner. One way to do this is to write them as a series of N/E ratios, as follows:

$$\frac{N_1}{E_1} \diagdown\!\!\!\!\diagup \frac{N_2}{E_2} \diagdown\!\!\!\!\diagup \frac{N_3}{E_3} \cdots \frac{N_n}{E_n} \diagdown\!\!\!\!\diagup \frac{N_1}{E_1}$$

The subscript n stands for the total number of stations in the traverse. The coordinates for the first station are repeated at the end of the sequence, but it really does not matter which is considered the first station (previously, we were using letter symbols—that is, A, B, etc.—instead of numbers to represent the stations).

To perform the computation, first sum the products of the adjacent diagonal terms in the northeast direction (upward and to the right; i.e., E_1N_2, E_2N_3, etc.). Then sum the adjacent diagonal terms in the southeast direction (downward to the right; i.e., N_1E_2, N_2E_3, etc.). Finally, take the difference between those two sums and divide that by 2; the result is the area in either square feet or square meters, depending on the system of units used. This procedure is illustrated for the loop traverse *ABCDE* of Figure 7-11 and Table 7-4. (*Note:* If the sequence of coordinate ratios follows a clockwise path around the traverse, the northeast sum must be subtracted from the southeast sum.)

$$\frac{857.00}{1371.35} \diagdown\!\!\!\!\diagup \frac{734.98}{691.17} \diagdown\!\!\!\!\diagup \frac{908.98}{100.00} \diagdown\!\!\!\!\diagup \frac{239.96}{208.89} \diagdown\!\!\!\!\diagup \frac{100.00}{1169.72} \diagdown\!\!\!\!\diagup \frac{857.00}{1371.35}$$

Sum the products of diagonal terms upward to the right:

$(1371.35)(734.98) + (691.17)(908.98) + (100.00)(239.96)$

$+ (208.89)(100.00) + (1169.72)(857.00) = 2,683,510$

Sum the products of diagonal terms downward to the right:

$(857.00)(691.17) + (734.98)(100.00) + (908.98)(208.89)$

$+ (239.96)(1169.72) + (100.00)(1371.35) = 1,273,529$

Take the difference between the two sums

$$2,683,510 - 1,273,529 = 1,409,981 \text{ ft}^2$$

Divide by 2

$$\text{Area} = \frac{1,409,981}{2} = 704,991 \text{ ft}^2$$

Divide by 43,560 ft²/ac

$$\text{Area} = \frac{704,991}{43,560} = 16.18 \text{ ac}$$

Irregular and Curved Boundaries

Sometimes part of a tract of land may be bounded by an irregular line, such as stream shoreline. And many properties are bounded by the curving portion of a road, that is, by the arc of a circle. The surveyor must be able to compute the enclosed area, even though direct traverse measurements cannot be made to coincide exactly with the irregular or curved part of the boundary. A method that makes use of a scaled drawing, and a device called a *planimeter*, is discussed in Section 10-7. In this section, methods generally used to approximate or compute these areas from field data are discussed.

Offset Measurements When part of a tract of land includes an irregular boundary segment, a loop traverse may be run along the straight-line segments and closed with a straight line established in close proximity to the irregular boundary (see Figure 7-17a). The position of the irregular boundary can then be determined by making perpendicular offset distance measurements (h), from the established traverse line to the boundary, at regular intervals (d).

The coordinate method is used to calculate the area enclosed within the looped straight-line courses. A method called the *trapezoidal rule* may then be used to approximate the area between the traverse line and the irregular boundary. The sum of the two areas represents the total enclosed area of the property. In the trapezoidal rule, it is assumed that the boundary line is actually straight between each offset interval distance (see Figure 7-17b). The smaller the interval d, the more accurate this assumption.

The area between the traverse line and the irregular boundary is approximated by summing all the trapezoidal areas formed by the boundary, the offset distances, and the offset interval(s). The formula for the area of a trapezoid is applied here as Equation 7-9. Because the constant offset interval d forms one of the bases of each trapezoid, it can be factored out, and the following formula can be written:

$$\text{Area} = (d)\left[\frac{h_1 + h_n}{2} + h_2 + h_3 + h_4 + \ldots + h_{n-1} \right] + \frac{h_1 d}{2} + \frac{h_n d}{2} \quad (7\text{-}9)$$

The triangular areas should also be included and are shown at the end of the equation. The use of the trapezoidal rule is illustrated in Example 7-3.

Example 7-3
Perpendicular offsets are measured at regular intervals of 5 m from a traverse line to a curved boundary. The values of the offset distances are given as follows: $h_1 = 3.5$ m, $h_2 = 7.2$ m, $h_3 = 9.7$ m, $h_4 = 12.4$ m, $h_5 = 16.7$ m, $h_6 = 13.5$ m, $h_7 = 7.9$ m, and $h_8 = 3.2$ m. The last interval is 2.7 m. Determine the area between the traverse line and the irregular boundary line.

Solution
From Equation 7-9, the trapezoidal rule, we get

$$A = 5 \times \frac{3.5 + 3.2}{2} + 7.2 + 9.7 + 12.4 + 16.7 + 13.5 + 7.9 = 354 \text{ m}^2$$

The area of the two end triangles is computed as

$$\frac{1}{2} \times 5 \times 3.5 + \frac{1}{2} \times 2.7 \times 3.2 = 13 \text{ m}^2$$

The total irregular area, then, is $354 + 13 = 370$ m² (rounded off).

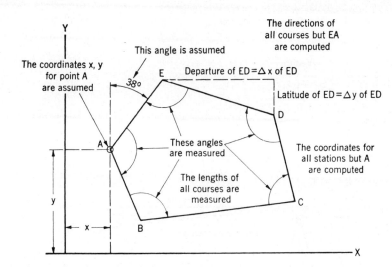

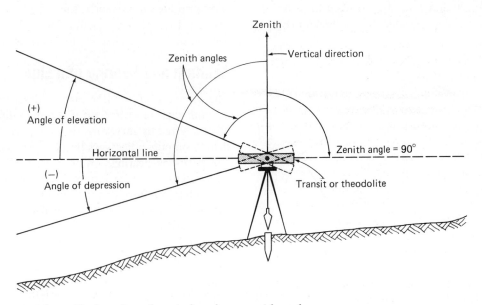

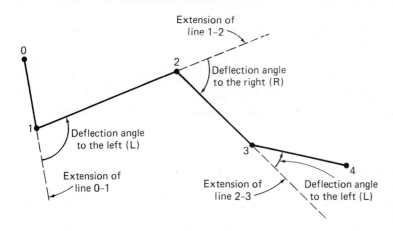

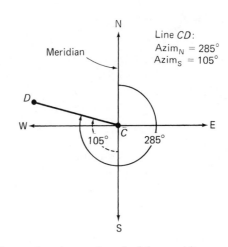

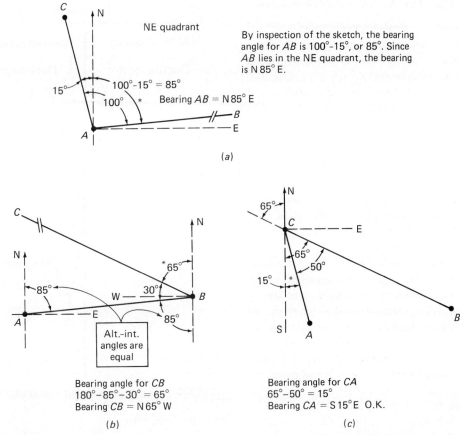

By inspection of the sketch, the bearing angle for *AB* is 100°-15°, or 85°. Since *AB* lies in the NE quadrant, the bearing is N 85° E.

NE quadrant

100°-15° = 85°

Bearing *AB* = N 85° E

(a)

Alt.-int. angles are equal

Bearing angle for *CB*
180°-85°-30° = 65°
Bearing *CB* = N 65° W

(b)

Bearing angle for *CA*
65°-50° = 15°
Bearing *CA* = S 15° E O.K.

(c)

FIGURE 6-13. Solution for Example 6-2; the symbol (*) marks the bearing angle being solved for.

is 46°30'. (This follows from the fact that either alternate interior angles are equal or the back bearing of *EF* has the same numerical value as its forward bearing.) The angle between line *FG* and the south end of the meridian line is the bearing angle of *FG*, or 14°45'. By inspection, the value of the deflection angle is the difference between a straight angle (180°) and the sum of the two bearing angles, or 118°45'. Because *FG* deflects in a clockwise direction from *EF* extended, the deflection angle should be designated as 118°45' *R*.

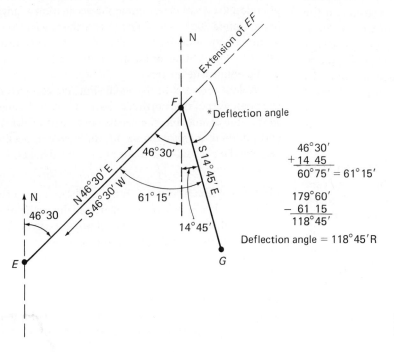

46°30'
+14 45
60°75' = 61°15'

179°60'
− 61 15
118°45'

Deflection angle = 118°45'R

FIGURE 6-14. Illustration for Example 6-3.

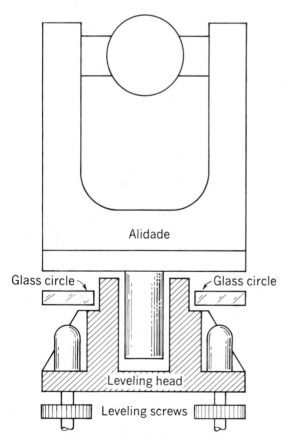

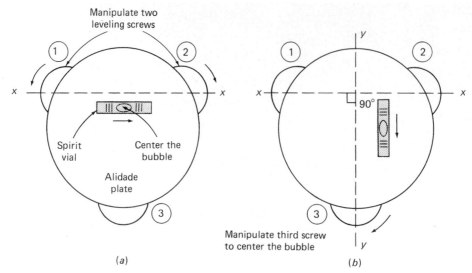

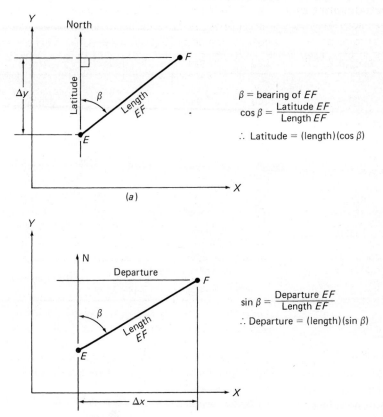

β = bearing of EF

$$\cos \beta = \frac{\text{Latitude } EF}{\text{Length } EF}$$

$\therefore$ Latitude = (length)(cos β)

$$\sin \beta = \frac{\text{Departure } EF}{\text{Length } EF}$$

$\therefore$ Departure = (length)(sin β)

FIGURE 7-8. Definition of the latitude and departure of a line.

onto the north–south axis of the survey. From basic right-angle trigonometry, it is computed as the product of the course length L and the cosine of the bearing angle β:

$$\text{Latitude} = \Delta y = L \cos (\beta) \qquad (7\text{-}1)$$

The *departure* of a traverse course is simply the X component of the line in a rectangular XY coordinate system (see Figure 7-8b). The X axis is usually the same as the *east–west* axis of the survey. A departure, then, may also be defined as the projection of a traverse course onto the east–west axis. From right-angle trigonometry, it is computed as the product of the course length L and the sine of the bearing angle β:

$$\text{Dep} = \Delta x = L \sin (\beta) \qquad (7\text{-}2)$$

Sign Convention   If the traverse course has a northerly (N) bearing, its latitude will have a positive sign (+); a positive latitude is sometimes called the *northing* of the line (see Figure 7-9). If the course has a southerly (S) bearing, its latitude will carry a negative (−) sign; it may also be called the *southing* of the line.

If a line has an easterly (E) bearing, its departure will have a positive sign; a positive departure may be called the *easting* of the line (see Figure 7-9). If the line has a westerly (W) bearing, its departure will be negative; it may be called the *westing* of the line.

When computing a traverse using bearing angles, it is necessary to "manually" apply the appropriate algebraic signs to the latitudes and departures. A line with a SE

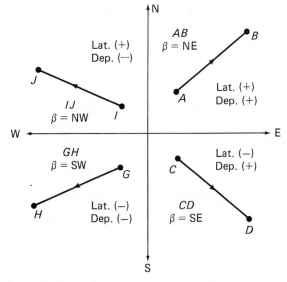

FIGURE 7-9. Algebraic sign convention for latitude and departure.

bearing, for example, would be assigned a negative latitude ($-\Delta y$) and a positive departure ($+\Delta x$).

The computations of latitudes and departures for the traverse shown in Figure 7-6 are summarized in Table 7-1. Note the format of this table—the data for each course are listed on the lines between the station names. The values of the trig functions are rounded to four decimal places for display only.

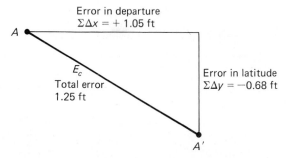

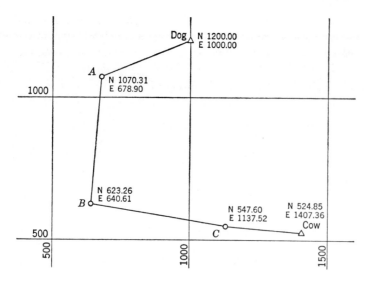

FIGURE 7-14. Adjusted connecting traverse plotted by coordinates.

Mapping   Natural and/or constructed topographic features are generally located by field measurements from the traverse stations or from points set at known distances along the traverse courses. The measurements may consist of any convenient combination of angles and distances; any two of these measurements will locate a point. The topics of mapping and plotting traverses are covered in detail in Chapter 9.

Inverse Computations

It is generally necessary to compute the new directions and lengths of the traverse courses that result from the adjustment of the traverse. The process is called *inversing*. This can be done using either the corrected latitudes and departures or the station coordinates. Inversing may also be used in connection with side-shot computations, as will be explained in the next section. In either case, the formulas that are used for inversing are derived from right-angle trigonometry and the Pythagorean theorem. They are as follows:

Inversing from corrected latitude and departure

$$\beta = \tan^{-1} \frac{|\mathrm{Dep}|}{|\mathrm{Lat}|} \tag{7-7a}$$

$$L = \frac{|\mathrm{Lat}|}{\cos B} = \frac{|\mathrm{Dep}|}{\sin B} = \sqrt{\mathrm{Lat}^2 + \mathrm{Dep}^2} \tag{7-7b}$$

where β = new bearing angle
Dep = corrected departure
Lat = corrected latitude
 L = new course length

Recall that θ^{-1} is the inverse or arctangent function. Also, the symbol "| |" stands for absolute (or positive) value. To compute L, use the formula containing Lat when Lat is larger than Dep, and vice versa. If either Lat or Dep is not available, compute it from the final station coordinates, or use the following formulas directly:

Inversing from coordinates (station S to station T)

$$\beta = \tan^{-1} \frac{|\mathrm{E}_T - \mathrm{E}_S|}{|\mathrm{N}_T - \mathrm{N}_S|} \tag{7-8a}$$

$$L = \sqrt{(\mathrm{E}_T - \mathrm{E}_S)^2 + (\mathrm{N}_T - \mathrm{N}_S)^2} \tag{7-8b}$$

where E_S and E_T = the eastings (X coordinates) of station S and station T, respectively

 N_S and N_T = the northings (Y coordinates) of station S and station T, respectively

It can be seen that Equations 7-7 and 7-8 are, in effect, the same: the latitude of a course is equivalent to the difference in the Y coordinates of the stations, ΔY, and the departure is equivalent to the difference in the X coordinates, ΔX (see Figure 7-15).

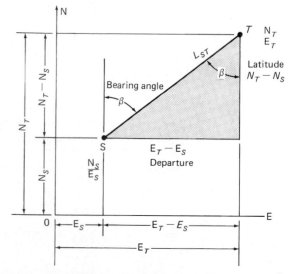

FIGURE 7-15. Geometry for the process of inversing between two points.

with appropriate algebraic signs. The result of the computation is double the area, which must be divided by 2.

The first step is to list the N and E (or Y and X) coordinates of all the stations in a systematic manner. One way to do this is to write them as a series of N/E ratios, as follows:

$$\frac{N_1}{E_1} \diagdown\diagup \frac{N_2}{E_2} \diagdown\diagup \frac{N_3}{E_3} \cdots \frac{N_n}{E_n} \diagdown\diagup \frac{N_1}{E_1}$$

The subscript n stands for the total number of stations in the traverse. The coordinates for the first station are repeated at the end of the sequence, but it really does not matter which is considered the first station (previously, we were using letter symbols—that is, A, B, etc.—instead of numbers to represent the stations).

To perform the computation, first sum the products of the adjacent diagonal terms in the northeast direction (upward and to the right; i.e., E_1N_2, E_2N_3, etc.). Then sum the adjacent diagonal terms in the southeast direction (downward to the right; i.e., N_1E_2, N_2E_3, etc.). Finally, take the difference between those two sums and divide that by 2; the result is the area in either square feet or square meters, depending on the system of units used. This procedure is illustrated for the loop traverse ABCDE of Figure 7-11 and Table 7-4. (*Note:* If the sequence of coordinate ratios follows a clockwise path around the traverse, the northeast sum must be subtracted from the southeast sum.)

$$\frac{857.00}{1371.35} \diagdown\diagup \frac{734.98}{691.17} \diagdown\diagup \frac{908.98}{100.00} \diagdown\diagup \frac{239.96}{208.89} \diagdown\diagup \frac{100.00}{1169.72} \diagdown\diagup \frac{857.00}{1371.35}$$

Sum the products of diagonal terms upward to the right:

(1371.35)(734.98) + (691.17)(908.98) + (100.00)(239.96)
+ (208.89)(100.00) + (1169.72)(857.00) = 2,683,510

Sum the products of diagonal terms downward to the right:

(857.00)(691.17) + (734.98)(100.00) + (908.98)(208.89)
+ (239.96)(1169.72) + (100.00)(1371.35) = 1,273,529

Take the difference between the two sums

$$2{,}683{,}510 - 1{,}273{,}529 = 1{,}409{,}981 \text{ ft}^2$$

Divide by 2

$$\text{Area} = \frac{1{,}409{,}981}{2} = 704{,}991 \text{ ft}^2$$

Divide by 43,560 ft^2/ac

$$\text{Area} = \frac{704{,}991}{43{,}560} = 16.18 \text{ ac}$$

Irregular and Curved Boundaries

Sometimes part of a tract of land may be bounded by an irregular line, such as stream shoreline. And many properties are bounded by the curving portion of a road, that is, by the arc of a circle. The surveyor must be able to compute the enclosed area, even though direct traverse measurements cannot be made to coincide exactly with the irregular or curved part of the boundary. A method that makes use of a scaled drawing, and a device called a *planimeter*, is discussed in Section 10-7. In this section, methods generally used to approximate or compute these areas from field data are discussed.

Offset Measurements   When part of a tract of land includes an irregular boundary segment, a loop traverse may be run along the straight-line segments and closed with a straight line established in close proximity to the irregular boundary (see Figure 7-17a). The position of the irregular boundary can then be determined by making perpendicular offset distance measurements (h), from the established traverse line to the boundary, at regular intervals (d).

The coordinate method is used to calculate the area enclosed within the looped straight-line courses. A method called the *trapezoidal rule* may then be used to approximate the area between the traverse line and the irregular boundary. The sum of the two areas represents the total enclosed area of the property. In the trapezoidal rule, it is assumed that the boundary line is actually straight between each offset interval distance (see Figure 7-17b). The smaller the interval d, the more accurate this assumption.

The area between the traverse line and the irregular boundary is approximated by summing all the trapezoidal areas formed by the boundary, the offset distances, and the offset interval(s). The formula for the area of a trapezoid is applied here as Equation 7-9. Because the constant offset interval d forms one of the bases of each trapezoid, it can be factored out, and the following formula can be written:

$$\text{Area} = (d)\left[\frac{h_1 + h_n}{2} + h_2 + h_3 + h_4 + \ldots + h_{n-1} \right] + \frac{h_1 d}{2} + \frac{h_n d}{2} \qquad (7\text{-}9)$$

The triangular areas should also be included and are shown at the end of the equation. The use of the trapezoidal rule is illustrated in Example 7-3.

Example 7-3

Perpendicular offsets are measured at regular intervals of 5 m from a traverse line to a curved boundary. The values of the offset distances are given as follows: $h_1 = 3.5$ m, $h_2 = 7.2$ m, $h_3 = 9.7$ m, $h_4 = 12.4$ m, $h_5 = 16.7$ m, $h_6 = 13.5$ m, $h_7 = 7.9$ m, and $h_8 = 3.2$ m. The last interval is 2.7 m. Determine the area between the traverse line and the irregular boundary line.

Solution

From Equation 7-9, the trapezoidal rule, we get

$$A = 5 \times \frac{3.5 + 3.2}{2} + 7.2 + 9.7 + 12.4 + 16.7 + 13.5 + 7.9 = 354 \text{ m}^2$$

The area of the two end triangles is computed as

$$\frac{1}{2} \times 5 \times 3.5 + \frac{1}{2} \times 2.7 \times 3.2 = 13 \text{ m}^2$$

The total irregular area, then, is $354 + 13 = 370$ m^2 (rounded off).

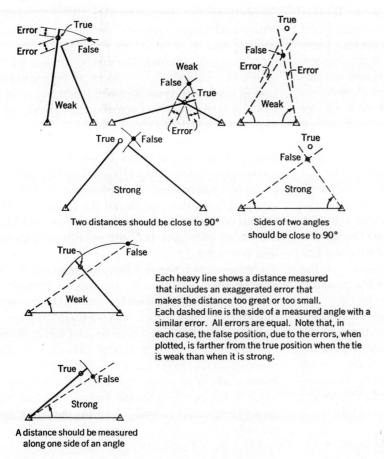

Each heavy line shows a distance measured that includes an exaggerated error that makes the distance too great or too small. Each dashed line is the side of a measured angle with a similar error. All errors are equal. Note that, in each case, the false position, due to the errors, when plotted, is farther from the true position when the tie is weak than when it is strong.

FIGURE 9-13. Strong and weak ties.

the order of their importance. Tie 1 is the most useful for an area map, and tie 2 for a strip map. These two types are used almost exclusively; the others are used under special circumstances.

Angle and Distance Ties Figure 9-14a shows the angle and distance method used to locate two buildings. Two corners of each building are located, and the building dimensions are measured along the sides of the buildings. The field notes for

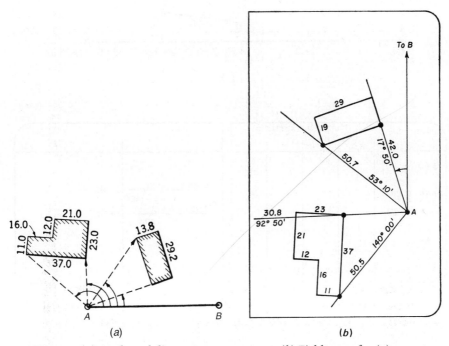

FIGURE 9-14. (*a*) Angle and distance measurements. (*b*) Field notes for (*a*).

the building location are shown in Figure 9-14b. If other buildings are to be built to connect these two existing structures, then the angles and distances must be measured very accurately. If the purpose is only to depict the relative location on a map, then the use of a woven cloth tape or stadia will provide sufficient accuracy for distance measurement. Stadia is a good method of angle and distance measurement for area maps of small areas; it is discussed in detail in the Appendix I.

Plus and Offset Ties   Figure 9-15a illustrates the plus and offset method of making ties for mapping. The traverse line is first marked off in *stations* (see Section 4-2); the stations are lined in with a transit or theodolite. The rear chainman holds the zero of the tape at station 1 + 00; the head chainman estimates the position on the traverse line from which a perpendicular projected from the line would meet the first building corner; in Figure 9-15, the "plus," or distance from station 1 + 00 for the corner, is observed to be +70.

Next, the *offset* from the traverse line is measured, usually with a cloth tape; in this example, it is observed to be a *left offset* of 18.1 ft. (Left and right are determined by facing forward, toward the increasing stations along the traverse line.) For the next corner, the rear chainman holds zero at 2 + 00, and the process is repeated. The dimensions of the building are also measured. A portion of typical field notes is shown in Figure 9-15b.

Estimating the Perpendicular   A reasonably good estimate of the perpendicular direction from the traverse baseline can be obtained by a trial-and-error method called *swinging the arms*. The surveyor stands on the line with arms outstretched, as shown in Figure 9-16a, and swings his or her arms forward; if not pointing to the building corner (or other feature), the surveyor moves as required along the line and repeats the process until a position is reached that lines up with the point to be located. Figure 9-16b shows a somewhat more accurate method, which makes use of a small optical device called a *double pentaprism*. The observer moves forward and back until the objects and the ends of the line are aligned in the window of the pentaprism, and he or she moves left and right until the point to be located is in line with them.

When very accurate offsets are required, the *swing-offset* method may be used. Assume, for example, that a perpendicular distance must be measured from point *P* to a line *AB* (see Figure 9-16c). Set up a transit at point *A*, and sight on point *B*. Swing a tape or level rod as shown; the instrument person will record the shortest distance observed on the tape or rod. On the other hand, to *establish line* at a certain perpendicular distance from *P*, the tape or rod is swung as before; the instrument person sights at the greatest angle reached while observing the proper mark on the rod.

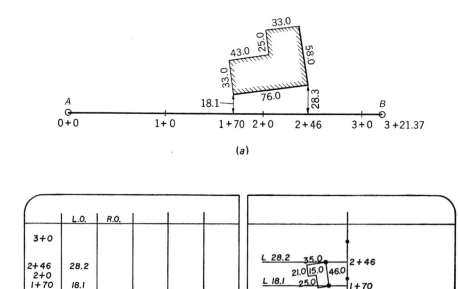

FIGURE 9-15.   (a) Plus and offset measurements. (b) Field notes.

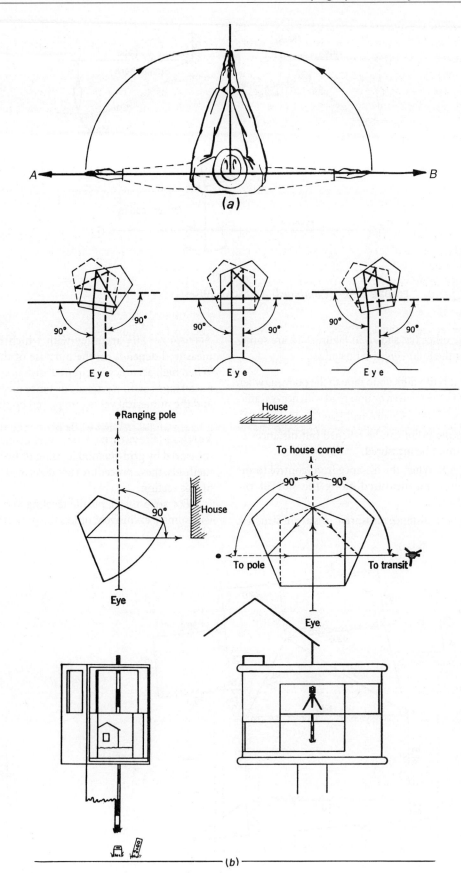

FIGURE 9-16. (*a*) Estimating a perpendicular by swinging the arms. (*b*) The double pentaprism for estimating right angles.

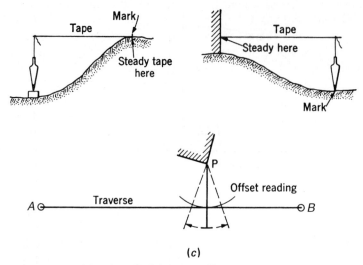

FIGURE 9-16. (*Continued*) (*c*) Swing offset.

Other Ties   The other ties shown in Figure 9-12 are sometimes used under the following circumstances:

Tie 3. When it is too difficult to tape to the point, as when the point is across a river, or on a road with heavy traffic.

Tie 4. For short distances between objects (see Figure 9-17).

Tie 5. When the point can be reached but distances to control cannot be measured.

Tie 6 through 8. When the distance from control to the point cannot be measured along the side of the measured angle.

Tie 9. When both distance measurements are obstructed.

Accuracy   The accuracy with which horizontal ties are measured depends on the purpose of the survey and map. When high accuracy is required, distances are measured with a steel tape (or an electronic distance measuring instrument) and the numerical values are placed on the map.

Vertical (Elevation) Ties   Vertical ties for area maps are measured by grid-method leveling or by radial/stadia survey methods; these procedures are described in subsequent parts of this section.

For strip maps, profile leveling and cross sectioning is used almost exclusively, unless the project is extensive enough

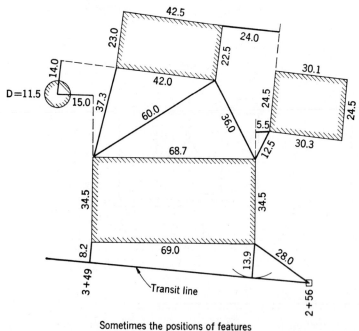

Sometimes the positions of features
are determined by measurements
from other features rather than
from the control line itself

FIGURE 9-17. Locating one feature from another.

to use photogrammetric methods. First, a connecting traverse and a line of benchmarks are established along the approximate centerline of the project. Then a cross section (a short profile) is measured at right angles to the traverse line, usually at each station and half station. These are carried out far enough on each side of the line to cover all possible earthwork that will be required to build the project. Right angles are often estimated by the swing-of-the-arms method. Pluses and offsets to topographic features are also determined.

The elevations along the baseline, as well as the cross-section elevations, can be measured using an automatic level; at each instrument position, a backsight must first be taken on a benchmark or turning point to establish the height of instrument (HI).

Differential leveling is carried out in a manner similar to profile leveling (see Section 5-5), except that more rod shots can usually be observed from one instrument position. Rod readings are taken at each stake and wherever a noticeable *break* in ground slope exists between stakes. The positions of breaks in slope, as well as other topo features, are located by rectangular offset measurements from the nearest grid lines. Breaks must not be omitted because in drawing the contours, it is assumed that the slope is uniform between points where elevations have been determined.

As shown in the field notes (Figure 9-18), the grid intersections are identified by their column and row positions (A1, C2, etc.). As with all leveling work, the first rod reading must be a backsight (+) on a point of known elevation; in this case, it is a city benchmark of elevation 58.791. The HI of the first instrument setup is determined

to be 59.86, and rod shots on all visible grid points are taken from that position. In addition, rod shots are taken on the sewer manholes (MH) in the street because those data will be needed for designing the service connection from any new house or building. (The *invert* elevations at the bottom of the pipes are obtained; this is explained further in Section 11-4.)

The solid black dots at the grid points of Figure 9-19 represent rod shots taken from the first instrument position. When obstructions prevent sighting other points or when the lines of sight become excessive, the level must be moved to a more convenient position. A suitable turning point must first be established before the instrument is moved. Then a new HI is determined, and the work continues as before; the open dots represent rod shots taken from the second instrument position. In this example, it can be seen that two breaks were observed, and their positions were noted in the field record. Finally, a new benchmark is set at grid point D4, a third and last instrument position is established, and the work is closed back on the starting benchmark with a small but acceptable error of closure.

In the office, the rectangular grid is drawn to a suitable scale, and the grid intersections are labeled. The elevation of each point is lettered in, frequently with the dot that marks the grid station also serving as the decimal point in the elevation value. An appropriate contour interval is selected, and the contour lines are sketched in by interpolation between the four sides of each grid square (as described in Section 9-2). (Often, elevations interpolated along grid diagonals do not agree with those interpolated on the sides,

PLOT PLAN PROP. A.G. SMITH					
Sta	+	HI	−	Rod	Elev.
BM	1.07	59.86			58.791
MH				11.62	48.24
MH				9.49	50.37
A1				5.4	54.5
A2				3.7	56.2
A3				1.9	58.0
A4				1.8	58.1
B1				3.4	56.5
B2				3.0	56.9
TP1	6.34	64.45	1.75		58.11
B3				5.1	59.3
B4				5.3	59.1
Brk				5.3	59.1
C1				5.4	59.0
C2				4.9	59.5
C3				4.0	60.4
C4				4.8	59.6
Brk				3.2	61.2
D1				4.7	59.7
D2				3.6	60.8
D3				4.6	59.8
BM-D4	4.16	63.37	5.24		59.21
BM			4.56		58.81
	11.57		11.55		

Ch & Recorder Roberts   Date
π Smith   Hazy
Rod Jones   72°F.
"R" in Corey F.H. Opp. Property   Level
West of Prop. Invert   Berger 12978
East. "   "   "

Enumeration

D
C
B
A
          1 2 3 4 Street

22' N from B2   Arith Ck.
                                58.79
                                +11.57
                                70.36
                                −11.55
20' N from C, 30' E from 2   58.81

Top Conc. Prop. Mon. N.E. Cor. Prop.
Error +.02

FIGURE 9-18. Form of field notes for a plot plan.

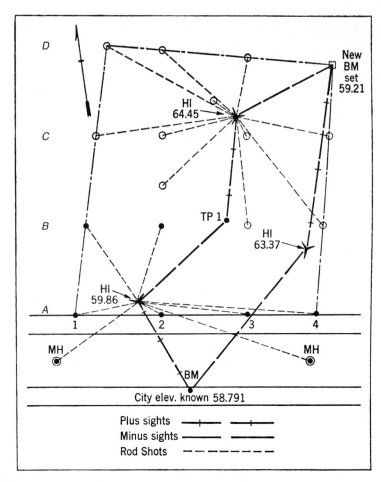

FIGURE 9-19. Leveling procedure for a plot plan.

due to the "warped" shape of the terrain.) A complete sketch of the contours located from the field notes shown in the preceding example is presented in Figure 9-20*a*; the grid elevation values would not be shown on the final plot plan. The procedure is further clarified by showing the location of only the 58-ft contour, in Figure 9-20*b*.

Radial Survey Field Methods

A radial survey typically begins with the establishment of a control network, usually a loop traverse, on or around the area to be mapped. Numerous side shots are taken from each control station to establish the horizontal and vertical positions of topographic features.

The locations of the traverse stations must be carefully planned to reduce field time and improve the accuracy of the survey. Adjacent stations must be intervisible. They should be placed around the parcel to be mapped, so that all important topographic features can be readily observed. (Sometimes it may be necessary to run a short open traverse from one of the loop-traverse stations to obtain additional details for the map.)

The traverse stations should preferably be located not more than about 500 ft (150 m) apart. It is generally best to err on the side of having too many stations rather than

establishing too few. Although this requires more setups, the shorter sight distances tend to reduce the field time and to improve accuracy.

With the advent of new and less expensive technology, surveyors have replaced the transit and level rod method with the total station instrument. Using a prism pole, typically 5 ft high and expandable up to 12 ft, the precision of the survey can be increased while the time to complete it is decreased. The procedures are basically identical; the major difference occurs in field data records. The traditional field book has been replaced by an on-board data collector, which is later connected to a desktop computer system at the office. There, the information is downloaded from the data collector, instantly reduced, and a map image produced. The survey data are coded in the field so that the computer recognizes the type of data point observed. Simply put, the field crews are effectively drafting the map in the field.

Choosing Points for Side Shots   One of the advantages of the stadia or radial method over the grid method of topo surveying is that only certain key points need be observed for locating contours. In general, these *control points* are *the points between which the ground has a reasonably uniform slope.*

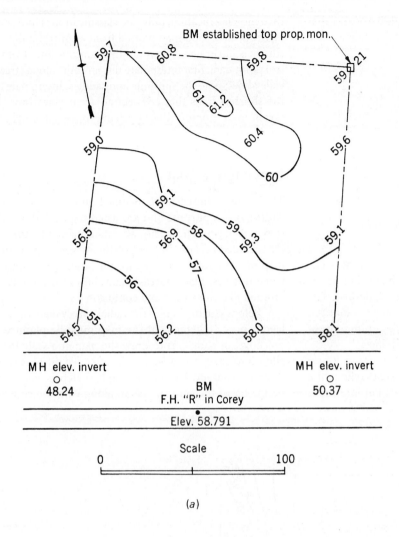

(a)

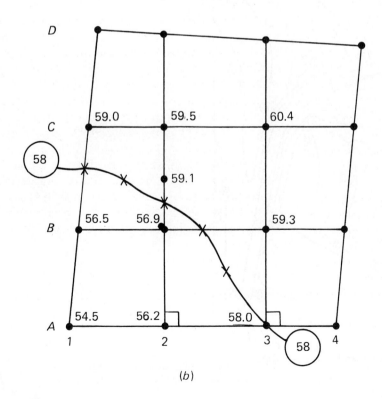

(b)

FIGURE 9-20. (a) Partially completed plot plan showing interpolated contour lines. (b) A detail of the plot plan showing the interpolation of the 58-ft contour line.

Some of the most common topographic features that are considered to be control points are listed as follows (see Figure 9-21):

1. Summits
2. Saddles (low points in ridges)
3. Depressions
4. Valley profiles
5. Ridge profiles
6. Boundary and building corners
7. Profiles along buildings and boundaries
8. Profiles along toes (bottoms) of slopes
9. Profiles along brows of hills (tops of slopes)
10. Profiles along shoulders

Because the ground rarely slopes uniformly, the accuracy of the map depends on how small a change in slope is considered significant for the contour interval desired. The ability to recognize and select control points, so that the desired map accuracy can be obtained with a minimum of field work, is a skill that develops with experience.

Figure 9-21 illustrates the typical control points found on a project site. The numbers in the small circles refer to the preceding list. Although many of the points fall into more

than one classification, only one classification is indicated. In Figure 9-22, a topo map plotted from a control point radial survey is illustrated. When plotting contour lines from control point data, first interpolate the contours along stream or valley lines; note the summits and saddles. Interpolate along the shortest lines that connect adjacent elevations. Then sketch in the contour lines freehand in the same manner as for the grid method.

Drawing the Map

The features chosen to be included on the map depend, of course, on its purpose and are usually specified before the survey is begun. Ordinarily, all data obtained by the survey are included because the cost of the survey is high, and the map may eventually be used for purposes never considered when it is first made. Occasionally, however, some data are omitted to avoid clutter and confusion.

Before starting to plot the radial survey data, the general layout or arrangement of the map must be planned. The objective, of course, is to draw the map at a scale that will allow it to be read and used for its intended purpose with the desired accuracy. Usually, a rough sketch is made of the perimeter of the control system along with the controlling

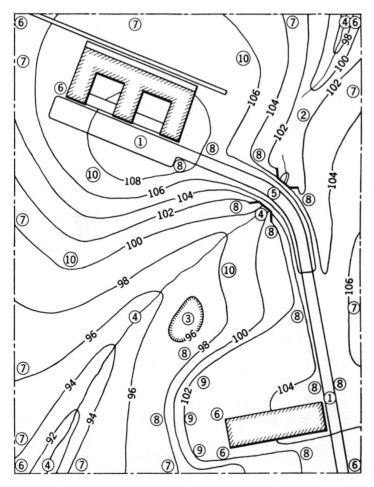

FIGURE 9-21. Key points for locating contours by stadia.

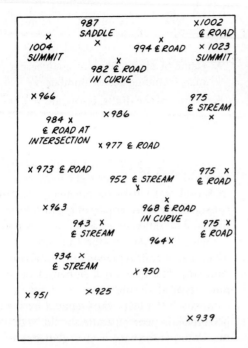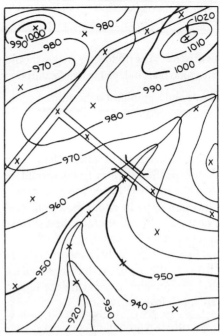

FIGURE 9-22. Plotting topography from control point data. (*Madsen, David A.; Shumaker, Terence M., Civil Drafting Technology, 1st Edition, © 1983. Reprinted by permission of Pearson Education, Inc., Upper Saddle River, NJ.*)

external topographic observations (see Figure 9-23). This serves as an aid in selecting a suitable scale so that the map will fit on the drawing paper.

As described in Section 9-1, the first step in actually drawing the map is to plot the control traverse at the chosen or specified scale. Either the coordinate method, the tangent-offset method, or the protractor method can be used. A protractor should be used with great care because this is the greatest source of error. Light construction lines are drawn at right angles through the traverse stations to represent the 0° azimuth and the quadrants; it is usually preferable to establish the 0° azimuth parallel to the side of the drawing paper, if possible. Naturally, the last line drawn should close onto the beginning station; if not, the stations should be shifted proportionately to eliminate the error.

After the traverse has been plotted and closed graphically, the elevation of each traverse station is marked on the paper.

The *side shots are then plotted by protractor and scale* from their respective stations. The protractor is used to lay out the azimuth of the shot (or the clockwise angle from the previous station), and the scale is used to lay out its distance from the station. As each side shot is plotted, its elevation is marked; often, the pencil point that marks its position is used as a decimal point in the marked elevation. As the plotting progresses, all topographic details are drawn and identified, to avoid any questions about which shots have been marked on the drawing.

Usually, the entire map must have a uniform standard of accuracy so that data may be determined anywhere on it with equally accurate results. When maps are used for design, it should be possible to determine distances, elevations, and angles from them by scaling. Because the survey on which a map is based can be readily made more accurate than can any drafting procedure, map accuracy is limited mainly by the accuracy of drafting.

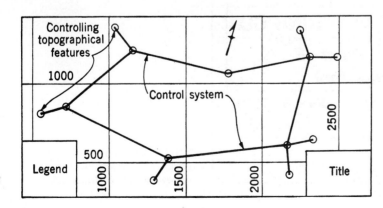

FIGURE 9-23. Sketch map with sheet arrangement completed.

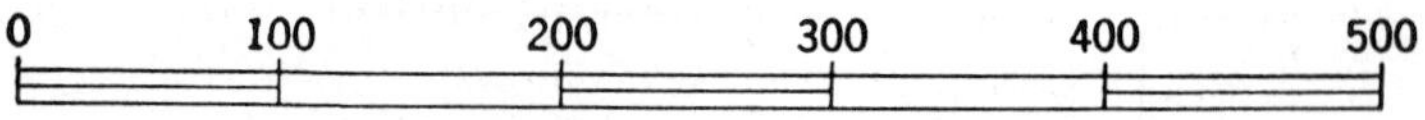

FIGURE 9-24. A graphical scale, in feet.

Standard Map Features   The following items should *always* be included on a topo map, independent of its purpose:

1. A statement of scale and a graphical indication of scale
2. A suitable title block and legend
3. A north arrow

Scale   The importance of a statement of scale, such as 1 in = 50 ft, or a representative fraction such as 1/600, should be obvious, particularly if the map will be used to read meaningful distance or location data. In addition, a graphical representation of scale is useful in case the map sheet shrinks or expands or is reproduced at an unknown scale. A graphical bar scale (see Figure 9-24) will change length in proportion to any change in the size of the drawing; distance on the map can be determined by comparing the length between two mapped points with the bar scale.

Title   An appropriate title is required, of course, to completely identify the map. Generally, the title should contain the following:

1. Identification and location of the area mapped
2. Name of the individual or company for whom the map is made

3. Name of the surveyor or engineering firm making the map, including license number
4. Names of the draftsperson and responsible engineer or surveyor
5. Date of the survey and/or map preparation

The title may be placed in any suitable location on the map, although the lower right-hand corner of the sheet is most common. Often, the statement of scale and/or graphical bar scale is included as part of the title. Examples of the same title used for different purposes are shown in Figure 9-25.

Figure 9-25a shows the kind of title that might be used by a consulting firm preparing the map for a manufacturing company. The title block shown in Figure 9-25b may be more typical of the form used by the manufacturing company if the map was prepared by the company's own personnel. In general, a title should be designed to give the maximum information at a glance, and should not be embellished with ornate details. Certain items, however, should be emphasized by larger and heavier letters so that the map can be quickly selected from others in a file (i.e., the name of the client and the location of the survey).

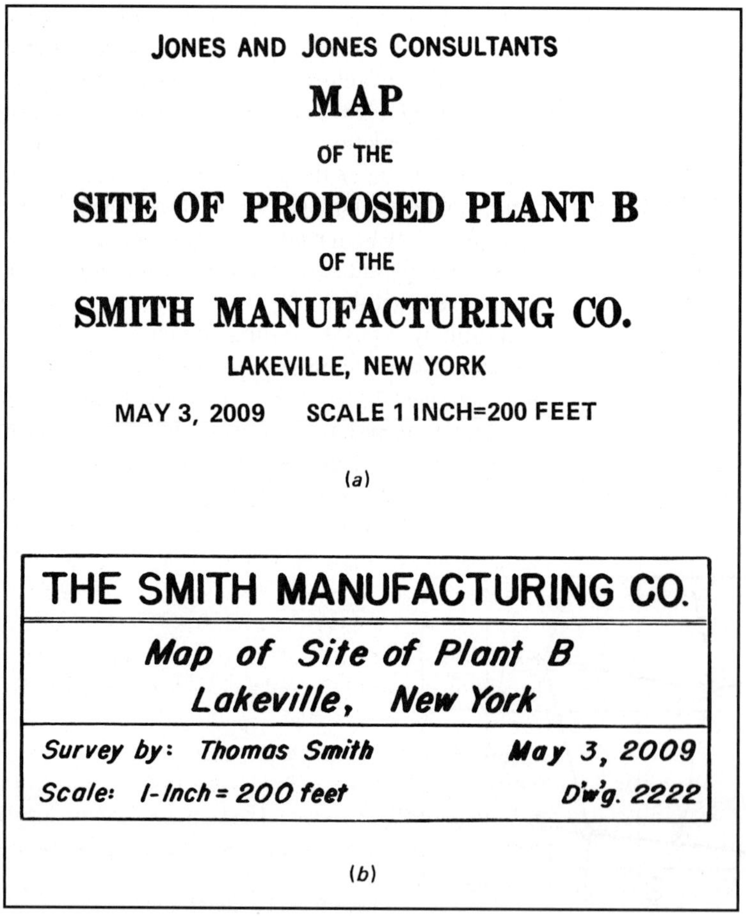

FIGURE 9-25. Typical map title blocks. The surveyor's license number should be included.

North Arrow For proper orientation when reading and using a map, it must have a noticeable (but not excessively ornate) north arrow, as shown in Figure 9-26. A note should be placed next to the arrow stating whether it represents true, magnetic, grid, or assumed north. If there is no note, it is generally assumed that the arrow points to true north.

Topographic Symbols The use of consistent symbols for representing small-scale topographic features is important for the clarity of the map; on large-scale maps, the features can usually be recognized and are easily labeled. Symbols are useful for indicating the locations of trees, for distinguishing between roads and paths, for outlining the limits of woods and swamps, and for accomplishing similar purposes. Some typical topographic symbols are shown in Figure 9-27. A list or *legend* that gives the meaning of these and any other symbols should be included on the map.

Lettering Generally, vertical letters are more quickly read than slant or inclined letters (although this is a matter of personal preference). Special lettering devices that guide the pen, such as the Leroy lettering device, are commonly used for uniformity and neatness in the appearance of the finished map.

Final Map The final map may be traced from the working drawing on which the traverse and radial shots were plotted; the control system can be omitted from the final drawing for clarity. Often, the work is done in ink. (Colored inks may sometimes be used to improve the appearance of a special-purpose map. Black ink might be used for buildings and roads, blue ink for water, green ink for vegetation, and brown ink for contour lines.)

True North

FIGURE 9-26. A typical north arrow for a map.

Computer-Automated Plotting Topographic maps can be prepared automatically, using a method commonly called *computer-aided drafting* (CAD). Surveyors are using modern CAD systems to produce high-quality maps, as well as plats. (A computer-generated subdivision plat is illustrated in Figure 8-9.) Contour lines can be plotted automatically (Figure 9-28) from *X*, *Y*, and *Z* coordinates that are stored electronically in the computer. The array of data is called a *digital terrain model*. The data can be collected in the field using "total-station" equipment, including an electronic field book.

A typical CAD workstation consists of a keyboard, digitizer board, printer, plotter, and monitor for graphic display. The graphic display screen can be used by the surveyor for editing data, or even for subdivision design; this process is called *interactive graphics*. Portions of large drawings can be *windowed*, or viewed on the screen at enlarged scales for interactive design. The finished map is prepared on a *drum plotter* using vellum or Mylar sheets; laser plotters provide the ability to produce different line weights and colors.

9-4 BASIC PHOTOGRAMMETRY

Topographic maps of relatively large land areas [i.e., roughly 75 ac (30 ha) or more] can usually be obtained in less time and at lower cost using *photogrammetry*, rather than using stadia or other field surveying methods. Photogrammetry involves making precise measurements of images on *aerial photographs* (photos taken from an aircraft) to determine the relative locations of points and objects on the ground. Distances and elevations can be accurately measured, and both planimetric and topographic maps can be prepared from the photos; map scales may vary from 1/1,000,000 to 1/250, and contour intervals as small as 1 ft (0.3 m) can be plotted.

Photogrammetry is often used by government agencies to prepare general-purpose topo maps. It is also a particularly important tool for preparing special-purpose maps that are used to plan and design highways, pipelines, reservoirs, flood-control systems, land-use projects, and other extensive infrastructure works. It can be useful in property surveying to provide rough base maps for relocating existing boundary lines. The point of beginning and other property corners of a tract of land may be identified and located with respect to identifiable features on the photo to facilitate the subsequent ground survey of the tract.

Although field surveying work is considerably reduced when photogrammetry is used for mapping, it is not eliminated completely. A number of clearly defined, well-distributed control points must be selected on the photographs and located on the ground for horizontal position and elevation by precise field survey methods. The positions are plotted on the map sheet and serve as reference for locating features from the photographs. The accuracy of a map prepared from aerial photos depends to a large extent on the density and accuracy of the ground control survey.

Photogrammetry is actually part of a more extensive discipline called *remote sensing*. In addition to conventional photography, remote sensing includes the use of data gathered from infrared and thermal scanning devices; remote sensing instruments can be carried in orbiting satellites as well as in airplanes. In addition to providing quantitative information for planimetric and topographic mapping purposes, remote sensing images allow identification and analysis of natural resources such as surface water, woodlands, soils, and farmland. Even water pollution can be detected using remote sensing. The qualitative examination and analysis of remote sensing data is called *photographic interpretation*. It is particularly useful for regional planning and resource management studies.

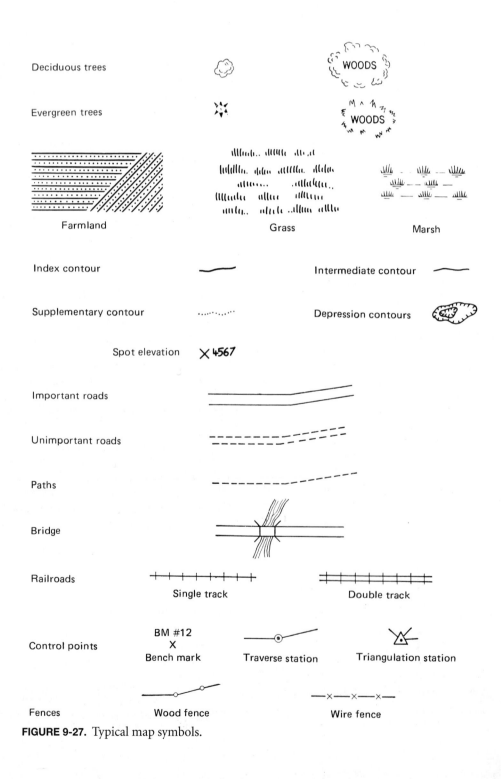

FIGURE 9-27. Typical map symbols.

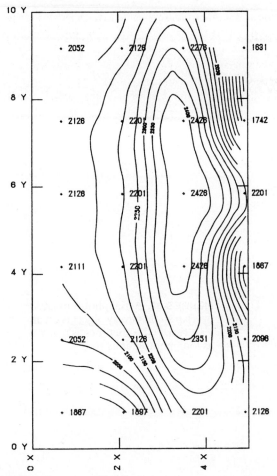

FIGURE 9-28. Contour lines generated automatically by a computer-controlled plotter. (*B. A. Barry, Construction Measurements,* © *1973. Reprinted with permission of John Wiley & Sons, Inc.*)

Basic Principles

Aerial photography can provide either *vertical photos* or *oblique photos*, depending on the orientation of the camera axis. Vertical photos are taken with the camera (or optical) axis aligned in the direction of gravity, whereas oblique photos are taken with the axis intentionally tilted away from a vertical position (see Figure 9-29). The aerial photograph

shown in Figure 1-3 is an example of a vertical photo. In a vertical photo, the photographic plane is parallel to the horizontal reference plane or datum; vertical photos are generally more useful for mapping purposes than oblique photos.

Aerial photographs are taken along a series of overlapping paths, or *flight strips*, as shown in Figure 9-30. The *end lap*, along the direction of flight, is about 60 percent; each pair of the adjacent overlapping photos is called a *stereopair*. By viewing stereopairs with special optical equipment, it is possible to observe a three-dimensional image of the overlap area, to discern ground relief, and to plot ground contour lines on a map. The *side lap* between adjacent flight strips is usually about 20 percent; two or more side-lapping strips are called a *block* of photos. A block of photos can be pieced together to form a composite *photomap* or *mosaic*. An aerial mosaic can be used directly as a planimetric map of the photographed area.

Vertical Photo Geometry To make meaningful measurements on an aerial photograph, it is necessary to know its scale. Figure 9-31 is a schematic diagram showing the basic geometry of a vertical photo taken over horizontal ground. The scale of the photo is, by definition, the ratio of the photo distance *ab* to the corresponding distance on the ground, *AB*. Because the ratios of corresponding sides of similar triangles are equal, we can write

$$\text{Scale} = \frac{ab}{AB} = \frac{f}{H} \qquad (9\text{-}1)$$

where f = image distance
H = object distance

The image distance is equal to the camera lens *focal length*, that is, the distance from the plane in which light rays are focused (converge to a point) to the center of the lens. The object distance is the height of the camera lens above the ground, or *flying height*.

It is seen from Equation 9-1 that, for a fixed camera focal length, the scale of the photograph varies inversely with the flying height; in other words, the greater the altitude of the camera above the ground, the smaller the photo scale. Also, for a fixed flying height, the photo scale increases with increasing camera focal length. Because the ground is not

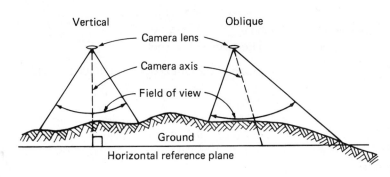

FIGURE 9-29. Vertical aerial photographs are most useful for mapping. The axis of the camera is aligned with gravity.

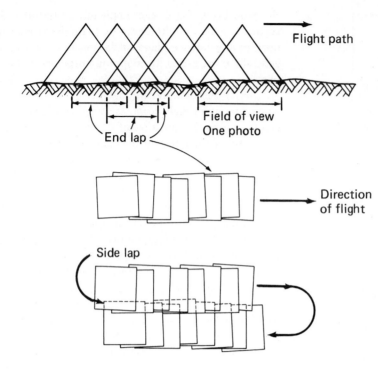

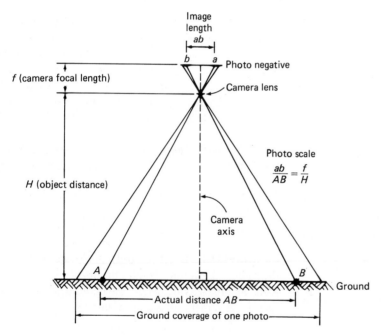

FIGURE 9-30. Aerial photos must overlap so that every object is on at least two, and sometimes as many as four, photographs.

FIGURE 9-31. The scale of a vertical photo.

likely to be perfectly level over large areas, the photo scale actually varies from point to point on the negative or print; for many applications, however, it is acceptable to use an average flying height for determining an average photographic scale.

Example 9-1

A camera with a 200-mm focal length is used to take a block of vertical aerial photographs. The average camera height above ground is 2000 m. Determine the photo scale.

Solution

Using Equation 9-1, we get

$$\text{Scale} = 0.200\,\text{m}/2000\,\text{m} = 1/10{,}000 \text{ or } 1{:}10{,}000$$

Example 9-2

It is required to obtain aerial photos of a large tract of land at a scale of 1 in = 2000 ft, using a camera with a 6-in focal length. What should the average flying height above ground be?

Solution
Using Equation 9-1, we can write

$$1\,in/2000\,ft = 6\,in/height$$
$$and\ Height = (6\,in)(32,000\,ft/in) = 12,000\,ft$$

It is possible to determine the scale of an aerial photo when the flying height or camera focal length is not known. For example, suppose the length of an airport runway seen on a vertical photo is measured to be 4.17 in. From ground survey measurements, or from a map of known scale, the actual length of the runway is found to be 1250 ft. The scale of the photo, then, is simply 4.17 in/1250 ft, or 1 in = 300 ft (1:3600). If the terrain is fairly level, it could be assumed that the computed scale is reasonably accurate for scaling the dimensions of other features on the photo.

Photo Coordinate System   The positions of features seen on a vertical photo can be measured in terms of rectangular coordinates. The coordinate system has its origin at a point called the *center of collimation* or *principal point*. This point is, in effect, the true center of the photo, where the light reflected from the ground strikes the photo negative at a right angle. Most aerial cameras usually have *fiducial marks* that photograph as silhouettes on the sides or in the corners of the photo (Figure 9-32).

The intersection of *fiducial lines* that connect opposite pairs of the fiducial marks is the center of collimation. The fiducial marks are set at fixed distances across the photograph so that any possible shrinkage or expansion of the photographic paper can be detected and corrected for. The location of any feature on the photo is defined by its X and Y coordinates, measured from the center of collimation. The X axis is usually the fiducial line parallel to the direction of flight. Distances and directions of lines located on the photo can be computed from the basic coordinate geometry formulas.

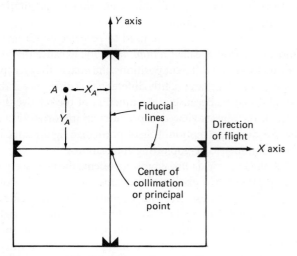

FIGURE 9-32. Side fiducial marks typically appear on an aerial photograph. Rectangular coordinates of images on the photo are measured from the principal point at the center of the photograph, located by the fiducial marks.

Photocoordinates can be measured with an ordinary engineer's scale. For better accuracy, a special *microrule* may be used; this micrometer device allows measurements to within ±0.0005 in. More sophisticated optical instruments, called *comparators*, can be used to determine photocoordinates with even greater precision.

Systematic errors due to lens distortion, refraction, and other sources can be reduced by suitable methods. Photocoordinates can be transformed to the state plane coordinate system if two or more ground "control" points of known position are visible on the photo.

Relief Displacement   The difference in the position of an object or point on a vertical photo compared with its true planimetric position is called *relief displacement*. It is caused by the change in elevation of the various ground features with reference to the datum plane (i.e., the average ground elevation). This can be seen by considering the photographic image of a tall vertical object, such as a smokestack, as shown in Figure 9-33. The paths of light from the bottom and top of the stack are different, causing the top of the stack to be seen in a different position on the photo than the bottom of the stack; in reality, of course, the top and bottom of the stack have one and the same rectangular coordinate position on the ground.

Relief displacement occurs in a radial direction, that is, along lines emanating from the center of the photo. At the center, there is no relief displacement at all; the farther the object is from the photo center, the greater the relief displacement is. From the geometry of a vertical photograph, the relationship among the amount of relief displacement, d, the flying height, H, the height of the displaced point, h, and the radial distance to the point, r, can be determined. This relationship can be used to compute the vertical heights of buildings and other objects seen on the photo, using the following equation:

$$h = \frac{d \times H}{r} \qquad (9\text{-}2)$$

The amount of displacement and the radial distance can be measured with a scale or microrule; the flying height above the ground must be known.

Example 9-3
For the smokestack illustrated in Figure 9-33, it is known that the camera height is 1000 ft above the base of the stack. The relief displacement from the bottom to the top of the stack is measured to be 1.95 in, and the radial distance from the center of collimation to the top of the stack is measured to be 5.45 in. Determine the height of the chimney above the ground.

Solution
Applying Equation 9-2, we get

$$h = \frac{1.95 \times 1000}{5.45} = 358\ ft$$

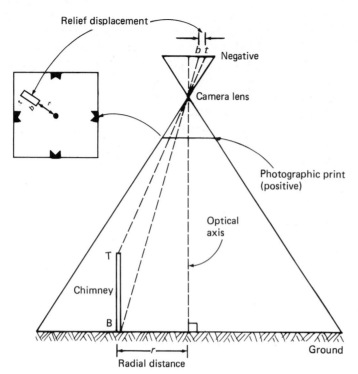

FIGURE 9-33. Because of relief displacement, the top of the chimney (T) and the bottom (B) appear displaced by the distance bt on the negative or photographic print.

The locations of points on a vertical photo can be adjusted with respect to relief displacement by laying off distances along radial lines equal to $d = rh/H$; these corrected positions can be used to determine true angles, lengths, and areas. Also, special instruments can be used to produce *orthophotos* from original vertical aerial photographs, using a process called *differential rectification*.

Rectification eliminates the relief displacements, effectively raising or lowering every image on the photo to the same horizontal plane. The resulting orthophoto is geometrically equivalent to a planimetric map, which shows the true positions of objects and points; in other words, after rectification, the top and bottom of the smokestack in Figure 9-33 would appear at the same position on the orthophoto. A mosaic of adjoining orthophotos can be constructed to form a large *orthophotomap*. Contours can then be superimposed on it to form a *topographic orthophotomap*. These maps are useful to civil engineers, technicians, planners, surveyors, geologists, foresters, and other professionals.

Stereoscopic Plotting of Topo Maps

One of the most significant applications of photogrammetry is the preparation of topographic maps that show the shape of the ground, as well as the positions of natural and cultural features, for large land areas. Special instruments called *stereoplotters* make it possible for an operator both to observe a three-dimensional image of the ground by viewing overlapping aerial photographs and to plot ground elevation contour lines on a map sheet. These instruments use the basic principles of *stereoscopic depth perception* in their operation.

Principles of Stereovision   Depth perception is the mental process of judging the relative distances of different objects in the field of view. There are various visual clues that enable a person to perceive depth or to see the world in three dimensions. One of the most important factors is the ability to use *binocular vision*, that is, the ability to see with two eyes.

Depth perception using binocular vision is called *stereoscopic viewing*. With binocular vision, the optical axes of the two eyes converge at a point when they focus on an object. The angle at which the lines of sight intersect is called the *parallactic angle*; the closer the object is to the viewer, the larger is the parallactic angle, and vice versa. Most people with normal vision have a remarkable ability to detect even slight changes in the parallactic angle, thereby facilitating accurate depth perception.

Another important clue used to perceive depth using binocular vision is called *retinal disparity*. Because the two eyes are located at different positions, the images they receive of any given object are slightly different; this difference is the retinal disparity. Because it is a function of the relative distance of the objects viewed, it provides an important visual clue for depth perception. It is of particular significance in photogrammetric stereoplotting applications.

A single vertical photograph represents the view seen by one eye. When two photos of the same area are made from slightly different positions, and arranged so that the left eye sees only the left photo and the right eye sees only the right photo, binocular vision is established; the viewer can then distinguish depth or relief in what appears to be a three-dimensional image. The two photographs are called a *stereopair*, as previously mentioned. A device called a *mirror*

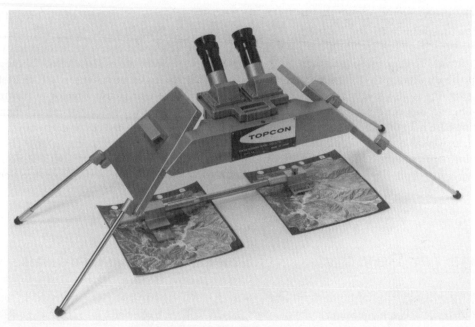

FIGURE 9-34. A mirror stereoscope used for making measurements on aerial photographs. (*Courtesy of Topcon Instrument Corporation of America.*)

stereoscope can be used to view a stereopair of aerial photographs in three-dimensional perspective (Figure 9-34).

There are many types of stereoscopic plotting instruments that vary in accuracy and cost.

Ground Control and Project Planning

Photogrammetry requires *ground control* to provide a way of orienting the photographic images to actual points on the ground. This makes it necessary to conduct field surveys for establishing a network of photogrammetric control points. The points must be clearly identifiable on the photos. Their horizontal and vertical positions on the ground (i.e., rectangular coordinates and elevations) must be accurately determined by control survey methods.

Usually, photogrammetric control surveys are conducted after the aerial photos have been obtained. This ensures that well-defined points at suitable locations on the photos can be selected before field work begins. Typical objects that provide suitable control positions are road intersections, manhole covers, building corners, etc. In areas where existing points suitable for control are not available, artificial positions or targets called *panel points* may be placed on the ground before the aerial photos are taken; this process is called *paneling*. The size of the target depends on the scale of the photo (Figure 9-35). It may be a painted plywood or heavy cloth cross placed with its center over the control position.

The cost of ground control work ranges from 25 to 50 percent of the total cost for a photogrammetric mapping project. Because accurate ground control is directly related

to the accuracy of the finished map, the control survey procedure should be very carefully planned. An appropriate degree of accuracy should be specified, and the required field procedures and techniques must be selected. Generally, the horizontal control points and elevation benchmarks are monumented and witnessed. State plane coordinates are best used for defining horizontal position,

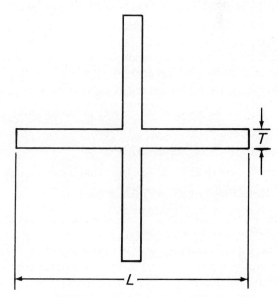

FIGURE 9-35. Photogrammetric panel point. The target dimensions depend on the photo scale. For example, at a scale of 1 in = 200 ft, L = 2 ft and T = 4 in; at a scale of 1 in = 2000 ft, L = 25 ft and T = 30 in.

and elevations should be referenced to mean sea level by differential leveling from National Geodetic Survey benchmarks.

Because the accuracy of a photogrammetric map also depends on the quality of the aerial photos used, thorough *flight planning* is also a very important aspect of a photogrammetric mapping project. A flight plan includes an existing base map that shows the entire area to be photographed, as well as written specifications related to camera and film requirements, flying height, end and side lap amounts, and so on. The flight plan depends largely on the basic purpose of the project and the desired scale of the finished map.

The number of overlapping flight lines should be minimized to reduce the expense of the photography; they are generally oriented north and south or east and west. The season of the year is also a factor in planning the project; normally, the photos are not taken when the ground is obscured by leaves on trees or deep snow. Consideration of weather conditions is also important. The best condition, of course, is a cloudless day with minimal atmospheric haze or smog and little wind or air turbulence.

Questions for Review

1. What is the chief characteristic of a topographic map?

2. What is the difference between a plat and a plot plan?

3. Define *scale* as it pertains to a map. What is an RF?

4. Which is a larger scale, 1:200 or 1:2000?

5. What is the first step in drawing a topographic map? List and briefly describe three methods to accomplish it.

6. Define *contour line* and *contour interval*.

7. What are five important rules for contour lines?

8. What is the basic assumption for contour line interpolation?

9. What is a horizontal tie? When is it strongest?

10. What is a double pentaprism used for?

11. Briefly describe the grid method of contour surveying.

12. Briefly discuss the basic principles of radial surveying.

13. What is trigonometric leveling?

14. What is the difference between HI and h.i.?

15. List five typical control points used for a topo survey.

16. List and briefly describe three items always shown on a map.

17. What is photogrammetry?

18. What are end lap and side lap? What is a stereopair?

19. Briefly describe two different ways to determine the scale of an aerial photograph.

20. What are fiducial marks?

21. What is relief displacement?

22. What is an orthophoto?

23. Briefly describe the basics of stereovision.

24. What is meant by *ground control* in photogrammetry?

Practice Problems

1. Convert a scale of 1 in = 50 ft to an RF.

2. Convert a scale of 1 in = 200 ft to an RF.

3. If a map scale is 1:10,000, what does a 1-in length represent in terms of feet? What does a 10-mm length represent in terms of meters?

4. If a map scale is 1:50,000, what does a 1-in length represent in terms of miles? What does a 1-cm length represent in terms of kilometers?

5. Using an engineer's scale, determine the distances represented by the following lines:

   _____ 1 in = 20 ft

   _____ 1 in = 200 ft

   _____ 1 in = 50 ft

   _____ 1 in = 4000 ft

   _____ 1:24,000

6. Using an engineer's scale, determine the distances represented by the following lines:

   _____ 1 in = 10 ft

   _____ 1 in = 1000 ft

   _____ 1 in = 500 ft

   _____ 1 in = 400 ft

   _____ 1:60,000

7. What should the scale of a map be if distances on it must be read to the nearest 1 ft?

8. What should the scale of a map be if distances on it must be read to the nearest 0.2 ft?

9. What should the RF of a map be if distances on it must be measured to the nearest 1 m?

10. What should the RF of a map be if distances on it must be measured to the nearest 1 dm?

11. Draw a grid 6 in wide by 7 in long with 1-in intersections, and place the given elevations at the intersections in the same arrangement as follows.

   a. Draw the 5-ft contours. (No depression contours needed.)

77.0	73.0	68.0	77.0	81.0	85.0	77.0
77.0	71.0	80.0	86.0	83.0	95.0	85.0
80.0	72.0	80.0	95.0	78.0	85.0	89.0
79.0	86.0	77.0	82.0	83.0	73.0	84.0
78.0	80.0	86.0	72.0	73.0	68.0	80.0
80.0	71.0	75.0	79.0	68.0	62.0	72.0
84.0	76.0	68.0	73.0	74.0	67.0	60.0
85.0	73.0	65.0	69.0	72.0	65.0	61.0

   b. Draw the 1-ft contours. (No depression contours needed.)

29.3	27.6	25.6	23.0	24.0	23.1	21.8
28.5	27.3	25.9	24.0	26.0	23.9	22.0
27.5	26.8	25.8	24.0	27.2	24.6	22.9
26.4	26.0	25.3	23.0	26.0	25.0	23.8
25.5	25.1	24.7	22.5	24.9	25.3	24.9
24.3	23.9	23.0	22.0	23.5	24.7	26.3
26.0	25.8	25.3	24.0	21.3	23.8	24.3
27.4	27.4	27.0	26.1	23.5	20.6	23.0

12. Draw a grid 15 cm wide by 17.5 cm long with 2.5-cm intersections, and place the given elevations at the intersections in the same arrangement as follows.

   a. Draw the 5-m contours. (No depression contours needed.)

22	17	28	40	47	52	57
27	24	22	33	41	46	51
35	32	28	27	34	42	49
45	41	37	31	37	43	49
50	52	48	40	36	42	50
45	46	46	42	44	49	52
34	30	38	45	50	55	60
23	34	45	50	55	60	65

   b. Draw the 1-m contours. (No depression contours needed.)

50.0	50.5	50.5	49.6	48.4	50.0	52.0
49.2	49.6	49.6	49.3	48.7	49.3	50.2
49.7	49.0	48.9	48.8	49.5	48.8	49.3
51.2	50.8	50.1	50.3	50.5	49.0	48.2
50.2	50.2	50.1	49.8	49.4	48.4	49.0
48.0	48.3	48.4	48.6	48.4	50.0	51.0
50.7	50.5	49.7	48.3	50.0	51.0	52.0
52.7	51.8	50.4	48.1	50.3	51.4	52.6

13. The data given in Figure 9-36 were taken in the order shown in parentheses during a grid-method leveling survey. The numbers along the lines of sight, next to the parentheses, are the rod readings. Place the data in standard field book form. Sketch the 1-ft contour lines on an appropriate grid.

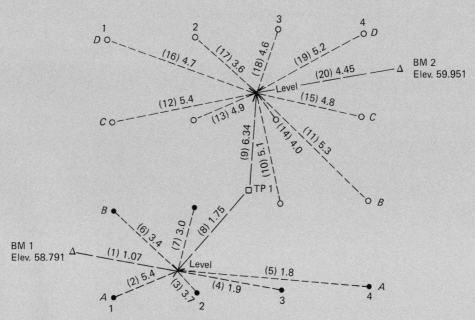

FIGURE 9-36. Illustration for Problem 13.

14. Draw a sketch illustrating an actual example of field conditions that make each of the following horizontal ties the best tie to use: Figure 9-12, ties 3, 5, and 7. Show ties.

15. Draw a sketch illustrating an actual example of field conditions that make each of the following horizontal ties the best tie to use: Figure 9-12, ties 4, 6, and 8. Show ties.

16. (a) Draw a sketch of the locus of a point that is exterior to a triangle and 10 ft from it. (b) Draw a sketch of the locus of a point that is equidistant from the two sides of an angle.

17. Sketch the 5-ft contours based on the control point elevations and stream location shown in Figure 9-37.

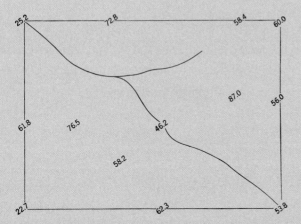

FIGURE 9-37. Illustration for Problem 17.

18. Sketch the 5-m contours based on the control point elevations and stream location shown in Figure 9-38.

19. A camera with a 6-in focal length is used to take a block of vertical aerial photographs. The average camera height above the ground is 1000 ft. Determine the photo scale.

20. It is required to obtain aerial photos of a large tract of land at a scale of 1:24,000, using a 150-mm focal-length camera. What should the average flying height above the ground be?

21. The distance between two major road intersections seen on a vertical photo is measured to be 6.54 in. From ground survey measurements, the actual distance is found to be 1308 ft. What is the scale of the photo?

22. The distance between two major road intersections seen on a vertical photo is measured to be 125 mm. From ground survey measurements, the actual distance is found to be 375 m. What is the RF of the photo?

23. The relief displacement of a tall building is measured to be 1.20 in from its base, as seen on a vertical photo taken from a camera height of 1500 ft. The radial distance from the center of collimation to the top of the building is 6.00 in. Determine the height of the building.

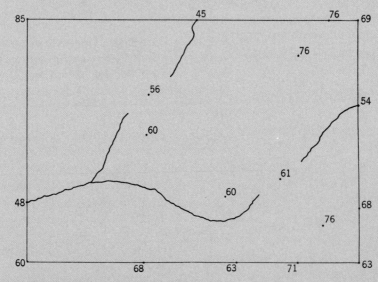

FIGURE 9-38. Illustration for Problem 18.

CHAPTER TEN

HIGHWAY CURVES AND EARTHWORK

CHAPTER OUTLINE

A frequent task for the surveyor is to stake out the position of a transportation route. This is usually for a new street or highway, but it could also be for a railway, for a long pipeline, or for a power transmission line. The "shape" or "geometry" of any transportation route is called its *alignment*. This includes both its *horizontal alignment* (i.e., a plan view) and its *vertical alignment* (i.e., a profile view). The vertical alignment is also called the *grade line*.

A straight-line section of a road or railway alignment is called a *tangent*. Naturally, as the horizontal or the vertical direction of the route changes, the tangent sections of its alignment must be connected by a series of gradual and smooth *curves* for a safe and comfortable ride (Figure 10-1). The shape of the curves must be computed by the surveyor so that they can be located on the ground for construction.

Surveyors are also called upon to compute the quantities of earthwork required to construct roadways. When the grade line lies above the existing ground surface, *embankment (fill)* is required; when the grade line lies below the existing ground, *excavation (cut)* is necessary (see Figure 10-1b).

This chapter focuses on horizontal and vertical curve geometry, that is, on the basic mathematics required to establish the location of curved sections of a roadway. It also covers common methods used to compute cross-section areas and earthwork volumes. Collecting the topographic data needed for design of the alignment and earthwork volume computations and doing the field work required to stake out the alignment make up the activity called *route surveying*.

10-1 ROUTE SURVEYS

Route surveying includes the field and office work required to plan, design, and lay out any "long and narrow" transportation facility. Most of the basic surveying concepts and methods described in the previous chapters apply to route surveying. Horizontal distances, elevations, and angles must be measured, maps must be drawn, and profile and cross-section views of the route must be prepared. Route surveying operations, however, typically include a reconnaissance, a preliminary, and a location survey.

The *reconnaissance survey* involves an examination of a wide area, from one end of the proposed route to the other. It is the first step in selecting alternative routes. For most projects, this would be done using existing small-scale maps and aerial photographs, although ground reconnaissance surveys may be used for the relocation of short sections of existing routes. In some cases, a complete topographic survey may be conducted so that an appropriate map can be prepared.

Matching up aerial photos to form a *strip mosaic* is done frequently to prepare the required map. For preliminary reconnaissance and planning, this can be an *uncontrolled* mosaic, that is, one in which reference to ground control stations has not been made. In relatively flat areas, a planimetric map is usually sufficient for this stage. Reconnaissance maps are used for comparing alternative "paper routes" before the actual survey or layout on the ground. Map scales range from 1 in = 2000 ft (1:24,000) to 1 in = 200 ft (1:2400).

The *preliminary survey* may be conducted on the ground with surveying instruments, or in the office, using aerial photogrammetry. Modern transportation routes are

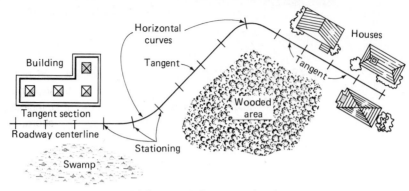

(a) Horizontal alignment—plan view

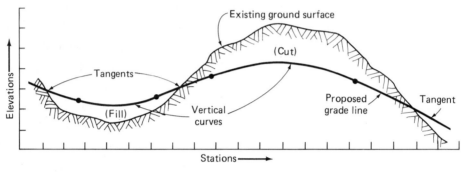

(b) Vertical alignment—profile view

FIGURE 10-1. The route alignment for a road or railway line comprises a connected series of tangents and curves.

usually located using low-altitude photogrammetric maps at a scale of 1 in = 50 ft (1:600) and 2-ft (0.5-m) contours. The maps generally cover about 1300 ft (400 m) in width, primarily along the alternate route corridor selected in the reconnaissance survey operation. In effect, conducting the preliminary survey using photogrammetry is a refinement of the reconnaissance effort. The state of the art of modern photogrammetry and computer applications is such that even the required earthwork (cut-and-fill) computations for roadway design can be done using data from aerial photography.

The basic product of the preliminary survey is the location of a baseline or connecting traverse. This is a series of straight lines that run along or near what will be the centerline of the final route. It is essentially the horizontal alignment of the route without the curves. Distances along the traverse are marked as stations and pluses and run continuously from the beginning point of the route. The angles at intersection points where the baseline tangents change direction are carefully measured by double centering. Data for drawing a profile of the traverse line are also obtained.

The design of the horizontal curves that connect the tangent sections of the baseline depends on several factors, including the topography and the maximum speed of vehicles using the route. After the curve computations have been made and appropriate field notes prepared, the horizontal alignment of the route can be laid out on the ground in a *location survey*. This includes setting stakes along the tangents and the curves of the route centerline (and often along an offset line as well). Because the stations and pluses of the final centerline run along

the curves as well as the tangents, new stations have to be computed for points on the final alignment. This is explained further and illustrated in Section 10-2.

As the staking of the centerline progresses, topographic data are collected, and property corners within the route boundaries or right-of-way (ROW) are located. Profile and cross-section data are obtained for final design, for preparation of engineering drawings, and for final estimates of earthwork quantities. The final *grade line* (vertical alignment) is established to balance cut-and-fill (excavation and embankment) quantities, as explained in Section 10-7. On the engineering drawings, the final horizontal alignment is shown in plan view, above the profile view of the vertical alignment (see Figure 1-14).

The plan view should include the bearings of the tangents, angles of intersection, stationing, and geometric data for each horizontal curve. It should also include topographic data within and adjacent to the ROW lines and any existing structures affected by the project. The profile view should include the existing ground surface, proposed route grade line, grades (slopes) of all the tangent sections, vertical curve data, and other pertinent information.

10-2 HORIZONTAL CURVES

The most common type of horizontal curve is a single arc of a circle, called a *simple curve* (Figure 10-2). Proceeding in the forward direction along the route (i.e., the direction of increasing station numbers), the curve connects the *back tangent* to the *forward tangent*. The curve, or arc, of length *L*,

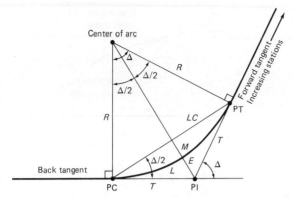

Center of arc

R

R

Δ

$\Delta/2$

$\Delta/2$

Back tangent

$\Delta/2$

PC

T

PI

L

M

E

LC

PT

T

Δ

Forward tangent—Increasing stations

FIGURE 10-2. The simple horizontal curve is an arc of a circle.

begins at the *point of curvature* (PC) and ends at the *point of tangency* (PT). Another terminology is sometimes used to describe the PC and PT, such as TC (*tangent to curve*) and CT (*curve to tangent*). Whatever notation is used, it is important to remember that the curve is literally tangent to the straight-line sections of the route at those points. Therefore, the *radius of the curve* (R), drawn from the center of the arc to the PC or PT, forms a right angle with the tangent section (see Section 3-1).

The tangent sections meet at a *point of intersection* (PI) and form an *intersection angle* (Δ). From plane geometry, this angle is also equal to the central angle between the two radius lines drawn to the PC and PT. Also, a line drawn from the center of the arc to the PI bisects Δ. The distance along that line from the curve to the PI is called the *external distance* (E). The distances from the PC to the PI and from the PI to the PT are equal, and are called the *tangent distance* (T). The straight line that connects the PC and the PT is called the *long chord* (LC). The distance from midpoint of the curve to the midpoint of the long chord is called the *middle ordinate* (M).

Computing the Curve

The equations that are used to compute the parts of a simple curve are derived from plane geometry and right-angle trigonometry. These equations are summarized as follows:

$$T = R \tan\left(\frac{\Delta}{2}\right) \qquad (10\text{-}1)$$

$$L = \frac{\pi R \Delta}{180} \qquad (10\text{-}2)$$

$$LC = 2R \sin\left(\frac{\Delta}{2}\right) \qquad (10\text{-}3)$$

$$E = R\left(\frac{1}{\cos\frac{\Delta}{2}} - 1\right) = T \tan\frac{\Delta}{4} \qquad (10\text{-}4)$$

$$M = R\left(1 - \cos\frac{\Delta}{2}\right) \qquad (10\text{-}5)$$

It should be noted that it is a good idea to use unrounded answers when using that value to generate another variable

in another formula. This eliminates cumulative round-off errors.

Example 10-1

A simple horizontal curve of radius 300 ft connects two tangents that form an intersection angle of 74°46′36″. Compute the parts of the curve, including the tangent distance, the length of arc, the long chord, the external distance, and the middle ordinate.

Solution

First, convert the intersection angle Δ to decimal form.

$$\Delta = 74°46'36'' = 74.7767°$$

$$\frac{\Delta}{2} = \frac{74.7767°}{2} = 37.3883° \quad \text{and} \quad \frac{\Delta}{4} = 18.6942°$$

Applying Equations 10-1 to 10-5 directly, we get

$$T = 300 \tan 37.3883° = 229.27 \text{ ft}$$

$$L = \frac{\pi \times 300 \times 74.7767}{180} = 391.53 \text{ ft}$$

$$LC = 2 \times 300 \times \sin 37.3883° = 364.33 \text{ ft}$$

$$E = 229.27 \times \tan 18.6942° = 77.58 \text{ ft}$$

$$M = 300 (1 - \cos 37.3883°) = 61.64 \text{ ft}$$

Example 10-2

A simple curve is to be laid out so that its middle ordinate is 30 m long. If the tangents intersect at an angle of 50°, what is the minimum radius required?

Solution

Applying Equation 10-5, we can write

$$30 = R\left(1 - \cos\frac{50}{2}\right) \quad \text{and} \quad R = \frac{30}{1 - \cos 25} = 320 \text{ m}$$

Example 10-3

The radius of a simple curve is half its tangent distance. What is the angle of intersection between the tangents?

Solution

Applying Equation 10-1, we get

$$\tan\frac{\Delta}{2} = \frac{T}{R} = 2$$

and

$$\Delta = 2 \times \tan^{-1} 2 = 126.87° = 126°52'12''$$

Degree of Curve   The "sharpness" of a simple curve can be defined by its *degree of curve* or *curvature*. The higher the degree of curvature, the sharper the curve. Degree of curve, D_a, may be considered equal to the *central angle subtended by a 100-ft length of arc* (Figure 10-3). This is called the *arc definition*. Because the circumference of a full circle comprising 360° is $2\pi R$, we can write the proportion $D_a/360 = 100/2\pi R$, from which we get

$$D_a = \frac{18000}{R\pi} \quad \text{and} \quad R = \frac{18000}{D_a\pi} \qquad (10\text{-}6)$$

where D_a is expressed in degrees and R is expressed in feet.

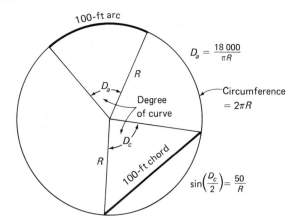

FIGURE 10-3. The degree of curve may be determined by the arc definition (D_a) or by the chord definition (D_c).

Also, because any two arcs of a given circle are proportional to the opposite central angles, we get $L = 100(\Delta/D_a)$, which is an alternate form of Equation 10-2.

The arc definition for degree of curvature is used primarily for roadway design applications. There is one other relationship for curvature called the *chord definition*, which is based on a 100-ft chord length instead of a 100-ft arc length (see Figure 10-3); it is used primarily for railway applications. For the chord definition, the relationship between the degree of curvature and the radius becomes $R = 50/\sin(D_c/2)$. For relatively flat curves, there is very little difference between the arc and chord definitions for degree of curve. For example, given a radius of 1000 ft, the value of $D_a = 5.723°$ and the value of $D_c = 5.732°$. Only the arc definition is used in this text.

It can be seen from Equation 10-6 that the curve radius varies inversely with the degree of curvature. In general, a sharp curve has a small radius and a large degree of curvature; a flat curve has a large radius and a small degree of curvature (Figure 10-4). The allowable degree of curvature for a road depends on the allowable vehicle speed and the type of road; maximum values may vary from about 20° for a 30-mi/h (48-km/h) road to about 2° for a 70-mi/h (112-km/h) highway.

Example 10-4

a. What is the degree of curve if the radius = 300 ft?

b. What would be the corresponding radius for a degree of curve = 5°?

Solution

a. Simply apply Equation 10-6 in the following form:

$$D_a = \frac{18,000}{R\pi} = \frac{5729.578}{300} = 19.099°$$

b. Simply apply Equation 10-6 as follows:

$$R = \frac{18,000}{5\pi} = 1145.92 \text{ ft}$$

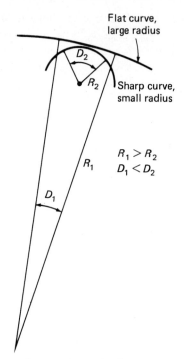

FIGURE 10-4. A sharp curve and a flat curve.

Stationing Along a Route

One of the goals of route design is to establish the stations of all the PCs and the PTs. The station of a PC is computed by simply subtracting T from the station of the PI. But to compute the station of the PT, the arc length L must be added to the station of the PC. This is because the final stationing along the route runs continuously along the tangents *and the curves*. The stations indicate the true centerline distances from the beginning point of the project.

The following expressions summarize the method for stationing along a simple curve:

$$\text{Station PC} = \text{station PI} - T \qquad (10\text{-}7)$$
$$\text{Station PT} = \text{station PC} + L \qquad (10\text{-}8)$$

Example 10-5

Consider the simple horizontal curve given in Example 10-1, with a tangent distance $T = 229.27$ ft and an arc length $L = 391.53$ ft. If the station of the PI is established as $7 + 47.64$, find the stations of the PC and the PT.

Solution

PI =	7 + 47.64	station of the PI
−T =	−(2 + 29.27)	minus *T* distance (Equation 10-7)
PC =	5 + 18.37	station of the PC
+L =	+(3 + 91.53)	plus curve length (Equation 10-8)
PT =	9 + 09.90	station of the PT

Restationing   After the first PT is established, the original stationing along the rest of the preliminary centerline traverse must be changed to reflect the difference between the straight-line distances and the length of the final route with curves. The original PI values are first used to compute the length of the following tangent section. Next, the tangent distances at each end of the section are subtracted from that length; the remaining length, S, is added to the previous PT station to establish the next PC. This procedure for restationing is illustrated in Example 10-6.

Example 10-6

A 2500-ft roadway centerline is established during a preliminary survey, as shown in Figure 10-5a. The three tangent sections are to be connected by two simple curves, the first with a radius of 700 ft and the second with a radius of 600 ft. Determine the stations of the PCs and the PTs, the total

The correct procedure is first to compute the distance S_1 (see Figure 10-5b) by subtracting T_1 and T_2 from the actual length of the tangent between the two PIs, as follows:

$$S_1 = (1200.00 - 500.00) - 220.71 - 133.02 = 346.27 \text{ ft}$$

Now S_1 can be added to the station of PT_1 to find the PC_2:

$$\text{Station } PC_2 = 706.90 + 346.27 = 1053.17 = 10 + 53.17$$

By adding the length of the second curve to the station of PC_2 (i.e., by applying Equation 10-8), we get the station of PT_2:

$$\text{Station } PT_2 = 1053.17 + 261.80 = 1314.97 = 13 + 14.97$$

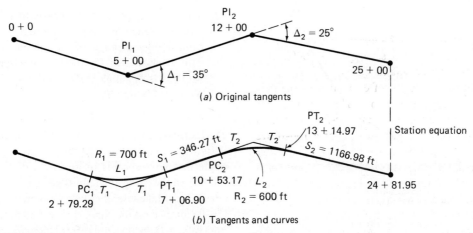

FIGURE 10-5. Restationing along a route centerline.

length of the centerline with curves, and the last station of the final route.

Solution
First, compute the values of T and L for each curve, as follows:

$$T_1 = 700 \times \tan\left(\frac{35}{2}\right) = 220.71 \text{ ft}$$

$$L_1 = \frac{\pi \times 700 \times 35}{180} = 427.61 \text{ ft}$$

$$T_2 = 600 \times \tan\left(\frac{25}{2}\right) = 133.02 \text{ ft}$$

$$L_2 = \frac{\pi \times 600 \times 25}{180} = 261.80 \text{ ft}$$

Now apply Equations 10-7 and 10-8 to establish PC_1 and PT_1:

$$\text{Station } PC_1 = 500.00 - 220.71 = 279.29 = 2 + 79.29$$

$$\text{Station } PT_1 = 279.29 + 427.61 = 706.90 = 7 + 06.90$$

At this point, many students make the mistake of simply subtracting the value of T_2 from the station of PI_2 to get the station of PC_2. This is incorrect because the original stationing along the tangent section from PI_1 to PI_2 has been altered by the first curve.

Finally, the total length of the centerline, including tangents and curves, is determined as follows:

$$S_2 = (2500.00 - 1200.00) - 133.02 = 1166.98 \text{ ft}$$

$$\text{Total length} = PT_2 + S_2 = 1314.97 + 1166.98 = 2481.95 \text{ ft}$$

It is seen, then, that the final centerline with the two curves is shorter than the original combined lengths of the straight tangent sections. The last station, originally 25 + 00.00, becomes station 24 + 81.95. This relationship is sometimes called the *station equation* or *equation of chainage*.

10-3 LOCATING A CURVE

Except for a very sharp circular curve (i.e., with a small radius), it is not practical to lay out the curve by simply swinging an arc from its center. One method for field location of a curve involves measurement of the *deflection angles* between the tangent and the points along the curve and measurement of the *chord lengths* between those points (Figure 10-6a). The necessary field instruments include a transit or theodolite and a steel tape or electronic data measuring instrument (EDMI). Sometimes an *offset method* may be used, particularly when there are short curves or when a transit is not available. It

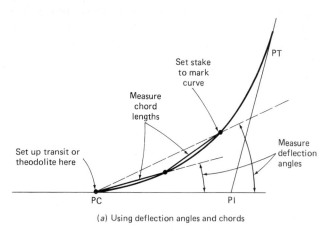

(a) Using deflection angles and chords

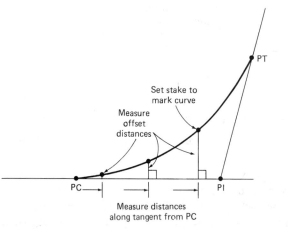

(b) Tangent-offset method

FIGURE 10-6. Two methods to lay out a simple horizontal curve.

involves measuring only horizontal distances—typically those along the back tangent and those offset at right angles from the tangent to stations on the curve (Figure 10-6b).

The most common method, which requires the use of an electronic total station, involves measuring distances and angles from a point near the curve. Rectangular coordinates of stations along the curve are computed in the office. The instrument is set up on a control point and backsights a second point in the control survey to orient the instrument to the construction project. If no control points are accessible, a random point can be set near the curve. The coordinates of the point over which the instrument is set up are first determined in the field by sighting on two nearby points of known position; this, in effect, is a distance–distance intersection problem. The required directions and distances to the coordinated points on the curve may then be computed by the process of inversing (automatically, by the "on-board" computer).

Deflection Angles and Chords

Because the deflection-angle and chord method is most frequently used for curve layout, it is described here in detail. A *deflection angle*, in the sense applied to a simple curve, is the angle measured at the PC from the back tangent

(prolonged) to a desired point on the curve. A *chord* is a straight line between two points on the curve. Briefly, the method involves setting up a transit (or theodolite) at the PC and orienting the circle by aiming at the PI with the scale set at zero. Points on the curve, usually at half-station or 50-ft intervals, are then staked out by measuring the computed chord length from each previous point set and by taking line from the transit when it is set at the proper deflection angle.

The deflection-angle method of curve layout is based primarily on the following geometric principles:

1. The angle between a tangent and a chord, measured at the point of tangency, is equal to one-half of the central angle or angle of arc subtended by the chord. This is illustrated in Figure 10-7a, where $a = a' = a'' = 1/2$ angle $MON = 1/2$ arc MN

2. The angle between two chords that intersect on the circumference of a circle is equal to one-half of the central angle or angle of arc subtended between them. This is shown in Figure 10-7b, where $a = 1/2$ angle MON, $b = 1/2$ angle MOP, and $c = b - a = 1/2$ angle $NOP = 1/2$ arc NP.

Deflection Angles   For a 100-ft arc, the central angle is, by definition, equal to the degree of curve, D_a. The deflection angle that corresponds to an interval of one full station (100 ft) on the curve, then, must be equal to half the degree of curve, $D_a/2$. Likewise, the deflection angle for a half-station (50-ft) interval on the curve is $D_a/4$, and for a quarter-station interval it is $D_a/8$. A useful formula for computing the deflection angle of any given length of arc, expressed in minutes of arc, may be written as follows:

$$a = \frac{\text{arc length}}{R} \times 1718.87 \qquad (10\text{-}9)$$

where a = deflection angle, minutes of arc

R = radius of curve, ft

The deflection angle to any point on the curve is equal to the sum of the incremental deflection angles for each subdivision of the arc. It should be noted that the final deflection angle measured at the PC, from the PI to the PT, must be one-half of the intersection angle Δ (Figure 10-8). This fact is always used as a check on the computation of deflection angles because their sum must equal $\Delta/2$.

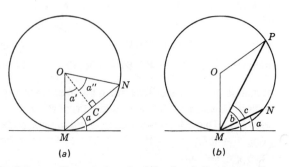

FIGURE 10-7. Geometric principles for deflection angles.

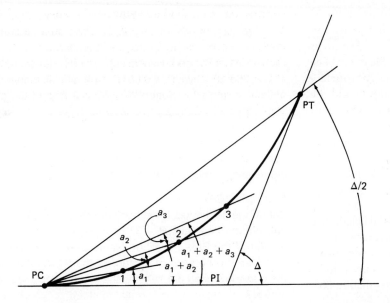

FIGURE 10-8. The deflection angle to any point on the curve is equal to the sum of the incremental deflection angles for each previous subdivision of the arc.

can be shown that the length of a chord is equal to twice the radius of the curve times the sine of half the angle subtended by the chord (Figure 10-9). In equation form, we get

$$\text{Chord length} = 2R \sin a \qquad (10\text{-}10)$$

Field Procedure   Usually, the tangents have already been marked on the ground by POTs (*points on tangent*), and the back tangent has been marked off in stations (see Figure 10-10). The first step in curve layout is to set a stake at the PI (assuming it is accessible). This involves a field procedure that is described in Section 11-5. After the PI has been staked out, the plus or station of the PI is determined and the intersection angle is measured.

From a specified value of R or D, the parts of the curve can be computed, including the tangent distance T and the curve length L. Stations of the PC and PT are determined (using Equations 10-7 and 10-8). Deflection angles for each point to be set on the curve and chord lengths are also computed and recorded in a field book (using Equations 10-9 and 10-10).

The PC and PT are staked out on the tangents by measuring the distance T from the PI. The instrument is

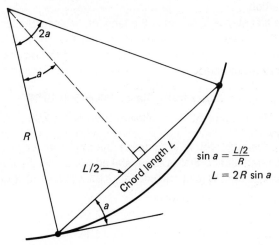

FIGURE 10-9. The length of a chord is equal to twice the radius times the sine of the chord's deflection angle.

Chord Lengths   Because the length of each chord is slightly less than the length of arc it subtends, the actual chord lengths to be laid out between the points set on the curve must be computed. From right-angle trigonometry, it

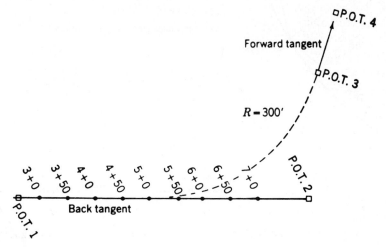

FIGURE 10-10. Beginning of a curve layout procedure.

set up over the PC and oriented by backsighting on the PI with the horizontal circle set at zero. The first deflection angle is turned, and the corresponding chord length is laid out from the PC to the first station on the curve. The second deflection angle is turned, and the appropriate chord length is laid out between the first station and the second station. This procedure is continued, setting off each successive deflection angle and measuring out the required chord length from the previous point, until the PT is set.

Because no surveying measurement is perfect, it is unlikely that the PT originally set by measuring the distance T along the tangent from the PI will correspond exactly to the PT set by the last deflection angle ($\Delta/2$) and chord length. The error of closure is measured, and the relative accuracy is computed (in the same manner as for a traverse survey, using Equation 2-3). The total length of the survey is taken to be $2T + L$. Generally, the accuracy should be better than 1:3000.

Example 10-7

A simple curve has a $D_a = 16°$ and its PC at station $25 + 50$. What are the deflection angles for stations $26 + 00$, $27 + 00$, and $28 + 00$? What is the chord length from the PC to station $26 + 00$ and from station $26 + 00$ to station $27 + 00$?

Solution

The deflection angle for a half-station interval is $D_a/4 = 4°$. This would be the angle turned from the PC toward station $26 + 00$, as shown in Figure 10-11. The chord length can be computed from Equation 10-10. The value of $R = 358.10$, and the chord length is $2 \times 358.10 \times \sin 4° = 49.96$ ft.

The deflection angle for a full-station interval is $D_a/2 = 8°$. The deflection angle for station $27 + 00$, then, is equal to the sum of that for the previous station and $8°$, or $12°$ (see Figure 10-11). The chord length subtended by an arc of 100 ft is $2 \times 358.10 \times \sin 8° = 99.68$ ft. In a similar manner, the deflection angle for station $28 + 00$ is $20°$, and the chord length from $27 + 00$ to $28 + 00$ is 99.68 ft.

Before staking out a curve, the surveying crew must have a suitable set of field notes that identifies a deflection angle and chord length for each point to be set on the curve (see Example 10-8).

Example 10-8

Set up the field notes for staking out the following curve at half-station intervals: $R = 300$ ft, $\Delta = 74° 46'36''$, and the station of the PI is $7 + 47.64$ (same as in Examples 10-1 and 10-5). If the error of closure at the PT is 0.02 ft after the curve is staked out, what is the relative accuracy of the survey?

Solution

The first step is to compute the tangent distance, the length of the curve, and the stations for the PC and PT. This was done in Examples 10-1 and 10-5, and the results are summarized here:

$T = 229.27$ ft	Station PC $= 5 + 18.37$
$L = 391.53$ ft	Station PT $= 9 + 09.90$

The next step is to compute the deflection angles for each half station that is to be staked out along the curve. Because the PC is at station $5 + 18.37$, the first 50-ft-point

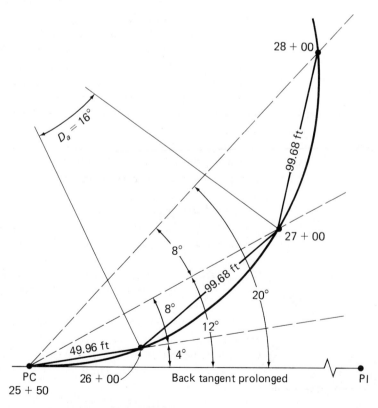

FIGURE 10-11. Illustration for Example 10-7.

mark on the curve will be at station 5 + 50.00. The arc length may be computed as follows:

$$\text{First 50-ft point} = 5 + 50.00$$
$$\text{Minus the plus of the PC} = \underline{5 + 18.37}$$
$$\text{Length of first arc} = \quad 31.63 \text{ ft}$$

Using Equation 10-9 to compute the first deflection angle to station 5 + 50.00, we get

$$a = \frac{\text{length of arc}}{R} \times 1718.87$$
$$= \frac{31.63}{300} \times 1718.87 = 181.24'$$

$a = 181.24' = 3°1.24' = 3°01'15''$ (to the nearest 15 seconds)

The second deflection angle (for station 6 + 00) equals the first deflection angle plus the angle that subtends a 50-ft interval along the arc. Again using Equation 10-9, we get (50/300)(1718.87) = 286.48' = 4°46.48' = 4°46'30'' (to the nearest 15 seconds). This value is added for each 50-ft point until the point just previous to the PT (9 + 00) is reached. The last length of arc to the PT (9 + 09.90) is equal to 9.90 ft. The increment in the deflection angle for this arc is (9.90/300)(1718.87) = 56.72' = 56'45'' (to the nearest 15 seconds).

The deflection angles for each station can now be computed, as shown in Table 10-1. The deflection angle computed for the PT should equal Δ/2, or 74°46'36''/2 = 37°23'18''. The small discrepancy between that angle and the value of 37°23'30'' computed in Table 10-1 is due to rounding off. A large error would indicate a mistake in computation.

Table 10-1. Deflection Angle Calculations

Station	Deflection Angle	
PC 5 + 18.37	0°00'00''	
	+ 3 01 15	(deflection for first arc)
5 + 50	3 01 15	
	+ 4 46 30	(deflection for 50-ft arc)
6 + 00	7 47 45	
	+ 4 46 30	
6 + 50	12 34 15	
	+ 4 46 30	
7 + 00	17 20 45	
	+ 4 46 30	
7 + 50	22 07 15	
	+ 4 46 30	
8 + 00	26 53 45	
	+ 4 46 30	
8 + 50	31 40 15	
	+ 4 46 30	
9 + 00	36 26 45	
	+ 56 45	(deflection for last arc)
PT 9 + 09.90	37°23'30''	

Three different values of chord lengths are to be computed: one for the chord subtended by the first arc of 31.63 ft, one for the chords subtended by 50-ft arcs, and one for the last arc of 9.9 ft. These may be found using Equation 10-10, as follows:

First arc: Chord length = 2 × 300 × sin 3°01'15'' = 31.62 ft

50-ft arc: Chord length = 2 × 300 × sin 4°46'30'' = 49.95 ft

Last arc: Chord length = 2 × 300 × sin 00°56'45'' = 9.90 ft

The field notes for staking out the curve (see Figures 10-12 and 10-13) are usually set up with the stations increasing from the bottom of the page upward, so that they can be read as if facing forward along the curve. The total length of the survey is 2T + L = 2 × 229.27 + 391.53 = 850 ft, and the relative accuracy is 1:850/0.02 = 1:42500.

Orientation on the Curve

It often occurs that some obstacle prevents sighting from the PC to distant points on a curve, as shown in Figure 10-14.

The computed deflection angles for the stations to be measured at the PC are as follows.

Station	Deflection Angles
PC	0
D	A
E	$a + b$
F	$a + b + c$

When the obstruction interferes, as in the line PC to E, the instrument is moved to station D. The telescope is reversed, and set at the deflection angle of the PC, which is zero, and the line of sight is aimed at the PC.

The telescope is then changed to direct so that it is sighting along the line PC to D prolonged. To set E, it must be turned through the angle $a + b$. But note that $a + b$ is the deflection angle computed for E. This is, of course, true for all stations from D to E, or, for that matter, for all stations on the curve, because E represents any station. Thus, with this procedure, the same list of deflection angles can be used as those originally computed. When this is the case, the instrument is said to be *oriented to the curve*. It was oriented by sighting PC with the deflection angle of PC (zero) set in the instrument.

To set stations beyond E, the instrument is moved to E. How can it be oriented to the curve? The deflection angle of D (angle a) is set in the instrument, and the line of sight is aimed at D with telescope reversed.

The telescope is then changed to direct so that it now aims along the prolongation of the line DE. Remember that the instrument still reads the angle a.

To set F, the instrument must be turned through the angle $b + c$ so that the total reading will be $a + b + c$, which is the deflection angle of F. Evidently, the instrument is now oriented to the curve. Thus, two rules can be stated.

To Orient to the Curve When the instrument is on the curve, aim at any other station on the curve, with the telescope

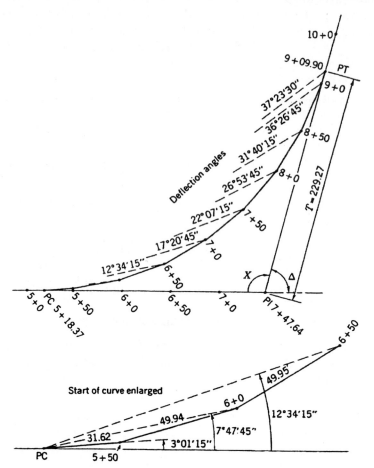

FIGURE 10-12. Illustration for Example 10-8.

Sta.	Chord	Deflec.	Curve Data
+50			$R = 300 \ L$
⊙+09.90 PT	9.90	37° 23' 30"	
9+0	49.95	36° 26' 45"	$\Delta = 74° 46' 36"$
+50	49.94	31° 40' 15"	
			$\frac{\Delta}{2} = 37° 23' 18"$
8+0	49.94	26° 53' 45"	$= 37° 23.30'$
+50	49.94	22° 07' 15"	
⊙+47.64 PI			$T = 229.27$
7+0	49.94	17° 20' 45"	
			$L = 391.53$
+50	49.94	12° 34' 15"	
6+0	49.94	7° 47' 45"	
+50	31.62	3° 01' 15"	
⊙+18.37 PC		0	
5+0			

FIGURE 10-13. Field notes for staking out the curve of Example 10-8.

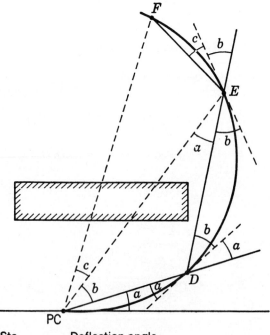

Sta.	Deflection angle
D	a
E	$a+b$
F	$a+b+c$

FIGURE 10-14. Orientation on the curve.

reversed for a point behind the instrument station or direct for a point ahead of the instrument station and with the angle set at the deflection angle of the station at which it is aimed.

When Oriented to the Curve When the instrument is oriented to the curve, any station can be set on the curve by setting the instrument at the deflection angle of the point to be set, with the telescope reversed for points behind and direct for points ahead. Also, after orientation, to establish a tangent to the curve at the instrument station, turn to the deflection angle of the instrument station.

When the PI Is Inaccessible Figure 10-15 shows what to do when the PI cannot be reached. Points A and B are set wherever convenient on the tangents. The distance AB and the angles A and B are measured. Then,

$$\Delta = A + B$$

$$\text{PI to } A = \frac{AB}{\sin \Delta} \sin B$$

$$\text{PI to } B = \frac{AB}{\sin \Delta} \sin A$$

The distance to be measured for setting PT by measuring from B is computed from the preceding by using the value for T, and PC to A is computed similarly.

Example 10-9

A simple horizontal curve, with $R = 1000.00$ ft, has an inaccessible PI (Figure 10-16). Point A is set at station $50 + 00$ on the back tangent, and point B is set on the forward tangent. The distance AB is measured as 752.50 ft; the angle at A is $23°30'$, and the angle at B is $36°15'$. Determine the stations of the PC and the PT.

Solution

$$\Delta = A + B = 23°30' + 36°15' = 59°45' = 59.75°$$

$$T = R \times \tan\left(\frac{\Delta}{2}\right) = 1000 \times \tan 29.875° = 574.45 \text{ ft}$$

$$\text{PI to } A = \frac{752.50}{\sin 59.75°} \times \sin 36.25° = 515.10 \text{ ft}$$

$$\text{PI to } B = \frac{752.50}{\sin 59.75°} \times \sin 23.50° = 347.36 \text{ ft}$$

Referring to Figure 10-16, we find the following:

$$\text{PC to } A = 574.45 - 515.10 = 59.35 \text{ ft}$$

$$L = \pi R\Delta/180 = \frac{\pi \times 1000 \times 59.75}{180} = 1042.83 \text{ ft}$$

Station $A =$	$50 + 00.00$
Minus	59.35
Station PC $=$	$49 + 40.65$
Plus L	$10 + 42.83$
Station PT	$59 + 83.48$

To locate the PT, measure B to PT $= 574.45 - 347.36 = 227.09$ ft along the forward tangent.

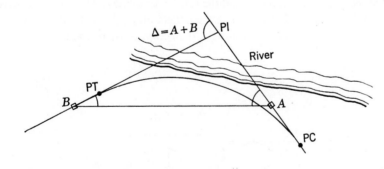

FIGURE 10-15. When the PI is inaccessible, random points A and B are set on the tangents so that the PC and PT can be located with reference to them.

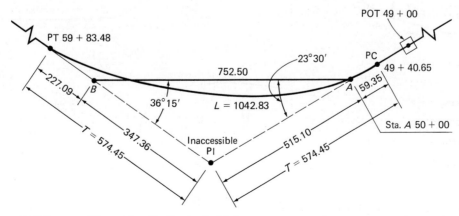

FIGURE 10-16. Illustration for Example 10-9.

10-4 COMPOUND AND REVERSE CURVES

Under certain conditions, route tangents may be connected by something other than the simple curve. A *compound curve*, for example, may be used in mountainous terrain to "fit" the route to the ground. This type of curve consists of two different simple curves joined at a common point of tangency (Figure 10-17a).

When two circular curves are joined together, but lie on opposite sides of a common tangent, they constitute a *reverse curve*, forming what is commonly called an S shape (Figure 10-17b). A reverse curve can serve as a means for shifting a route alignment partly sidewise. Reverse curves may be used on low-speed roadways in mountainous country, and they are usually acceptable for collector streets in suburban residential areas because of their pleasing appearance and tendency to slow down traffic. They are not suitable, however, for major arterial roads or highways.

A *spiral* or *transition curve* provides a gradual change in curvature from a straight tangent to a circular curve or to another tangent (Figure 10-17c). It is especially useful for rapid-transit or railway routes, and for highway exit ramps, to avoid a sudden and uncomfortable change in curvature.

A spiral is a curve with a constantly changing "radius" or curvature; its radius decreases uniformly from infinity, at the point on the tangent where it begins, to that of the circular curve it meets. *Superelevation*—the raising or "banking" of the outer edge of a highway pavement, or the rail of a track, to resist the effect of centrifugal force when moving along a curved path, can be gradually provided on the spiral. In Figure 1-14, a spiral begins at the TS (*tangent to spiral*) and ends at the SC (*spiral to circle*). A full discussion of spiral curve geometry is beyond the scope of this text.

The Compound Curve

A compound curve comprising circular arcs with two different radii is shown in Figure 10-18. Point *P*, where the arcs join, is the *point of compound curve* (PCC). The dashed line *GH* is a common tangent. Subscript 1 refers to the circular curve of smaller radius.

The angle Δ is measured; R_1 and R_2 and either Δ_1 or Δ_2, are given. To find the curve data for the two curves, the following are computed:

From the figure:

$$\Delta_1 = \Delta - \Delta_2 \quad \text{or} \quad \Delta_2 = \Delta - \Delta_1$$

$$t_1 = R_1 \tan 1/2\ \Delta_1 \qquad t_2 = R_2 \tan 1/2\ \Delta_2$$

$$GH \text{ (the common tangent)} = t_1 + t_2$$

$$VG = \sin\Delta_2\ \frac{GH}{\sin\Delta}$$

$$VH = \sin\Delta_1\ \frac{GH}{\sin\Delta}$$

$$T_1 = AV = VG + t_1$$

$$T_2 = VB = VG + t_2$$

To stake out the curve, the deflection angles and the chords are computed for the two curves separately. When *P* is reached, the transit is oriented to the second curve by aiming it so that the vernier reads zero when pointed along the imaginary common tangent *GH*. To accomplish this, aim at any point on the first curve with the telescope reversed and the vernier set to the *right* (if the first curve is a left curve) at the deflection angle of the PCC on the first curve minus the deflection angle of the point sighted. To

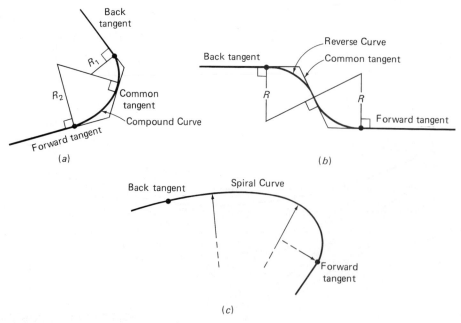

(a)

(b)

(c)

FIGURE 10-17. Different kinds of horizontal curves.

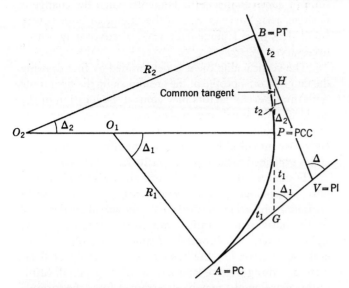

FIGURE 10-18. Nomenclature for the compound curve.

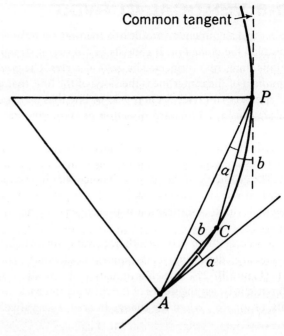

FIGURE 10-19. To orient to the point of compound curvature.

prove this, in Figure 10-19, let C be any point on the first curve. On the first curve,

$$\begin{array}{rl} \text{Deflection angle of } P = & a + b \\ -\text{Deflection angle of } C = & a \\ \hline \text{Result} = & b \end{array}$$

Thus, if b is set off to the right and aimed at C, when the transit is then turned to zero, the telescope will be on the common tangent and the vernier will read zero. Accordingly, once oriented in this way, the deflection angles computed for the second curve can be used.

The Reverse Curve

A reverse curve that connects point A on the back tangent to point B on the forward tangent is illustrated in Figure 10-20.

In the field, the distance AB and the angles a and b are measured. Because it is always an advantage to use the largest radius possible, the best method is to use equal radii.

$$\cos c = \frac{SO_2}{O_2O_1} = \frac{R \cos a' + R \cos b'}{2R}$$

But $a' = a$ and $b' = b$, sides perpendicular in the same order. Substituting and dividing both numerator and denominator by R,

$$\cos c = 1/2 \,(\cos a + \cos b)$$
$$AB = R \sin a + 2R \sin c + R \sin b$$
$$R = \frac{AB}{\sin a + 2 \sin c + \sin b}$$
$$\Delta_1 = a + c \qquad \Delta_2 = b + c$$

The curves are computed separately. The first curve is staked out and, at the PRC (*point of reverse curve*), the transit is oriented to the second curve as in the compound curve.

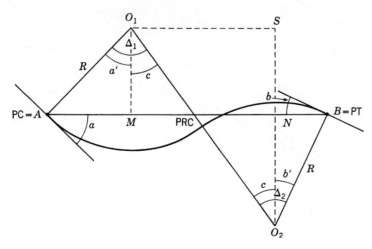

FIGURE 10-20. Nomenclature for the reverse curve.

10-5 VERTICAL CURVES

The vertical alignment or profile of a roadway centerline is also called the *grade line*. It consists of a series of straight sections (tangents) connected by *vertical curves*. The *grade* or *gradient* of the centerline is the slope of the line, that is, the "rise over run" (see Section 9-2). A line that increases in elevation in the forward direction of stationing has a positive gradient ($+g$); a line that slopes downward in the forward direction has a negative gradient ($-g$). The vertical curves are segments of *parabolas* instead of circular arcs. The geometry of the parabola is such that it provides a constant rate of change in slope between two adjoining tangents, which is desirable for passenger comfort and safety.

A vertical curve may be either a *crest* (*summit*) *curve* or a *sag curve*, depending on the tangent grades that it connects (Figure 10-21). The change in grade is the algebraic difference between the slopes of the forward and back tangents, or $g_2 - g_1$. When the change in grade is negative, a summit curve connects the tangents; when the change is positive, a sag curve is used. If the change in slope is very small (less than 1 percent), a vertical curve may not be necessary.

The vertical alignment is determined by first drawing the tangents on a profile of the ground along the final route centerline. Several factors may control the location of the grade line, but usually the tangents are located to balance the required volumes of earthwork excavation (cut) and embankment (fill); this is discussed briefly in Section 10-1 and is explained further in Section 10-7.

Distances along a vertical curve are measured horizontally, and *the length of a vertical curve is taken to be its horizontal projection*. Vertical curves for a road are designed on the basis of minimum required stopping or passing sight distances, rider comfort, drainage control, and general appearance. On the basis of one or more of these factors, a design curve length is usually specified. Minimum curve lengths may be determined from the formula $L_{min} = K(g_2 - g_1)$, where the gradients are expressed in

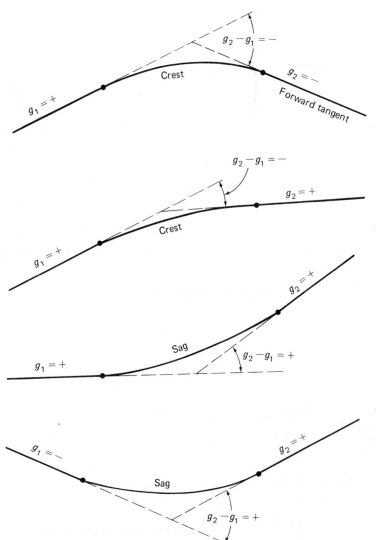

FIGURE 10-21. Vertical curves: crest and sag.

percent and K depends on the design speed; typical values of K are as follows:

Speed, mi/h	Minimum Value of K	
	Summit Curve	**Sag Curve**
40	50	50
50	80	70
60	150	100

For example, if the back tangent gradient is -3 percent and the forward tangent gradient is $+4$ percent, for a 50-mi/h roadway the minimum vertical curve length would be $(70)[4 - (-3)] = (70)(7) = 490$ ft. Usually, the length is selected in full-station or half-station increments; a 500-ft-long vertical curve may be selected in this case.

Elevations on Tangents

To mark the vertical alignment in the field (set gradestakes), the surveyor must have field notes that list the elevations of the grade line at each station along the route centerline. (These may be "finish elevations" of the pavement, or they may be elevations of the *subgrade*—the base of the roadway.) It is necessary to apply the geometric properties of a parabolic curve to compute the elevations of stations along the curve. The formulas and procedure for this are described in the next part of this section. First, the procedure for simply determining tangent gradients and a series of elevations along a tangent is illustrated in Example 10-10.

Example 10-10
Three tangent sections of a grade line are shown in profile view in Figure 10-22. Determine the gradient of each tangent section and the elevation at each full station along the tangents.

Solution
The gradient or slope is equal to "rise over run." From the data shown in Figure 10-22, we get

$$g_1 = \frac{720.00 - 738.50}{1400 - 1000} = \frac{-18.5}{400} = -0.04625 = -4.625\%$$

$$g_2 = \frac{732.00 - 720.00}{1700 - 1400} = \frac{12}{300} = 0.040 = 4.00\%$$

$$g_3 = \frac{714.50 - 732.00}{1975 - 1700} = \frac{-17.5}{275} = -0.06364 = -6.364\%$$

The difference in elevation between two points on a tangent of gradient g is equal to gX, where X is the distance between the points. The elevations at full stations along the three tangents in this example can be computed as shown in Table 10-2.

Computing the Curve

The point where two tangents meet is called the *point of vertical intersection* (PVI). The point on the back tangent where the vertical curve begins is called the *point of vertical curve* (PVC) or the *beginning of vertical curve* (BVC). The point where the curve joins the forward tangent is called the *point of vertical tangency* (PVT) or the *end of vertical curve* (EVC). A vertical axis through the PVI bisects the curve length L into two equal parts (Figure 10-23).

A straight line drawn between the PVC and the PVT is called the *long chord*. From the geometry of a parabola, the elevation of the curve at the station of the PVI is midway

Table 10-2. Elevations on Tangents

Station	Computations	Elevation
10 + 00		= 738.50
11 + 00	738.50 + (−.04625)(100)	= 733.88
12 + 00	738.50 + (−.04625)(200)	= 729.25
13 + 00	738.50 + (−.04625)(300)	= 724.63
14 + 00	738.50 + (−.04625)(400)	= 720.00
15 + 00	720.00 + (0.040)(100)	= 724.00
16 + 00	720.00 + (0.040)(200)	= 728.00
17 + 00	720.00 + (0.040)(300)	= 732.00
18 + 00	732.00 + (−0.06364)(100)	= 725.64
19 + 00	732.00 + (−0.06364)(200)	= 719.27
19 + 75	732.00 + (−0.06364)(275)	= 714.50

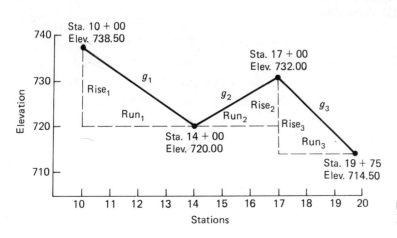

FIGURE 10-22. Illustration for Example 10-10: tangent elevations.

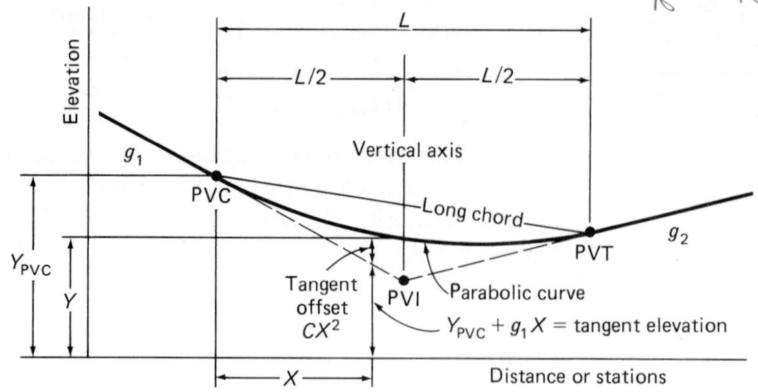

FIGURE 10-23. Nomenclature for a vertical parabolic curve.

between the PVI and the midpoint of the long chord. The vertical distance between a tangent and the curve is sometimes called a *tangent offset* or *tangent correction*. The tangent offsets are proportional to the squares of the distances from the PVC, and the offsets from the back and forward tangents are symmetrical with reference to the PVI.

There are several methods for computing grade-line elevations at stations along a vertical parabolic curve. Although they differ in the form of organizing the computations, they are each based on the same fundamental geometric properties of the parabola.

Typically, the station and elevation of the PVI are first located on a profile and the length of the curve, L, is selected as previously described. Then the stations and the elevations of the PVC and PVT are determined, using the following relationships:

$$\text{Station PVC} = \text{station PVI} - \frac{L}{2} \qquad (10\text{-}11)$$

$$\text{Elevation PVC} = \text{elevation PVI} \pm g_1\left(\frac{L}{2}\right) \qquad (10\text{-}12)$$

$$\text{Station PVT} = \text{station PVI} + \frac{L}{2} \qquad (10\text{-}13)$$

$$\text{Elevation PVT} = \text{elevation PVI} \pm g_2\left(\frac{L}{2}\right) \qquad (10\text{-}14)$$

(*Note:* In Equations 10-12 and 10-14, use + for a sag curve and − for a summit curve.)

A parabolic curve may be expressed as a quadratic equation. In surveying terminology (Figure 10-23), the equation can be written as

$$Y = Y_{\text{PVC}} + g_1 X + \frac{r}{2}X^2 \qquad (10\text{-}15)$$

where $r = \dfrac{g_2 - g_1}{L}$

and Y = elevation of any point on the curve, ft (m)

Y_{PVC} = elevation of the PVC, ft (m)

X = horizontal distance of the point from the PVC, ft (m) or stations

r = rate of change of grade

g_1 = gradient of the back tangent, decimal or percent

g_2 = gradient of the forward tangent, decimal or percent

L = length of the curve, ft (m) or stations

The combined terms $Y_{\text{PVC}} + g_1 X$ in Equation 10-15 give elevations along the back tangent (and the back tangent prolonged); the term $(r/2)X^2$ is, in effect, a vertical tangent offset that, when added to the back tangent elevation, gives the curve elevation. The sign of r will be negative (−) for a summit curve and positive (+) for a sag curve. (*Note:* $C = r/2$ in Figure 10-23.)

Example 10-11

The data for a summit vertical curve given on a roadway plan and profile sheet are as follows: PVI station = 11 + 02.43, PVI elevation = 43.32 ft, back tangent grade g_1 = + 6.00 percent, forward tangent grade g_2 = − 2.00 percent, and curve length L = 550 ft (Figure 10-24). Grade stakes are to be set at the PVC, at the PVT, and at half-station intervals along the curve. Set up a table to show curve elevations at those points.

Solution

1. Compute the stations and elevations of the PVC and PVT. Because L = 550, the horizontal distance to each from the PVI is $L/2$ = 550/2 = 275 ft, or 2 + 75.00 stations. Applying Equations 10-11 to 10-14, we get

Station PVC = (11 + 02.43) − (2 + 75.00) = 8 + 27.43

Elevation PVC = 43.32 − (0.06)(275) = 43.32 − 16.5

$\qquad$ = 26.82

Station PVT = (11 + 02.43) + (2 + 75.00) = 13 + 77.43

Elevation PVT = 43.32 − (0.02)(275) = 43.32 − 5.5

$\qquad$ = 37.82

2. Compute the value of r/2.

$$\frac{r}{2} = \frac{(-0.02 - 0.06)}{2 \times 550} = -7.2727 \times 10^{-5}$$

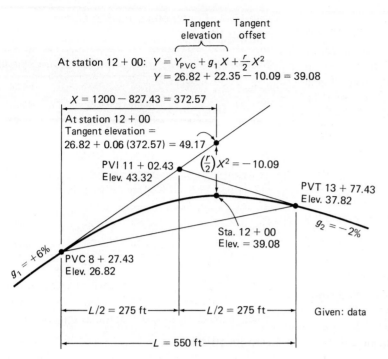

At station $12 + 00$: Tangent elevation, Tangent offset

$$Y = Y_{PVC} + g_1 X + \frac{r}{2}X^2$$
$$Y = 26.82 + 22.35 - 10.09 = 39.08$$

$X = 1200 - 827.43 = 372.57$

At station $12 + 00$
Tangent elevation =
$26.82 + 0.06 (372.57) = 49.17$

PVI $11 + 02.43$
Elev. 43.32

$\left(\frac{r}{2}\right)X^2 = -10.09$

PVT $13 + 77.43$
Elev. 37.82

$g_2 = -2\%$

Sta. $12 + 00$
Elev. = 39.08

$g_1 = +6\%$

PVC $8 + 27.43$
Elev. 26.82

$L/2 = 275$ ft $L/2 = 275$ ft

$L = 550$ ft

Given: data

FIGURE 10-24. Illustration for Example 10-11; a typical computation is shown for station $12 + 00$.

3. Set up a table for computing the curve (Table 10-3). The distance from the PVC to the first point on the curve is $850 - 827.43 = 22.57$ ft. Half-station points are listed from $8 + 50$ to $13 + 50$, and the last point is the PVT, at station $13 + 77.43$.

    In Table 10-3, the values of $g_1 X$ and $(r/2)X^2$ are rounded off to the nearest hundredth of a foot. The curve elevation at each point is obtained by adding those values to the elevation of the PVC, 26.82 ft. For example, at station $11 + 00$, $g_1 X = (0.06)(272.57) = 16.35$, $(r/2)X^2 = (-7.2727 \times 10^{-5})(272.57)^2 = -5.40$, and the curve elevation equals $26.82 + 16.35 + (-5.40) = 37.77$ ft. Computations

are facilitated by using a calculator that can store and recall the values of g_1 and $r/2$.

As a check on the curve computations, it should be noted that the elevation of the PVT (37.82) computed using Equation 10-15 matches that obtained from Equation 10-14. Also, the elevation at the PVI is $26.82 + (0.06)(275) + (-7.2727 \times 10^{-5})(275)^2 = 37.82$ ft. This matches the curve elevation at that station computed as being halfway between the elevations at the middle of the long chord and the PVI, as follows: $(26.82 + 37.82)/2 = 32.32$ ft, the elevation at the middle of the long chord, and $(43.32 + 32.32)/2 = 37.82$ ft, the elevation on the curve.

Table 10-3. Elevations on a Summit Curve—Example 10-1

Station	X	$g_1 X$	$(r/2)X^2$	Curve Elevation
PVC $8 + 27.43$	0.00	0.00	0.00	26.82
$8 + 50$	22.57	1.35	−0.04	28.13
$9 + 00$	72.57	4.35	−0.38	30.79
$9 + 50$	122.57	7.35	−1.09	33.08
$10 + 00$	172.57	10.35	−2.17	35.00
$10 + 50$	222.57	13.35	−3.60	36.57
$11 + 00$	272.57	16.35	−5.40	37.77
$11 + 50$	322.57	19.35	−7.57	38.60
$12 + 00$	372.57	22.35	−10.09	39.08
$12 + 50$	422.57	25.35	−12.99	39.18
$13 + 00$	472.57	28.35	−16.25	38.92
$13 + 50$	522.57	31.35	−19.86	38.31
PVT $13 + 77.43$	550.00	33.00	−21.99	37.82

Example 10-12

The data for a vertical curve in sag appearing on a roadway plan and profile sheet are as follows: the PVI station = 21 + 25.00, the PVI elevation = 82.79 ft, the back tangent grade g_1 = −5.00 percent, the forward tangent grade g_2 = +3.00 percent, and the curve length L = 450 ft. Grade stakes are to be set at the PVC, at the PVT, and at half-station intervals. Set up a table to compute curve elevations at those points (see Table 10-4).

Solution

In this example, tangent gradients will be expressed as given, that is, in percent instead of in decimal form, and distances will be expressed in stations. For instance, $L/2$ is written as 2.25 stations instead of as 225 ft. Following the procedure outlined in Example 10-11, we get

Station PVC = (21 + 25.00) − (2 + 25.00) = 19 + 00.00

Elevation PVC = 82.79 + 5 × 2.25 = 94.04

Station PVT = (21 + 25.00) + (2 + 25.0) = 23 + 50.00

Elevation PVT = 82.79 + 3 × 2.25 = 89.54

$$\frac{r}{2} = \frac{g_1 - g_2}{[2L]} = \frac{[3 - (-5)]}{[(2)(4.5)]} = 0.88889$$

High or Low Point

It is sometimes required to find the station and the elevation of the highest point on a summit curve, or the lowest point on a sag. For example, it may be necessary to determine the clearance beneath a bridge, the depth of cover over a buried pipeline, or the required location of a storm-water drainage inlet in a sag curve. These points, called *vertical curve turning points*, do not occur at the station of the PVI unless the back and forward tangent grades are equal. The following formula may be used to compute the distance of the turning point X' from the PVC:

$$X' = \frac{g_1 L}{g_1 - g_2} \tag{10-16}$$

Table 10-4. Elevations on a Sag Curve— Example 10-12

Station	X	$g_1 X$	$(r/2)X^2$	Curve Elevation
PVC 19 + 00	0.00	0.00	0.00	94.04
19 + 50	0.50	−2.50	0.22	91.76
20 + 00	1.00	−5.00	0.89	89.93
20 + 50	1.50	−7.50	2.00	88.54
21 + 00	2.00	−10.00	3.56	87.60
21 + 50	2.50	−12.50	5.56	87.10
22 + 00	3.00	−15.00	8.00	87.04
22 + 50	3.50	−17.50	10.89	87.43
23 + 00	4.00	−20.00	14.22	88.26
PVT 23 + 50	4.50	−22.50	18.00	89.54

The computed value of X' is used in Equation 10-15 to determine the curve elevation at the turning point.

Example 10-13

The data given for a vertical sag curve on a roadway plan and profile sheet are as follows: PVI station = 32 + 11.61, PVI elevation = 54.18 ft, back tangent gradient g_1 = −4.00 percent, forward tangent gradient g_2 = 7.00 percent, and length of curve L = 600 ft. Determine the curve elevations at half-station intervals along the curve, and compute the station and elevation of the lowest point.

Solution

Following the general procedure outlined in the two previous examples, we get the following (see Figure 10-25 and Table 10-5):

Station PVC = (32 + 11.61) − (3 + 00) = 29 + 11.61

Elevation PVC = 54.18 + 4 × 3.00 = 66.18 ft

Station PVT = (32 + 11.61) + (3 + 00) = 35 + 11.61

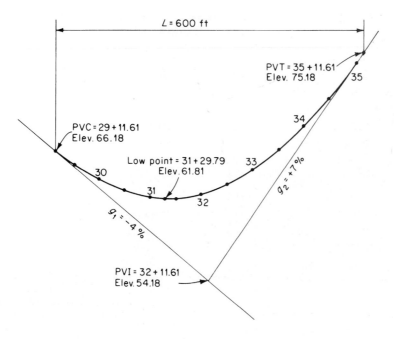

FIGURE 10-25. Illustration for Example 10-13.

Table 10-5. Elevations on a Sag Curve—
Example 10-13

Station	X	g_1X	$(r/2)X^2$	Curve Elevation
PVC 29 + 11.61	0.00	0.00	0.00	66.18
29 + 50	0.3839	−1.54	0.14	64.78
30 + 00	0.8839	−3.54	0.72	63.36
30 + 50	1.3839	−5.54	1.76	62.40
31 + 00	1.8839	−7.54	3.25	61.89
31 + 50	2.3839	−9.54	5.20	61.84
32 + 00	2.8839	−11.54	7.63	62.27
32 + 50	3.3839	−13.54	10.50	63.14
33 + 00	3.8839	−15.54	13.83	64.47
33 + 50	4.3839	−17.54	17.62	66.26
34 + 00	4.8839	−19.54	21.86	68.50
34 + 50	5.3839	−21.54	26.57	71.22
35 + 00	5.8839	−22.54	31.74	74.38
PVT 35 + 11.61	6.0000	−24.00	33.00	75.18

Elevation PVT $= 54.18 + 7 \times 3.00 = 75.18$

$$\frac{r}{2} = \frac{g_1 - g_2}{[2L]} = \frac{[7 - (-4)]}{[(2)(6.00)]} = 0.91667$$

From Equation 10-16, the distance from the PVC to the low point on the curve is $X' = g_1L/(g_1 - g_2) = (-4)(6)/(-4 - 7) = -24/ - 11 = 2.1818$ stations

$$\text{Station of the PVC} = 29 + 11.61$$
$$+2 + 18.18$$
$$\text{Station of the low point} = 31 + 29.79$$

Applying Equation 10-15, we compute the elevation of the low point to be

$$Y = 66.18 + (-4)(2.1818) + 0.91667(2.1818)^2 = 61.81 \text{ ft}$$

Example 10-14

Determine the location and elevation of the high point on the curve given in Example 10-11.

Solution

$$X' = \frac{0.06 \times 550}{[0.06 - (-0.02)]} = \frac{33}{0.08} = 412.50 \text{ ft}$$

Station of the high point $= (8 + 27.43) + (4 + 12.50)$

$$= 12 + 39.93$$

$$Y = 26.82 + 0.06 \times 412.50 + (-7.2727 \times 10^{-5})(412.50)^2$$
$$= 39.20 \text{ ft}$$

10-6 CURVES THROUGH FIXED POINTS

Sometimes it is necessary to design a curve that has established tangents so that it passes through a predetermined point or elevation. For example, a horizontal curve may have to be laid out to cross a stream at a special location, or to pass no closer than a certain distance from a particular building or other feature. The grade line along a vertical curve may have to meet the existing elevation of an intersecting road, or a minimum amount of clearance may be specified for an underground utility or an overhead structure at a particular station along the route. The following examples illustrate solutions to problems of this type.

Example 10-15

Determine the radius of a simple curve that will connect the given tangents and pass through point P, which is located from the PI by distance and angle measurements as shown in Figure 10-26.

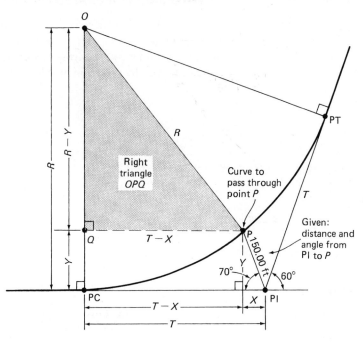

FIGURE 10-26. Illustration for Example 10-15; designing a horizontal curve to pass through a fixed point.

Solution

The angle and distance measurements from the PI allow the computation of distances X and Y by trigonometry, as follows:

$$X = 150.00 \times \cos 70 = 51.30 \text{ ft}$$

$$Y = 150.00 \times \sin 70 = 140.95 \text{ ft}$$

Applying the Pythagorean theorem to right triangle OPQ, we can write $R^2 = (T - X)^2 + (R - Y)^2$. And because $T = R \tan (\Delta/2) = R \tan 30 = 0.5774 R$, we can also write $R^2 = (0.5774 R - 51.30)^2 + (R - 140.95)^2$. After squaring and combining terms, we get the following quadratic equation: $R^2 - 1023.25R + 67484 = 0$. Solving this with the quadratic formula (Appendix C), with $a = 1.00$, $b = -10023.25$, and $c = 67484$, we get the following:

$$R = \frac{-(-1023.25) \pm \sqrt{1023.25^2 - 4(1.00)(67484)}}{(2)(1.00)}$$

(The smaller root or solution to the quadratic equation, 70.86 ft, is not physically possible for this particular problem.)

Example 10-16

A vertical curve is to connect two tangents that intersect at station 21 + 00, as shown in Figure 10-27. The elevation of the curve at station 22 + 00 must be equal to or greater than 108.00 ft to provide adequate cover over an underground pipeline. What is the required length of curve?

Solution

The distance (in stations) from the PVC to station 22 + 00 can be expressed as $X = L/2 + 1.00$. Also, the elevation of the PVC can be expressed as $100.00 + 5(L/2)$, and $r/2 = (g_2 - g_1)/[2L] = [3 - (-5)]/[2L] = 8/[2L] = 4/L$

Applying Equation 10-15 and substituting these expressions for Y_{PVC}, X, and $r/2$, we can write the following equation:

$$108.00 = (100.00 + 2.5L) + (-5)(0.5L + 1.00)$$
$$+ (4/L)(0.5L + 1.0)^2$$

Rearranging terms and simplifying the expression, we get

$$L^2 - 9L + 4 = 0$$

Solving with the quadratic formula, we get $L = 8.53$ stations (the smaller root, 0.47, is clearly not feasible for this problem). For convenience in computing the curve, L could be rounded off up to 9.00 stations or 900 ft; this would raise the curve elevation at station 22 + 00 slightly above the 108.00-ft minimum.

Check: $Y = 100 + (5)(4.5) + (-5)(5.5) + (8/18)(5.5)^2$
$= 108.44 \text{ ft}$

10-7 EARTHWORK COMPUTATIONS

The movement of soil or rock from one location to another for construction purposes is called *earthwork*. A volume of earth that is *excavated*, that is, removed from its natural location, is called *cut*. Excavated material that is placed and compacted in a different location is called *embankment* or *fill*. The construction of the grade line for a new road or railway typically involves much cut and fill (see Figure 10-1); the *grading*, or reshaping, of the ground for a building site also involves cut and fill. Surveyors are often called on to measure earthwork quantities in the field and to compute the volumes of cut and fill.

Earthwork quantities or volumes are measured in terms of cubic yards (yd^3) or cubic meters (m^3). Generally, the volume is computed as the product of an area and a depth or distance. The area may be that of a roadway cross section or that enclosed within a particular contour line; the distance or depth is that between the cross-section stations, or the contour interval. The first part of this section deals with the computation of irregular areas; the second part covers the computation of volumes and the balancing of cut-and-fill quantities.

Cross Sections and Areas

As previously defined, a *cross section* is a short profile taken perpendicular to the centerline of a roadway or other facility (Section 5-5). The cross section at a station along a road will typically show the profile of the original ground

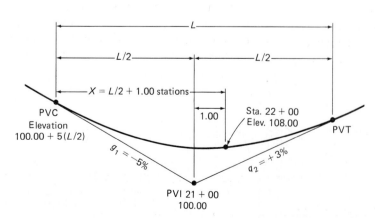

FIGURE 10-27. Illustration for Example 10-16; designing a vertical curve to pass through a fixed point.

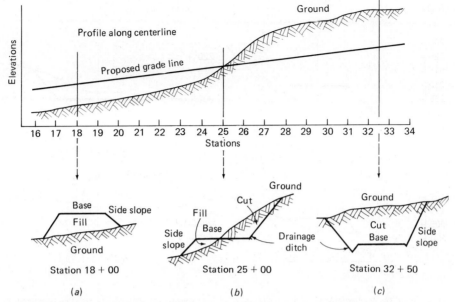

FIGURE 10-28. Typical cross sections: (*a*) embankment or fill, (*b*) mixed or sidehill, and (*c*) excavation or cut.

surface, the *base* of the roadway, and the *side slopes* of the cut or fill. The base is the horizontal line to which the cut or fill is first constructed; its width depends primarily on the number of lanes and the width of roadway shoulders (Figure 10-28).

A *side slope* is expressed as the ratio of a horizontal distance to a corresponding unit of vertical distance for the cut or fill slope (Figure 10-29). This ratio depends largely on the type of soil and on the natural *angle of repose* at which it remains stable. A side slope of 1:1 is possible for some compacted embankment sections, whereas a flatter ratio of 2:1 or more is typical for a side slope in a cut section. Of course, a vertical concrete retaining wall may be built to hold back the soil where very flat side slopes would require excessively wide right-of-way acquisition. (Note that the definition of *side slope* is opposite that of *gradient*, which is "rise over run," as explained in Section 9-2.)

Plotting Cross Sections   Route cross sections are usually plotted to scale on a special grid or "cross-section paper"; a typical scale is 1 in = 5 ft (1:60) for both the vertical and the horizontal axes. Sometimes the vertical scale is exaggerated if the depth of cut or fill is very shallow.

For wide sections with flat side slopes, a horizontal scale as small as 1 in = 20 ft (1:240) may be used to conserve space on the paper. A cross section is usually drawn for each half-station or quarter-station interval along the route, and the station number is recorded just below the section view (Figure 10-30).

To draw a section, a vertical line is first drawn to represent the route centerline (the symbol ℄ is often used to identify a centerline). Enough space must be left between adjacent centerlines so that the cross sections do not overlap on the drawing. The vertical scale is positioned individually for each section, and the existing terrain elevations are plotted from the cross-section field notes (see Figure 10-30). The base elevation is taken from the proposed alignment profile drawing; it is drawn to the appropriate scaled width as a horizontal line, bisected by the centerline. The side slopes are then drawn at the specified inclination, from each end of the base to the existing terrain line.

For preliminary earthwork computations, it is sufficient to use a cross section with the simple horizontal base. For more accurate work, a *template section* is superimposed on each cross section. The template is a plastic or paper

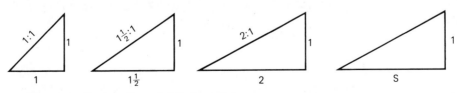

FIGURE 10-29. Designation of side slope, S:1.

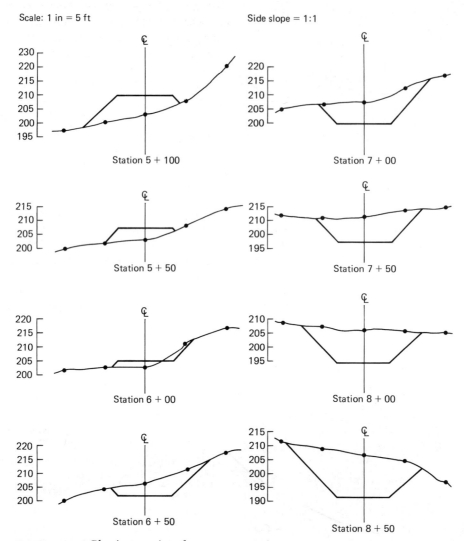

Scale: 1 in = 5 ft   Side slope = 1:1

Station 5 + 100

Station 5 + 50

Station 6 + 00

Station 6 + 50

Station 7 + 00

Station 7 + 50

Station 8 + 00

Station 8 + 50

FIGURE 10-30. Plotting a series of route cross sections.

form representing the constant shape of the finished section, which includes the thickness, crown, and superelevation of the pavement, shoulders, and drainage swales (Figure 10-31). The template section increases the cross-sectional area of earthwork in a cut section, and decreases the area in a fill section. This, in turn, affects the respective earthwork volumes.

Section Areas   The area enclosed in a section by the natural terrain, the side slopes, and the base can be determined in several ways. These include approximate methods such as simply counting the number of enclosed grid boxes. In a method called *stripping*, the section is divided into several vertical strips, or "slices," of constant width. The sum of the altitudes of the strips is determined by placing a long strip of

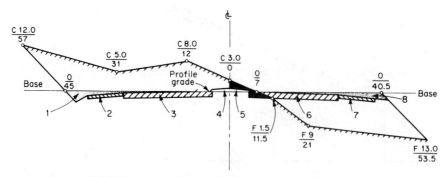

FIGURE 10-31. Sidehill section with template. Areas numbered 1–7 constitute the constant shape of the road surfacing.

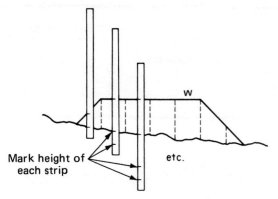

FIGURE 10-32. Cross-section area by stripping.

paper successively over each slice, as shown in Figure 10-32, and marking the accumulated heights. The total length of the paper strip is multiplied by the constant width (w) of a section or slice to compute the area of the cross section.

Plane geometry may be used to compute a cross-section area by first dividing the section into regular shapes, including triangles and trapezoids. The dimensions of those figures can be determined by scaling or from field note data, and their areas computed from basic geometric formulas. The sum of those areas is the area of the cross section.

Area by Planimeter A *planimeter* is an instrument that will measure the area of a plane figure of any shape when the tracer point of the instrument is moved around the perimeter or edge of the figure. The planimeter is used by surveyors and civil engineering technicians for determining storm drainage basin areas, checking property survey areas, determining areas of roadway cross sections, and performing other tasks. It is particularly useful for measuring the areas of irregularly shaped figures, and accuracies better than ±1 percent can be obtained under most circumstances.

An electronic planimeter displays area measurements in digital readout directly in square inches or square centimeters; it can be instantly set on zero, and most models are designed to facilitate the cumulative adding and averaging of areas (Figure 10-33a). A mechanical planimeter includes a graduated

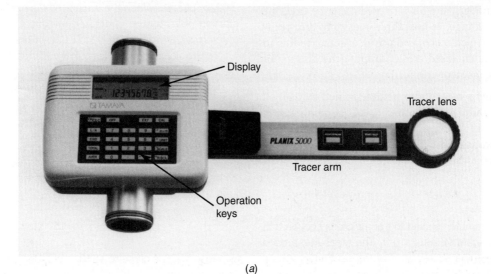

(a)

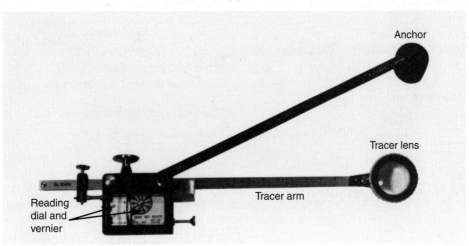

(b)

FIGURE 10-33. (*a*) An electronic planimeter. (*b*) A conventional mechanical polar planimeter. (*Courtesy of Sokkia Corporation.*)

drum and a disk that is read to four digits with a vernier; most have an adjustable tracer arm, making it possible to set the instrument so that the drum and disk readings are related to the area by a convenient ratio (Figure 10-33b). For some electronic planimeters, and most mechanical planimeters, it is necessary to convert the instrument reading to an area that is related to the scale of the drawing used.

Some general requirements for the use of a planimeter are to

1. Perform all work on a smooth, horizontal surface.
2. Select and mark a starting point on the perimeter of the figure. Movement of the tracer arm around the figure should begin and end *exactly* at that point. It is more important to start and stop at the same point than to precisely follow the perimeter.
3. Trace the perimeter in a clockwise direction (so that the readings increase). If the tracer point strays slightly off the perimeter, compensate by moving off to the other side of the line to make the areas of the errors about equal.
4. To avoid blunders, and for increased accuracy, trace the figure until you get at least three consistent area readings with the planimeter, and use an average reading to compute the enclosed area. Compute the average of only those consistent area readings.

Areas of polygons can also be determined by using a digitizer tablet and CAD software. This is done by simply marking each point defining the polygon with a mouse. The computer software then determines a coordinate for the points and automatically calculates the area by the coordinate method.

Example 10-17
An electronic planimeter is used to trace a cross section that was drawn to a scale of 1 in = 10 ft. The measured area is 34.56 in^2. What is the scaled area of the section in square yards?

Solution
Because 1 in = 10 ft, we can write (1 in)^2 = (10 ft)^2 and

$$1 \text{ in}^2 = 100 \text{ ft}^2$$

The cross-section area, then, is

$$34.56 \text{ in}^2 \times \frac{100 \text{ ft}^2}{1 \text{ in}^2} = 3456 \text{ ft}^2$$

and

$$3456 \text{ ft}^2 \times \frac{1 \text{ yd}^2}{9 \text{ ft}^2} = 384 \text{ yd}^2$$

Example 10-18
An electronic planimeter is used to trace the shoreline of a lake that was drawn to a scale of 1:2000. The measured area is 123.45 cm^2. What is the scaled area of the lake in hectares?

Solution
Because the drawing scale is 1:2000, we can write

$$1 \text{ cm} = 2000 \text{ cm} \times \frac{1 \text{ m}}{100 \text{ cm}} = 20 \text{ m}$$

and

$$(1 \text{ cm})^2 = (20 \text{ m})^2 \quad \text{or} \quad 1 \text{ cm}^2 = 400 \text{ m}^2$$

The area of the lake, then, is

$$123.45 \text{ cm}^2 \times \frac{400 \text{ m}^2}{1 \text{ cm}^2} = 49\,380 \text{ m}^2$$

and

$$49\,380 \text{ m}^2 \times \frac{1 \text{ ha}}{10\,000 \text{ m}^2} = 4.94 \text{ ha}$$

Example 10-19
A mechanical planimeter is used to trace the boundary of a tract of land drawn to a scale of 1 in = 50 ft. The instrument is calibrated so that 1 unit on the planimeter scale equals 0.02 in^2 of area. When the tracer point is positioned over the starting point on the perimeter, the initial planimeter scale reading is 2345 units (the 2 is read on the drum, the 34 is read on the disk, and the last digit, 5, is read on the vernier). After tracing the perimeter once, the reading is 3855 units; the final reading after tracing the figure three times around is 6845. What is the scaled area of the tract of land in acres (1 ac = 43,560 ft^2)?

Solution
For once around the figure, the area corresponds to 3855 − 2345 = 1510 planimeter units. The average for three times around is

$$\frac{6845 - 2345}{3} = 1500 \text{ units}$$

Because 1500 is close to 1510, a blunder is not likely. The area is

$$1500 \text{ units} \times \frac{0.02 \text{ in}^2}{1 \text{ unit}} = 30 \text{ in}^2$$

Because 1 in = 50 ft, we get

$$1 \text{ in}^2 = 2500 \text{ ft}^2$$

The area of the tract, then, is computed to be

$$30 \text{ in}^2 \times \frac{2500 \text{ ft}^2}{1 \text{ in}^2} \times \frac{1 \text{ ac}}{43\,560 \text{ ft}^2} = 1.72 \text{ ac}$$

The Coordinate Method   A method for computing the area enclosed by a loop traverse using station coordinates is described in Section 7-3. The same procedure is often applied to determine the area of a cross section.

The "coordinates" for a point on the edge or perimeter of the section are the depth of cut or fill, relative to the base, and the distance of the point from a vertical axis, usually the centerline. Depths above the base may be considered positive, and those below the base negative. Distances to the right of the centerline are taken as positive, and those to the left are negative. The pairs of numbers are arranged as a series of ratios, and the area is computed as for a traverse. Selected points generally include the ends and center of the base, the points where the side slopes meet the ground surface, and any terrain break points. The coordinates can be scaled from the plotted cross section or can be computed from cross-section field notes.

Example 10-20

The earthwork section shown in Figure 10-34 has six coordinated points, expressed as the ratio of the depth of cut to the horizontal distance of the point from the centerline (Y/X), in feet. Compute the cross-sectional area, in square yards.

Solution

It is convenient to use the center of the base, with coordinates 0/0, as a starting and ending point. First, arrange the coordinates in a series by moving counterclockwise around the cross section:

Pt. 1	Pt. 2	Pt. 3	Pt. 4	Pt. 5	Pt. 6	Pt. 7	Pt. 1
$\dfrac{0}{0}$	$\dfrac{0}{20}$	$\dfrac{6}{32}$	$\dfrac{6.2}{0}$	$\dfrac{8.5}{-28}$	$\dfrac{8.9}{-42}$	$\dfrac{0}{-20}$	$\dfrac{0}{0}$

The sum of the products of diagonal terms upward to the right is

$$20 \times 6 + 32 \times 6.2 + (-28)(8.9) = 69.2$$

The sum of the products of terms downward to the right is

$$(6.2)(-28) + (8.5)(-42) + (8.9)(-20) = -708.6$$

The difference between the two sums is $69 - (-709) = 778 \, \text{ft}^2$.

Because 778 ft² represents the *double area* (see Section 7-3), we compute the cross-sectional area to be

$$\frac{778 \, \text{ft}^2}{2} \times \frac{1 \, \text{yd}^2}{9 \, \text{ft}^2} = 43.2 \, \text{yd}^2$$

Instead of using plus or minus signs for depths below or above the base, sometimes the letter C is used to designate cut and F to indicate fill (see Figure 10-3). Wooden slope stakes or grade stakes would be labeled to indicate the amount of cut or fill and the distance left or right of the centerline. For instance, a stake at point 3 in Example 10-20 would be marked C 6/32. (Slope staking and grade staking are described in Chapter 11.)

Example 10-21

The following notes describe the ground at a section in fill:

F 11.8	F 14.3	F 15.8	F 16.3
-42.5	-32.0	0	65.4

The base is 50 ft wide. Sketch the section and label the points with coordinates. Compute the area.

Solution

A sketch of the cross section is shown in Figure 10-35. The area is computed as follows:

$\dfrac{0}{0}$	$\dfrac{0}{-25}$	$\dfrac{-11.8}{-42.5}$	$\dfrac{-14.3}{-32.0}$	$\dfrac{-15.8}{0}$	$\dfrac{-16.3}{65.4}$	$\dfrac{0}{25}$	$\dfrac{0}{0}$

$$(-25)(-11.8) + (-42.5)(-14.3) + (-32.0)(-15.8) = 1408$$

$$(-11.8)(-32.0) + (-14.3)(0) + (-15.8)(65.4) + (-16.3)(25) = -1063$$

$$[1408 - (-1063)]/2 = 1236 \, \text{ft}^2 = 137 \, \text{yd}^2$$

Earthwork Volumes

Cross-section areas are computed for the purpose of determining the volumes of cut or fill between adjacent sections. One of the most common methods for computing the volume of cut or fill is to use the *average end-area formula*, expressed as follows (Figure 10-36):

$$\text{Volume} = \frac{(A_1 + A_1)(L)}{2} \qquad (10\text{-}17)$$

where $A_1, A_2 =$ areas of adjacent sections, ft² or m²
$L =$ distance between stations, ft or m

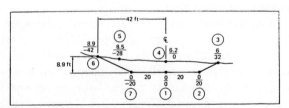

FIGURE 10-34. Coordinates of points on a section are written as the ratio of height from the base to distance from the centerline. For example, point 6 is 8.9 ft above the base and 42 ft left of the centerline. (In a fill section, a point below the base would have a negative sign.)

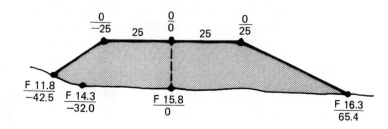

FIGURE 10-35. Illustration for Example 10-21.

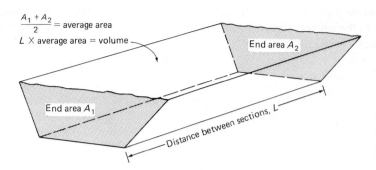

$\dfrac{A_1 + A_2}{2}$ = average area

L × average area = volume

End area A_2

End area A_1

Distance between sections, L

FIGURE 10-36. The average end-area method can provide a reasonable approximation of earthwork volume along a route.

Although the average end-area formula gives only approximate volumes, it is accurate enough for most practical applications. The accuracy can be increased, if necessary, by using more sections (i.e., reducing L) or by using a more precise prismoidal volume formula.

Example 10-22

Compute the volume of fill between station 4 + 00, where the section area $A = 123$ ft^2, and station 5 + 00, where $A = 234$ ft^2.

Solution

Applying Equation 10-17, we get

$$\text{Volume} = \frac{123 + 234 \times 100}{2} = 17\,850 \text{ ft}^3$$

and

$$17\,850 \text{ ft}^3 \times \frac{1 \text{ yd}^3}{27 \text{ ft}^3} = 661 \text{ yd}^3$$

(*Note:* Cubic feet are divided by 27, *not* 9, to get cubic yards!)

At a point where the grade line intersects the ground, a transition from cut to fill, or from fill to cut, must occur; that point is called the *grade point*. The cross section at the grade point may be a sidehill section (see Figure 10-28*b*). For *preliminary* earthwork computations, it is usually acceptable to consider the net area at the grade point to be zero. The station of the grade point can be taken from the vertical alignment profile drawing. A net volume of cut or fill can be computed between stations on each side of the grade point.

Example 10-23

At station 6 + 00, the cross-section area is 100 ft^2 of fill. At station 7 + 00, the area is 150 ft^2 of cut. The grade point is at station 6 + 35. What is the net volume of cut or fill between stations 6 + 00 and 7 + 00?

Solution

The volume of fill between station 6 + 00 and the grade point is

$$\text{Fill} = \frac{100 + 0}{2} \times 35 = 1750 \text{ ft}^2$$

The volume of cut between the grade point and station 7 + 00 is

$$\text{Cut} = \frac{0 + 150}{2} \times 65 = 4875 \text{ ft}^3$$

The net quantity of earthwork between full stations 6 + 00 and 7 + 00 is approximately $(4875 - 1750) \div 27 = 116$ yd^3 of cut. (After slope stakes have been set and transition points have been more accurately located, more accurate earthwork computations can be made if necessary.)

The Mass Diagram   One of the objectives in vertical alignment design is to balance the volumes of cut and fill. This is to minimize the quantity of earth that must either be "borrowed" from somewhere else and hauled to the site or be disposed of off-site. The preliminary grade line can be located on the profile so that earthwork appears to be balanced, but this is difficult to do visually because of the effect of *shrinkage*. Shrinkage refers to the decrease in volume of soil due to compaction in an embankment. For example, if 1 yd^3 of soil is excavated from its natural position and then compacted in a fill, it may occupy a volume of only 0.8 yd^3. It would be characterized as having a shrinkage of 20 percent, or a shrinkage factor of 0.8.

A *mass diagram* may be used to determine the extent to which cut and fill are balanced in a preliminary alignment design. The mass diagram is also useful to evaluate haul distances and to plan the overall earthwork operation. It is simply a graph that depicts the accumulation of cut-and-fill quantities along the route (Figure 10-37). Volumes of cut are positive, and volumes of fill are negative. The fill volumes are adjusted for shrinkage so that all volumes shown on the diagram are equivalent to natural or "in situ" soil conditions.

The ordinates (y values) are the cumulative algebraic sums of earthwork volume starting at station 0 + 00. The abcissas (x values) are the stations. The ordinates are connected by a smooth curve to form the mass diagram. Usually, the mass diagram is plotted directly below the profile of the grade line; this facilitates visualization of earthmoving activities. Some general characteristics of the mass diagram are shown in Figure 10-37 and are summarized as follows:

1. The mass curve rises from left to right in areas of cut.
2. The mass curve falls from left to right in areas of fill.

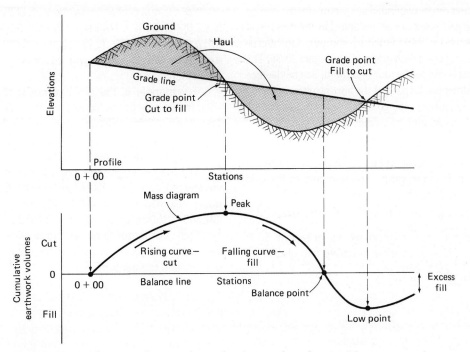

FIGURE 10-37. The mass diagram for evaluating earthwork quantities.

3. Grade points on the profile correspond to the peaks of crests and the low points in sags (or valleys) of the mass diagram.

4. Peaks occur at transitions from cut to fill; low points occur at transitions from fill to cut.

5. Any horizontal line that intersects the mass curve at two points is a *balance line*; the volume of cut equals the volume of fill between the stations of the balance points.

The amount of "unbalance," that is, the extra cut or fill along a route or section of a route, is seen as the ordinate value of the mass diagram at the last station. If this is excessive, the designer will adjust the position of the grade line in an attempt to bring the volumes of cut and fill into closer agreement; the mass diagram will then be replotted to check the balance. Sometimes, however, balancing cut and fill may be of secondary importance in alignment design; for example, a fixed grade intersection elevation may control the position of the grade line at a particular section of the route.

Volume by the Grid Method   When fill material must be hauled to a jobsite from an outside source, such as for embankment construction, the source is called a *borrow pit*. Payment for borrow is generally on a unit price basis (i.e., dollars per cubic yard or cubic meter), and the surveyor is called on to measure the quantity of the material excavated from the borrow pit. This is done by the *grid method* (Figure 10-38). A set of permanent marks or stakes are established just outside the borrow pit area to form a grid of small squares; the squares are usually 50 ft (15 m) or 25 ft (7.5 m) in size.

Rod shots are taken at the intersections of the grid, before and after excavation, and each change in elevation is computed. For one square, the volume of borrow is approximately equal to the average of the elevation change at the corners times the area of the square. For example, if the changes in elevations at the corners of a 50-ft square are 3.5, 3.9, 4.7, and 5.2 ft, the excavated volume is simply $(3.5 + 3.9 + 4.7 + 5.2)/4 \times (50 \text{ ft})^2 = 4.3 \text{ ft} \times 2500 \text{ ft}^2 = 10,800 \text{ ft}^3 = 400 \text{ yd}^3$. (Quantities computed in cubic feet must be divided by 27 ft^3/yd^3 to convert the volume to cubic yards.)

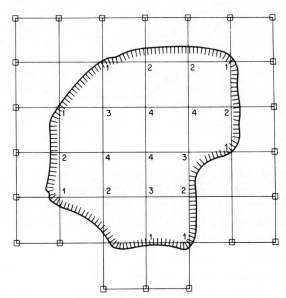

FIGURE 10-38. Grid method for computing volumes of excavation at a borrow pit.

Adjacent squares can be combined as a group, and the change in elevation at each grid point can be multiplied by the number of grid squares it touches, to avoid repetitive computations; this is illustrated by the numbers at each grid point in Figure 10-38. The sum of these results is divided by four and multiplied by the area of one square. Volumes for the parts of the borrow pit not covered by a full grid square may be computed by taking the product of the figure area (e.g., a triangle) and the average depth of cut.

Example 10-24

For the borrow pit grid shown in Figure 10-39, compute the excavated volume, in cubic yards. The numbers at the grid points represent the depth of cut, in feet.

Solution

The grid figures can be grouped as six adjacent 50-ft squares (1, 2, 4, 5, 6, and 9), three separate triangles (3, 8, and 10), and a 50×25 ft rectangle.

For the group of squares, the sum of the corners is $(1.8) + (2 \times 2.0) + (1.6) + (2 \times 1.9) + (4 \times 2.2) + (3 \times 2.3) + (2.1) + (1.5) + (3 \times 2.1) + (3 \times 2.4) + (1.8) + (1.2) + (1.8) = 48.8$ ft. The total volume excavated within those grid squares is $(48.8/4)(50 \times 50) = 30{,}500$ ft^3.

For triangle 3, the average cut is $(1.6 + 2.3 + 2.1)/2 = 2.0$ ft. The area of the triangle is $1/2 \times 50 \times 50 = 1250$ ft^2. The approximate volume, then, is area $\times$ height $= 2.0$ ft $\times 1250$ ft$^2 = 2500$ ft^3. For triangles 8 and 10, the volumes are 2000 ft^3 and 2500 ft^3, respectively.

For the rectangle, the average cut is 1.425 ft, and the volume is 1.425 ft $\times 1250$ ft$^2 = 1781$ ft^3. Summing the computed volumes and dividing by 27, we get a total volume of $(30{,}500 + 2500 + 2000 + 2500 + 1781)/27 = 39{,}281$ ft^3/27 $\approx$ 1450 yd^3. For larger grids, especially when there are more individual groups of areas, it is helpful to set up the computations in tabular form.

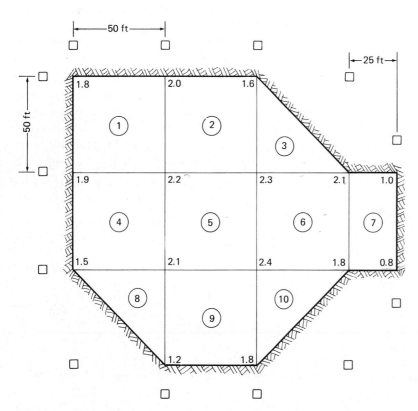

FIGURE 10-39. Illustration for Example 10-24.

Questions for Review

1. Outline and briefly discuss the general procedure for performing a route survey.

2. What kinds of curves are usually used to connect tangents along the horizontal alignment of a roadway? What kinds of curves are used along the vertical alignment?

Why are different types of curves used for the horizontal and vertical alignments?

3. Make a sketch of a horizontal curve and label the key parts.

4. Make a sketch of a vertical curve and label the key parts.

5. Define *degree of curve*. How does it vary with the curve radius?

6. Briefly describe how to determine the station on the back tangent where a horizontal curve begins, and the station on the forward tangent where it ends.

7. What is meant by *restationing* a route baseline?

8. Briefly describe a common procedure for laying out a horizontal curve and determining the relative accuracy of the work.

9. Sketch and label a compound curve and a reverse curve.

10. Define the terms *gradient*, *summit curve*, and *sag curve*.

11. How are distances measured along the vertical alignment? How does the "length" of a vertical curve differ from that of a horizontal curve?

12. What is a vertical curve turning point? Why is it sometimes necessary to compute its position?

13. Under what circumstances might it be necessary to design a horizontal or vertical curve to pass through a fixed point or elevation?

14. What are cut and fill?

15. What is a planimeter? Briefly describe how it is used.

16. Briefly describe the average end-area method for computing earthwork quantities.

17. What is the mass diagram, and what is it used for? Briefly describe its general characteristics.

18. Briefly describe the grid method for computing volume.

Practice Problems

1. A simple horizontal curve of radius 750 ft connects two tangents that intersect at an angle of 66°30'. Compute the parts of the curve, including T, L, LC, E, and M.

2. A simple horizontal curve of radius 125 m connects two tangents that intersect at an angle of 105°40'. Compute the parts of the curve, including T, L, LC, E, and M.

3. What is the degree of curve (arc definition) in Problem 1?

4. What is the degree of curve (arc definition) in Problem 2?

5. A simple curve is to be laid out so that its middle ordinate is at least 75 ft. If the tangents intersect at an angle of 40°, what is the highest degree of curve that can be used?

6. A simple curve is to be laid out so that its external distance is 35 m or less. If the tangents intersect at an angle of 80°, what is the smallest degree of curve that can be used?

7. The radius of a simple curve is twice its tangent distance. What is the angle of intersection?

8. The radius of a simple curve is equal to the length of the long chord. What is the angle of intersection?

9. For the simple curve in Problem 1, if the station of the PI is 22 + 50, what are the stations of the PC and the PT?

10. For the simple curve in Problem 2, if the station of the PI is 12 + 00, what are the stations of the PC and the PT?

11. Given:

    Tangent 1, 0 + 00 to 12 + 50, azimuth = 53°30'

    Tangent 2, 12 + 50 to 19 + 00, azimuth = 79°00'

    Tangent 3, 19 + 00 to 28 + 75, azimuth = 24°30'

    The tangents are to be connected by simple curves, each with a degree of curvature = 8°. Determine the stations of the PCs and the PTs along the final route, and determine the equation of chainage at the endpoint.

12. Given:

    Tangent 1, 0 + 00 to 15 + 75, bearing = S33°30' E

    Tangent 2, 15 + 75 to 23 + 00, bearing = S49°00' E

    Tangent 3, 23 + 00 to 38 + 00, bearing = S14°30' W

    The tangents are to be connected by simple curves, each with a degree of curvature = 6°. Determine the stations of the PCs and the PTs along the final route, and determine the equation of chainage at the endpoint.

13. A simple curve with $D_a = 18°$ has its PC at station 10 + 50. What are the deflection angles for stations on the curve of 11 + 00, 12 + 00, and 13 + 00, from the PC? What is the chord length from the PC to station 11 + 00, and from station 11 + 00 to station 12 + 00?

14. A simple curve with $D_a = 12°$ has its PC at station 15 + 25. What are the deflection angles for stations on the curve of 16 + 00, 16 + 50, and 17 + 00, from the PC? What is the chord length from the PC to station 16 + 00, and from station 16 + 00 to station 16 + 50?

15. Given, for a simple curve: $R = 350$ ft, $\Delta = 72°34'30''$ and the station of the PI = 22 + 41.64. Set up the field notes for staking out the curve with deflection angles and chords.

16. Given for a simple curve: $R = 400$ ft, $\Delta = 66°18'24''$, and the station of the PI = 48 + 25.32. Set up the field notes for staking out the curve with deflection angles and chords.

17. Given for a simple curve: $R = 500$ ft, $\Delta = 58°08'40''$, and the station of the PI = 38 + 17.25. Set up the field notes for staking out the curve with deflection angles and chords.

18. Given for a simple curve: $R = 600$ ft, $\Delta = 42°34'28''$, and the station of the PI = 28 + 37.42. Set up the field notes for staking out the curve with deflection angles and chords.

19. The PI of a simple horizontal curve with $R = 750$ ft is not accessible. Point A is established on the back tangent at station 75 + 00, and point B is set on the forward tangent. The distance AB is measured as 322.33 ft, the angle at A is measured as 32°15', and the angle at B is determined to be 41°30'. Determine the stations of the PC and the PT.

20. The PI of a simple horizontal curve with $R = 1200$ ft is not accessible. Point A is established on the back tangent at station 115 + 00, and point B is set on the forward tangent.

The distance AB is measured as 987.65 ft, the angle at A is measured as 43°45′, and the angle at B is determined to be 39°30′. Determine the stations of the PC and the PT.

21. Given, for a compound curve: plus of PI = 14 + 29.31, $\Delta = 97°35'15''$; the first radius $R_1 = 400'$, $\Delta_1 = 63°22'18''$, $R_2 = 800'$. Compute the pluses of PC, PCC, and PT and the length T_2.

22. Given for a compound curve: plus of PI = 12 + 87.93, $\Delta = 98°32'54''$, the first radius $R_1 = 300'$, $\Delta_1 = 62°18'34''$, $R_2 = 600'$. Compute the pluses of PC, PCC, and PT and the length T_2.

23. Given for a reverse curve: plus PC = A = 1729.38, $a = 47°29'14''$, AB = 276.82, $b = 22°34'16''$. Compute Δ_1, Δ_2, plus PRC, and plus PT.

24. Given for a reverse curve: plus PC = A = 1532.71, $a = 44°32'10''$, AB = 283.17', $b = 25°17'20''$. Compute Δ_1, Δ_2, plus PRC, and plus PT.

25. For a preliminary vertical alignment of a roadway, the straight tangent sections are established as follows:

    Station 0 + 00, tangent elevation = 1055.00
    Station 23 + 00, tangent elevation = 1107.75
    Station 40 + 00, tangent elevation = 1056.75
    Station 65 + 00, tangent elevation = 1156.00

    Determine the gradient of each tangent and the elevation at 1000-ft intervals along the tangents.

26. For a preliminary vertical alignment of a roadway, the straight tangent sections are established as follows:

    Station 0 + 00, tangent elevation = 73.00
    Station 9 + 50, tangent elevation = 49.25
    Station 22 + 25, tangent elevation = 93.00
    Station 29 + 00, tangent elevation = 105.00

    Determine the gradient of each tangent and the elevation at 500-ft intervals along the tangents.

27. A vertical parabolic curve has its PVI at station 29 + 25.00 and elevation 87.52. The grade of the back tangent is 2.5 percent, the grade of the forward tangent is −4.5 percent, and the curve length is 550 ft. Set up a table showing curve elevations at the PVC, at the PVT, and at half-station points along the curve. Compute the station and elevation of the curve turning point.

28. A vertical parabolic curve has its PVI at station 14 + 75.00 and elevation 76.29. The grade of the back tangent is 3.4 percent, the grade of the forward tangent is −4.8 percent, and the curve length is 450 ft. Set up a table showing curve elevations at the PVC, at the PVT, and at half-station points along the curve. Compute the station and elevation of the curve turning point.

29. A vertical parabolic curve has its PVI at station 18 + 50.00 and elevation 69.32. The grade of the back tangent is −2.8 percent, the grade of the forward tangent is 5.6 percent, and the curve length is 600 ft. Set up a table showing curve elevations at the PVC, at the PVT, and at half-station points along the curve. Compute the station and elevation of the curve turning point.

30. A vertical parabolic curve has its PVI at station 10 + 00.00 and elevation 54.71. The grade of the back tangent is −3.2 percent, the grade of the forward tangent is 5.8 percent, and the curve length is 500 ft. Set up a table showing curve elevations at the PVC, at the PVT, and at half-station points along the curve. Compute the station and elevation of the curve turning point.

31. A simple curve is to connect two tangents with an angle of intersection = 40°. The curve must pass through a point that is located 125.00 ft from the PI, at an angle of 70° from the back tangent, measured at the PI. Determine the required degree of curvature (arc definition).

32. A simple curve is to connect two tangents with an angle of intersection = 80°. The curve must pass through a point that is located 50.00 m from the PI, at an angle of 30° from the back tangent, as measured at the PI. Determine the required curve radius.

33. A vertical curve is to connect two tangents that intersect at station 50 + 00 and elevation 500.00 ft. The back tangent gradient is −4 percent, the forward tangent gradient is 2 percent, and the elevation of the curve at station 48 + 50 must be equal to at least 510 ft. What is the required length of curve?

34. A vertical curve is to connect two tangents that intersect at station 30 + 50 and elevation 800.00 ft. The back tangent gradient is 3 percent, the forward tangent gradient is −5 percent, and the elevation of the curve at station 32 + 50 must be equal to at most 785.00 ft. What is the required length of curve?

35. A planimeter is used to trace a cross section that was drawn to a scale of 1 in = 5 ft, and the measured area is 22.50 in². What is the scaled area, in square yards?

36. A planimeter is used to trace the perimeter of a lake that was drawn to a scale of 1 in = 500 ft, and the measured area is 32.50 in². What is the scaled area, in acres?

37. A planimeter is used to trace a cross section that was drawn to a scale of 1:50, and the measured area is 122.50 cm². What is the scaled area, in square meters?

38. A planimeter is used to trace the perimeter of a lake that was drawn to a scale of 1:10,000, and the measured area is 222.22 cm². What is the scaled area, in hectares?

39. A mechanical planimeter is used to trace the boundary of a tract of land drawn to a scale of 1 in = 100 ft. It is calibrated so that 1 unit on the planimeter scale equals 0.025 in² of area. When the tracer point is positioned over the starting point on the perimeter, the initial reading is 3456 units. After tracing the perimeter once, the reading is 4970; the final reading after tracing the figure four times is 9536. What is the scaled area of the tract, in acres?

40. A mechanical planimeter is used to trace the boundary of a tract of land drawn to a scale of 1 in = 2000 ft. It is calibrated so that 1 unit on the planimeter scale equals

0.03 in² of area. When the tracer point is positioned over the starting point on the perimeter, the initial reading is 5678 units. After tracing the perimeter once, the reading is 6233; the final reading after tracing the figure two times is 6798. What is the scaled area of the tract, in acres?

41. By the method of coordinates, determine the cross-sectional areas of the sections shown in Figure 10-40. Compute the volume of earthwork between the sections.

42. By the method of coordinates, determine the cross-sectional areas of the sections shown in Figure 10-41. Compute the volume of earthwork between the sections.

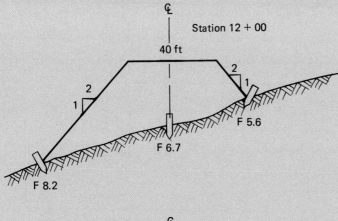

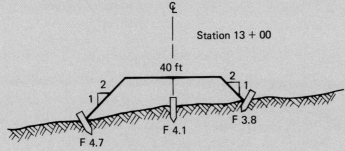

FIGURE 10-40. Illustration for Problem 41.

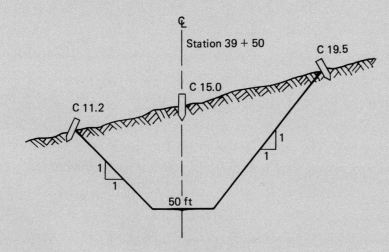

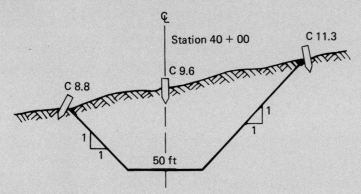

FIGURE 10-41. Illustration for Problem 42.

43. Sketch a mass diagram for the roadway grade line shown in Figure 10-42.

44. Sketch a mass diagram for the roadway grade line shown in Figure 10-43.

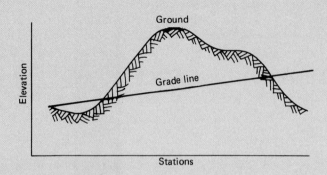

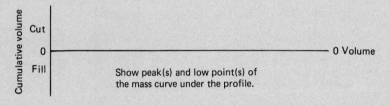

Show peak(s) and low point(s) of the mass curve under the profile.

FIGURE 10-42. Illustration for Problem 43.

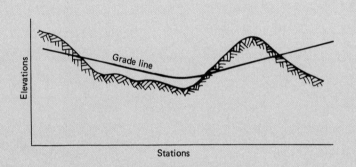

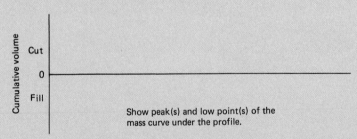

Show peak(s) and low point(s) of the mass curve under the profile.

FIGURE 10-43. Illustration for Problem 44.

45. For the borrow pit shown in Figure 10-44, compute the excavated volume in cubic yards. The numbers at the grid points represent the depths of cut, in feet.

46. For the borrow pit shown in Figure 10-45, compute the excavated volume in cubic meters. The numbers at the grid points represent the depths of cut, in meters.

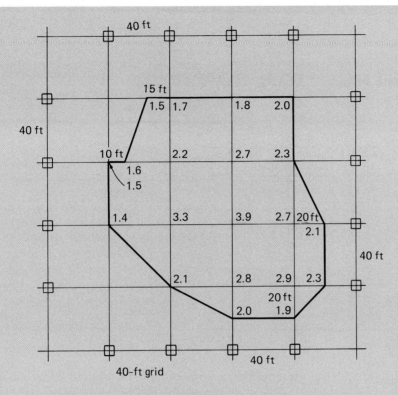

FIGURE 10-44. Illustration for Problem 45.

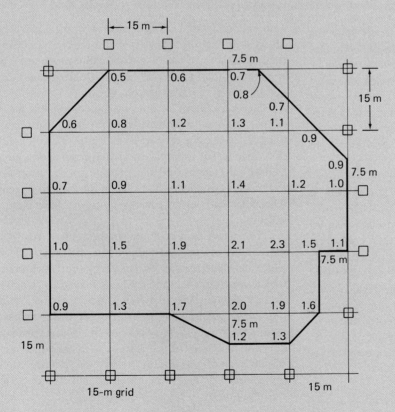

FIGURE 10-45. Illustration for Problem 46.

CONSTRUCTION SURVEYS

One of the most common tasks for the surveyor is to mark on the ground the locations of buildings, roads, pipelines, and other projects that are to be built. The proposed locations are shown on a site plan by the designer (a civil engineer or architect), generally by giving appropriate distances and directions from the site boundary lines or from horizontal and vertical control monuments. The surveyor must transfer these given (or scaled) distances from a drawing into the field, with a suitable degree of accuracy. Naturally, the accuracy required to temporarily mark the position of a house for foundation excavation is not as great as that required to mark the exact position of an anchor bolt for securing a bridge girder to a pier.

This task of marking the positions of proposed infrastructure is called *construction surveying*. It may also be called *location surveying* or *construction stakeout*. The marks placed by the surveyor typically are wooden stakes or hubs, and they may serve as references for either horizontal location, vertical location, or both. The vertical location or elevation of future construction is called the *grade*. (This should not be confused with the word *gradient*, which is the equivalent of *slope*; sometimes the phrase *rate of grade* is also used to express slope, that is, the ratio of a change in elevation to a corresponding horizontal distance.) Placing reference marks or stakes to establish the location and elevation of a project to be built is sometimes called *giving line and grade*.

The stakes set by the surveyor serve as reference points for the construction contractor who is responsible for actually building the project. Carpenters, masons, and other skilled craftspersons can make relatively short measurements from the stakes to locate the exact position and height of concrete

formwork, a roadway curb, the depth of a foundation, or other major components of the facility to be built.

The location survey process begins before the contractor starts work, and usually continues throughout the entire construction period. The surveyor must gauge her or his work so that the necessary marks are always available to the builder for each day's operation, but never so far ahead of the work that the marks might be destroyed in the rough and tumble of the construction process.

Stakes for line or location are sometimes set at the actual position called for in the plans, but these can serve only temporarily because they are soon disturbed by the construction activity. For example, the actual corners of a house or building may be staked out preceding excavation for the foundation (see Figure 11-1). They will have to be replaced when formwork for the concrete footings is to be built in the excavation.

The actual field positions are best referenced by more permanent marks that will not be disturbed and from which construction can be located by short measurements with a carpenter's rule and level (see Figure 11-2). Stakes for line are generally *offset* between 3 and 6 ft (1 and 2 m) from the actual position of the facility for this purpose (see Figure 11-3). An *offset line* parallels the actual construction line, and is marked at full-station, half-station, or quarter-station intervals, depending on the type and dimensions of the project (see Figure 11-4). House corners are generally staked out with 10-ft (3-m) offsets to avoid disturbance by foundation excavation.

Construction surveying involves the application of many of the basic techniques described earlier in this text. In fact, the field procedure for *marking line and distance*, that is,

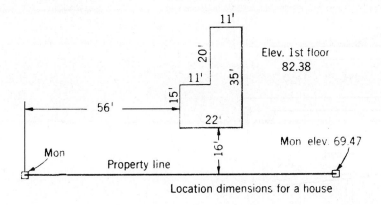

Location dimensions for a house

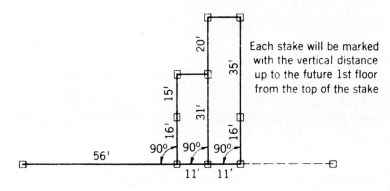

Each stake will be marked with the vertical distance up to the future 1st floor from the top of the stake

FIGURE 11-1. One method for staking out the corners of a house, showing stakes set and angles and distances measured.

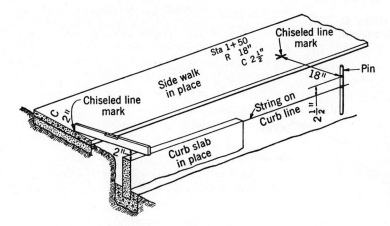

FIGURE 11-2. Setting pins to give line and grade for curb.

setting stakes or other marks at certain distances on a given line, was already described in Section 4-2. The process of locating or staking out a horizontal curve, as described in Section 10-3, is another example of a layout or construction survey application. In this chapter, the basic procedures for establishing line and grade using traditional instruments, as well as modern electronic and laser devices, are discussed and illustrated. Although it is not possible to cover all field layout problems, some of which can get quite complex and require special techniques, this chapter will serve as a useful introduction to the very dynamic and challenging task of construction surveying.

11-1 ESTABLISHING LINE

The process of giving line consists in establishing a direction by turning a predetermined angle and placing a series of marks along the line at predetermined distances. The angle may be established with a transit or theodolite, and the distances are laid out with a steel tape or by electronic distance measurement (EDM). As previously mentioned, the field procedure for measuring the distances and setting the marks is discussed in Section 4-2. In this section, the procedures for setting a predetermined angle and establishing direction are discussed.

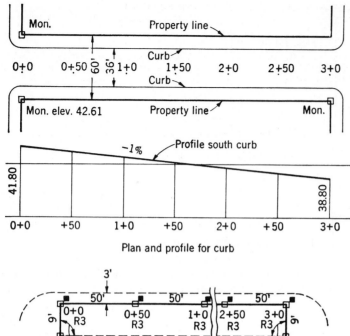

Plan and profile for curb

One method of placing line and grade stakes

The line stakes are set every 50 feet
3 feet back from future face of curb

Legend   Line stakes □
          Grade stakes ■

FIGURE 11-3. Staking out a curb. Often only one set of stakes are used for both line and grade.

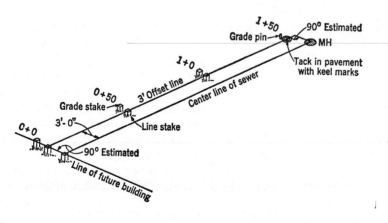

FIGURE 11-4. Offset-line and grade stakes for a sewer. (One set of stakes may be used for both line and grade.)

Setting a Predetermined Angle

An angle can be established by setting up an instrument at the angle point, or vertex, and proceeding as follows:

1. Point at the reference mark and lock the instrument on line.
2. Set zero using the "set 0" button on the instrument.

3. Turn the instrument and accurately set the predetermined value of the angle.
4. Set a stake or other mark on the new line (see Section 4-2).

When greater accuracy is required, the angle established by one turn of the instrument must be measured by repetition and the mark adjusted accordingly. The distance the mark must be shifted is computed by trigonometry:

$$D = R \tan \delta \qquad (11\text{-}1)$$

where D = distance the mark is moved perpendicular to the line

R = distance from the instrument to the mark

δ = difference between the predetermined angle and the angle measured by repetition

Example 11-1

A mark is to be set at an angle of exactly 90°00'00" from a given baseline and at a distance of 400.00 ft from the instrument position. After setting the mark, the angle is measured by repetition and determined to be 90°00'20" (see Figure 11-5). What distance should the mark be shifted so that the angle is exactly 90°00'00"?

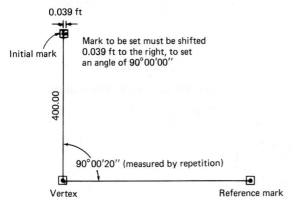

FIGURE 11-5. Establishing an accurate angle for direction.

Solution

The angular error is equal to 20 seconds. Applying Equation 11-1, we get

$$D = 400.00 \tan\left(\frac{20}{3600}\right) = 400.00 \times 0.000097 = 0.039\,\text{ft}$$

(Note that 1° = 3600".)

Establishing Direction

When the direction of a line is to be established either by turning an angle from a mark or by merely pointing at a mark on a line, if more than one mark is available, the mark at the greatest distance from the instrument should be used to establish the original direction of the line of sight. In general, *the direction of a line should be established from a line longer than itself.*

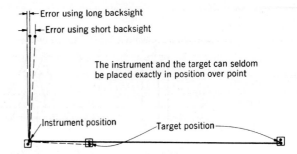

FIGURE 11-6. Using a long backsight reduces error.

The instrument can never be set up exactly over a point, nor can the signal or target be placed exactly over its mark. Obviously, the longer the line sighted, the less these errors will affect direction (see Figure 11-6).

The instrument is always subject to possible motion. Changes in temperature, settlement of the tripod, vibration, and readjustment of stresses in the tripod are contributing causes. Therefore, whenever a series of marks are to be set on a line, the direction of the line of sight should be frequently checked by pointing at the original mark, and should always be checked after the last mark is set.

It is clear that the line of sight must be pointed repeatedly at certain marks. When these marks cannot be seen, much time is wasted by sending someone with a plumb bob or a range pole to them whenever a sight is necessary. This can be avoided by establishing clearly visible foresights for these points. For example, instead of a tack, a finishing nail can be driven so that its head is about 1/4 in. (6 mm) above the top of the original stake. Also, a plumb bob, or some other device can be rigged over the mark (see Figure 11-7).

In lieu of these, after *taking line* by pointing on a plumb bob, look for an object that happens to be anywhere on line. Letters on signboards are especially useful for this purpose. If an object is not available, choose any flat vertical surface on line. Set two pencil marks in line on this surface, one about 6 in. (200 mm) above the other. Using a pencil and yellow keel (lumber crayon), construct a target that is easily found and identified, and that offers a precise line centered on these marks (see Figure 11-8).

For major construction projects, important lines should be permanently marked with monuments, and permanent foresights should be built at each end of the line.

11-2 ESTABLISHING GRADE

Marking elevations is usually called *giving grade* and *grade staking*. It consists in setting marks such as tops of stakes, nails in vertical surfaces, and keel marks at required elevations. Marks may also be set at convenient elevations, with

Save with
elevated nail

Plumb bob
marking point

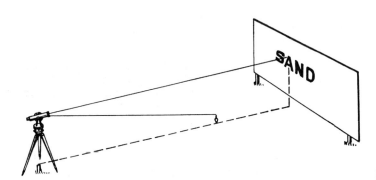

FIGURE 11-7. Typical foresights.

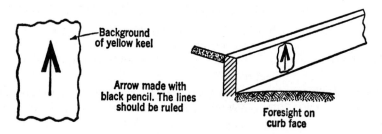

Background
of yellow keel

Arrow made with
black pencil. The lines
should be ruled

Foresight on
curb face

FIGURE 11-8. A type of foresight
that is easily established.

indications of the vertical heights at which the actual grade is to be established above or below them. As previously mentioned, marks for grade are usually placed in the vicinity of the work and transferred into position by carpenter's levels and rules. Grade can be transferred over relatively large offset distances using a board or string line and level (see Figure 11-9).

Three methods of giving grade, called *setting grade marks*, *shooting in grade*, and *indicating cuts and fills*, are discussed here.

Setting Grade Marks

When support is available at the proper elevation, it is possible to set marks exactly at the proposed grade. However, this method is time consuming and not often utilized any longer. Starting at a benchmark, a line of levels is carried to the vicinity of the work. The instrument is thus brought into a

position at a known height of instrument (HI) from which the rod held on the mark may be observed.

The *grade rod* (GR) is then determined. Grade rod is *the reading on the level rod that would be obtained from the present instrument position if the bottom of the rod were placed on the proposed grade.* It is computed as follows (see Figure 11-10):

$$GR = HI - grade \qquad (11-2)$$

where grade is the required or proposed elevation of construction.

The rod target is set at the value of the grade rod. If the top of a wooden stake is to be used for a mark, the stake is driven down until, when the rod is placed on it, the target appears on the line of sight. This is a trial-and-error process. When the stake is driven to the proper depth, it may be covered with blue keel; these stakes are sometimes called *blue tops*. Sometimes the letter G is placed on the stake to indicate

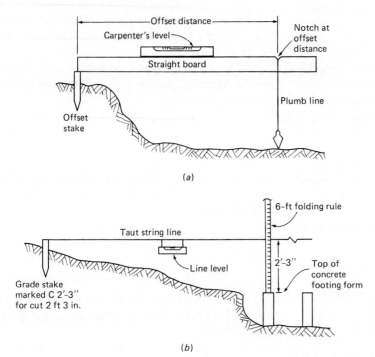

(a)

(b)

FIGURE 11-9. Line and grade can be easily transferred from the surveyor's stakes to the work, using builder's tools.

that the top is at the required grade. The station may be marked on the side of a nearby guard stake.

When a grade mark is to be placed on a vertical surface instead of the top of a stake or hub, the rod is held against the surface and moved up or down until the target is on the line of sight. A pencil mark or nail is then placed at the bottom of the rod (Figure 11-11).

Obviously, several grades can be established from one instrument position. The line of levels can then be carried to other locations and more grades set. Finally, the line of levels must be carried to the original or to another benchmark for a check on the work.

Example 11-2

The HI of a level is 75.37 ft. A blue-top stake is to be set to mark a required grade of 68.50 ft in a location where the existing ground is only slightly lower than the required grade. At what value should the rod target be set so that the stake can be driven to the proper depth?

Solution

The target should be set at grade rod. Using Equation 11-2,

$$GR = 75.37 - 68.50 = 6.87 \text{ ft}$$

The stake is driven, with frequent checking, until the target at 6.87 is on the line of sight of the instrument. The top of the stake, which may be an inch or 2 (25–50 mm) above the ground surface, is then at the required grade.

Support not Available   Very often, support is not available in the vicinity of the work on which the actual grade can be marked. For example, the actual grade for a foundation footing that is meant to be 3 ft (1 m) below the ground surface cannot be marked on the ground. Likewise, the grade for the first-floor

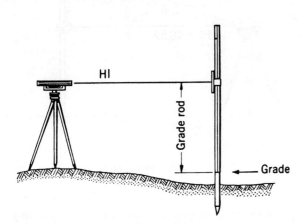

FIGURE 11-10. Setting a stake at grade.

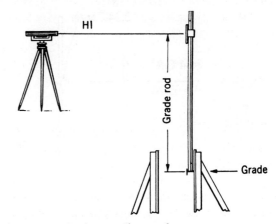

FIGURE 11-11. Setting a nail at grade.

slab of a building that is designed to be 2 ft (600 mm) above existing grade cannot be marked by a blue top because the stake would protrude excessively above the existing ground.

Under these circumstances, it is customary to set grade stakes, place the rod on top of the stakes, and take a reading to determine the elevation of the stakes. The cut or fill is then determined and the stakes (or guards) are marked accordingly. When the required grade is above the grade mark, the letter F precedes the amount of fill needed at that point; for example, F 3′6″ indicates that the required grade is 3.5 ft above the top of the grade stake or mark. The letter C precedes the amount of cut required at the point, when the required grade is below the grade mark; for example, C 2′0″ indicates that 2.0 ft of excavation is needed at that point to reach the grade.

If the grade rod value is larger than the rod setting, the grade will be below the top of the stake by the difference. In this case, the stake will be marked *cut,* or C with the number of feet and tenths. This may be stated as follows:

$$C = GR - \text{rod} \qquad (11\text{-}3)$$

If the grade rod value is less than the target setting on the rod, the grade will be above the top of the stake by the difference. In this case, the stake will be marked fill, or F with the number of feet and tenths. This may be stated as follows:

$$F = \text{rod} - GR \qquad (11\text{-}4)$$

Thus, when the ground is not at the right height for setting a stake at grade, the problem is to determine how many half feet to add to or subtract from the grade rod value. This is clarified in the following examples.

Example 11-3

It is required to set a stake to mark a grade of 46.94 ft. The HI is determined to be 55.28 ft, and the reading of the rod on the stake is 3.34 ft. Determine the appropriate target setting and the amount of cut or fill to be marked on the stake.

Solution

First, apply Equation 11-2 to compute grade rod as follows:

$$GR = HI - \text{grade} = 55.28 - 46.94 = 8.34 \text{ ft}$$

Because the rod on the stake reads 3.34, it is clear that the required grade is several feet below the ground (see Figure 11-12).

In this case, the grade rod value is larger than the rod setting. Applying Equation 11-3, we compute the amount of cut to be

$$C = 8.34 - 3.34 = 5.0 \text{ ft} = 5'0''$$

Example 11-4

It is required to set a stake to mark a grade of 42.27 ft. The HI is determined to be 48.52 ft, and the reading of the rod on the stake is 9.75 ft. Determine the amount of cut or fill to be marked on the stake.

Solution

First, apply Equation 11-2 to compute grade rod, as follows:

$$GR = HI - \text{grade} = 48.52 - 42.27 = 6.25 \text{ ft}$$

Because the rod on the stake reads 9.75, it is clear that the required grade is several feet above the ground (see Figure 11-13).

In this case, the grade rod value is less than the rod setting. Applying Equation 11-4, we compute the amount of fill to be

$$F = 9.75 - 6.25 = 3.5 \text{ ft} = 3'6''$$

Indicating Cuts and Fills

The most rapid and, in many ways, the best method of giving grade is to indicate the cuts or fills measured from convenient objects near the work. Usually the tops of line stakes (centerline or offset) or other line marks are used.

The elevations of the tops of the line stakes or of other objects chosen are determined by profile leveling. The values of the cuts or fills are computed by comparing the elevation of each mark with the grade at that particular position. They are computed in hundredths of a foot, reduced to inches, and marked on the stakes or near the marks (see

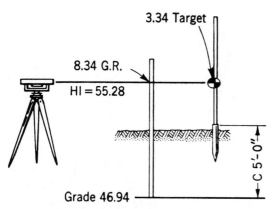

FIGURE 11-12. Setting a grade stake when the supporting ground is too high above grade.

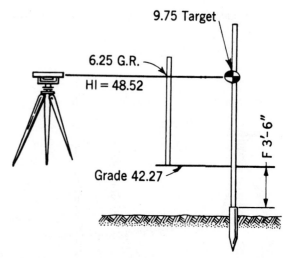

FIGURE 11-13. Setting a grade stake when the supporting ground is too far below grade.

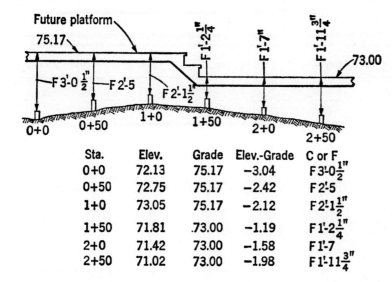

Sta.	Elev.	Grade	Elev.-Grade	C or F
0+0	72.13	75.17	−3.04	F 3'-0$\frac{1}{2}$"
0+50	72.75	75.17	−2.42	F 2'-5
1+0	73.05	75.17	−2.12	F 2'-1$\frac{1}{2}$"
1+50	71.81	.73.00	−1.19	F 1'-2$\frac{1}{4}$"
2+0	71.42	73.00	−1.58	F 1'-7
2+50	71.02	73.00	−1.98	F 1'-11$\frac{3}{4}$"

FIGURE 11-14. Giving grade by indicating cut or fill.

Figure 11-14). The required "cuts and fills" are sometimes provided in tabular form on a *cut sheet*. The cut sheet is referenced to the grade stakes by either stationing or consecutive numbering (see Table 11-1).

When the required grade is above the grade of the stake, the letter "F" precedes the amount of fill needed at that point. For example, F 3'6" indicates that the required grade

is 3.5 ft above the top of the grade stake. The letter "C" precedes the amount of cut required at the point when the required grade is below the grade mark. For instance, C 2'4" indicates that 2.33 ft of excavation is needed at that point to reach grade. The tops of the stakes or other objects are usually covered with keel to indicate that grade should be measured from those points.

Table 11-1. Typical Cut Sheet

Sta.	Stake Elevation	Proposed Elevation	Difference	Cut	Fill	Remarks
Inlet 8	411.40	398.61	−12.79	12' − 9$\frac{1}{2}$"		7' off grate
	411.40	394.93	−16.47	16' − 5$\frac{5}{8}$"		7' off inv
	411.39	398.61	−12.78	12' − 9$\frac{3}{8}$"		12' off grate
	411.39	394.93	−16.46	16' − 5$\frac{1}{2}$"		12' off inv
Inlet 9	400.51	398.61	−1.90	1' − 10$\frac{3}{4}$"		10' off grate
	400.51	394.25	−6.26	6' − 3$\frac{1}{8}$"		10' off inv in
	400.51	394.00	−6.51	6' − 6$\frac{1}{8}$"		10' off inv out
	399.77	398.61	−1.16	1' − 1$\frac{7}{8}$"		15' off grate
	399.77	394.25	−5.52	5' − 6$\frac{1}{4}$"		15' off inv in
	399.77	394.00	−5.77	5' − 9$\frac{1}{4}$"		15' off inv out
Inlet 10	376.38	375.50	−0.88	0' − 10$\frac{1}{2}$"		10' off grate
	376.38	373.45	−2.93	2' − 11$\frac{1}{8}$"		10' off inv
	375.54	375.50	−0.04	0' − 0$\frac{1}{2}$"		15' off grate
	375.54	373.45	−2.09	2' − 1$\frac{1}{8}$"		15' off inv
Inlet 11	371.65	373.00	1.35		1' − 4$\frac{1}{4}$"	10' off grate
	371.65	371.50	−0.15	0' − 1$\frac{3}{4}$"		10' off inv
	371.33	373.00	1.67		1' − 8"	15' off grate
	371.33	371.50	0.17		0' − 2"	15' off inv

(Continued)

Table 11-1. Typical Cut Sheet   *(Continued)*

Sta.	Stake Elevation	Proposed Elevation	Difference	Cut	Fill	Remarks
Inlet 12	356.78	355.60	−1.18	$1' - 2\frac{1}{8}''$		10' off grate
	356.78	353.85	−2.93	$2' - 11\frac{1}{8}''$		10' off inv in
	356.78	351.65	−5.13	$5' - 1\frac{1}{2}''$		10' off inv out
	356.77	355.60	−1.17	$1' - 2''$		14' off grate
	356.77	353.85	−2.92	$2' - 11''$		14' off inv in
	356.77	351.65	−5.12	$5' - 1\frac{1}{2}''$		14' off inv out
MH 1	382.84	384.00	1.16		$1' - 1\frac{7}{8}''$	10' off rim
	382.84	369.67	−13.17	$13' - 2''$		10' off inv in
	382.84	369.30	−13.54	$13' - 6\frac{1}{2}''$		10' off inv out
	382.84	381.00	−1.84	$1' - 10\frac{1}{8}''$		10' off inv in
	383.13	384.00	0.87		$0' - 10\frac{1}{2}''$	15' off rim
	383.13	369.67	−13.46	$13' - 5\frac{1}{2}''$		15' off inv in
	383.13	369.30	−13.83	$13' - 10''$		15' off inv out
	383.13	381.00	−2.13	$2' - 1\frac{1}{2}''$		15' off inv in

As a convenience to the builder, cut or fill may be indicated in feet, inches, and fractions of an inch because this is the way most carpenter's rules are graduated.

Because 1 in. equals $8\frac{1}{3}$ hundredths of a foot, for practical purposes 1/8 in. can be taken to be 1 hundredth of a foot. The quarters of a foot can be expressed accurately in inches and hundredths of a foot as follows:

0 in. = 0 hundredths, or 0.00 ft

3 in. = 25 hundredths, or 0.25 ft

6 in. = 50 hundredths, or 0.50 ft

9 in. = 75 hundredths, or 0.75 ft

12 in. = 100 hundredths, or 1.00 ft

By adding 8 to or subtracting it from the nearest quarter point, the inch values in hundredths of a foot can be computed to within one-third of a hundredth. This is shown in Table 11-2.

To reduce hundredths to inches, choose the nearest inch value and correct for the odd hundredths by calling them eighths of an inch. The error is never greater than 0.0005 ft. For example:

0.89 ft = 0.92 ft − 0.03 ft = 11 in. − $\frac{3}{8}$ in. = $10\frac{5}{8}$ in.

0.44 ft = 0.42 ft + 0.02 ft = 5 in. + $\frac{2}{8}$ in. = $5\frac{1}{4}$ in.

0.71 ft = 0.75 ft − 0.04 ft = 5 in. − $\frac{4}{8}$ in. = $8\frac{1}{2}$ in.

Signals for Giving Grade   The only signals used for giving grade that are not used for profile leveling are "up" and "down." Up is signaled by moving the hand upward from shoulder height, usually with the index finger pointed up. Down is signaled by lowering the hand from waist height, with the index finger pointed down. Large, slow motions indicate large amounts, and vice versa. Usually, the estimated distance is signaled immediately afterward in hundredths of a foot.

11-3 SLOPE STAKING

The procedure for giving line and grade for the construction of earthwork side slopes is called *slope staking*. It is most commonly used for locating the edges of highway cuts and fills that exceed 3 ft (1 m) in depth. *Slope stakes* mark the line of intersection of the side slope and the existing ground surface.

Table 11-2. Converting Hundredths to Inches

Inch	Quarter Points	Computations	Inch Values Hundredths of a Foot
0	0		0
1		0 + 8	8
2		25 − 8	17
3	25		25
4		25 + 8	33
5		50 − 8	42
6	50		50
7		50 + 8	58
8		75 − 8	67
9	75		75
10		75 + 8	83
11		100 − 8	92
12	100		100

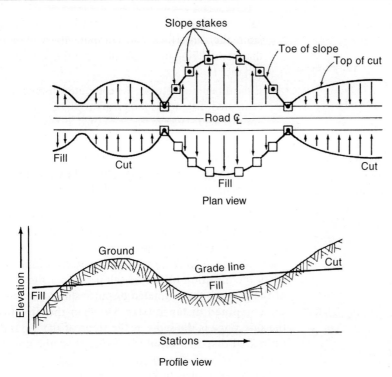

Plan view

Profile view

FIGURE 11-15. Slope stakes mark the line where cut or fill side slopes intersect the original ground surface. (The arrows in plan view show the downward direction of the slope.)

This line, called the *toe of slope* for embankment or the *top of cut* for excavation, is usually an irregular line due to the changing terrain and grade of construction (see Figure 11-15). The earthwork contractor must know where these outer limits of cut and fill are before construction can start.

A slope stake is placed on each side of every centerline stake, usually at 50-ft (15-m) intervals along the route; each slope stake is marked with both the horizontal distance (left or right) of the centerline and the vertical distance from the existing ground at the stake to the elevation of the base (see Figure 11-16). For example, a stake marked F 15.1/58.1 R is 58.1 ft (m) to the right of the centerline and 15.1 ft (m) below the finish grade of the base. Each stake is also marked with the station number. Slope stakes are usually driven so that they are inclined slightly outward from the embankment or excavation, although some surveyors may incline a stake inward for cut, toward the excavation. Generally, reference stakes are also driven about 10 ft (3 m) beyond the actual slope intercepts (also called the *catch points*), out of the way of the earthmoving machines.

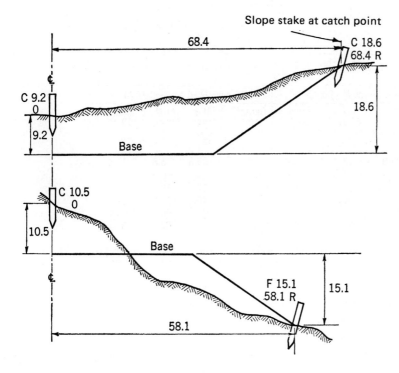

FIGURE 11-16. Marks on stakes for slope staking. Note that C (cut) or F (fill) is not the cut or fill at the stake, but the vertical distance from the ground at the stake to the elevation of the base. Generally, the stakes are offset from the actual catch points.

The position of a slope stake depends on the

1. Elevation of the base
2. Width of the base
3. Slope of the sides
4. Elevation of the ground where the stake is placed

Slope intercepts can be located from plotted cross sections by scaling the distances from the centerline to the positions where the side slopes intersect the ground. Slope intercepts can also be located in the field by a trial-and-error process. Even when the intercepts are predetermined from cross-section data, their position must be checked in the field and adjusted, if necessary, by the trial-and-error process. An error of up to 0.5 ft (0.15 m) in the distance from the centerline is usually acceptable for rough grading.

Field Procedure

The trial-and-error field procedure for slope staking can be outlined as follows:

1. Compute grade rod at the centerline (using Equation 11-2).
2. Compute cut (C) or fill (F) at the centerline (using either Equation 11-3 or Equation 11-4).
3. Compute the distance D to the catch point that would occur if the ground were level: $D = B/2 + S$ (C or F), where B is the width of the base and S is the side slope.
4. Estimate the distance to the actual catch point.

5. Take a rod shot on the ground at the estimated distance from the centerline, and compute the cut or fill at that point. Using that value of cut or fill, recompute the distance D.
6. If the difference between the computed distance and the estimated distance is larger than ±0.5 ft (0.15 m), try another value close to the computed distance and repeat steps 4 and 5.
7. If the computed distance is within ±0.5 ft (0.15 m) of the estimated distance, mark the stake with the amount of cut or fill and the computed distance.

The first estimate (step 4) for the distance from the centerline to the catch point may be based on the scaled value from the plotted cross-section data, or it may be based on the judgment of the surveyor. As a general rule, when the direction of the side slope is opposite the slope of the ground, the estimated distance should be less than the computed distance (step 3); when the direction of the side slope is the same as the slope of the ground, the estimated distance should be more than the computed distance. The number of trials needed may vary; in the following examples, three trials are used to illustrate the procedure. Once the first slope stakes are set, the trials for slope stakes at the remaining stations become more accurate.

Example 11-5

Locate the catch points by trial-and-error for the section in cut shown in Figure 11-17.

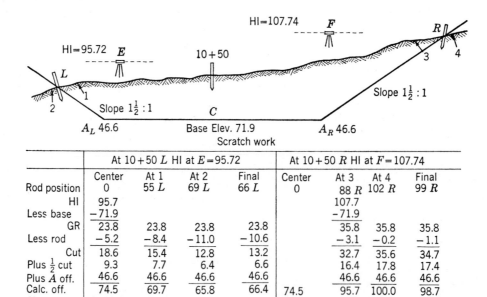

Scratch work

	At 10+50 L HI at E=95.72				At 10+50 R HI at F=107.74			
	Center	At 1	At 2	Final	Center	At 3	At 4	Final
Rod position	0	55 L	69 L	66 L	0	88 R	102 R	99 R
HI	95.7					107.7		
Less base	−71.9					−71.9		
GR	23.8	23.8	23.8	23.8		35.8	35.8	35.8
Less rod	−5.2	−8.4	−11.0	−10.6		−3.1	−0.2	−1.1
Cut	18.6	15.4	12.8	13.2		32.7	35.6	34.7
Plus $\frac{1}{2}$ cut	9.3	7.7	6.4	6.6		16.4	17.8	17.4
Plus A off.	46.6	46.6	46.6	46.6		46.6	46.6	46.6
Calc. off.	74.5	69.7	65.8	66.4	74.5	95.7	100.0	98.7
Slopes	Opposite	Move less			Same	Move more		
Try	55	69	66	O.K.	88	102	99	O.K.

	Mark stakes	C 13.2	C 18.6	C 34.7
		66.4 L	0	98.7 L

FIGURE 11-17. Illustration for Example 11-5; a section in cut.

Solution

In Figure 11-17, the first HI is located at E, and its elevation is found from previous leveling to be 95.72. The scratch work is then started. A rod shot will be first taken on the ground beside the center stake, hence the notation zero for the rod position. See scratch work below the drawing.

1. Compute the grade rod. This is the theoretical rod reading that would occur if the rod were standing on the desired grade elevation when read from a given HI. In this case, the HI is 95.72, and the desired elevation is that of the base, as shown on the plans, 71.9. The formula is

$$\text{GR} = \text{HI} - \text{grade}$$
$$\text{HI} = 95.7$$
$$\text{Less base} = -71.9$$
$$\text{GR} = 23.8$$

Follow the first scratch-work column.

2. Read the rod when held on the ground beside the center stake (reading, 5.2). Compute the cut at the centerline. The formula is

$$\text{Cut} = \text{GR} - \text{rod}$$
$$\text{GR} = 23.8$$
$$-\text{Rod} = -5.2$$
$$\text{Center cut} = 18.6$$

This means that the base is 18.6 ft below the ground at the center stake C.

When the grade rod, 23.8, and the centerline cut, 18.6, are known, the first slope stake can be set.

To Set the Left Grade Stake L

Estimate the offset to the left grade stake (L). This may be a guess based on experience. If the volumes have been determined on an electronic computer or the cross sections have been plotted, a very close estimate will be available from these sources. A practical field method, shown in the scratch work, is as follows:

Compute the offset to L that would occur if the ground were level. This would be the offset to A_L (46.6) plus $1\frac{1}{2}$ times the center cut.

	For a $1\frac{1}{2}$:1 Slope	For a 2:1 Slope
Center cut	18.6	18.6
Plus $\frac{1}{2}$ center cut (or plus center cut for 2:1 slope)	9.3	18.6
A offset	46.6	46.6
Calculated offset to stake L	74.5	83.8

But the ground slopes downward, so that the cut at stake L would be less than the center cut. Hence, the offset would be somewhat less than 74.5 for the $1\frac{1}{2}$:1 slope. Try, for example, 55. The rod is held at offset 55, as shown on the drawing at 1. The offsets are usually measured with a woven tape.

The offset for this rod reading is computed in the second column. Its value is 69.7.

The Key Procedure

It is now known that the cut measured at 55 should occur at 69.7. This indicates that the rod should be moved from its position at 55 toward 69.7. Should it be moved more or less than the whole distance? *To know what to do is the key.* Here are the rules:

1. When the slopes are opposite, move less.
2. When the slopes are the same, move more.

The two slopes are the slope of the ground and the side slope of the earthwork. They are opposite when one slopes down and the other up. They are the same when both slope up or both slope down. In the example, they are opposite, so move the rod less than called for.

For example, try 69 (2 in the drawing).

At 69, the calculated offset turns out to be 65.8. The rod should be moved from 69 toward 65.8 but, as before, not all the way. Try 66. Here the calculated distance is 66.4. This is near enough to the actual rod position. A difference of 0.5 or less is near enough.

Set the stake at the *calculated offset* (66.4), and assume that the rod reading is the same as at 66. Therefore, mark the stake C 13.2/66.4 L, as shown below the scratch work.

To Set the Right Grade Stake R

From the previous work, the cut at the center is known to be 18.6; so with level ground, the calculated offset is 74.5 as before. But here the slopes are the same; therefore move more.

For example, try 88, shown at 3. The calculated offset is 95.7. Move from 88 toward 95.7 and more.

Try 102. The calculated offset is 100.0. Move from 102 toward 100.0 and more.

Try 99. The calculated offset is 98.7, which is near enough.

Example 11-6

Locate the catch points by trial and error for the section in fill, shown in Figure 11-18.

Solution

$$\text{GR} = \text{HI} - \text{grade} = 70.57 - 75.4 = -4.8$$
$$\text{Fill} = \text{rod} - \text{GR} = 13 - (-4.8) = 17.8$$

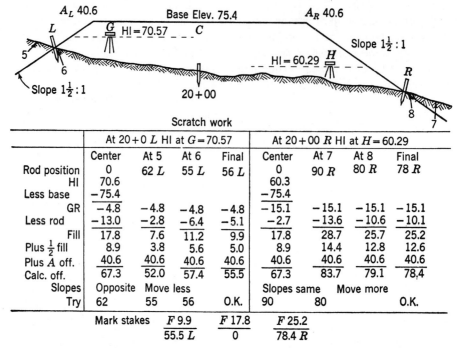

FIGURE 11-18. Illustration for Example 11-6; a section in fill.

	At 20+0 L HI at G=70.57				At 20+00 R HI at H=60.29			
	Center	At 5	At 6	Final	Center	At 7	At 8	Final
Rod position	0	62 L	55 L	56 L	0	90 R	80 R	78 R
HI	70.6				60.3			
Less base	−75.4				−75.4			
GR	−4.8	−4.8	−4.8	−4.8	−15.1	−15.1	−15.1	−15.1
Less rod	−13.0	−2.8	−6.4	−5.1	−2.7	−13.6	−10.6	−10.1
Fill	17.8	7.6	11.2	9.9	17.8	28.7	25.7	25.2
Plus $\frac{1}{2}$ fill	8.9	3.8	5.6	5.0	8.9	14.4	12.8	12.6
Plus A off.	40.6	40.6	40.6	40.6	40.6	40.6	40.6	40.6
Calc. off.	67.3	52.0	57.4	55.5	67.3	83.7	79.1	78,4
Slopes	Opposite	Move less			Slopes same	Move more		
Try	62	55	56	O.K.	90	80		O.K.

Mark stakes	F 9.9	F 17.8	F 25.2
	55.5 L	0	78.4 R

The trials are shown in Table 11-3. Note that the center cut and calculated offset were taken from HI at H as well as from G as a check.

Example 11-7

Locate the catch points by trial-and-error for the sidehill or mixed section shown in Figure 11-19.

Solution

Here the surveyor must use judgment. By observing the ground, one must realize that, despite the fact that at the center there is fill, at the left side the ground is so high that cut will be required. Therefore, the slopes are the same and the move is *more*, not less, and the cut offset for A (46.6) is used.

The trials are shown in Table 11-4.

Field Notes   The last rod shot taken, where the slope stake is to be set, is recorded in the rod column. The elevation is computed, and the cut or fill is computed from this elevation and the required grade elevation. The formula is as follows:

$$\text{Cut} = \text{ground elevation} - \text{grade elevation}$$

(Minus indicates fill.)

These values should check with the cuts or fills computed by the grade rod method.

On the right-hand side is the record of the marks placed on the slope stakes (Figure 11-20).

Table 11-3

Rod Position	Calculated Offset	Move	Try
0	67.3	Less	62 L
62 L	52.0	Less	55 L
55 L	57.4	Less	56 L
56 L	55.5	O.K.	
0	67.3	More	90 R
90 R	83.7	More	80 R
80 R	79.1	More	78 R
78 R	78.4	O.K.	

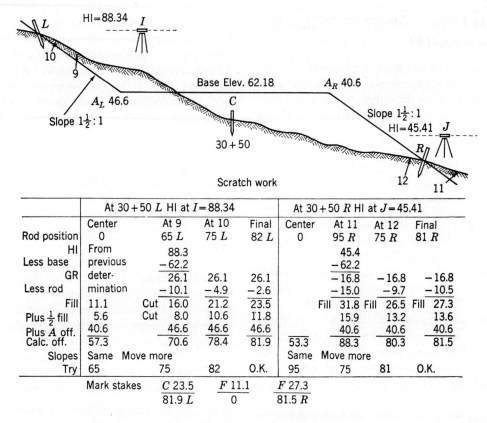

Scratch work

	At 30 + 50 L HI at I = 88.34				At 30 + 50 R HI at J = 45.41			
	Center	At 9	At 10	Final	Center	At 11	At 12	Final
Rod position	0	65 L	75 L	82 L	0	95 R	75 R	81 R
HI	From	88.3				45.4		
Less base	previous	−62.2				−62.2		
GR	deter-	26.1	26.1	26.1		−16.8	−16.8	−16.8
Less rod	mination	−10.1	−4.9	−2.6		−15.0	−9.7	−10.5
Fill	11.1	Cut 16.0	21.2	23.5	Fill 31.8	Fill 26.5	Fill 27.3	
Plus $\frac{1}{2}$ fill	5.6	Cut 8.0	10.6	11.8		15.9	13.2	13.6
Plus A off.	40.6	46.6	46.6	46.6		40.6	40.6	40.6
Calc. off.	57.3	70.6	78.4	81.9	53.3	88.3	80.3	81.5
Slopes	Same	Move more			Same	Move more		
Try	65	75	82	O.K.	95	75	81	O.K.

Mark stakes	$\dfrac{C\ 23.5}{81.9\ L}$	$\dfrac{F\ 11.1}{0}$	$\dfrac{F\ 27.3}{81.5\ R}$

FIGURE 11-19. Illustration for Example 11-7; a mixed section.

Table 11-4

Rod Position	Calculated Offset	Move	Try
0	57.3	More	65 L
65 L	70.6	More	75 L
75 L	78.4	More	82 L
82 L	81.9	O.K.	
0	53.3	More	95 R
95 R	88.3	More	75 R
75 R	80.3	More	81 R
81 R	81.5	O.K.	

Sta.	+	HI	−	Rod	Elev.	Gds	C, F	L	₵	R
10 + 50 ₵		95.72		5.2	90.5	71.9	C 18.6		$\dfrac{C18.6}{0}$	
66.4 L				10.6	85.1	71.9	C 13.2	$\dfrac{C13.2}{66.4}$		
		107.74								
98.7 R				1.1	106.6	71.9	C 34.7			$\dfrac{C34.7}{98.7}$
20 + 00 ₵		70.57		13.0	57.6	75.4	F 17.8		$\dfrac{F17.8}{0}$	
55.5 L				5.1	65.5	75.4	F 9.9	$\dfrac{F9.9}{55.5\,L}$		
₵		60.29		2.7	57.6	75.4	F 17.8		$\dfrac{F17.8}{0}$	
78.4 R				10.1	50.2	75.4	F 25.2			$\dfrac{F25.2}{78.4\,R}$
30 + 50 ₵		88.34		2.6	85.7	62.2	C 23.5	$\dfrac{C23.5}{81.9\,L}$	$\dfrac{F11.1}{0}$	
81.9 L										
		45.41								
81.5 R				10.5	34.9	62.2	F 27.3			$\dfrac{F27.3}{81.5}$

FIGURE 11-20. Suggested field notes for slope staking. Standard field leveling notes are used except when any position (HI) is reached from which one or more slope stakes are set.

11-4 BUILDING AND PIPELINE STAKEOUT

In addition to giving line and grade for roadway tangents and curves, two of the most common construction applications for the surveyor are the stakeout of new buildings and underground pipelines. In this section, traditional procedures for these applications, using baseline offsets and batter boards, are described; procedures that make use of EDM and lasers are discussed in Section 11-5.

Staking Out a Building

Naturally, a property survey must precede the stakeout of any structure on a parcel of land to accurately locate boundary lines. Constructing a building that encroaches on a neighboring lot can be a very costly mistake. In addition to the property boundaries, the *building lines* (or *setbacks*) specified in the local building code must be located; a setback is the minimum required distance between a new building and a front or side property line. For a single-family suburban home, which usually does not require a very high degree of accuracy in its location, the surveyor may only stake out the building lines (Figure 11-21). The builder can then locate the house anywhere within those lines. For most projects, especially where land values are high and lots are small, the layout must be more thorough; all the building corners and column foundation positions must be accurately located and referenced.

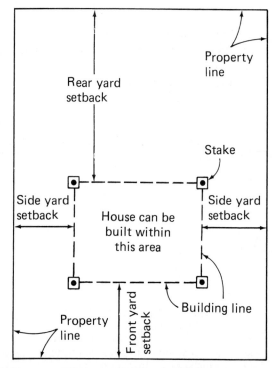

FIGURE 11-21. Minimum "yard setback" distances are specified in most local land-use ordinances. The allowable building limits or lines may be marked as shown by surveyor's stakes.

A common method for staking out a building makes use of several perpendicular offsets measured from a predetermined baseline. The baseline serves as a reference to control the position of the proposed structure; it may be a property line (see Figure 11-1), or it may be the centerline of a large facility. The designer shows the position of the building on the site plan in relation to the baseline.

As previously mentioned, stakes may first be driven at the actual locations of the building corners, but these will be destroyed as soon as construction begins. They are useful, however, as an initial check on the position and orientation of the building. Generally, the building corners must be referenced so that they can be easily relocated after excavation, as well as periodically during the construction process.

Batter Boards   A standard method for temporarily referencing the building corners, as well as the first-floor or basement slab elevation, makes use of the *batter board*. A batter board is simply a horizontal wooden plank fastened to two vertical posts (see Figure 11-22). The land surveyor retained by the owner may be required only to set offset stakes at each corner of the building and to set a benchmark; the builder is then generally responsible for setting up the batter boards using the land surveyor's reference marks.

A pair of batter boards are built offset from each corner so that opposite boards will support a wire, string, or carpenter's line; the line will delineate the exterior faces of the building (Figure 11-23). The string lines are stretched taut between two nails driven into the tops of opposite boards, which are usually set at the same elevation so that the line will be level. Sometimes all the boards are set at an elevation that is a specific height above the basement floor elevation. The string lines then establish both line and grade. The carpenters and masons can readily make measurements from the string lines using plumb bobs and

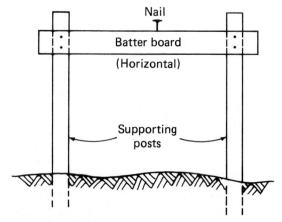

FIGURE 11-22. A batter board may be used by the builder to guide line and grade of the work. Nails support a string stretched between opposite batter boards to give line. The top of the batter board may be used as a reference for grade.

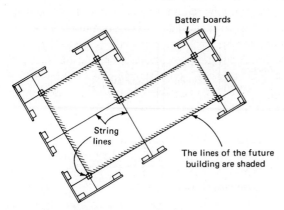

FIGURE 11-23. String lines stretched between opposite batter boards delineate or outline the faces of the walls or of the foundations for a proposed building.

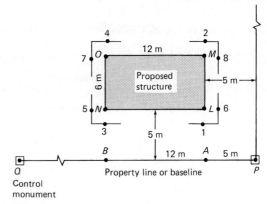

FIGURE 11-25. Setting up batter boards for staking out a building.

folding rules to transfer the corners into the excavation, to set concrete foundation forms, and to align the walls. The intersection of two strings marks the position of a corner; this position is easily transferred vertically with the plumb-bob cord. The string lines can be removed so not to interfere with the work, and then replaced as necessary to again give line and grade.

Sometimes, the surveyor indicates the fill from each corner stake up to the first-floor elevation. In this case, the building contractor adjusts the wire using a plumb bob to set the alignment and a rule to measure up from the stake. The line marks may be transferred from the stakes to the batter boards with a transit, and the grade of the first floor may be marked directly on the batter board (Figure 11-24).

The layout procedure for a simple rectangular structure, shown in Figure 11-25 follows:

1. Set up an instrument at monument P; take line on Q; set stakes at A and B.
2. Set up an instrument at A; *backsight on* Q; turn 90°; set stakes at corners L and M; set batter boards and nails at 1 and 2.

3. Set up an instrument at B; backsight on Q; turn 90°; set stakes at corners N and O; set batter boards and nails at 3 and 4.
4. Measure diagonals LO and NM and check with length computed using the Pythagorean theorem; restake if necessary.
5. Set up an instrument at L; backsight on N; set nail 5; plunge scope and set nail 6.
6. Set up an instrument at M; backsight on O; set nail 7; plunge scope and set nail 8.

This is an example of only one possible approach to the problem. Building stakeout can be time consuming, and every effort should be made to plan the work in the office to minimize the number of instrument setups. A procedure based on the use of precalculated angle and distance measurements made from a few selected points, instead of baseline and offset measurements, may speed up the work; this method is described in Section 11-5.

Column Footings   In buildings of any appreciable size, the structural frame may include steel columns that are supported by concrete *footings* or piers (see Figure 11-26).

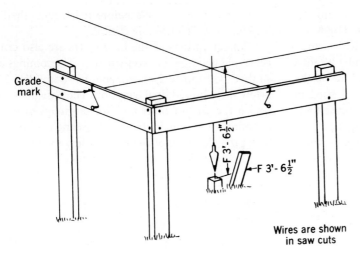

FIGURE 11-24. A plumb bob at the intersection of two batter board string lines locates the original corner stake position.

Wires are shown in saw cuts

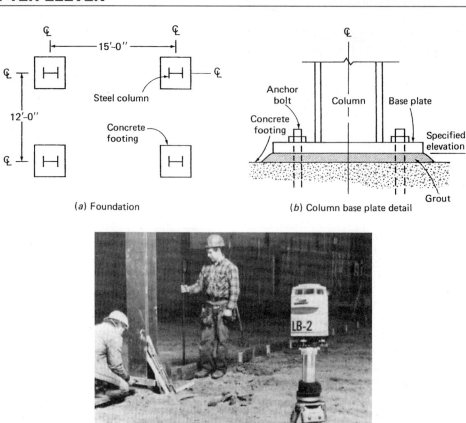

(a) Foundation

(b) Column base plate detail

(c)

FIGURE 11-26. (*a, b*) The construction surveyor must accurately locate the footing and column positions for a proposed structure. (*c*) Laser instruments are often used to establish construction elevations. (*Courtesy of Laser Alignment, Inc.*)

The center-to-center distances between adjacent columns are generally shown by the designer on the building foundation plan. The columns must be located with a high degree of accuracy, generally to within a few hundredths of a foot (a few millimeters) of the distances called for on the plan. Baseline offsets and batter boards may be used to locate, stake out, and build the forms for the concrete footings, as previously described for the building corners.

The columns are set in place on steel *base plates*, which serve to spread the weight supported by the column uniformly over the surface of the concrete footing. The base plates are fastened to the footing with several steel *anchor bolts*. The anchor bolts must pass through holes punched or drilled through the base plates. Because the bolts are usually

set in the fresh concrete before it hardens, their proper location and alignment are critical.

The elevations of the base plates are also critical for achieving good-quality construction. The footings are built so that their top surfaces are about 1–2 in. (250–500 mm) below the required final elevation. The base plates are then set on the anchor bolts and are shimmed to the correct elevation. Traditional differential leveling methods are used to set the elevation of the plate. When the plate is in final position, cement grout is forced under the plate to fill the space created by the shims.

In addition to locating the columns in plan and elevation, the construction surveyor is also called on to ensure that the columns are placed in a truly vertical position. This can be done by using a plumb bob or by aligning the top of the column with its base, using an instrument.

Line and Grade for a Sewer

Flow in a storm sewer or in a sanitary sewer is called *open channel gravity flow*. The flow capacity of a given diameter pipe depends primarily on the slope or gradient of the *flow line*. The flow line is the bottom inside surface of the pipe or drainage channel. Naturally, pipes or channels constructed on steep slopes have greater capacities than those built on shallow slopes. The determination of proper slope is one of the major factors in sewer design. The slope is shown on the engineering drawings so that the builder can excavate the trench and place the pipe at the gradient needed to provide its design flow capacity.

Whenever the pipeline changes in slope, diameter, or direction, a *manhole* is built to provide access both for sewage flow measurement and sampling and for pipeline inspection and maintenance. The length of pipeline between two manholes is called the *reach* of the sewer. The designer shows the pipe *invert elevation* at each end of a reach to guide the builder in placing the pipe at the required slope (Figure 11-27). The invert is a point on the bottom inside surface of a pipe or channel; the locus of inverts forms the flow line. (The terms *invert* and *flow line* are often used synonymously.)

Batter boards have traditionally been used to give line and grade for a gravity flow pipeline. (Lasers are frequently used in present-day construction—see Section 11-5.) The pipe is first located by a series of stakes that are usually set at 50-ft (15-m) intervals and offset 3–6 ft (1–2 m) from the pipe centerline (see Figure 11-4). These line stakes may also be used to control grade or separate grade stakes may be set by the surveyor. As the trench is excavated, its depth is

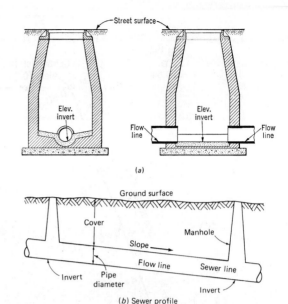

FIGURE 11-27. The surveyor is often called on to give line and grade for a sewer. Pipe invert elevations are usually shown on the plans to the nearest 0.01 ft (3 mm).

checked periodically by measurements from the grade stakes. After a section of trench is opened to a depth slightly greater than that required for the flow line, a series of batter boards are placed across the trench at uniform intervals (Figure 11-28).

The batter boards are set at a constant elevation above the pipe flow line or invert (e.g., 7 ft—0 in.), and a string line is run between the boards so that it is directly over the pipe centerline. The string line will have a slope equal to that of the pipeline. It is then simple for the workers to place the pipe sections into the trench in the proper position on a bed of sand and gravel, and to adjust the pipe invert while making periodic measurements from the string line.

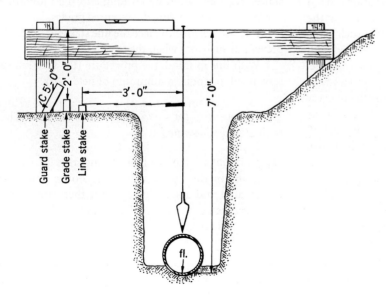

FIGURE 11-28. A batter board set up across the trench for a pipeline. *Note: Wall bracing is required in trenches greater than 5900 deep.*

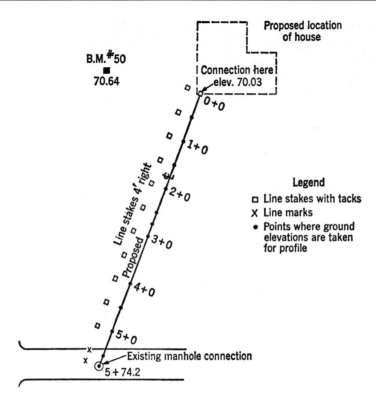

Proposed location of house

B.M. #50
70.64

Connection here
elev. 70.03

0+0

1+0

2+0

3+0

4+0

5+0

Line stakes 4' right

Proposed

Legend
□ Line stakes with tacks
X Line marks
● Points where ground elevations are taken for profile

Existing manhole connection
5+74.2

FIGURE 11-29. Plan illustrating an example for a pipeline location.

Field Location Example Suppose that it is necessary to build a new sewer from a house to an existing manhole (Figure 11-29). It is assumed that the flow line (fl) must be at least 3 ft (1 m) below the ground surface, and the minimum slope should be 0.004. A manhole should be placed at any change in gradient. The fl elevation at the house is given as 70.03 on the plans. The invert elevation of the existing manhole must be determined during the preliminary survey by opening the manhole cover and observing a rod held on the flow line.

The data from a preliminary survey are plotted to give a profile of the ground from the house to the manhole (Figure 11-30). On the profile, a straight line representing a possible flow line is drawn from the known elevation (70.03) of the flow line at the house to any point not below the manhole connection (60.52). It is discovered that such a line comes too near the ground. Other flow lines are tried with various locations and elevations for breaks in rate of grade, the object being to find an arrangement that complies with the specifications and requires a minimum quantity of excavation and number of manholes. In this case, a break in the rate of grade of the flow line located at about station 2 + 30 at an elevation of about 62.1 (as indicated by scaling) will solve the problem. It will require one new manhole (at 2 + 30). The existing connection at the street manhole can be used. Its fl elevation is 60.52.

It is now necessary to compute grades for the intervening points. The grades must be such that they will produce absolutely straight slopes for the flow line. For this purpose, an *exact* position and elevation must be assumed for the invert of the new manhole. Accordingly, station 2 + 30 and elevation 62.10 are chosen, and the grades are computed by proportion. This completes the plan (see Figure 11-30).

It is decided to give grade by indicating the cut from the top of the line stakes. It is to be remembered that cut is the distance from the top of the line stakes down to the flow line. It is *not* the excavation, which would be the distance from the ground down to the bottom of the trench.

To indicate cuts, the elevations of the tops of the line stakes must be found by leveling and the individual cuts computed by subtracting the required grades.

It is also decided to place the line stakes at a 4-ft offset to prevent disturbance when the trench is excavated.

With this in mind, the procedure (the location survey) is planned to require a minimum of field work.

Field Procedure for Field-Location Problem The field steps are the following:

1. Stake out a 4-ft offset line, placing stake 0 + 0 beside the point in the house where the house connection is located and a stake every 50 ft thereafter. Carry the measurement to a point beside the manhole, and determine its plus.

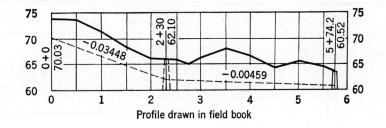

Profile drawn in field book

Computations of Grades

	Station	Grade	Station	Grade	Grade used
Start........	0 + 0	70.03	0 + 0	70.03	70.03
End.........	2 + 30	62.10		− 1.724	
Diff........	230	− 7.93	+ 50	68.306	68.31
				− 1.724	
Rate $= \dfrac{-7.93}{230} = -.03448$			1 + 0	66.582	66.58
				− 1.724	
			+ 50	64.858	64.86
				− 1.724	
Change in grade = distance × rate			2 + 0	63.134	63.13
50(−0.03448) = −1.724				− 1.034	
30(−0.03448) = −1.034			+ 30	62.10	62.10
				− 0.092	
	Station	Grade	+ 50	62.008	62.01
				− 0.230	
Start........	2 + 30	62.10	3 + 0	61.778	61.78
End.........	5 + 74.2	60.52		− 0.230	
Diff........	344.2	− 1.58	+ 50	61.548	61.55
				− 0.230	
Rate $= \dfrac{-1.58}{344.2} = -0.00459$			4 + 0	61.318	61.32
				− 0.230	
			+ 50	61.088	61.09
				− 0.230	
Change in grade = distance × rate			5 + 0	60.858	60.86
20(−0.00459) = −0.092				− 0.230	
50(−0.00459) = −0.230			+ 50	60.628	60.63
24.2(−0.00459) = −0.111				− 0.111	
			+ 74.2	60.52	60.52

FIGURE 11-30. Pipeline location example: computations and profile.

2. Find the elevation of the ground at each 50-ft point along the true line and at all breaks in ground slope. The rod is held on the ground at an estimated 4 ft from and opposite to each offset stake. This places the rod at the true position on the construction line. The rod is read to tenths.

3. At the same time, determine the elevation of the tops of each of the offset-line stakes. On these, the rod is read to hundredths.

4. Draw the profile of the ground elevations and determine the grade profile for the flow line.

5. Compute the cuts and mark the stakes.

6. Measuring along the offset line, place a stake for the new manhole, find the elevation of the top of the stake set and mark the cut for the invert.

The form of notes is shown in Figure 11-31.

						Chief Smith π Jones	H.C. Cole R.C. Doe	Fair 60° Date			
HOUSE CONNECTION											
Sta	+	HI	−	Rod	Elev	Grade	Cut	Mark Stk.			
						Nail in	Maple	Near House			
BM#50	6.78	77.42			70.64						
0+0 S				3.15	74.27	70.03	4.24	C 4'-2⅞"			
G				3.2	74.2						
+50 S				4.00	73.42	68.31	5.11	C 5'-1⅜"			
G				4.5	72.9						
1+0 S				5.41	72.01	66.58	5.43	C 5'-5⅛"			
G				6.0	71.4						
+50 S				9.15	68.27	64.86	3.41	C 3'-4⅞"			
G				9.3	68.1						
2+0 S				11.04	66.38	63.13	3.25	C 3'-3"			
G				11.1	66.3						
TP#1	4.03	70.50	10.95		66.47						
+50 S				4.39	66.11	62.01	4.10	C 4'-1¼"			
G				4.5	66.0						
+75 G				5.5	65.0						
3+0 S				4.07	66.43	61.78	4.65	C 4'-7⅞"			
G				4.1	66.4						
+50 S				2.35	68.15	61.55	6.60	C 6'-7¼"			
G				2.5	68.0						
4+0 S				4.18	66.32	61.32	5.00	C 5'-0"			
G				4.1	66.4						
+50 S				6.13	64.37	61.09	3.28	C 3'-3⅜"			
G				6.2	64.3						
5+0 S				5.22	65.28	60.86	4.42	C 4'-5"			
G				5.2	65.3						
+50 S				5.90	64.60	60.63	3.97	C 3'-11⅝"			
G				5.9	64.6						
+74.2 S				6.90	63.60						
G				6.9	63.6						
Connect				9.98	60.52						
TP#2	5.89	72.92	3.47		67.03						
BM#50			2.29		70.63						
BM#50	7.42	78.06			70.64						
2+30 S				11.81	66.25	62.10	4.15	C 4'-1¾"			
BM#50			7.42		70.64						

FIGURE 11-31. Field notes for the location of a pipeline (Figure 11-30).

11-5 ADDITIONAL LAYOUT PROCEDURES

Every construction project is different, particularly with regard to the shape and topography of the construction site, and the position of the proposed facilities thereon. The common layout operations of giving line and grade have been described in the preceding sections. The construction surveyor must be thoroughly familiar with these basic procedures, and must also have the ability to deal with other layout problems that may be unique to a specific site or project. A few of the additional procedures that may be used by the surveyor to lay out a proposed project are described in this section, including the use of random control points and laser devices for grading operations.

Miscellaneous Alignment Methods

The field procedures described here are frequently used as part of location survey operations. These include double centering, bucking in, setting a very close point, and setting a point of intersection.

Double Centering   It is often necessary to extend or *prolong a straight line* beyond a given endpoint. For example, line AB must be prolonged from B to C by setting a mark at C (Figure 11-32). One way to do this is to set up a transit or theodolite at point A, sight point B, and then simply raise the telescope slightly to set point C on line. But this method is generally unsatisfactory for a long prolongation, due to

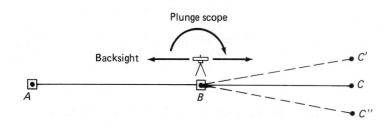

FIGURE 11-32. The method of double centering. Set a mark for C halfway between C' and C".

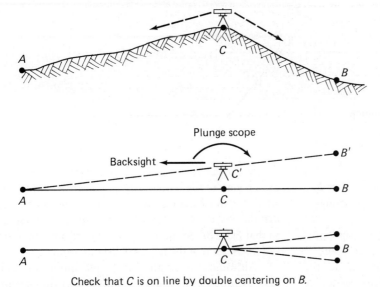

Check that C is on line by double centering on B.

FIGURE 11-33. Bucking in over a hill.

potential instrumental error. Also, gently rolling terrain may interfere with the visibility of C from station A.

The preferred method for prolonging any straight line is called *double centering.* Applied to line AB in Figure 11-33, the instrument is set up over point B instead of point A. A *backsight is taken on A,* the telescope is plunged or reversed (transited) and point C' is set. If the instrument is in perfect adjustment, this one operation will give correct results. But if the instrument is out of adjustment, particularly if the line of sight is not perpendicular to the horizontal axis, this one step will not accurately set C' on the straight line AB prolonged.

To prolong the line by double centering, the procedure described here is repeated with the telescope in the opposite positions. In other words, after setting point C' by plunging the scope from direct to reverse, a second backsight is taken on point A with the scope still in the reverse position. The scope is then plunged again, and point C" is set. Any gap between C' and C" is due to instrumental error. The final point C is then set halfway between the two marks. Of course, it is best to keep the instrument in proper adjustment at all times. But it is also good practice to perform surveying operations as though there still may be some instrumental error, to maintain accuracy in the work and to avoid blunders.

Bucking in Between Two Points It is sometimes necessary to establish a point on a line *between* two given marks when it is impossible to set up over either one of the marks, or when the marks are not intervisible because of a hill between them. The usual field procedure to solve this problem is a trial-and-error method called *bucking in* (also called *balancing in* or *wiggling in*).

In Figure 11-33, it is required to set point C between marks at A and B by bucking in between the two given marks. Set up the transit or theodolite at point C', judged to be approximately on line. Choosing the most distant mark,

say point A, backsight on A, transit the scope, and set B'. Measure the distance from B to B'. Estimate the ratio of AC to AB and move the instrument from C' to C after computing the distance as follows: $CC' = BB'(AC/AB)$.

Repeat the procedure until B' falls on B. When BB' becomes small, the position B' must be established by double centering. When the direct and reversed sights are equally spaced on each side of B, the instrument is on line and C can be set directly under the plumb bob or optical plummet.

Setting a Point Close to the Instrument The telescope cannot be lowered far enough or focused close enough to set a point on line nearer the instrument than about 3 ft (1 m). To set a point closer than that, the following procedure may be followed (Figure 11-34): Set up at A and set point C on line. Set up on C, point at A, *and set B* on line.

Setting a Point of Intersection It is often necessary to establish a point at the intersection of two fixed lines. A common example of this is setting the point of intersection (PI) of two route tangents, say, lines AB and CD (Figure 11-35).

Set up at C, and then set E by double centering. Set F on line; E and F should be as close together as possible and yet

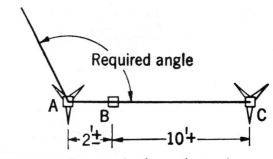

FIGURE 11-34. To set a point close to the transit.

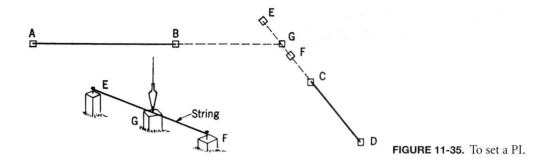

FIGURE 11-35. To set a PI.

lie on opposite sides of *AB* prolonged. Tie a string from *E* to *F*. Set up at *B*, and set a stake at *G* on line *AB* prolonged, under the string line.

The stake should be driven down until the top is just touched by the string when it is replaced between *E* and *F*. Draw a pencil line on the top of the stake, just under the string. Locate the PI accurately on the pencil line by double centering from *B*.

Avoiding an Obstacle on Line

A property line or a construction survey baseline marked at both ends may be blocked or obstructed between the marks by buildings, trees, or other existing features. In some cases, it may be possible to avoid the obstacle by setting a point on high ground from which a line may be established over it, or by setting a station on it (see Figure 11-36). Distance can be carried over the obstacle by measuring slope distances with tape or EDM.

Other methods for avoiding the obstacle on line include using either a *rectangular offset*, an *equilateral-triangle offset*, a *parallel offset*, a *random line*, or a *random traverse*.

Rectangular Offset   Suppose it is required to carry line and distance accurately from *AB* to *CD* across an obstacle such as a small building (Figure 11-37). At point *B*, backsight on *A*, turn 90°, and set point *E* at a whole number of feet (meters) from *B*, but far enough to clear the obstacle. Set the instrument over mark *E*, point toward a *swing offset* equal in length to *BE* from *A*, and then set *G* by double centering (see Figure 9-16c

for a review of the swing-offset method). Aim at *G*, and then set *F* at a convenient number of feet or meters from *E* such that the obstacle is cleared. At point *F*, turn 90° and set point *C* so that *FC* = *BE*. At mark *C*, point toward a swing offset from *G*. Finally, set *D* at the required distance from *C*.

Although this method is simple and accurate, it may take as much as 2 hours to complete. A quicker method would be simply to turn four 90° angles at *B*, *E*, *F*, and *C* to get back on line. But some accuracy will be sacrificed if the sight distances are short.

Equilateral-Triangle Offset   Set up at 2, backsight on 1, and turn 120° to set point 3 at a convenient distance from 2 (see Figure 11-38). From point 3, backsight on 2, and turn 60° to set point 4 such that 3-2 = 3-4. From point 4, backsight on 3, and turn 120° to get back on line. Finally, set point 5 at the required distance from point 4. From the geometry of an equilateral triangle, 2-4 = 3-2 = 3-4.

Parallel Offset   Sometimes the entire length of a line is obstructed, and it is necessary to establish a new line parallel to it, called a *parallel offset line* (see Figure 11-39). Set a mark at *C* by estimating a position opposite point *A*. *Point a swing offset equal to AC* at *B*, turn 90°, and measure a swing offset at *A* (usually a very small distance). If the swing offset from *A* is large, move *C* back to *C'* and repeat the process. If it is small, add the value to measurements along the offset line from *C*.

Random Line   When a parallel offset line cannot be used, a *random line* can be used instead to establish points between

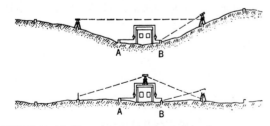

FIGURE 11-36. To measure over an obstacle.

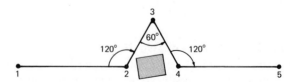

FIGURE 11-38. An equilateral-triangle offset to prolong a line.

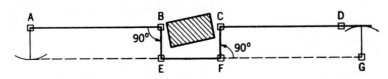

FIGURE 11-37. A rectangular offset to prolong a line.

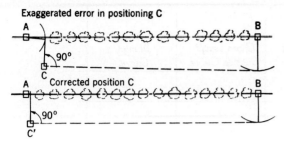

FIGURE 11-39. To establish a line parallel to an obstructed line.

the ends of an obstructed line (Figure 11-40). Set C at a random spot but visible from A. Measure the angle ACB. Compute any other desired positions, such as D and E, from the proportions:

$$\frac{FD}{AF} = \frac{GE}{AG} = \frac{CB}{AC}$$

Stake out the required points by turning the same angles, that is, $AFD = AGE = ACB$.

Random Traverse   Any obstructed line can be replaced with a random traverse (Figure 11-41). The obstructed line is taken to be a missing side of a loop traverse, and its length

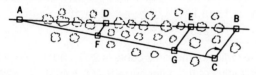

FIGURE 11-40. To establish an obstructed line by a random line.

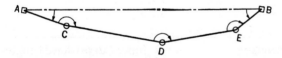

FIGURE 11-41. To establish a line by a random traverse.

and direction are computed by traverse computation techniques, that is, by closing the loop with the missing side and inversing between the endpoints of the line (see Section 7-2 to review traverse computations).

Circular Offsets and Curbs

The deflection angle procedure for staking out a circular curve is described in Section 10-3. The construction of road pavements and curbs generally requires the setting of stakes offset from the route centerline, so that they will not be disturbed during the construction process. The circular offset lines are usually from 3 to 6 ft (1–2 m) beyond the location of the edge of pavement or the back of curb. The stakes generally are set at either quarter-station or half-station intervals along the offset curve, to the right and to the left.

The offset circular arcs are parallel to the arc of the centerline; the central angle between any two radii is the same for parallel arcs. The design radius is usually taken as that of the route centerline. The stations of all the points of curvature (PCs) and points of tangency (PTs) (i.e., for the centerline, the right, and the left offset) are computed using the design radius. But the PCs of the right and left offset arcs lie on the same radial line; likewise for the PTs (see Figure 11-42). Therefore, *the stations of the offset PCs and PTs are the same as for those on the centerline arc (the design curve)*, even though offset curve lengths are not the same as the centerline length.

Deflection angles computed using the design curve data are the same for the offset curves. But because chord lengths are a function of arc radius, the chord lengths used to lay out an offset curve must be computed on the basis of the actual radius to that curve. Field notes for stakeout would be set up showing the common deflection angles and the different chord lengths for each point on the offset curves.

Example 11-8

Set up the field notes for stakeout of circular curves offset 5 ft from the edges of a 40-ft-wide pavement. The intersecting

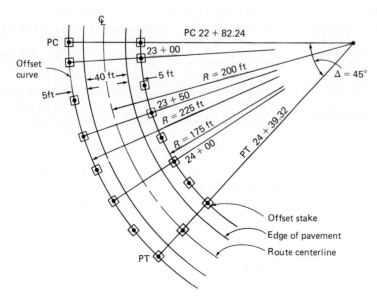

FIGURE 11-42. Offset curves.

Station	Deflection Angle	Chord Length Inside Curve	Chord Length Outside Curve	Design Curve
PT 24 + 38.32	22° 31′	12.00 ft.	15.43 ft.	
24 + 25	20° 33′	21.86	28.11	
24 + 00	16° 58′	21.86	28.11	Data
23 + 75	13° 23′	21.86	28.11	△ = 45° 00′
23 + 50	9° 48′	21.86	28.11	R = 200 ft.
23 + 25	6° 13′	21.86	28.11	T = 82.84 ft.
23 + 00	2° 38′	16.06	20.65	L = 157.08 ft.
PC 22 + 81.64				

FIGURE 11-43. Field notes for Example 11-8 and Figure 11-43.

angle of the curve is 45°, the centerline radius is 200.00 ft, and the station of the PI is 23 + 64.48. Stakes are to be set at the PCs and PTs and at quarter-station (25-ft) intervals along the offset curves (see Figure 11-43).

Solution

First, compute the tangent distance T, the arc length L, and the stations of the PCs and PTs, with centerline as the design curve (see Sections 10-2 and 10-3 for a review of the simple circular curve):

$$T = R \tan \frac{\Delta}{2} = 200 \tan \frac{45}{2} = 82.84 \text{ ft}$$

$$L = \frac{\pi R \Delta}{180} = \frac{\pi \times 200 \times 45}{180} = 157.08 \text{ ft}$$

Station PC = 2364.48 − 82.84 = 2281.64 (or 22 + 81.64)
Station PT = 2281.64 + 157.08 = 2438.72 (or 24 + 38.72)

Now compute the deflection angles as follows:

For the quarter-station (25-ft) intervals along the curves,

$$a = \frac{arc\ length}{R} \times 1718.87 = \frac{25}{200} \times 1718.87 = 214.86$$

$$= 3.581° = 3°35' \text{ (rounded off to the nearest minute of arc)}$$

The length of arc from the PC to the first quarter-station point, 23 + 00.00, is 2300.00 − 2281.64 = 18.36 ft. The first deflection angle from the PC to station 23 + 00.00 is then computed to be

$$a = \frac{arc\ length}{R} \times 1718.87 = \frac{18.36}{200} \times 1718.87$$

$$= 157.79' = 2°38'$$

The length of arc from the last quarter-station point, 24 + 25.00, to the PT is 2438.72 − 2425.00 = 13.72 ft. The last

deflection angle from the station 24 + 25.00 to the PT is then computed to be

$$a = \frac{13.72}{200} \times 1718.87 = 117.91'' = 1°58'$$

The radius of the inner curve is 200 − 40/2 − 5 = 175 ft and the radius of the outer curve is 200 + 40/2 + 5 = 225 ft. Chord lengths are computed with the formula

$$\text{Chord length} = 2R \sin a$$

as follows:

Stations	Inner Curve Chord Lengths
PC to 23 + 00	$2 \times 175 \times \sin 2.630° = 16.06$ ft
23 + 00 to 23 + 25, etc.	$2 \times 175 \times \sin 3.581° = 21.86$ ft
24 + 25 to PT	$2 \times 175 \times \sin 1.965° = 12.00$ ft

	Outer Curve Chord Lengths
PC to 23 + 00	$2 \times 225 \times \sin 2.630° = 20.65$ ft
23 + 00 to 23 + 25, etc.	$2 \times 225 \times \sin 3.581° = 28.11$ ft
24 + 25 to PT	$2 \times 225 \times \sin 1.965° = 15.43$ ft

Field notes for curve stakeout are illustrated in Figure 11-43.

Curb Returns   The circular arc formed by a curb at a street intersection is called a *curb return* or a *radius curb*. The radius of the circular arc depends on traffic volume and speed and is usually specified by local building codes; typically, the radii may vary from about 25 ft (8 m) for local streets to about 60 ft (18 m) for arterial roads. It is best for streets to intersect at right angles, but angles ranging from

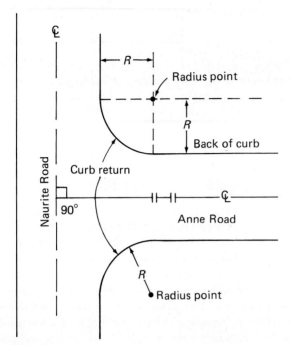

FIGURE 11-44. Curb returns for streets intersecting at a right angle.

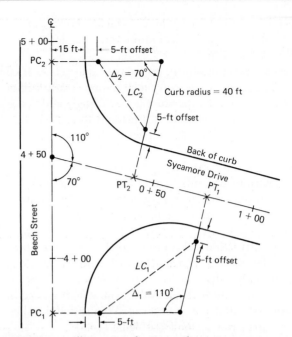

FIGURE 11-45. Illustration for Example 11-9.

60° to 120° are generally acceptable for modern design. The curb returns for streets that intersect at 90° are quarter circles.

Because the radius of a curb return is relatively small, the curve can be laid out by swinging an arc from the circle center (the *radius point*) with a tape. The radius point is easily located by finding the intersection of two straight lines, each of which is parallel to one of the centerlines and distant from it by the amount of the radius plus half the street width (Figure 11-44).

Stations for the PCs and PTs of the curb returns are computed with reference to the street centerlines; the design radius is equal to half the street width plus the curb radius. Stakes are offset 3–6 ft (1–2 m) from the back of each curb, at its PC and PT. As a check on the work, the long chord (*LC*) distance between the PC and PT offset stakes may be computed and measured. The radius used to compute the *LC* is not that of the centerline, but is the curb radius minus the offset distance.

When the streets do not intersect at a right angle, the curb returns are computed using the supplementary deflection angles. A uniform gradient along the curb from the PC to the PT is usually established by the builder.

Example 11-9

Sycamore Drive intersects Beech Street at an angle of 70°, at station 4 + 50 along the centerline of Beech and station 0 + 00 along the centerline of Sycamore (Figure 11-45). Both roads are 30 ft wide, and each curb return radius is to be 40 ft. Determine the PC stations along Beech Street and the PT stations along Sycamore Drive for the curbs, and compute the *LC* distances if stakes are offset 5 ft from the back of each curb.

Solution

$$\text{Design } R = 1/2 \text{ street width} + \text{curb radius}$$
$$= 30/2 + 40 = 55 \text{ ft}$$

Now compute the PC stations along Beech Street as follows:

$$\Delta_1 = 110°$$

$$T_1 = R \tan \frac{\Delta_1}{2} = 55 \tan \frac{110}{2} = 78.55 \text{ ft}$$

$$\text{Station PC}_1 = (4 + 50) - 78.55 = 3 + 71.45$$

$$\Delta_2 = 180 - 110 = 70° \quad \text{(supplementary angles)}$$

$$T_2 = R \tan \frac{\Delta_2}{2} = 55 \tan \frac{70}{2} = 38.51 \text{ ft}$$

$$\text{Station PC}_2 = (4 + 50) + 38.51 = 4 + 88.51$$

Compute the PT stations along Sycamore Drive as follows:

$$\text{Station PT}_1 = (0 + 00) + 78.55 = 0 + 78.55$$

$$\text{Station PT}_2 = (0 + 00) + 38.51 = 0 + 38.51$$

The long chords are computed as follows:

$$R = \text{curb radius} - \text{offset} = 40 - 5 = 35$$

$$LC_1 = 2R \sin\left(\frac{\Delta_1}{2}\right) = 2 \times 35 \times \sin\left(\frac{110}{2}\right) = 57.34 \text{ ft}$$

$$LC_2 = 2R \sin\left(\frac{\Delta_2}{2}\right) = 2 \times 35 \times \sin\left(\frac{70}{2}\right) = 40.15 \text{ ft}$$

Radial Stakeout Surveys

The phrase *radial survey* is used to describe the process of making several angle and distance measurements from a single point or station of known position (i.e., coordinates). A second coordinated station is necessary for a reference backsight. A third fixed point is useful for checking the work and for adjusting the data to minimize random errors. A radial survey is particularly useful on open terrain where there are few or no obstructions to the required lines of sight.

The use of an electronic total station greatly facilitates the radial survey procedure because angle and distance measurements can be quickly made with one pointing of the line of sight. A radial survey can be used to determine the positions of control traverse stations or of topographic features. And it can be used to lay out the positions of predetermined points such as the corners of a building, slope stakes, or circular curve offset lines. When used for construction layout, the process may be called a *radial stakeout survey*.

Construction stakeout by radial survey techniques is also called the *angle and distance method*. This procedure can significantly reduce the total time required for a construction layout; much fewer instrument setups are required compared with those generally used in the traditional baseline-offset layout method (see Figure 11-46).

This survey operation is particularly useful when an electronic tacheometer (a total station) is used. For many construction projects, especially complex ones, the locations of key points may be shown on the engineering drawings by rectangular coordinates rather than by the traditional baseline-offset distances. Of course, the coordinates are really offsets from two perpendicular baselines, called the X and Y (or N and E) coordinate axes. But this *coordinate method* of construction location is very compatible with the radial stakeout survey, as explained here.

The electronic tacheometer can be set up at a *random* location, but one that gives unobstructed lines of sight over a large portion of the project site. The instrument person has to simply point on two established (and coordinated) control stations and observe and record the distances to them. Then the on-board computer (or a programmable handheld computer) is used to quickly solve for the coordinates of the random control station (in effect, solving a distance–distance intersection type problem—see Section 7-4). This is called resectioning.

With the position of the instrument then known, the surveyor simply inputs into the computer the design coordinates of any point to be staked out. The computer quickly solves the problem by inversing between that point and the random control point (see Section 7-2), and displays the required direction and distance from the instrument to the stake position. A backsight on a control station is taken, the proper angle is turned, and the computed distance is set operating the EDM in its tracking mode. The work can then be checked from a second instrument setup, if necessary.

Use of Lasers for Line and Grade

A *laser* is a bright beam of monochromatic (single color) light. The laser beam is generated in such a way that the light waves are in step with each other; the beam therefore retains its power over long distances and spreads out only very slightly as it travels. An intense beam of laser light can be made powerful enough to cut through steel. The beam can also be generated with power levels low enough for safe use in many applications. The straight beam of a low-power laser is particularly useful as a tool for giving line and grade in construction surveying.

A *single-beam* laser projects a narrow "string line," easily visible as a bright (red) dot on a flat surface or target, regardless of the lighting conditions. The laser instrument can be mounted on a tripod and the laser beam oriented in a horizontal direction: in this configuration, the instrument can serve as an *electronic level* (Figure 11-47). An adjustable column may be attached to the tripod so that the laser beam can be accurately set at a specific height, or HI.

The single-beam laser can be used to give line. Once aimed at a foresight, the position of the line can be found without the need of a person at the instrument. It is therefore especially useful when many points must be set on line, particularly when they are set at irregular location intervals.

With a fine-adjustment micrometer knob, the laser beam can be inclined at a specific slope or gradient for "shooting in grade." Because the beam can be set at a predetermined slope, lasers are quite useful for aligning pipelines such as sewers. A tripod-mounted laser can be set up over a manhole, and the beam can be set at the design slope of the flow line. This eliminates the need for batter

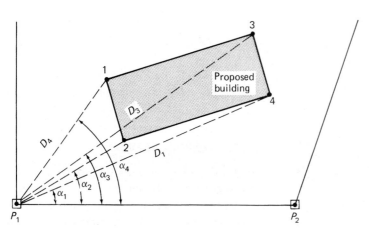

FIGURE 11-46. Radial stakeout of building corners. Stations P_1 and P_2 are coordinated control points. In this simple example, only one instrument setup is required at P_1.

(a)   *(b)*

FIGURE 11-47. (*a, b*) Self-leveling pipe-laying lasers that can be mounted in a manhole, on top of the pipe barrel, or on a tripod over the pipe. (*Courtesy of AGL Corporation.*)

boards and string line. The laser beam could be used for guiding trench excavation as well as for setting pipe inverts at the proper grade.

Some laser devices are suitable for installation in the manhole; the laser beam is set at the required gradient, and the workers align the pipe sections by observing the beam on a special target placed in the far end of the pipe section. The horizontal alignment or location of the pipeline must initially still be set using traditional methods with a transit or a theodolite.

A *rotating-beam laser* is an especially useful construction survey tool. This type of instrument has an internal optical system that rotates the laser beam and thereby generates a flat reference surface over an open area, instead of a single line. The reference plane can be oriented in a horizontal, vertical, or sloped position (Figure 11-48). In a horizontal position, it can be used to level floor slabs; in a sloped position, uniform grades for parking lot or airport pavements can be controlled.

When the beam is set to generate a vertical plane, it can be used to align walls and columns.

Most modern rotating laser are "self-leveling" and are equipped with a safeguard system that automatically turns off the laser if it is accidentally knocked too much out of level, to prevent inaccurate readings. The speed of rotation of the beam can be controlled up to about 8 rev/second on some models. A zero speed setting is usually provided, thus allowing the instrument also to be used as a single-beam laser. When rotating, the laser can typically provide a constant reference plane for accurately controlling grade over about 6.5 ac (2.5 ha) of the construction site (i.e., over about a 300-ft, or a 100-m, radius). The beam diameter is only about 3/8 in. (9 mm) at that distance.

The graduated level rod used in conjunction with a laser device may be equipped with a sliding battery-powered laser beam detector or sensor, allowing the rod to be read within ±0.01 ft (3 mm) at a distance of 100 ft (30 m) from the laser

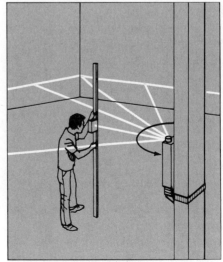

Establishing a vertical plane   Establishing a horizontal plane

FIGURE 11-48. The rotating laser beam can be leveled horizontally (or plumbed vertically) to establish a constant reference plane at a construction site. (*Courtesy of CST/Berger, Illinois.*)

device. On some models, the sensor will seek the beam and give an audible signal or beep, thus indicating when the scale can be read. This is useful for differential leveling, that is, determining unknown elevations. The sensor can also be clamped at a predetermined height on the level rod and used for setting grade marks, controlling excavation depth, setting forms, and executing many other construction layout tasks.

Projected upward in a vertical direction, a single laser beam provides a long narrow column of light that can facilitate surveying operations. It is, in effect, an *inverted plumb bob*, or a *laser range pole*. The beam is not visible to the eye,

but because it ionizes air particles in its path, it can be detected by a special electronic receiving device. Using the laser beam as a plumb line is particularly helpful for work in rough terrain. Sighting on the vertical beam with a theodolite-mounted electronic receiving device allows the surveyor to establish a line between the laser and the receiver, even though hills, trees, or buildings may prevent visual observations to be made.

The basic advantage of lasers in construction surveying is that they provide rapid and accurate alignments with a smaller field crew.

Questions for Review

1. What is construction surveying?

2. What is meant by *giving line and grade*?

3. What is an offset line used for?

4. Should the direction of a line be established from a line longer than itself? Why?

5. Describe the use of a foresight for establishing direction.

6. Make a sketch showing how line and grade can be transferred from the surveyor's marks to the construction work using simple builder's tools.

7. Describe the process of shooting in grade.

8. What is slope staking? What is a catch point?

9. Outline the field procedure for locating catch points.

10. Define the terms *setback*, *building line*, and *baseline*, with regard to building stakeout.

11. What is a batter board? How is it used?

12. Outline the procedure for laying out a sewer line.

13. Briefly describe the procedures for double centering, bucking in, setting a point very close to the instrument, and setting a PI.

14. List and briefly outline five methods for avoiding an obstacle on line.

15. What is a curb return? Briefly describe how it is laid out.

16. What is a radial stakeout survey?

17. Describe how a single-beam laser may be used in construction surveying applications.

18. Describe how a rotating-beam laser may be used in construction surveying applications.

Practice Problems

1. A mark is to be set at an angle of 70°00′00″ from a given line at a distance of 500 ft from the instrument. After setting the mark, the angle is measured by repetition

and determined to be 69°59′30″. How far should the mark be shifted so that the angle is set at 70°00′00″?

2. A mark is to be set at an angle of 80°00′00″ from a given line at a distance of 200 m from the instrument. After setting the mark, the angle is measured by repetition and determined to be 80°00′40″. How far should the mark be shifted so that the angle is set at 80°00′00″?

3. Compute the grades at each half station and full station for a uniform gradient between the positions indicated:

Station:	0 + 00	6 + 73.41
Grade:	29.68	34.25

4. As in Problem 3 for

Station:	6 + 29.7	12 + 16.5
Grade:	51.26	72.49

5. The HI of a level is 567.89 ft. A blue top is to be set to mark a grade of 558.12 ft. What is the value of grade rod?

6. The HI of a level is 123.45 m. A blue top is to be set to mark a grade of 121.87 m. What is the value of grade rod?

7. It is required to set a stake to mark a grade of 45.49 ft. The HI of the level is 53.56 ft and the rod on stake reads 4.32 ft. Determine the amount of cut (C) or fill (F) to be marked on the stake.

8. It is required to set a stake to mark a grade of 53.72 ft. The HI of the level is 60.05 ft and the rod on stake reads 10.93 ft. Determine the amount of cut (C) or fill (F) to be marked on the stake.

9. Write out a set of notes for setting a grade stake at each station, at a certain number of feet, or feet and half

feet, above or below grade (as in Figure 11-14) for the following:

(a)				(b)			
HI	Station	Grade	Rod on Ground	HI	Station	Grade	Rod on Ground
37.28	0 + 0	32.61	8.2	81.29	0 + 0	80.32	1.4
	0 + 50	33.01	5.4		0 + 50	81.32	1.0
	1 + 0	33.41	2.3		1 + 0	82.32	0.6
	1 + 50	33.81	1.7		1 + 50	83.32	1.7
39.46	2 + 0	34.21	3.5		2 + 0	84.32	1.9
	2 + 50	35.61	4.7	92.42	2 + 50	85.32	2.8
	3 + 0	36.01	5.6		3 + 0	86.32	3.2
	3 + 50	36.41	7.2		3 + 50	87.32	4.2
	4 + 0	36.81	9.7		4 + 0	88.32	6.7
	4 + 50	37.21	10.6		4 + 50	89.32	7.8

10. Compute the cuts and fills to be written on the marks for the following data:

(a)			(b)		
Station	Grade	Elevation Mark	Station	Grade	Elevation Mark
0 + 0	35.64	35.27	0 + 0	47.28	46.17
0 + 50		39.42	0 + 50		41.62
1 + 0		46.25	1 + 0		45.10
1 + 50	Uniform	47.31	1 + 50	Uniform	40.83
2 + 0	Slope	46.22	2 + 0	Slope	36.15
2 + 50		47.38	2 + 50		42.14
3 + 0		55.20	3 + 0		34.75
3 + 50		59.71	3 + 50		35.29
4 + 0		59.64	4 + 0		32.67
4 + 50	62.64	64.28	4 + 50	29.28	33.48

11. Convert the following dimensions from feet and hundredths to equivalent values in feet and inches:

(a)		(b)	
2.69	5.60	3.52	6.25
4.79	3.87	4.76	7.81
8.21	1.83	9.23	2.94
7.93	0.36	10.16	5.06
6.08	9.27	8.72	6.67

12. Convert the following dimensions in feet and inches to equivalent values in feet and hundredths:

(a)		(b)	
7 ft $2\frac{1}{2}$ in.	3 ft $5\frac{1}{4}$ in.	2 ft $6\frac{3}{4}$ in.	4 ft $6\frac{1}{8}$ in.
4 ft $9\frac{3}{4}$ in.	8 ft $8\frac{5}{8}$ in.	1 ft $10\frac{1}{8}$ in.	7 ft $2\frac{7}{8}$ in.
5 ft $7\frac{5}{8}$ in.	9 ft $4\frac{1}{8}$ in.	3 ft $7\frac{5}{8}$ in.	5 ft $4\frac{3}{4}$ in.
6 ft $4\frac{7}{8}$ in.	2 ft $6\frac{1}{2}$ in.	6 ft $3\frac{1}{2}$ in.	8 ft $7\frac{3}{8}$ in.
4 ft $3\frac{3}{8}$ in.	10 ft $7\frac{3}{4}$ in.	9 ft $8\frac{1}{2}$ in.	10 ft $5\frac{1}{4}$ in.

13. In the following, state whether the slopes are the same or opposite and whether to move the rod more or less than the distance computed as if the ground were level: (*a*) downhill cut, (*b*) downhill fill, (*c*) uphill cut, and (*d*) uphill fill.

14. In the following table, fill in the "Try" column. Assume that the side slopes are 1.5:1.

Cut or Fill	Ground Slope	Rod Position	Calculated Offset	Try
C	Up steep	70	55	
F	Up steep	75	85	
C	Down steep	80	90	
F	Down steep	75	60	
F	Up medium	70	55	
C	Up medium	75	85	
F	Down medium	80	90	
C	Down medium	75	60	

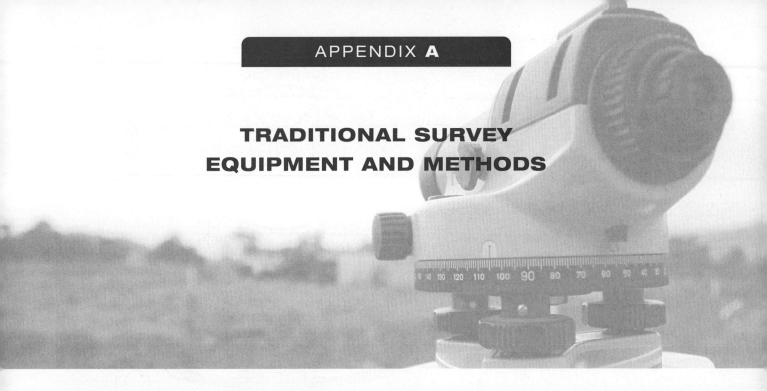

TRADITIONAL SURVEY
EQUIPMENT AND METHODS

TRANSIT CONFIGURATION

Rapidly changing technology and the need to collect and process data more quickly require today's surveyors to use field techniques and equipment that did not exist just 5 or 10 years ago. However, to be truly able to "retrace" the footsteps of the surveyors that have come before us, it is important to have an understanding of the equipment and techniques they used in performing their surveys. This understanding provides an insight into why there might be discrepancies between field measurements performed 50 or even just 20 years ago and today.

A full discussion of all the older instruments and field methods is beyond the scope of this book. However, the *transit*, an optical device used primarily for angular measurement, was such a key instrument in nearly every type of surveying activity in part of the nineteenth and most of the twentieth centuries, that no land development or engineering project of any importance could be designed or constructed without its use. And knowledge of its configuration and operation can provide an insight into the underlying motions and operations of modern angular measurement instruments.

The *theodolite* (described in Section 6.4) is an instrument that largely replaced the transit for angular measurement toward the latter part of the twentieth century. (Although modern electronic total stations have now largely supplanted the theodolite, it is still used in some surveying tasks.) Transits evolved as American-style instruments that were used most extensively in the United States. Theodolites are primarily of European design. They have several features in common and operate on the same fundamental principles. The key difference between the transit and the theodolite is primarily that of precision; theodolites typically provide greater precision in angular measurements than the transits. Angle readings on theodolites are taken from enclosed graduated glass circles and micrometer scales, which are viewed through an internal magnifying optical system. Transits have exterior graduated metal circles and *vernier scales* that are used for angle readings.

When properly operated, transits can measure horizontal angles to very high levels of accuracy, but angles must be observed using certain repetitive and time-consuming procedures. They can also measure vertical angles to about ±10 seconds. When equipped with *stadia hairs* (described later), transits can also measure horizontal distances to the level of accuracy required for topographic mapping. And equipped with a compass, they can determine magnetic bearings within ±15 minutes of arc.

A transit consists of three fundamental parts: the *alidade* at the top, the *horizontal circle* in the middle, and the *leveling head* at the base (Figure A-1). These three parts are operated by two clamps, each equipped with a slow-motion (tangent) screw. The upper clamp clamps the horizontal circle to the alidade, and the lower clamp clamps the horizontal circle to the leveling head. When a clamp has been tightened, the appropriate tangent screw can be used to make a fine setting.

The alidade is mounted on a tapered spindle called the *alidade spindle* or *inner center*. The essential parts of the alidade are the *telescope*, which is actually a telescopic line of sight that rotates in a vertical plane on the horizontal elevation axis, and the *A and B verniers*, which act as indexes for reading the horizontal circle. A *vertical circle* is mounted on the telescope axis, which turns with the telescope, and vertical angles are read with a *vertical-circle vernier*, which is mounted on one standard. Two *plate levels* (spirit levels) are mounted horizontally, at right angles, on or near the upper plate. They are used to place the vertical or *azimuth axis* in the direction of gravity. A telescope spirit level is attached to the bottom of the telescope. Usually a compass is mounted on the upper plate.

1. A vernier
2. azimuth axis
3. x vernier
4. center of half ball
5. elevation or horizontal axis
6. footplate
7. graduations of horizontal circle
8. half ball
9. half ring
10. horizontal circle (lower plate)
11. inner center, or alidade spindle
12. leveling screw
13. lower clamp screw
14. lower clamp drum contact
15. lower tangent screw for
    slow motion
16. nub for lower clamp
17. nub for upper clamp
18. outer center
19. plate level
20. shifting plate
21. shoe
22. telescope
23. threads for triped
24. upper clamp screw
25. upper clamp drum contact
26. upper plate
27. upper tangent screw for slow motion
28. vertical circle
29. vertical-circle vernier
30. window, glass
31. telescope level
32. vertical tangent screw for
    slow motion
33. focusing screw for focusing
    on object sighted
34. eyepiece focusing ring

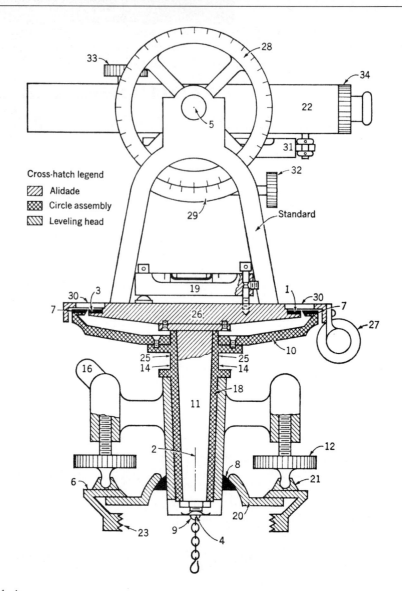

Cross-hatch legend

▨ Alidade
▩ Circle assembly
▨ Leveling head

FIGURE A-1. Principle parts of the transit design.

The horizontal circle (lower plate) is mounted on a *hollow* tapered spindle or *outer center*, the inner surface of which acts as a bearing for the alidade spindle; the outer surface turns in a bearing in the leveling head. This arrangement is called the *double center*. The horizontal circle is graduated in degrees and usually halves or thirds of a degree and numbered throughout, every 10°, usually both clockwise and counterclockwise, starting from a common zero. It is read to varying degrees of precision from 1 minute to 10 seconds by two verniers mounted on the alidade 180° apart.

The leveling head contains the tapered bearing for the outer center. Four *leveling screws* are threaded into the arms of the leveling head and press *shoes* down against the *footplate*. This action tends to raise the leveling head and thus pulls a *half ball*, attached to the end leveling-head bearing, upward into a socket in the *shifting plate*, which in turn is upward against the underside of the footplate. At the bottom of the footplate are the threads by which the instrument is screwed to the tripod. When the leveling screws are loosened,

the shifting plate drops and the whole upper assembly can be shifted anywhere within a circle of about 3/8 in., or 10 mm, in diameter, so that the instrument can be placed exactly in the desired horizontal position.

A small chain, with a hook at the lower end to hold the plumb-bob cord, hangs from a small half ring attached to a cap that is screwed to the lower end of the leveling-head bearing. In a well-designed instrument, the ring is placed at the center of curvature of the half ball. In leveling the instrument, the whole assembly above the footplate rotates slightly around the center of curvature of the half ball. If, as is often the case, the half ring is too low, the plumb bob is moved horizontally when the instrument is leveled and thus moved off the point where it had been originally placed.

The alidade spindle, the outer center, and the leveling-head bearing combine to form the vertical or *azimuth axis*. This is also called the *standing axis*. Thus, the circle and the alidade can turn in azimuth independently of each other.

Two journals, one at each end of the telescope axle (the horizontal axle that supports the telescope), fit in bearings at the tops of the standards and thus form the horizontal or *elevation axis*. When the telescope is aimed up and down, it turns on this axis, which is also called the *tilting axis*.

The Motions   Three *motions* control the movements of the transit. Each motion consists of a *clamp* and a *tangent screw*. When the clamp is tightened, a *gib* is forced against a drum on the circle assembly or on the telescope axle. The tangent screw then becomes operative and provides a slow motion between the two parts clamped together. The *lower motion* joins the horizontal circle and the leveling head. The *upper motion* joins the horizontal circle and the alidade. The *vertical motion* joins the telescope axle with the standard and thus controls the vertical angle of the telescope. Each tangent screw acts on a nub between it and an opposing spring. When a tangent screw is turned, the relative positions of the two parts clamped together are changed very slightly.

The Telescopic Sight   The telescopic sight of an engineer's transit is similar to that of the level (see Section 5-2). The transit telescope generally has slightly less magnifying power. Also, the transit telescope is supported by the standards so that the scope may be rotated or *transited* a full 360° around its horizontal axis.

As shown in Figure A-1, the telescope has an attached spirit bubble tube that can be used to level the line of sight. It may be used when the scope is in a direct or *normal position* (with the spirit tube underneath the scope) or when it is in an inverted or *reversed position* (i.e., "plunged" 180°, with the tube on top of the scope). Although the engineer's transit may be used for leveling, its spirit bubble vial is less sensitive than that on a level, and excellent accuracy is therefore more difficult to obtain.

The telescopic sight of a transit is focused in the same manner as that of the level (see Section 5-2).

The horizontal circle of a transit is divided and graduated automatically on a large wheel. Modern dividing machines can space the graduations very uniformly, but the circle can never be exactly centered on the wheel. Therefore, the graduations on one part of the circle may be slightly closer together than the graduations on the opposite side of the circle. This is called *eccentricity* of the circle.

As mentioned previously, the circle may be read by two verniers (called *A* and *B*), which are mounted 180° apart on the alidade. When an angle is determined by averaging the readings of the two verniers, the effect of the circle's eccentricity is eliminated. This occurs because if the *A* vernier is used to read graduations that are too close together, the *B* vernier will then be used to read graduations that are proportionally too far apart.

By reading the two verniers and using an average value instead of a single reading, the accuracy of the work may be increased; for the most reliable and accurate results, then, both verniers of the transit should be used. Generally, however, only the *A* vernier is read for ordinary surveying work.

Transit Verniers

The basic principle of a vernier was already described in Section 5-2 with regard to level rod targets. Verniers, in general, are devices for determining readings smaller than the least division on the main scale with which they operate. They consist of an auxiliary scale that is moved along the main scale. On the level rod, the main scale is straight; on the transit circle, it is curved. But the basic design and function of a straight and a curved vernier are the same.

The 1-Minute Vernier   When the horizontal circle of a transit is graduated in half degrees, that is, divisions 30 minutes in length, the vernier is usually designed so that the direction of the alidade can be read to ±1 minute of arc. In this case, the vernier consists of a series of 30 uniform divisions, each division being 1/30 shorter than a division on the horizontal circle; the whole vernier scale of 30 divisions, then, spans exactly 29 divisions of the horizontal circle.

The *least count* of a vernier is the ratio of the smallest division on the main scale to the number of divisions on the vernier. For the vernier previously described, the least count is 30 minutes ÷ 30 divisions = 1 minute per vernier division. Because an angle or azimuth may be read directly to 1 minute with this kind of vernier, it is called a *1-minute vernier*. A transit with this kind of vernier is called a *1-minute transit*.

The Double Vernier   An example of a *double vernier*, the type commonly found on the engineer's transit, is shown in Figure A-2. A double vernier has a complete set of divisions running both ways, right and left, from a common zero line or index (labeled *A* or *B*). With a double vernier, an angle may be read either clockwise or counterclockwise, depending on whether the angle is turned to the right or to the left.

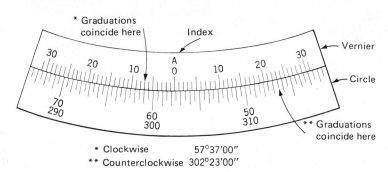

* Clockwise   57°37'00"
** Counterclockwise   302°23'00"

FIGURE A-2. Double direct 1-minute vernier.

Facing the double vernier, you would observe the index to move to the left as an angle is turned clockwise; it would move to the right as an angle is turned to the left. With this in mind, it can be seen that, for a clockwise angle, the set of divisions to the left of the index mark is used. For a counterclockwise angle, the divisions to the right of the index are used. A rule to remember is that *the vernier to be used (left or right) is the one whose numbers increase in the same direction as the numbers observed on the horizontal graduated circle.*

Reading the Vernier   Referring to Figure A-2, assume that a clockwise angle has been turned. If the zero mark or index of the *A* vernier coincided exactly with the 57°30′ graduation of the circle, the value of the angle would be just that, 57°30′. But the index is beyond that value, to the left of the half-degree mark.

If the alidade were turned only 1 minute (1/30 of a division on the circle) beyond that half-degree mark, the next graduation on the vernier to the left of the index would coincide exactly with one of the graduations on the circle. The reading would then be 57°30′ plus 1 minute (as counted on the vernier), or 57°31′. As it is, the seventh-minute graduation on the vernier coincides with a graduation of the circle. The reading of the clockwise angle is, therefore, 57°30′ plus 7′, or 57°37′.

In general, a transit vernier is read as follows: *Find the vernier division that lines up exactly with any line on the horizontal circle. Add the value of that vernier line to the angle on the circle at the index mark, observed to the least count of the circle* (e.g., the nearest 30 minutes on a 1-minute transit).

A counterclockwise angle can also be read on the vernier shown in Figure A-2, using the set of divisions to the right of the index. We first note that the angle is somewhat more than 302°, but not quite 302°30′, because the index is to the left of the half-degree mark. We then observe that the twenty-third vernier division to the right coincides exactly with a graduation on the circle. The value of the angle then is 302°23′. Notice that the sum of both the clockwise angle and the counterclockwise angle, 57°37′ + 302°23′, equals 360°, as it must.

Measuring Vertical Angles Using a Transit

Angles are commonly measured in a vertical plane for stadia and trigonometric leveling surveys, where the slope distances must be reduced to horizontal distances. The horizontal cross hair and the graduated vertical arc or circle and its adjacent vernier are used for this purpose. It should be noted that on most transits the vernier is on the outside of the vertical circle, just the opposite of its inside position on the horizontal circle. Care must be taken to read the scale correctly.

On the engineer's transit, vertical angles are measured with reference to the horizon; when the telescope bubble

tube is centered, the vernier on the vertical circle should read 0°00′. If it does not, the reading that is observed when the bubble is centered is the *index error* of the vertical circle. It is important to take note of its sign (plus if above the horizon and minus if below the horizon). This value, with its sign changed, is the *index correction*. It must be applied to all vertical angles observed with that instrument. For example, if the index error was −02′, and a vertical angle to a given point was observed to be +16°43′, the corrected angle would be +16°45′.

If the transit has a full vertical circle and the telescope can be plunged, it is best to observe the vertical angle twice, once with the scope direct and once reversed. In this way, an index correction need not be applied. By averaging the two readings, the index error in the position of the vernier is eliminated; in one position it is positive and in the other it is negative, so that in the average it cancels out.

Principles of Stadia Surveying

The traditional American transit is a versatile instrument. In addition to measuring horizontal and vertical angles, it is also capable of measuring horizontal and vertical distances using the *stadia method*. When using the stadia method (*tacheometry*), distance, direction, and elevation are all measured in essentially one operation. Taping of distances is not required. This method was very useful for topographic mapping small- or medium-sized parcels of land of variable terrain before the advent of modern total stations. Stadia surveying is not a very precise method of making field measurement. Distances can be determined with an accuracy of about 1/1000 at best. But this is sufficient for most topographic surveys.

A transit (or theodolite) used for stadia work must have a special reticle or set of cross hairs (see Figure A-3a). The cross hairs consist of central horizontal and vertical cross hairs, with two additional shorter *stadia hairs* that are equally spaced above and below the horizontal one. The geometric principle underlying stadia is that the corresponding sides of similar triangles are proportional. The stadia hairs are carefully placed in the reticle so that their lines of sight separate at a rate of 1–100, from a point at the center of a modern, internal-focus transit or theodolite (see Figure A-3b).

Because the lines of sight diverge at the rate of 1–100, the vertical length observed between the stadia hairs on a level rod held 100 ft (or 100 m) away would be 1.00 ft (or 1.00 m). At a horizontal distance of 200 ft, the *stadia intercept*, as it is called, would be 2.00 ft, and so on. Because the distance of a vertical rod from the instrument is always 100 times the vertical intercept observed on the rod, horizontal distances between the rod and the instrument are easily determined when the transit telescope is level. For example, if the bottom stadia hair intercepts the rod at 2.00 ft, and 3.58 ft is observed at the top stadia hair, then the horizontal distance is simply

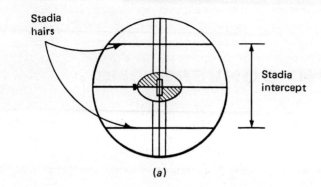

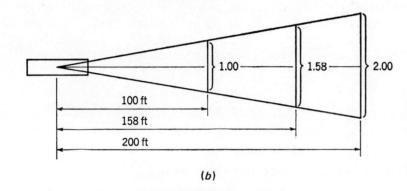

(b)

FIGURE A-3. (a) View through transit telescope of stadia hairs and level rod. (b) The distance to the rod is equal to 100 times the stadia intercept.

$100 \times (3.58 - 2.00) = 158$ ft. The perpendicular distance D between the rod and the instrument station is always $100 \times S$, where S is the observed stadia intercept.

One of the chief advantages of stadia surveying is that both horizontal and vertical distances can be measured even when the telescope line of sight is not horizontal; it is necessary, however, to determine the vertical angle for each observation. The process of determining elevations by measuring both a horizontal distance and a vertical angle is called *trigonometric leveling* (see Section 5-6).

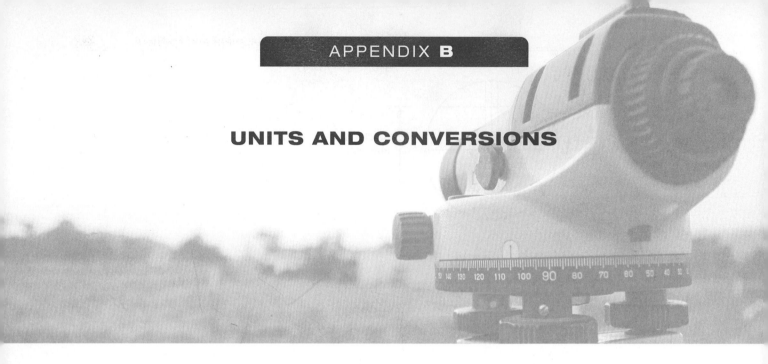

UNITS AND CONVERSIONS

LENGTH

U.S. Customary System

1 foot (ft) = 12 inches (in)

1 yard (yd) = 3 feet (ft)

1 mile (mi) = 5280 feet

1 chain (ch) = 66 feet

1 chain = 100 links (lk) = 4 rods (rd)

1 mile = 80 chains

1 fathom (fm) = 6 feet

SI Metric System

1 meter (m) = 1000 millimeters (mm)

1 meter = 100 centimeters (cm)

1 meter = 10 decimeters (dm)

1 kilometer (km) = 1000 meters

1 millimeter = 0.001 meter

1 centimeter = 0.010 meter

1 decimeter = 0.100 meter

U.S. Customary and SI Metric Equivalences

1 inch = 25.4 millimeters*

1 foot = 0.3048 meter*

1 mile = 1.609344 kilometers

1 meter = 39.37009 inches

1 meter = 3.2808399 feet

1 kilometer = 0.62137119 mile

(Note: * denotes that an *exact* equivalence for U.S. survey foot conversion is 1200/3937 m.)

Example Conversions:

1. Convert a distance of 567.89 ft to its equivalent in meters.

$$567.89 \text{ ft} \times \frac{0.3048 \text{ m}}{1 \text{ ft}} = 173.09 \text{ m}$$

2. Convert a distance of 2.34 km to its equivalent in miles.

$$2.34 \text{ km} \times \frac{0.62137119 \text{ mi}}{1 \text{ km}} = 1.45 \text{ mi}$$

AREA AND VOLUME

U.S. Customary System

1 square yard (yd^2) = 9 square feet (ft^2)

1 cubic yard (yd^3) = 27 cubic feet (ft^3)

1 acre (ac) = 10 square chains

1 acre = 43,560 square feet

1 square mile (mi^2) = 640 acres

SI Metric System

1 square kilometer (km^2) = 10^5 square meters (m^2)

1 square kilometer = 100 hectares (hs)

1 hectare = 10,000 square meters

1 hectare = 100 acres

1 acre = 100 square meters

U.S. Customary and SI Metric Equivalences

1 square yard = 0.8361274 square meter

1 cubic yard = 0.764555 cubic meter

1 square meter = 10.76 square feet

1 hectare = 2.4710538 acres

1 square kilometer = 0.3861 square mile

1 square meter = 1.19599 square yards

1 cubic meter = 1.30795 cubic yards

1 square foot = 0.0929368 square meter

1 acre = 0.40468564 hectare

1 square mile = 2.59 square kilometers

Example Conversions:

1. Convert an area of 34.56 ac to its equivalent in hectares.

$$34.56 \text{ ac} \times \frac{1 \text{ ha}}{2.4710538 \text{ ac}} = 13.99 \text{ ha}$$

2. Convert a volume of 1234.5 m^3 to cubic yards.

$$1234.5 \text{ m}^3 \times \frac{1.30795 \text{ yd}^3}{1 \text{ m}^3} = 1614.7 \text{ yd}^3$$

ANGLES

One complete revolution or a full circle contains:

360 degrees (°)

or 400 grads (also called *gons*)

or 2π radians (rads)

1 degree = 60 minutes (′)

1 minute = 60 seconds (″)

1 grad = 100 centigrads (°) = 100 centesimal minutes

1 centigrad = 100 decimilligrads (°°) = 100 centesimal seconds

A right angle = 90 degrees = 100 grads = $\pi/2$ radians

1 degree = 1.1111111 grads = 0.0174533 radian

1 grad = 0.9 degree = 0.015708 radian

1 radian = 57.29578 degrees = 63.661949 grads

Convert 12°23′34″ to degrees and decimals of a degree:

34″/60 = 0.5666667′   23.5666667′/60 = 0.3927778°

Therefore,

12°23′34″ = 12.3928°   (rounded to 1/10,000 degree)

Convert 56.5432° to degrees, minutes, and seconds:

0.5432 × 60′ = 32.592′   0.592′ × 60 = 35.52″

Therefore,

56.5432° = 56°32′36″   (rounded to seconds)

See Chapter 2, "Measurements and Computations."

FORMULAS

QUADRATIC FORMULA

To solve a quadratic equation in the form of $ax^2 + bx + c = 0$, apply the following formula:

$$x = \frac{-b \pm \sqrt{b^2 - 4ac}}{2a}$$

RIGHT TRIANGLES

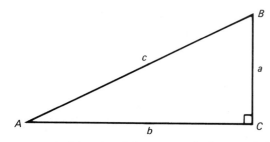

FIGURE C-1. A right triangle has one angle that equals 90°.

$$C = A + B = 90°$$

$\sin A = \cos B = a/c$	$\cos A = \sin B = b/c$	$\tan A = \cot B = a/b$
$A = \arcsin (a/c)$	$A = \arccos (b/c)$	$A = \arctan (a/b)$
$B = \arccos (a/c)$	$B = \arcsin (b/c)$	$\cot A = \tan B = b/a$

Note: The inverse function arcsin may also be written as $\sin^{-1}$, etc.

$$\text{cotangent} = \frac{1}{\text{tangent}} \left(\text{or } \cot A = \frac{1}{\tan A} \right)$$

$$\text{secant} = \frac{1}{\text{cosine}} \text{ or } \left(\sec A = \frac{1}{\cos A} \right)$$

$$\text{cosecant} = \frac{1}{\sin} \text{ or } \left(\csc A = \frac{1}{\sin A} \right)$$

$a = \sqrt{c^2 - b^2}$	$b = \sqrt{c^2 - a^2}$	$c = a^2 + b^2$
$a = b \tan A$	$b = a \tan B$	$c = a/\sin A$
$a = c \sin A$	$b = c \cos A$	$c = \dfrac{b}{\cos A}$
$a = c \cos B$	$b = c \sin B$	$c = \dfrac{a}{\cos B}$
$a = b/\tan B$	$b = a/\tan A$	$c = \dfrac{b}{\sin B}$

$$\text{Area} = \frac{ab}{2} = \left(\frac{a}{2}\right) \sqrt{c^2 - a^2} = \left(\frac{b}{2}\right) \sqrt{c^2 - b^2}$$

$$\text{Area} = \frac{a^2}{2} \cot A = \frac{b^2}{2} \tan A = \frac{c^2}{2} \sin A \cos A$$

$$= \frac{c^2}{4} \sin 2A$$

$$\text{Perimeter} = a + b + c$$

OBLIQUE TRIANGLES

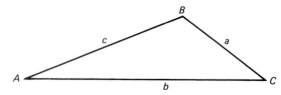

FIGURE C-2. An oblique triangle does not include a right angle.

Law of sines:

$$\frac{a}{\sin A} = \frac{b}{\sin B} = \frac{c}{\sin C}$$

Law of cosines:

$$a^2 = b^2 + c^2 - 2bc \cos A$$
$$b^2 = a^2 + c^2 - 2ac \cos B$$
$$c^2 = a^2 + b^2 - 2ab \cos C$$

$$a = b\left(\frac{\sin A}{\sin B}\right) = c\left(\frac{\sin A}{\sin C}\right)$$
$$= \sqrt{b^2 + c^2 - 2bc \cos A}$$
$$A = \arccos \frac{b^2 + c^2 - a^2}{2bc}$$

$$b = a\left(\frac{\sin B}{\sin A}\right) = c\left(\frac{\sin B}{\sin C}\right)$$
$$= \sqrt{a^2 + c^2 - 2ac \cos B}$$
$$B = \arccos \frac{a^2 + c^2 - b^2}{2ac}$$

$$c = a\left(\frac{\sin C}{\sin A}\right) = b\left(\frac{\sin C}{\sin B}\right)$$
$$= \sqrt{a^2 + b^2 - 2ab \cos C}$$
$$C = \arccos \frac{a^2 + b^2 - c^2}{2ab}$$

$$A = 180° - B - C \quad B = 180° - A - C$$
$$C = 180° - A - B$$

$$\text{Area} = \sqrt{s(s-a)(s-b)(s-c)}$$

$$\text{where } s = \frac{a+b+c}{2}$$

$$\text{Area} = \left(\frac{ab}{2}\right)\sin C = \left(\frac{bc}{2}\right)\sin A = \left(\frac{ac}{2}\right)\sin B$$

$$\text{Area} = \frac{a^2 \sin B \sin C}{2 \sin A}$$

$$\text{Perimeter} = a + b + c$$

INTERSECTION FORMULAS

Intersection problems are introduced in Section 7-4; the essential approach to evaluating those problems is to "solve triangles," that is, to apply the laws of sines, cosines, and right-angle trigonometry. The formulas presented here are derived from those laws, and they may be used directly to save time in obtaining solutions. The most common source of error in using formulas like these is in losing track of the proper algebraic signs of the various terms. It is most helpful to make a clear sketch of the problem before attempting the solution.

Bearing–Bearing Problem

Known: Coordinates of points A and B
Bearings of lines AC and BC

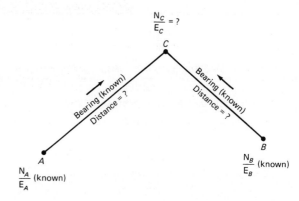

FIGURE C-3. Bearing–bearing intersection problem.

Unknown: Distances AC and BC
Coordinates of point C

$$\text{Distance } AC = \frac{(\Delta E)(\cos \overline{CB}) - (\Delta N)(\sin \overline{CB})}{\sin C}$$

$$\text{Distance } BC = \frac{(\Delta E)(\cos \overline{AC}) - (\Delta N)(\sin \overline{AC})}{\sin C}$$

$$\text{Northing } C = \text{northing } A + AC \cos \overline{AC}$$
$$= \text{northing } B + BC \sin \overline{BC}$$
$$\text{Easting } C = \text{easting } A + AC \sin \overline{AC}$$
$$= \text{easting } B + BC \cos \overline{BC}$$

where $\Delta E =$ difference in east coordinates
from A to $B = E_a - E_A$
$\Delta N =$ difference in north coordinates
from A to $B = N_a - N_A$
$\overline{CB} =$ bearing angle of line CB
(CB is the back direction of BC)
$\overline{AC} =$ bearing angle of line AC
$C =$ intersection angle at station C

Note: The algebraic signs of the trig functions depend on the quadrant of the bearing used, as follows:

Quadrant 1 (NE): sin is + and cos is +
Quadrant 2 (SE): sin is − and cos is +
Quadrant 3 (SW): sin is − and cos is −
Quadrant 4 (NW): sin is + and cos is −

Example C-1

Station A	N450.00/E350.00
Station B	N500.00/E775.00
Bearing AC = N 27°47′25″ E	
Bearing CB = S 60°57′35″ E	

Solution

$$C = 27°47'25'' + 60°57'35'' - 88°45'00''$$

$$\text{Distance } AC = \frac{(775-350)(\cos 60.96) - (500-450)(\sin 60.96)}{\sin 88.75}$$

$$\text{Distance } AC = \frac{(425)(+0.4854243) - (50)(-0.8742787)}{0.9997497}$$

$$= 250.08$$

$$\text{Distance } BC = \frac{(775 - 350)(\cos 27.79) - (500 - 450)(\sin 27.79)}{\sin 88.75}$$

$$\text{Distance } BC = \frac{(425)(+0.8846601) - (50)(+0.4662365)}{0.9997497}$$

$$= 352.76$$

Northing $C = 450.00 + (250.08)(0.8846601) = 671.24$

Easting $C = 350.00 + (250.08)(0.4662365) = 466.60$

Note: Compare the solution to this problem with that of Example 7-6 and Figure 7-22 in Section 7-4.

Distance–Distance Problem

Known: Coordinates of points A and B
                  Distances AC and BC

Unknown: Bearings of AC and BC
                  Coordinates of C

$$\text{Angle } A = 2 \arccos \sqrt{\frac{S(S - BC)}{(AB)(AC)}}$$

where $S = \dfrac{AB + BC + AC}{2}$.

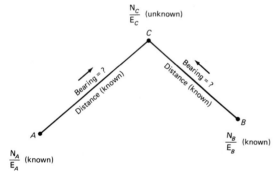

FIGURE C-4. Distance–distance intersection problem (e.g., locate the intersection of two curves).

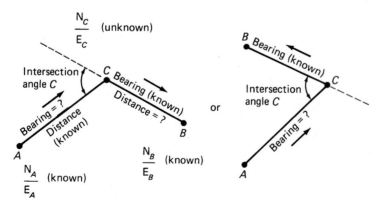

Example C-2

     Station A N800.00/E650.00
     Station B N1125.00/E1250.00
     Distance $AC = 334.56$
     Distance $BC = 468.13$

Solution

First determine the direction and length of AB by inversing:

     Bearing $AB = \text{N } 61°33'25'' \text{ E}$ Distance $AB = 682.37$

Now solve for

$$S = \frac{(682.37 + 468.13 + 334.56)}{2} = 742.53$$

$$\text{Angle } A = 2 \arccos \sqrt{\frac{742.53(742.53 - 468.13)}{(682.37)(334.56)}}$$

$$= 2 \cos^{-1} 0.9447178 = 2(19.140431) = 38.2809°$$

$$= 38°16'51''$$

Note: Compare this value of A to that obtained in Example 7-7; the rest of the solution for this is identical to that of Example 7-7.

Bearing–Distance Problem

Known: Coordinates of points A and B
                  Length of line AC
                  Bearing of line CB

Unknown: Bearing of line AC
                  Length of line CB
                  Coordinates of point C

$$\text{Intersection angle } C = \arcsin \frac{\Delta E(\cos \overline{CB}) - \Delta N(\sin \overline{CB})}{AC}$$

where ΔE, ΔN, and $\overline{CB}$ are defined as for the preceding bearing–bearing problem; the algebraic signs of the trig functions depend on the quadrant the line is in.

Use angle C to solve for the bearing of AC; inverse between points C and B to compute the length of CB. Compute the coordinates of C by adding the latitude and longitude of AC (or BC) to the coordinates of A (or B).

FIGURE C-5. Bearing–distance intersection problem (e.g., traverse or intersection of a curve and a line).

Areas of Plane Figures

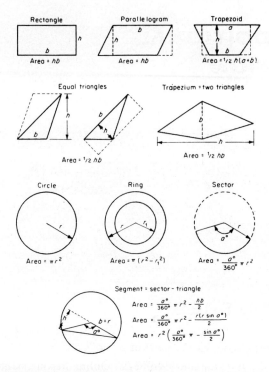

Rectangle
Area = hb

Parallelogram
Area = hb

Trapezoid
Area = $\frac{1}{2} h(a+b)$

Equal triangles
Area = $\frac{1}{2} hb$

Trapezium = two triangles
Area = $\frac{1}{2} hb$

Circle
Area = πr^2

Ring
Area = $\pi (r^2 - r_1^2)$

Sector
Area = $\frac{a°}{360°} \pi r^2$

Segment = sector - triangle
Area = $\frac{a°}{360°} \pi r^2 - \frac{hb}{2}$
Area = $\frac{a°}{360°} \pi r^2 - \frac{r(r \sin a°)}{2}$
Area = $r^2 \left(\frac{a°}{360°} \pi - \frac{\sin a°}{2} \right)$

FIGURE C-6. Areas of plane figures.

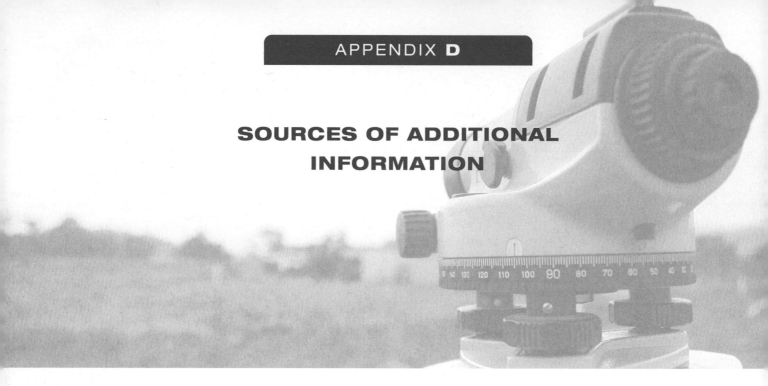

SOURCES OF ADDITIONAL INFORMATION

TEXTBOOKS

J. M. Anderson and E. M. Mikhail, *Surveying: Theory and Practice*, McGraw-Hill Book Company.

B. F. Kavanagh, Prentice-Hall, *Surveying with Construction Applications*, 4th ed., 2001.

F. H. Moffit and J. D. Bossler, *Surveying*, 10th ed., Harper and Row, 1997.

P. R. Wolf and C.G. Ghilani, *Elementary Surveying: An Introduction to Geomatics*, 10th ed., Addison-Wesley, 2001.

WEB SITES

American Congress on Surveying and Mapping (ASCM) http://www.ascm.net

Land Surveying and Geomatics Online Resources http://surveying.mentabolism.org/

National Society of Professional Surveyors http://nsps.org

Point of Beginning Magazine http://pobonline.com

Professional Surveyor Magazine http:www.profsurv.com

Virtual Museum of Surveying http://surveyhistory.org

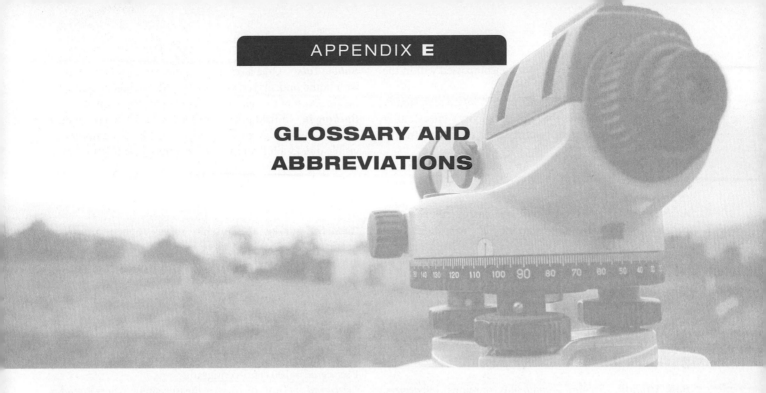

GLOSSARY AND ABBREVIATIONS

Most of the technical terms and abbreviations related to the subject of surveying are new to the beginning student. These terms are defined where they are first introduced in the text. Sometimes, however, students may read certain sections or chapters of the book out of sequence. This glossary can then be useful in providing a quick and brief definition of an unfamiliar term. It can also serve as a review and study aid. (The glossary term cross-references are in *italics*.)

The definitions here are intentionally brief; further discussion of each term can be found in the appropriate sections of the text. A list of commonly used surveying abbreviations follows these glossary definitions.

GLOSSARY

A

Accidental Error A small, unavoidable, random measurement error that is not caused by a *blunder* or *systematic errors*.

Accretion Gradual deposition of soil along the bank of a stream, gradually increasing the size of the adjacent property along the shore.

Accuracy Degree of perfection obtained in the results of a measurement, or, the closeness of the measured value to the "exact" value.

Acre The U.S. Customary unit for land *area*; one acre is equivalent to 43,560 sq. ft.

Acute Angle An *angle* less than 90 *degrees*.

Add Tape A *steel tape* that has the tenths- and hundredths-of-a-foot marks (or millimeter graduations) only extending beyond (or in back of) the zero mark, numbered backward.

Adjoiners Neighboring property owners identified in a *metes and bounds* boundary description.

Adjusting a Level Circuit See *Closing a Level Circuit*.

Adjusting a Traverse See *Closing a Traverse*.

Adverse Possession The taking possession of someone else's property by open and continuous *encroachment* for a statutory period of time.

Aerial Photograph A photograph taken from an aircraft in flight for the purpose of *photogrammetry*.

Alidade The top or upper part of a *transit* or *theodolite*, which includes the *standard, telescope, vertical circle, compass,* and *spindle*.

Alignment of a Route See *Horizontal Alignment* and *Vertical Alignment*.

Altitude See *Elevation*.

Analytical Stereoplotter An instrument that allows an operator to view pairs of *aerial photographs* in three-dimensional perspective to plot *contours*.

Angle A *plane* figure formed by the intersection of two *straight lines*, measured in units of *degrees, grads,* or *radians*.

Angle of Depression A *vertical angle* measured below a *horizontal* reference line.

Angle of Elevation A *vertical angle* measured above a *horizontal* reference line.

Angle to the Left An *angle* turned in a counterclockwise direction.

Angle to the Right An *angle* turned in a clockwise direction.

Annual Variation Yearly changes in *magnetic declination*.

Arc The curved portion of a *circle* between the ends of any *chord* in the circle.

Arc An SI metric unit of *area*, where 1 arc = 100 square meters.

Area   The two-dimensional space encompassed within the boundary of a closed figure.

Automatic Level   A *level* with an internal *optical compensator* that automatically takes over (using gravity's effect), after approximate leveling of the instrument, to set and maintain a truly *level line of sight*.

Average End-Area Formula   An equation for computing the volume of *earthwork (cut* or *fill)* between adjacent *cross-sections* of a highway or railway route.

Avulsion   A sudden and very noticeable change in the location of a shoreline that does not relocate the *riparian boundary line*.

Azimuth   A direction of a line expressed as the clockwise *angle* between the line and a given reference direction or *meridian*.

Azimuth Axis   The *vertical* axis of a *transit*, passing through the *alidade spindle* and the *leveling head*; also called the *standing axis*.

B

Back Azimuth   *Forward azimuth* plus (or minus) 180 *degrees*.

Back Direction   The direction opposite to which fieldwork is carried out.

Back Tangent   A *straight-line* section of a roadway or railway *alignment* that precedes a connecting curve and subsequent *forward tangent*.

Backsight   In *leveling*, the *rod reading* on a point of known elevation; also called a *plus sight*. Generally, a sight on a preceding point.

Banking   See *Superelevation*.

Barometric Leveling   A method of determining land *elevations* in preliminary surveys using barometers (called *altimeters*) to measure air pressure.

Batter Boards   *Horizontal* boards, each attached to two *vertical* posts, used during the *construction layout* of the corners of a building.

Bearing   Direction of a line expressed as the *angle* from the north or the south end of the *meridian*, whichever is nearest, to the line.

Benchmark   A secure and permanent point of known *elevation*, usually above sea level, used to establish elevations of other points.

Bisector   A line that divides another line (or *angle*) into two equal parts.

Blue Top   A wooden stake set in the ground so that the top (painted blue) of the stake is at the required *elevation* or *grade* of construction.

Blunder   A significant but avoidable mistake in a surveying measurement caused by human inattention or carelessness.

Borrow   In *earthwork* calculations, the volume of soil or rock that must be moved to a construction site from somewhere else.

Boundary Survey   See *Property Survey*.

Bowditch Rule   See *Compass Rule*.

Breaking Tape   A field procedure to measure *horizontal distances* over steeply sloping terrain, using one or more intermediate marks on line.

Bubble Tube   On a *level* or *theodolite*, a glass container filled with liquid and shaped so that when the bubble is centered, the direction of the telescopic *line of sight* is horizontal.

Bucking In   A field procedure used to establish a point on a line between two given marks when the points are not inter-visible due to a hill and when it is impossible to set up over either of the marks.

C

Cadastral Survey   A boundary survey applied to the U.S. *Public Lands Survey System*, or to identification of property in political subdivisions.

Celestial Sphere   The imaginary spherical shell formed by the sky.

Centesimal System   A system of angular measurement used in some countries, in which a complete rotation (full *circle*) is divided into 400 grades or *grads*.

Centi-centigrad   A unit of angular measurement, where 1 *centigrad* = 100 centi-centigrads.

Centigrad   A unit of angular measurement, where 1 *grad* = 100 centigrads.

Central Angle   The *angle* between two radii of a *circle*, with the angle's *vertex* at the center of the circle.

Chain   A historical American unit of distance measurement; one chain equals 66 feet; see also *Gunter's Chain*.

Chaining   A term sometimes used to describe the field procedure of *taping horizontal distances*; derived from *Gunter's Chain*.

Chicago Rod   A type of *level rod* consisting of three sliding sections; when the sections are unextended, it is more compact and portable than a *Philadelphia rod*.

Chord   A *straight-line* segment with its endpoints on the *perimeter* of a circle.

Chorobate   An ancient device used for *leveling*, from Roman times through the middle ages, which depended on the free surface of water in a trough to establish a *line of sight*.

Circle   A closed *plane* figure formed by a curved line, every point of which is equally distant from a single point inside the figure.

Circumference   The total length of the curved line that forms a *circle*.

Class of Accuracy   See *Order of Accuracy*.

Closing a Level Circuit   A mathematical procedure to distribute the *error of closure* among the intermediate *benchmarks* and to adjust the circuit so that the final observed benchmark elevation matches correctly.

Closing a Traverse   A mathematical procedure to eliminate geometric inconsistency in *traverse station coordinates* due to an *error of closure*.

Closing the Horizon   A procedure for checking *horizontal* angular measurements at a point by measuring the unused *angle* that completes the *circle*.

Closure   See *Error of Closure*.

Cloth Tape   See *Nonmetallic Tape*.

Coincidence Setting   See *Index Centering*.

Compass   A pivoted, freely swinging magnetic needle that rotates to align itself with the Earth's magnetic field.

Compass Rule   A mathematical method of distributing *errors* and adjusting the *coordinates* of a *traverse* so that it "closes" on a known point.

Compass Variation   See *Magnetic Variation*.

Complimentary Angles   Two *angles* whose sum is equal to a *right angle*.

Compound Curve   A roadway curve consisting of two *simple curves* with different radii, joined at a point of common tangency.

Connecting Traverse   A *traverse* that begins and ends at different points (or lines) of known position (or direction).

Construction Survey   A survey performed to mark the position on the ground of building corners, road locations, and other newly designed facilities and structures to be built.

Contour Interval   The constant *vertical* distance represented between successive *contour lines* on a *topographic map*.

Contour Line   A line on a *topographic map* showing points of equal *elevation*.

Control Survey   See *Horizontal Control* and *Vertical Control Surveys*.

Coordinate Geometry   A branch of mathematics in which geometric shapes are defined and studied algebraically in a *rectangular coordinate* system.

Coordinate Method   A computational method used to calculate the enclosed area in a *loop traverse* when the *coordinates* of each station is known.

Coordinate Transformation   A mathematical procedure to convert survey station *coordinates* from one reference system to another, usually to an SPCS.

Coordinates   See *Rectangular Coordinates* and *Polar Coordinates*.

Cosecant   In *trigonometry*, the reciprocal of the *sine* function.

Cosine   In *trigonometry*, a function of an *angle* equal to the ratio of the side adjacent to the angle to the *hypotenuse* of a *right triangle*.

Cotangent   In *trigonometry*, the reciprocal of the *tangent* function.

Course   The *straight line* between two *traverse stations*.

Course Departure   The *x*-component of a *traverse* line in a *rectangular coordinate* system.

Course Latitude   The *y*-component of a *traverse* line in a *rectangular coordinate* system. (Not to be confused with *Geographic Latitude*.)

Crest Curve   See *Summit Curve*.

Cross Hairs   Two intersecting *perpendicular lines* seen through a telescopic eyepiece of a surveying instrument to establish a *line of sight*.

Cross Section   In *route surveys*, a relatively short *profile* view of the ground or pavement, drawn *perpendicular* to the route centerline.

Cross-Section Leveling   A field procedure for obtaining relatively short *profile* views of the ground, *perpendicular* to the main route centerline.

Cubit   An ancient unit for *distance* measurement, equal to the length of a human forearm.

Cumulative Error   See *Systematic Error*.

Curb Return   The circular *arc* formed by a curb at a street intersection.

Curvature   See *Degree of Curve*.

Cut and Fill   In *earthwork*, *excavation* and *embankment* sections along a transportation route that establish the route's *vertical alignment*.

Cut Sheet   A table indicating depth of excavation or fill required to reach grade on a construction project.

Cut Tape   A *steel tape* marked every foot, with only the first and last foot intervals graduated in tenths and hundredths of a foot.

D

Data Reduction   The mathematical procedure of converting all distance and angle measurements of a *traverse* into station coordinates.

Datum   See *Horizontal Datum* and *Vertical Datum*.

Decimal System   A number system based on the number 10.

Declination   See *Magnetic Declination*.

Declination Arc   A scale on a *compass* that can be rotated to mark the *magnetic declination* so the compass reads true (or geographic) *bearings*.

Deflection Angle   A *horizontal angle* between the extension of a back or preceding line and the succeeding or next line forward.

Degree (of Arc)   A unit of angular measurement in which a complete rotation is equivalent to 360 degrees and a right angle equals 90 degrees.

Degree of Curvature   An angle that describes the "sharpness" of a *simple curve*; sharp curves have higher degrees of curves than "flat" curves.

Depression Contour   A *contour line* that encloses low ground with no drainage path.

Diameter   A *straight line* that passes through the center of a circle and has its two ends on the circle; the longest *chord* of a circle.

Differential Leveling   See *Leveling*.

Direct Elevation Rod   A type of *level rod* graduated to provide direct elevation readings, facilitating *topographic* or *construction surveys*.

Direct Reading Scale   A type of internal optical scale in a *theodolite*, read by looking through a small eyepiece mounted adjacent to the *telescope*.

Direction Theodolite   A *theodolite* that has only an *upper motion* with a single clamp and *tangent screw*, connecting the *alidade* to the *leveling head*.

Distance   See *Horizontal Distance*, *Vertical Distance*, and *Slope Distance*.

Diurnal Variation   Daily changes in *magnetic declination*.

Double Centering   A procedure used to accurately extend or prolong a *straight line* beyond a given endpoint using a *transit* or *theodolite*.

Double Meridian Distance Method   A computational method used to calculate the enclosed area in a *loop traverse* with adjusted latitudes and departures.

Double Sighting   See *Repeating the Angle*.

Double Vernier A *vernier* with a complete set of divisions running both ways, right and left, from a common zero line or index; *angles* may be read either clockwise (right) or counterclockwise (left).

Doubling the Angle See *Repeating the Angle.*

Drawing Scale The ratio between the length of a line on a drawing (or a *map*) and the actual distance that line represents in reality.

Dumpy Level An early type of *level* used in the United States that has the *bubble tube* attached directly to a relatively long *telescope.*

E

Earthwork The movement of soil or rock from one location to another for construction, including *excavation, embankment,* and *fill.*

Easement A legal right to use someone else's land for a specific purpose.

Electronic Data Collector An electronic recording device that automatically collects, stores, and displays data acquired by electronic surveying instruments to which it is attached.

Electronic Distance Measuring Instrument An instrument that quickly and accurately measures distances using a beam of electromagnetic waves (usually *laser* light).

Electronic Level An instrument that uses electronic digital image processing and a special bar-coded *level rod* to determine, record, and display elevations.

Electronic Total Station A surveying instrument with a combined digital electronic *theodolite,* an *electronic distance measuring device,* and a built-in computer that can process and record measurement data.

Elevation A *vertical* distance measured above or below a *benchmark* or reference surface (usually *mean sea level* (MSL)).

Elevation Axis The *horizontal* axis around which a *transit's* *telescope* rotates in a *vertical plane.*

Embankment Excavated soil placed and compacted in a different location for construction purposes; also called *fill.* See also *Earthwork.*

Encroachment The process of using and gradually taking possession of land belonging to someone else.

Engineer's Scale A *drawing scale* in the form of an *equivalence,* where a length of one unit on the scale is equivalent to a specified number of other units in the field (e.g., 1 in. = 2000 ft).

Engineer's Transit See *Transit.*

Equilateral Triangle A *triangle* that contains three sides of equal length.

Equivalence Scale A type of a *drawing scale,* also called an *engineer's scale.*

Error The difference between a measured quantity and its "exact" or "true" value, not due to *blunders.*

Error of Closure In *leveling circuits* and *control traverses,* the error or difference between the observed final position and the "true" position.

Excavation Removal of soil or rock from its natural location for the purpose of construction. See also *Earthwork.*

Exterior Angle An *angle* measured on the outside of a closed *polygon.*

Eyepiece A lens that magnifies the *cross hairs* in a telescope and that must be focused on them according to the observer's eyesight.

F

Fiberglass Tape See *Nonmetallic Tape.*

Field Book A small notebook (or clipboard and pad) used to record original data and sketches made at the time of measurement in the field.

Fill See *Embankment* and *Cut and Fill.*

Florida Rod A type of *level rod* consisting of only one section 10 ft long.

Focusing Lens A lens that can be moved back and forth inside a telescopic tube to focus the image on the *cross hairs.*

Forced Centering The exchange of a *target* or reflecting *prism* with a *theodolite* on a *tribrach,* maintaining a leveled and centered position.

Foresight In *leveling,* a *rod* reading on a point of unknown *elevation;* also called a *minus sight.* Generally, a sight on a forward point.

Forward Azimuth See *Azimuth.*

Forward Direction The direction in which fieldwork is carried out.

Forward Tangent A *straight-line* section of a road or railway *alignment* that follows a connecting curve with the *back tangent.*

Full Station Stations marked at intervals of exactly 100 ft (or 10 m in SI).

G

Geodetic Surveying A surveying method that takes Earth's curvature into account in measurements and *data reduction.*

Geographic Latitude The angular distance, north or south from the Earth's equatorial plane, of a point on the Earth's surface. (Not to be confused with *Course Latitude.*)

Geometry A branch of mathematics concerned with the properties of and relationships among lines, angles, surfaces, and solids.

Global Positioning System or Global Navigation Satellite System A system of orbiting satellites that continuously broadcast radio signals, used to determine the coordinates and elevation of any point on the Earth's surface.

Grad A unit of angular measurement in which a complete rotation is divided into 400 grads, and a right angle equals 100 grads.

Grade The *vertical* position or *elevation* of a point.

Grade Line The *vertical alignment* or *profile* of the centerline of a roadway or other type of transportation route.

Grade Rod The reading on a *level rod* that would be seen from the given instrument position if the bottom of the rod were placed at the required *grade* of construction.

Grade Staking Setting wooden stakes (or other marks) at required *elevations* to serve as reference points for construction.

Gradient The *slope* of rate of change in *grade* or *elevation* of a line.

Gravity A physical property of mass, manifested by a force of attraction directed toward the center of the Earth (i.e., *vertical* direction).

Grid-Method Leveling A field procedure used to determine the *topography* of a small, uncluttered, gently sloping parcel of land.

Gun A slang term for a transit, a theodolite, or a level mounted on a tripod.

Gunter's Chain A chain of 100 heavy wire links with a length of 66 ft, used to measure distances until the introduction of modern *steel tapes*.

H

Hand Level A small metal or plastic tube with a *horizontal* line across the open end, a small peephole in the front, a *spirit bubble*, and a prism to reflect the split view of the bubble onto the *line of sight*, used for rough *elevation* measurements, making *vertical ties*, etc.

Hectare SI metric unit of *area*; one hectare equals 10 000 square meters.

Height See *Elevation*.

Height of Instrument The *elevation* or height of the *horizontal* line of sight through the telescope of a *level, transit*, or other surveying instrument.

High Rod A term describing the use of a *level rod* in its extended position when *leveling* over steeply sloping terrain.

Horizontal A direction *perpendicular* to the *vertical* direction (i.e., at a *right angle* to the direction of gravity).

Horizontal Alignment A connected series of straight lines and curves projected onto a *horizontal* plane on a drawing, locating the centerline of a route.

Horizontal Angle An angle between two lines of sight measured in a plane that is *horizontal* at the point of observation.

Horizontal Axis See *Elevation Axis*.

Horizontal Circle The middle part of a *transit*, between the *alidade* and *leveling head*, graduated in *degrees* (of arc) and fractions of a degree.

Horizontal Control Survey A very accurate survey performed to establish a large network of fixed *stations* on the ground from which other less-accurate surveying measurements are made in the future.

Horizontal Curve Arcs of circles or spirals that connect the straight-line sections (back and forward *tangents*) of the *horizontal alignment* of a road or highway route.

Horizontal Datum A basis for *horizontal control* comprising the *coordinates* of a point and the direction of a baseline passing through the point.

Horizontal Distance A length measured along a *level surface*.

Horizontal Tie A *horizontal* distance measurement that is used to locate the position of natural and cultural features to be shown on a map.

Hydrographic Survey A survey performed to map the shorelines and water depths of a river, lake, or harbor.

Hypotenuse The long side, opposite the 90-degree angle, in a *right triangle*.

I

Index Centering A procedure followed when using a *theodolite* to read an observed *angle* with high *precision*, by manipulating a knob to center the circle degree graduation mark between the double index lines; also called *coincidence setting*.

Index Error The reading observed on the *vertical circle* of a *transit* when the *telescope bubble tube* is centered.

Inertial Positioning System An electromechanical device, which can be used to determine *coordinates* of survey points.

Inscribed Angle The *angle* formed between two *chords* that meet at a point on a *circle*.

Instrument Person In a surveying crew, the person using the *tripod-mounted level, transit, theodolite*, or *electronic total station*.

Instrumental Error A *systematic error* due to an imperfection or maladjustment of the measuring instrument.

Interior Angle An *angle* measured on the inside of a closed *polygon*.

Interpolation of Contours The process of estimating intermediate ground *elevation* values between observed data points to sketch *contour lines* on a *map*.

Invar A steel alloy relatively insensitive to temperature changes, used in some *steel tapes* and *leveling rods* for increased *precision*.

Inverse Computations Surveying computations that result in the direction and length of a line, starting with the *coordinates* of the line's endpoints.

Inverse Trig Function An expression relating an unknown *angle* to a known value of one of its *trig* functions.

Invert Elevation The *elevation* of the bottom inside surface of a sewer pipe or storm drain, established in the design and layout of pipelines.

Isogonic Chart A *map* showing *magnetic declination contour lines* and *secular variation* contour lines.

Isosceles Triangle A *triangle* that contains two sides of equal length.

K

Keel A yellow lumber crayon used to make marks on paved surfaces.

L

Land Survey See *Property Survey*.

Laser An intense narrow beam of light, used in *electronic distance measurement instruments* and for establishing *line and grade*.

Latitude See *Course Latitude* and *Geographic Latitude*.

Least Squares Method A mathematical procedure for adjusting the *coordinates* of a *traverse* so that it "closes." See *Closing a Traverse*.

Lenker Rod See *Direct Elevation Rod*.

Level *Horizontal*. Also, the instrument used to make *leveling* surveys.

Level Book One of two *field books* maintained when *running levels*, kept by the *instrument person*.

Level Circuit   A *leveling* survey that ends on either the starting *benchmark*, or another known benchmark, to check for *blunders* and determine the *error of closure* and *order of accuracy*.

Level Rod   A graduated rod held vertically at a point to measure *elevation*.

Level Surface   A curved surface to which the direction of *gravity* is normal, or *perpendicular*, at all points.

Leveling   Measurement of the *elevations* of a continuous series of points.

Leveling Head   The lower part of a *level, transit,* or *theodolite,* or *EDMI* on which the *leveling screws* operate; also called the *footplate*.

Leveling Screws   Three (or four) screws on the *leveling head* of a *level, transit,* or *EDMI,* used to level the instrument by rotating the screws.

Libella   An ancient surveying instrument used to establish a *level line,* using a triangular A-frame and a plumb-bob line at the *vertex*.

Line and Grade   Placing stakes or other reference marks in the field to establish the location, direction, and *elevation* of proposed construction.

Line of Levels   See *Level Circuit*.

Line of Sight   A straight line observed through a telescopic *eyepiece,* defined by the *cross hairs* and the optical center of the *objective lens*.

Linear Interpolation   For drawing contour lines based on the assumption that the ground slopes uniformly between adjacent *contour lines.* See *Interpolation of Contour Lines*.

Link   A historical American unit of distance; one link is 0.01 chain or 7.92 in. (See also *Gunter Chain*.)

Link Traverse   See *Connecting Traverse*.

Local Attraction   Disturbance of the direction of a *compass* needle due to nearby magnetic materials or power lines.

Location Survey   See *Construction Survey*.

Loop Traverse   A *traverse* that starts and ends at the same point or *station,* thus forming a *polygon*.

Lovar   A steel alloy relatively insensitive to temperature changes, used in some *steel tapes* and *leveling rods* for increased *precision*.

Lower Motion   A clamp and *tangent screw* that controls the motion of the *horizontal circle* relative to the *leveling head* of a *theodolite*.

M

Magnetic Azimuth   An *azimuth* measured with reference to a *magnetic meridian*.

Magnetic Bearing   A *bearing* measured with reference to a *magnetic meridian*.

Magnetic Declination   The true *bearing* of a pivoted, freely swinging magnetic needle (called a *compass*).

Magnetic Meridian   An imaginary line parallel to the direction taken by a pivoted, freely swinging *compass* needle.

Map   See *Planimetric Map* and *Topographic Map*.

Map Scale   See *Drawing Scale* and *Representative Fraction*.

Mass Diagram   In *earthwork* calculations, a graphical technique used to balance *cut-and-fill* quantities along a proposed transportation route.

Mean Sea Level   A primary reference level or *datum* for measuring elevations of points on land, determined by averaging the hourly elevations of the sea over a long period of time. Or, the position the ocean would take if tides and currents were eliminated.

Measuring Wheel   A wheel mounted on a rod and attached to an *odometer,* used for rough *distance* measurement by rolling the wheel along the line to be measured.

Mechanical Error   See *Systematic Error*.

Mensuration   Measurement of distances, areas, and volumes.

Meridian   A fixed reference direction. See *True Meridian* and *Magnetic Meridian*.

Metes and Bounds   A method for fully identifying and describing a parcel of land, including boundary line distances, directions, and *adjoiners*.

Micrometer Scale   A type of internal optical scale in a *theodolite,* requiring use of a knob on the instrument for *index centering* to read an angle.

Minus Sight   See *Foresight*.

Minute (of Arc)   An angular distance equal to one-sixtieth (1/60) of a *degree*.

Mirror Stereoscope   A device used to view a *stereopair* of *aerial photographs* in three-dimensional perspective.

Monument   See *Benchmark*.

Most Probable Value   The average value of a series of repeated measurements.

N

Natural Errors   *Random errors* not due to instrumental or personal causes.

Nonmetallic Tape   Tapes made of fiberglass, synthetic yarn, or cloth, for use when relatively low-accuracy distance measurements are required.

Normal Position   The position of the *transit telescope* with the *spirit bubble tube* underneath the scope.

Normal Tension   The pull on the tape required so that *systematic errors* due to incorrect tension and *sag* should cancel each other when *taping*.

O

Objective Lens   A lens at the forward end of a telescope that forms an image of the sighted target within the telescopic tube.

Oblique Photo   An *aerial photograph* taken with the optical axis of the camera unaligned with the *vertical* direction.

Oblique Triangle   A *triangle* that does not contain a right (90%) angle.

Obtuse Angle   An *angle* greater than 90°.

Odometer   An instrument used for measuring distances by relating the number of turns of a wheel to the linear distance covered.

Offset Line In *construction surveying*, a line located parallel to the actual construction line, but offset 1 to 2 m so as not to be disturbed.

Optical Compensator In an *automatic level*, a pendulum-type of device that uses the force of gravity to set and maintain a truly *level line of sight*.

Optical Micrometer A measuring device used with modern *precise tilting levels* to improve *precision*.

Optical Plummet A small, vertical telescopic sight in the *spindle* of a *theodolite*, used to set up the instrument directly over a point or *station*.

Order of Accuracy A federal standard level of *accuracy* for *horizontal or vertical control surveys*.

Orient to the Curve To set a transit on a curve with the vernier set at the appropriate deflection angle to proceed setting forward points on the curve.

P

Pace The length of one natural footstep while walking a level line.

Pacing A procedure for approximate *distance* measurement involving counting paces (single steps) while walking along a line to be measured.

Parabola A curve used in the *vertical alignment* of a transportation route, providing a constant rate of change of *slope* between *tangents*.

Parallax Occurs when the image of a *level rod* is not focused exactly on the plane of the *cross hairs*, causing the *rod reading* to vary as the observer's eye is moved up or down.

Parallel Lines *Straight lines* in the same *plane*, which do not meet or intersect, no matter how far they are prolonged.

Parallel Plate Micrometer An optical device built in or attached to a modern *tilting level*, allowing very precise *vertical* displacements to be measured.

Parallelogram A *quadrilateral* with each pair of opposite sides *parallel*.

Peg Book One of two *field books* maintained when *running levels*, kept by the *rodperson*.

Perimeter The border or boundary of a two-dimensional *plane* figure; also, the total length of the border.

Perpendicular Lines Lines intersecting to form a *right angle*.

Philadelphia Rod A type of *level rod* consisting of two sliding sections; when the rod is fully extended, its front face reads continuously from 0 at the bottom to 12 ft at the top. (Metric rods are also available.)

Photogrammetry Making precise measurements of images on *aerial photographs* to determine the relative locations of points and objects on the ground.

Plane A perfectly flat (two-dimensional) surface.

Plane Surveying A method of surveying measurement and computation methods that neglects the curvature of the Earth's surface.

Planimeter A mechanical or electronic instrument used to trace *perimeters* of plane figures of any shape, thereby measuring areas on maps.

Planimetric Map A drawing that shows the horizontal positions of natural and cultural features on the land (but does not show *surface relief*.)

Plat A drawing that shows the *metes and bounds* of a parcel of land, along with any buildings, fences, *adjoiners*, and other features.

Plot Plan See *Site Plan*.

Plumb In a *vertical* direction.

Plumb-Bob A small weight, freely suspended at the end of a string, used to establish the *vertical* direction over a point or survey *station*.

Plunge the Scope Turning the *transit telescope* 180° around the *elevation axis*, from *normal position* to *reversed position*.

Plus Sight See *Backsight*.

Point of Beginning A permanent marker on the boundary of a parcel of land that is used to start a *metes and bounds* description of the property.

Point of Curvature The intersection of a *back tangent* and a *horizontal curve* along the *alignment* of a transportation route; also called *tangent to curve* or *beginning of curve*.

Point of Intersection The intersection of the *back tangent* and the *forward tangent* in the *horizontal alignment* of a road or other transportation route.

Point of Reverse Curve The point where two *reverse curves* meet.

Point of Tangency The intersection of a *horizontal curve* and a *forward tangent* along the *alignment* of a transportation route; also called *curve to tangent* or *end of curve*.

Point of Vertical Curve The intersection of a *back tangent* and a *vertical curve* along the *vertical alignment* of a transportation route.

Point of Vertical Intersection The intersection of the *back tangent* and the *forward tangent* in the *vertical alignment* of a road or other transportation route.

Point of Vertical Tangency The intersection of a *vertical curve* and a *forward tangent* along the *vertical alignment* of a transportation route.

Polar Coordinates A pair of numbers (r, A) that describe the location of a point at a distance r from the origin and at an angle A from the x-axis.

Polygon A closed plane figure with three or more straight sides.

Precise Level See *Tilting Level*.

Precise Level Rod A *level rod* constructed in one solid section with an attached, graduated *invar–steel* strip, used for *precise leveling* surveys.

Precise Leveling High *order of accuracy* leveling for *vertical control*, requiring the use of special *leveling* instruments, *rods*, and field methods.

Precision The degree of refinement or perfection used in a measurement.

Preliminary Survey See *Reconnaissance Survey*.

Principal Meridian A *meridian* unique to each State for reference of *quadrangles, townships*, and *sections*, in the U.S. *Public Land Survey System*.

Prism A solid made up of several plane faces; see *Reflecting Prism.*

Prism Pole An adjustable height pole with attached bull's-eye *spirit level* and *reflecting prisms* for electronic distance measurement.

Profile A drawing that shows a *vertical cross section* or "side view" of the ground surface or roadway pavement along a *route survey.*

Profile Leveling The process of determining the *elevations* of a series of points on the ground, at mostly uniform intervals along a continuous line or route.

Property Survey A survey performed to establish the location of boundary lines and property corners on the ground.

Protractor A plastic circular or semicircular device with graduations in *degrees* used to measure or draw *angles* on a drawing.

Public Domain Land Land owned by the U.S. federal government.

Public Land Survey System In the United States, a rectangular framework created for surveying and describing large land parcels, primarily in mid-western and far western states.

Pythagorean Theorem A mathematical formula which states that in a *right triangle*, the square of the *hypotenuse* equals the sum of the squares of the other two sides.

Q

Quadrangle The largest parcel of land subdivision in the U.S. *Public Land Survey System*, approximately 24 miles on a side, subdivided into 16 smaller tracts called *townships.*

Quadrilateral A closed *plane* figure with four sides and four angles.

R

Radial Shot An extra measurement of distance and direction to a point in the vicinity of a control traverse station; also called a *Side Shot.*

Radial Stakeout *Radial survey* methods used for *construction surveys.*

Radial Survey Useful in open terrain, the process of making several angle and distance measurements from a single point or *station* of known position.

Radian A unit of angular measurement in which a complete rotation is equivalent to 2π radians (1 radian is equivalent to 57.3°).

Radius A line from the center of a *circle* to any point on the circle.

Random Error See *Accidental Error.*

Reciprocal Leveling A procedure for *running levels* accurately over obstacles, where the *backsight* and *foresight* distances must be different, using two instrument setups.

Reconnaissance Survey A *preliminary survey* conducted to get approximate or rough data regarding a tract of land.

Recording Electronic Tachometer See *Electronic Distance Meter.*

Rectangle A *parallelogram* with four *right angles.*

Rectangular Coordinates A pair of numbers (x, y) representing distances of a point from the origin (intersection point) of two perpendicular lines (axes) serving to describe the location of the point.

Reflecting Prism The corner of a solid glass cube, used to reflect *laser* light back to an *electronic distance measurement instrument.*

Reflector See *Reflecting Prism.*

Refraction Slight bending of light (and a *line of sight*) in the atmosphere.

Relative Accuracy For *horizontal* distance measurement, the ratio of *closure* to the true distance.

Reliction Gradual receding of water in a lake or stream as the water body dries up, moving the *riparian boundary* and increasing the area of a parcel of land on the shore.

Relief Displacement In *photogrammetry*, the difference in position of an object or point on a *vertical photo* compared with its true *planimetric* position.

Repeating an Angle The process of measuring an angle with a *transit* or *theodolite* more than once (an even number of times), with the telescope reversed half of the time, to increase *precision*, reduce the effect of *systematic errors*, and eliminate *blunders.*

Repeating Theodolite A *theodolite* with two independent *upper* and *lower motions.*

Representative Fraction A *map scale* expressed as a ratio of map distance to actual distance, with the number 1 in the numerator of the ratio.

Resurvey A *property survey* performed to relocate the original boundary lines for previously described and monumented land parcels.

Reticule (or Reticle) A component of a modern telescopic sight that provides the *cross hairs* near the rear of the telescopic tube.

Reverse Curve An "S-shaped" curve composed of two opposite *simple curves* in the *horizontal alignment* of a transportation route.

Reversed Position The "plunged" or "transited" position of the *transit telescope* with the *spirit bubble tube* on top of the telescope.

Right Angle An *angle* of 90° (or 100 grads, or $\pi/2$ radians).

Right-Angle Trig Trigonometric functions and relationships among the sides and *angles* of a *right triangle.*

Right of Way An *easement* that gives the right to pass across the land or use the land for other purposes (e.g., storm drainage).

Right Triangle A *triangle* with one interior angle of 90°.

Riparian Boundary A land boundary line (either high water mark or centerline of a stream) of property adjacent to a body of water.

Riparian Rights Certain privileges the owner of property adjacent to a body of water has with respect to the use of the water.

Rod A historical American unit of distance; one rod equals 0.25 chain or 16.5 ft. See also *Level Rod.*

Rod Reading A number observed through a *level* where the *level rod* appears to be intersected by the horizontal cross hair of the telescope.

Rod Shot In *profile leveling*, a series of *foresights* on the level rod held at stations along the profile line to determine ground *elevations*.

Rodperson In a surveying crew, the person who holds the *leveling rod* in a *vertical* direction over the surveyed points.

Rotating-Beam Laser An instrument with an internal optical system that continuously rotates a *laser* beam, generating a flat reference surface.

Rotation of Axes One of the steps in *coordinate transformation* involving a rotation of the *meridian* of the reference coordinate system.

Route Survey A survey for the design and construction of relatively "long and narrow" engineering projects (e.g., roads, railways, and pipelines).

Running Description A *property survey* description that gives the direction and length of each boundary line in sequence, starting at a POB.

Running Levels A procedure used to determine the *elevations* of two or more widely separated points for *vertical control* or *profile surveys*.

S

Sag A *vertical distance* between the horizontal and the midpoint of a *steel tape* held *horizontally* between two points on the ground.

Sag Curve A *vertical curve* in a *route survey* with a positive change in *grade* between the forward and back *tangents*.

San Francisco Rod A type of *level rod* consisting of three sliding sections; when the sections are unextended, it is more compact and portable than a *Philadelphia rod*.

Scale See *Drawing Scale*.

Sea-Level Datum See *Mean Sea Level*.

Secant In *trigonometry*, the reciprocal of the *cosine* function.

Second (of Arc) An angular distance equal to one-sixtieth (1/60) of a *minute* of arc.

Section A unit of land in the U.S. *Public Land Survey System* about 1 square mile in area; there are 36 sections in a *township*.

Sector A figure formed by an *arc* of a *circle* and its *subtended* central *angle*.

Secular Variation A long-term change in *magnetic declination*.

Segment The figure formed by a *chord* and an *arc* of a *circle*.

Self-Leveling Level See *Automatic Level*.

Self-Reading Rod *Level rods* that can be read directly by the *instrument person*.

Setback The minimum required distance between a new building and the front or side property lines, per local building codes.

Sexagesimal System A number system based on the number 60 in which a complete rotation (full *circle*) is divided into 360 *degrees of arc*.

Shooting in Grade In *construction surveys*, setting a grade mark wherever desired by holding a *level rod* at each point and raising or lowering the rod until the *target* is on the line of sight of the *transit* where the *height of instrument* is equal to the target setting.

Shrinkage In *earthwork* calculations, the decrease in volume of soil due to compaction in an *embankment*.

Side Shot An extra measurement of distance and direction from a *traverse station* to another point that is not part of the traverse.

Side Slope In a route *cross section*, the ratio of a horizontal distance to a corresponding unit of vertical distance for a *cut* or *fill* slope.

Significant Figures The number of sure or certain digits in a measurement, plus one estimated digit.

Simple Curves A single arc of a circle, the most common type of a *horizontal curve* used in *route surveys*.

Sine In *trigonometry*, a function of an *angle*, equal to the ratio of the side opposite the angle to the *hypotenuse* of a *right triangle*.

Site Plan A special-purpose *topographic map* that shows all buildings, roads, and other facilities to be constructed on a parcel of land.

Slope The rate of change in grade or elevation of a line; rise over run. See *Gradient*.

Slope Distance A distance measured in a direction other than *horizontal*, which eventually will be reduced (converted) to a horizontal distance.

Slope Stakes Wooden stakes that mark the line where *cut* or *fill side slopes* intersect the original ground surface.

Slope Staking The procedure for giving *line and grade* for the construction of *earthwork side slopes* or locating the edges of roadway *cuts* and *fills* that exceed 3 ft (1 m) in depth.

Slow Motion Screw See *Tangent Screw*.

Spindle A tapered metal cylinder on the *alidade* of a transit, also called the *inner center*, which fits into the hollow *outer center* of the *leveling head* and allows rotation around the *azimuth axis*.

Spiral Curve In *horizontal alignment*, it provides a gradual change in *curvature* from a *tangent* to a curve or another tangent; useful for railway routes or highway exit ramps to avoid sudden changes in curve.

Spirit Leveling See *Leveling*.

Spirit Vial See *Bubble Tube*.

Square A *rectangle* with four equal sides.

Stadia Hairs Two short, *horizontal cross hairs* in the *reticle* of a *telescope*, equally spaced above and below the central horizontal cross hair.

Stadia Survey A procedure for measuring direction, distance, and *elevation* in one operation, using only a *transit* and *level rod*, for mapping.

Standard A cast metal frame on the *alidade* of a *transit* that supports the *telescope* and *vertical circle*, allowing rotation of the telescope around the *elevation axis*.

Standard of Accuracy See *Order of Accuracy*.

Standing Axis See *Azimuth Axis*.

State Plane Coordinate System   A rectangular coordinate grid with central meridian and origin unique to each State in the United States for horizontal control surveys.

Station   See *Stationing*.

Stationing   A standard system for clearly identifying marks set on a line of measured distances; the marks are called *stations*.

Steel Tape   A narrow ribbon of steel, typically 100 ft (or 30 m long), stored and carried on an open-reel case, graduated throughout its entire length in feet, tenths, and hundredths of a foot (or in meters and millimeters), used to measure *horizontal* (and *slope*) distances.

Stereopair   A pair of overlapping *aerial photographs* for viewing a three-dimensional image of the ground.

Stereoplotter   An instrument that makes it possible both to observe a three-dimensional image of the ground by viewing overlapping *aerial photographs* and to plot *contour lines* on a *topographic map*.

Straight Angle   An angle of 180° (or 200 grads, or π radians).

Straight Line   The shortest line joining two points.

Stride   Two paces or steps. See *Pacing*.

Subdivision   The division of a large tract of land into two or more smaller parcels for sale as separate building lots.

Subtended Angle   An *arc* subtends (forms) a *central angle* between two radii from the center of the *circle* to the ends of the arc.

Summit Curve   A *vertical curve* in a *route survey* with a negative change in *grade* between the forward and back *tangents*.

Superelevation   The raising or *banking* of the outer edge of a roadway pavement or railway transportation route to resist the effect of centrifugal forces along a curved path.

Supplementary Angles   Two *angles* whose sum is equal to the sum of two *right angles*.

Surface Relief   The overall "shape" of the land (e.g., hills or valleys), shown on a *topographic map*.

System of Rectangular Surveys   See *Public Land Survey System*.

Systematic Error   An *error* caused by imperfections in the measuring equipment, by the method of measurement, or by certain natural conditions.

T

Tangent   A straight line that touches or meets a curve at only one point. See also *Forward Tangent* and *Back Tangent*. Also, a trigonometric function of an *angle* equal to the ratio of the opposite side to the adjacent side in a *right triangle*.

Tangent Screw   A slow-adjustment screw on surveying instruments, to provide fine control of the direction of the telescope by turning a knob.

Tape   See *Steel Tape* and *Nonmetallic Tape*.

Tape Clamp Handle   A metal device used for providing a firm grip on a *steel tape* at any intermediate point without causing damage to the tape or injury to the surveyor from the steel edge.

Tape Thermometer   A special thermometer, attached to a *steel tape*, to account for tape expansion or contraction when high *accuracy* is required.

Taping   The field procedure of measuring *distances* with a *steel tape*.

Target   A readily visible object with a clearly marked point for setting a *line of sight* that can be centered over a point in a *tribrach* on a tripod; see also *Target Rod*.

Target Rod   A *level rod* with a movable target and vernier scale that can be set by the *rodperson* at a position indicated by the *instrument person*, and read with greater *accuracy* by the rodperson.

Telescope   On *levels*, *transits*, *theodolites*, and *total stations* to magnify an image and obtain a *line of sight* on a *rod*, point, or *target*.

Tension Handle   A spring-balance and handle attached to the forward end of a *steel tape* to indicate whether the correct tension (pull) is applied to the tape.

Theodolite   A compact instrument for measuring angles accurately, with internal *micrometer scales* for precise reading of the circles.

Three-Wire Leveling   For *precise leveling* surveys, a procedure that makes use of the central and *stadia cross hairs*; the three readings are averaged.

Tilting Axis   See *Elevation Axis*.

Tilting Level   A modern *level* equipped with an attached (or internal) *parallel plate micrometer*, used for *precise leveling* surveys.

Topographic Map   A scale drawing (also called a topo map) showing *surface relief* and the locations of all natural and cultural features on the land.

Topographic Survey   A survey performed to determine the "shape" of the land and the locations of all existing natural and cultural features (e.g., streams, lakes, and houses) depicted on a *topographic map*.

Total Station   See *Electronic Total Station*.

Township   A tract of land in the U.S. *Public Land Survey System* about 6 miles on a side, further subdivided into 36 *sections*.

Transit   A traditional American-style optical surveying instrument used primarily to measure *horizontal* and *vertical angles*.

Transit Rule   A mathematical method of distributing *errors* and adjusting the *coordinates* of a *traverse* so that it "closes."

Transit the Scope   See *Plunge the Scope*.

Transition Curve   See *Spiral Curve*.

Translation of Axes   One of the steps in *coordinate transformation*, involving a displacement of the origin of the reference coordinate system.

Trapezium   A *quadrilateral* in which no two sides are *parallel*.

Trapezoid   A four-sided plane figure with only one pair of opposite sides *parallel*.

Trapezoidal Rule   A mathematical method used to approximate the area enclosed between a *traverse* line and an irregular natural boundary line.

Traverse   An interconnected series of lines (*courses*) running between a series of points on the ground (*stations*) for horizontal control.

Triangle   A three-sided *polygon*.

Triangulation   The determination of the positions of horizontal control *stations* covering large areas, relying primarily on angular measurement.

Tribrach   The base of a *theodolite*, with a special release mechanism that allows the instrument to be easily exchanged with a *target* or *reflector* without disturbing the leveled and centered position.

Trigonometric Leveling   A method used to determine the difference in *elevation* between two points indirectly by measuring a *vertical* or *zenith angle* and the *slope distance* between the two points, and using *trig*.

Trigonometry (Trig)   A branch of mathematics concerned with the relationships among the sides and angles of a triangle; abbreviated "trig."

Trilateration   The computation of *rectangular coordinates* of survey *stations* using only distance measurements and *trigonometry*.

Tripod   A three-legged wooden or aluminum stand on which *levels*, *transits*, *theodolites*, *total stations*, and so on are securely mounted.

True Azimuth   An *azimuth* measured with reference to a *true meridian*.

True Bearing   A *bearing* measured with reference to a *true meridian*.

True Meridian   An imaginary line that passes through a point on the Earth's surface and the Earth's geographic north and south poles.

Turning Point   A temporary mark or point conveniently located to serve as an intermediate reference when *running levels*.

U

Unit Pace   A person's average *pace* length expressed as ft/pace or m/pace.

Upper Motion   A clamp and *tangent screw* that controls motion of the *horizontal circle* relative to the *alidade* of a theodolite.

V

Vernier Scale   A short graduated scale mounted parallel to the main scale to be read, used to provide more precise readings of the main scale.

Vertex   The intersection of two sides of a *plane* figure; high point of a *triangle*.

Vertical   The direction of *gravity* (i.e., toward the center of the Earth).

Vertical Alignment   A *profile* view of the final *grade line* of a transportation route.

Vertical Angle   An *angle* between two *lines of sight* measured in a *vertical* plane at the point of observation.

Vertical Circle   A graduated metal disk on the *alidade* of a *transit* used to measure *vertical angles*.

Vertical Control Datum   A *level surface*, line, or point used as a reference from which the *elevations* of other points are determined.

Vertical Control Survey   A very accurate survey performed to establish a large network of *benchmarks* on the ground from which other, less-accurate, surveying measurements are made in the future.

Vertical Curve   A segment of a *parabola* in a *vertical* plane, used to connect the forward and back *tangents* of a highway route.

Vertical Distance   A length measured along the direction of *gravity*.

Vertical Motion   A clamp and *tangent screw* that controls the vertical angle of a transit or theodolite telescope.

Vertical Photo   An *aerial photograph* taken with the optical axis of the camera aligned in the *vertical* direction.

Vertical Tie   A *vertical distance* measurement for determining the *elevation* of a point to be shown on a *topographic* map.

W

Waving the Rod   A procedure used to assure that the *level rod* is in the *vertical* direction when the rod reading is taken.

Witnessing a Point   A field procedure for referencing or locating a control point with *horizontal ties* so that it can be relocated in the future.

Z

Zenith   The point on the *celestial sphere* vertically above a given point.

Zenith Angle   A *vertical angle* measured using the *zenith direction* as a zero reference line; also called *zenith distance*.

Zenith Direction   The upward *vertical direction*, which is used as a reference for measuring *vertical angles* with a *transit* or *theodolite*.

Zenith Distance   See *Zenith Direction*.

ABBREVIATIONS AND SYMBOLS

BLM	Bureau of Land Management		NSRS	National Spatial Reference System
BM	benchmark		NW	northwest
BS	backsight		°	degree
c	centigrad		PC	point of curvature
CAD	computer-aided drafting		PCC	point of compound curve
CADD	computer-aided design and drafting		PE	professional engineer
cc	centi-centigrad		PI	point of intersection
COGO	coordinate geometry		POB	point of beginning
CT	curve to tangent		PP	professional planner
DMD	double meridian distance		PRC	point of reverse curve
E	east		PT	point of tangency
EDM	electronic distance measurement		PVC	point of vertical curvature
EDMI	electronic distance measuring instrument		PVI	point of vertical intersection
ETI	electronic tachometer instrument		PVT	point of vertical tangency
FS	foresight		RF	representative fraction
g	grad		ROW	right of way
GIS	geographic information system		S	south
GPS	global positioning system		SC	spiral to curve
GR	grade rod		SE	southeast
HI	height of instrument		SI	System International
IPS	inertial positioning system		SPCS	state plane coordinate system
LS	land surveyor (or licensed surveyor)		SW	southwest
MD	meridian distance		TC	tangent to curve
MSL	mean sea level		TP	turning point
N	north		US	United States
NAVD88	North American Vertical Datum of 1988		USGS	United States Geological Survey
NE	Northeast		W	west
NGS	National Geodetic Survey		Δ	delta
NGVD29	National Geodetic Vertical Datum of 1929			

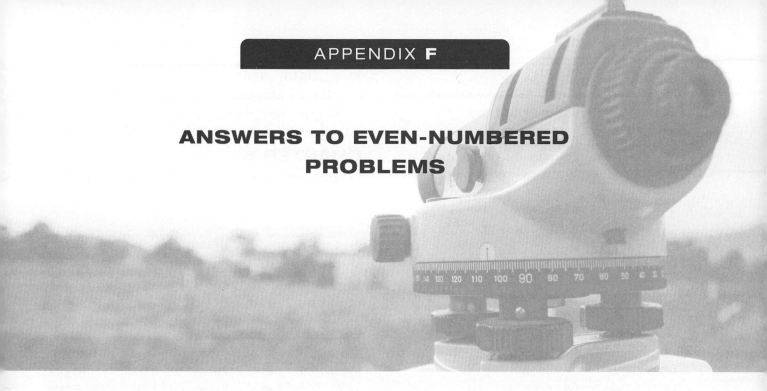

ANSWERS TO EVEN-NUMBERED PROBLEMS

(Rounded off to an appropriate number of significant figures.)

CHAPTER 2

2. a. 0.75°   **b.** 77.39708°

4. a. 86°39′   **b.** 27°32′35.8″

6. 111°26′07″; 61°39′25″

8. a. 45.75° × (1°/0.9°) = 50.83°
  b. 123.1234° × (1°/0.9°) = 136.8038°

10. a. 23° × (0.9°/1°) = 21°
  b. 75.245° × (0.9°/1°) = 67.721°
  c. 150.7654° × (0.9°/1°) = 135.6889°

12. a. 67.35 ft × (0.3048 m/1 ft) = 20.53 m
  b. 246.864 m × (1 ft/0.3048 m) = 809.921 ft
  c. 75 ch 3 rds 20 lk − 75.95 ch = 5012.70 ft
  d. 1.23 ml × (1 km/0.621 ml) = 1.98 km

14. a. 75 500 ft² × (1 ac/43 560 ft²) = 1.73 ac
  b. 10.5 ac × (1 ha/2.47 ac) = 4.25 ha
  c. 10.5 ha × (2.471 ac/1 ha) = 25.9 ac
  d. 750 ac × (1 mi²/640 ac) = 1.2 mi²
  e. 5.3 mi² × (1 km²/0.3861 mi²) = 14 km²

16. a. 500 ft² × (1 yd²/27 ft²) = 18.5 yd²
  b. 150 yd² × (1 m²/1.30795 yd²) = 115 m²

18. a. 3   **b.** 4   **c.** 5   **d.** 4   **e.** 5
  f. 3   **g.** 2   **h.** 4   **i.** 4   **j.** 4

20. 282.47

22. 640

24. 45.0; 246 000; 0.123; 261; 34.0

26. Average = 85.94 m;

$$E_\infty = 1.96 \times \sqrt{0.0486/30} = \pm\, 0.079 \text{ m}$$

28. $E = 0.066 \times \sqrt{3} = 0.114$ m

30. 1:640

32. 1:1100

34. 1:3800; 1:28 000; 1:6400; 1:13 000; 1:17 000; 1:2500

36. $C = 2500/5000 = 0.5$ ft

38. E_∞ for 100 m = 0.110 m

CHAPTER 3

2. a. $x = 3$;   **b.** $t = -6/7$;   **c.** $y = 2$;
  d. $n = -1/2$;   **e.** $x = 1/26$

4. a. $x = \pm\, 5$;   **b.** $x = 3, x = -4$;
  c. $x = 2.851, x = -0.351$;   **d.** no real solution;
  e. $y = 0.4684, y = -2.135$

6. a. $x = 1, y = -3/2$;   **b.** $x = 0, y = 1$;
  c. $x = -1.889, y = 1.444$

8. a. 165 m²;   **b.** 1400 ft²;   **c.** 165 m²;
  d. 2864 ft²;   **e.** 1227 m²;   **f.** 3474 ft²

10. a. opp = 294.76 ft, adj = 322.96 ft, $B = 47°36′48″$
  b. hyp = 393.23 m, adj = 187.75 m, $B = 28°31′13″$
  c. hyp = 441.45 ft, opp = 258.05 ft, $B = 54°13′43″$
  d. $A = 66°55′11″$, $B = 34°59′22″$, adj = 169.71 m
  e. $A = 55°00′38″$, $B = 34°59′22″$, opp = 386.40 ft
  f. $A = 53°18′15″$, $B = 36°41′45″$, hyp = 459.54 m

12. a. $C = 71°21′22″$, $b = 168.04$ ft, c = 282.82 ft
  b. $C = 67°15′44″$, $a = 320.89$ m, $b = 387.77$ m
  c. $B = 73°20′30″$, $C = 81°35′14″$, $c = 533.93$ ft
  d. $B = 49°23′22″$, $C = 71°19′15″$, $c = 497.10$ m
  e. $B = 64°09′12″$, $C = 60°08′13″$, $a = 391.82$ ft
  f. $B = 93°00′26″$, $C = 19°54′53″$, $a = 438.79$ m
  g. $A = 32°13′45″$, $B = 58°00′28″$, $C = 89°45′47″$

14. Building height = 214 ft

16. 78°41′24″; 101°18′36″; 229.46 ft

18. 20 m

20. $BC = 85.828$ m; $CD = 304.08$ m; $DA = 249.99$ m

22. 26°19′14″; 21°35′43″; 132°05′03″

24. 620 ft

26. 375.7 ft

28. **a.** $\sin(10+20) = \sin 30 = 0.500$
    $(\sin 10)(\cos 20) + (\cos 10)(\sin 20) = 0.500$
  b. $\cos(10-20) = \cos(-10) = 0.9848$
    $(\cos 10)(\cos 20) + (\sin 10)(\sin 20) = 0.9848$
  c. $\tan(10+20) = \tan 30 = 0.5774$
$$\frac{(\tan 10 + \tan 20)}{1 - [(\tan 10)(\tan 20)]} = 0.5774$$

30. $CD = \sqrt{70^2 + 50^2} = 86.02 = 86$

32. $y = 25$

34. $y = -0.7143x + 15.7143$

36. Intersection point: (5, 2.5)

38. $(x-3)^2 + (y-4)^2 = 49$

40. $(x-3)^2 + 36 = 49$
    $x^2 - 6x + 9 + 36 = 49$
    $x^2 - 6x - 4 = 0$
    $x = 6.6$ and $x = -0.6$
    Intersection points: (6.6, 10) and (−0.6, 10)

CHAPTER 4

2. **a.** $CD = 33.3$ m   **b.** 135.5 paces

4. **a.** Average unit pace = 0.85 m/pace (omit 96)
  b. $E_{95} = 1.3$ paces; relative accuracy = 1:90

6. **a.** 351.12 ft (107.02 m);
  b. 565.62 ft (172.40 m);
  c. 909.48 ft (277.21 m)

8. +76.543

10. $C_L = 29.992 - 30.000 = -0.008$ m
    Correct distance = $123.456 - 0.033 = 123.423$ m

12. $C_L = 99.990 - 100.000 = -0.010$ ft
    Correct distance = $250.000 + 0.025 = 250.025$ ft

14. $C_t = (1.116 \times 10^{-3})(65.432)(28 - 20)$
      $= 0.0058$ m $= 0.006$ m
    Correct distance = $65.432 + 0.006 = 65.438$ m

16. $C_L = 99.990 - 100.000 = -0.010$ ft/100 ft
    $C_t = (6.5 \times 10^{-6})(100)(25 - 68) = -0.028$ ft/100 ft
    Total correction per 100 ft = -0.038 ft
    Slope distance = $223.456 + (-0.038)(2.23456)$
          $= 223.371$ ft
    Horizontal distance = $\sqrt{223.371^2 - 17.25^2}$
          $= 222.70$ ft

18. $C_L = 99.990 - 100.000 = -0.010$ ft per 100 ft
    $C_t = (6.5 \times 10^{-3})(100)(95 - 68) = 0.030$ ft per 100 ft
    Total correction per 100 ft = 0.02 ft
    Distance to be laid out = $300.00 - 0.02 \times 3 = 299.98$ ft

20. $C_L = 15.005 - 15.000 = 0.005$ m per 15 m
    25.00 m $+ 0.005 \times 25/15 = 25.01$ m
    50.00 m $+ 0.005 \times 50/15 = 50.02$ m

CHAPTER 5

2. No. 1 (ft):   **a.** 1.410   **b.** 1.326   **c.** 1.218
      d. 1.064   **e.** 0.945

  No. 2 (m):   **a.** 1.010   **b.** 0.983   **c.** 0.950
      d. 0.903   **e.** 0.868

  No. 3 (ft):   **a.** 1.580   **b.** 1.666   **c.** 1.779
      d. 1.929   **e.** 2.040

  (*Note:* For rod no. 3, the readings are the final digits of elevation)

4. **a.**

Station	BS	HI	FS	Elevation
BM 10	3.45	756.65		753.20
TP 1	4.68	758.97	2.36	754.29
TP 2	6.85	764.59	1.23	757.74
TP 3	9.63	772.43	1.79	762.80
BM 20			2.46	769.97
Sum =	24.61		7.84	

  b.

Station	BS	HI	FS	Elevation
BM 10	1.567	201.567		200.000
TP 1	1.345	199.333	3.579	197.988
TP 2	1.136	197.709	2.760	196.573
TP 3	0.987	196.121	2.575	195.134
TP 4	0.876	194.942	2.055	194.066
BM 20			1.579	193.363
Sum =	5.911		12.548	

Check: Elevation BM 20 = $200.000 + 5.911 - 12.548$
          $= 193.363$ O.K.

6. **a.**

Station	BS (−)	HI	FS (+)	Elevation
BM 10	3.45	749.75		753.20
TP 1	4.68	747.43	2.36	752.11
TP 2	6.85	741.81	1.23	748.66
TP 3	9.63	733.97	1.79	743.60
BM 20			2.46	736.43
Sum =	24.61		7.84	

Check: Elevation BM 20 = $753.20 - 24.61 + 7.84 = 736.43$ O.K.

b.

Station	BS (−)	HI	FS (+)	Elevation
BM 10	1.567	198.433		200.000
TP 1	1.345	200.667	3.579	202.012
TP 2	1.136	202.291	2.760	203.427
TP 3	0.987	203.879	2.575	204.866
TP 4	0.876	205.058	2.055	205.934
BM 20			1.579	206.637
Sum =	5.911		12.548	

Check: Elevation BM 20 = 200.000 − 5.911 + 12.548
= 206.637 O.K.

8. a.

Station	BS	HI	FS	Elevation	Error
BM 4	0.806	26.039		25.233	
TP 1	1.454	25.176	2.317	23.722	
BM 9	1.841	24.020	2.997	22.179	
TP 2	2.298	25.206	1.112	22.908	
TP 3	3.187	26.648	1.745	23.461	
BM 4			1.418	25.230	0.003
Sum =	+ 9.586		− 9.589		0.003

Distance $K = 40$ m $\times 10 = 400$ m $= 0.4$ km
3 mm accuracy

b.

Station	BS	HI	FS	Elevation	Error
BM 16	2.226	21.241		19.015	
TP 1	0.536	19.267	2.510	18.731	
TP 2	3.089	21.529	0.827	18.440	
BM 40	2.814	21.707	2.636	18.893	
TP 3	1.656	21.367	1.996	19.711	
BM 16			2.417	18.950	0.065
Sum =	+ 10.321		− 10.386		0.065

Distance $K = 40$ m $\times 10 = 400$ m $= 0.4$ km
65 mm

c.

Station	BS	HI	FS	Elevation	Error
BM 6	2.167	24.917		22.750	
TP 1	1.459	25.444	0.932	23.985	
TP 2	1.672	26.320	0.796	24.648	

BM 11	1.470	24.851	2.939	23.381	
TP 3	1.839	23.647	3.043	21.808	
BM 6			0.906	22.741	0.009
Sum =	+ 8.607		− 8.616		0.009

Distance $K = 40$ m $\times 10 = 400$ m $= 0.4$ km
9 mm

10. a.

Station	BS	HI	FS	Elevation	Error
BM	2.300	14.300		12.000	
TP 1	2.088	15.278	1.110	13.190	
TP 2	2.506	16.132	1.652	13.626	
TP 3	3.257	17.556	1.833	14.299	
TP 4	0.497	15.387	2.666	14.890	
BM			3.384	12.003	0.003
Sum =	+ 10.648		− 10.645		0.003

Distance $K = 50$ m $\times 10 = 500$ m $= 0.5$ km
3 mm

b.

Station	BS	HI	FS	Elevation	Error
BM	2.58	28.92		26.34	
TP 1	2.25	28.24	2.93	25.99	
TP 2	1.63	27.88	1.99	26.25	
TP 3	2.81	28.17	2.52	25.36	
TP 4	1.94	26.97	3.14	25.03	
TP 5	2.81	27.52	2.26	24.71	
BM			1.18	26.34	0.00
Sum =	+14.02		−14.02		0.00

c.

Station	BS	HI	FS	Elevation	Error
BM	0.528	28.462		27.934	
TP 1	1.290	26.925	2.827	25.635	
TP 2	1.684	26.101	2.508	24.417	
TP 3	2.762	27.455	1.408	24.693	
TP 4	2.549	28.100	1.904	25.551	
BM			0.170	27.930	0.004
Sum =	+ 8.813		− 8.817		0.004

Distance $K = 50$ m $\times 10 = 500$ m $= 0.5$ km
4 mm

12. **a.**

Station	BS	HI	FS	Rod	Elevation
BM 16	1.715	21.600			19.885
0 + 00				3.90	17.70
0 + 30				2.47	19.13
0 + 60				1.43	20.17
0 + 90				2.56	19.04
TP 1	1.144	21.514	1.230		20.37
1 + 20				4.15	17.36
1 + 50				3.90	17.61
1 + 80				3.23	18.28
TP 2	1.914	20.953	2.475		19.039
2 + 10				1.98	18.97
2 + 40				1.83	19.12
2 + 70				1.65	19.30
3 + 00				3.54	17.41
BM 17			1.591		19.362
Sum =	+4.773		−5.296		

Check: Elevation BM 48 = 19.885 + 4.773 − 5.296
$$= 19.362 \text{ O.K.}$$
Error = 19.365 − 19.362 = 0.003 m = 3 mm

b.

Station	BS	HI	FS	Rod	Elevation
BM 27	2.860	22.610			19.750
0 + 00				3.29	19.32
0 + 30				1.92	20.69
0 + 60				0.67	21.94
0 + 90				0.37	22.24
TP 1	0.390	21.320	1.680		20.930
1 + 20				0.20	21.12
1 + 50				0.06	21.26
1 + 80				1.83	19.49
2 + 10				2.80	18.52
TP 2	0.887	20.217	1.990		19.330
2 + 40				1.61	18.61
2 + 70				0.94	19.28
3 + 00				0.52	19.70
BM 48			0.951		19.266
Sum =	+ 4.137		− 4.621		

Check: Elevation BM 48 = 19.760 + 4.137 − 4.621
$$= 19.266 \text{ O.K.}$$
Error = 19.270 − 19.266 = 0.004 m = 4 mm

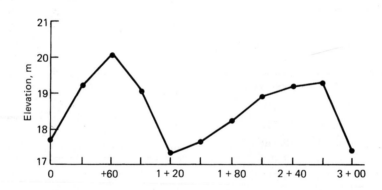

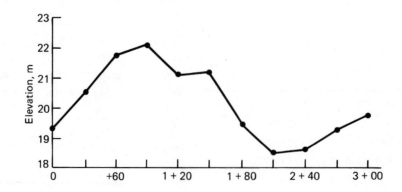

14. Elevation BM $10A = 376.296$ (errors cancel out in BS and FS shots)

16. Error of closure $= 0.04$ m $= 40$ mm
Adjusted elevations:
BM $30A$: $567.89 - 0.415 \times 0.04 = 587.87$
BM $30B$: $576.43 - 0.510 \times 0.04 = 576.41$
BM $30C$: $543.21 - 0.685 \times 0.04 = 543.18$

CHAPTER 6

2. **a.** $100°40'$
   b. $49°30'$
   c. $89°50'$
   d. $94°50'$

4. **a.** $-2°35'25''$
   b. $-18°15'45''$
   c. $17°27'12''$

6.

Bearing	Azim_N	Azim_S
a. N 30°40′ E	30°40′	210°40′
b. N 59°50′ W	300°10′	120°10′
c. N 9°20′ W	350°40′	170°40′
d. N 40°20′ W	319°40′	139°40′
e. N 10°30′ E	10°30′	190°30′
f. S 0°30′ E	179°30′	359°30′
g. S 89°40′ E	90°20′	270°20′
h. S 70°00′ W	250°00′ - 180	70°00′
i. S 20°40′ W	200°40′ ÷ 180	20°40′
j. S 29°30′ E	150°30′	330°30′
k. N 19°60′ W	340°10′	160°10′
l. S 49°30′ E	130°30′	310°30′

8. **a.** S 30°40′ W   **b.** 300°10′
   c. 170°40′   **d.** S 40°20′ E
   e. 190°30′   **f.** N 0°30′ W
   g. 270°20′   **h.** 70°00′
   i. N 20°40′ E   **j.** 330°30′
   k. 340°10′   **l.** 310°30′

10. (1) $+53.47$ ft; (2) -10.69 ft; (3) -8.74 ft

12. $\text{Azim}_N\ IH = 112°15'$; $\text{Azim}_N\ HG = 185°00'$; $\text{Azim}_N\ GF = 292°15'$

14. *PQ:* N 43°39′ W; *QR:* S 77°50 W; *RO:* S 12°32′ E

16. **a.** $G = 118°01'$; $H = 31°32'$; $I = 30°27'$
    b. $J = 108°30'$; $K = 37°45'$; $L = 33°45'$

18. True Azim $= 130°15'$; true bearing $= $ S 49°45′E

20. Compass bearing $= $ N 88°50′ W; True Azim $= 277°45'$

22.

	Interior Angles				
A	**B**	**C**	**D**	**E**
88°30′	40°15′	40°15′	50°15′	89°00′
−22°15′	−22°45′	+51°45′	+31°45′	+32°15′
66°15′	−17°30′	92°00′	−82°00′	121°15′
	179°60′		180°00′	
	162°30′		98°00′	

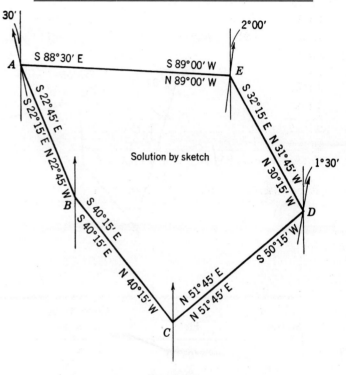

Solution by sketch

Computation by Interior Angles

A = 66°15′	BC − S 40°15′ E
B = 162°30′	92°00′
C = 92°00′	CD N 51°45′ E
D = 98°00′	+98°00′
E = 121°15′	−149°45′
Sum = 539°60′	179°60′
	DE −N 30°15′ W
180	121°15′
×3	S 91°00′ W
540	EA −N 89°00′ W
	66°15′
	AB − S 22°45′ E
	162°30′
	−139°45′
	179°60′

24. a. $0.0191° = 00°01'09'' \approx 01'$
   b. $0.0095° = 0.57° \approx 34''$

CHAPTER 7

2.

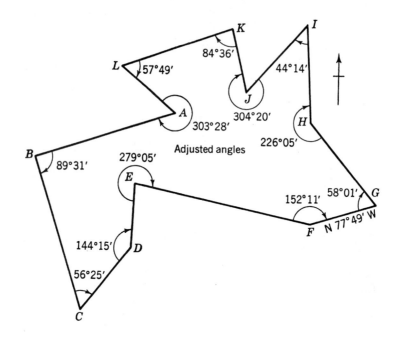

Station	Field	Correction, minutes	Adjusted	Course	Bearings
A	303°30′	−2	303°28′	FG	N 77°49′ E
B	89°33′	−2	89°31′	GH	N 44°10′ W
C	56°27′	−2	56°25′	HI	N 1°55′ E
D	144°17′	−2	144°15′	IJ	S 46°09′ W
E	279°07′	−2	279°05′	JK	N 9°31′ W
F	152°13′	−2	152°11′	KL	S 75°05′ W
G	58°03′	−2	58°01′	LA	S 47°06′ E
H	226°07′	−2	226°05′	AB	S 76°22′ W
I	44°16′	−2	44°14′	BC	S 14°07′ E
J	304°22′	−2	304°20′	CD	N 42°18′ E
K	84°38′	−2	84°36′	DE	N 6°33′ E
L	57°51′	−2	57°49′	EF	S 74°22′ E
	1796°264′		1796°240′		
	+ 4°−240′				
	1800°24′				
	−1800°				
Error	+24′				

4.

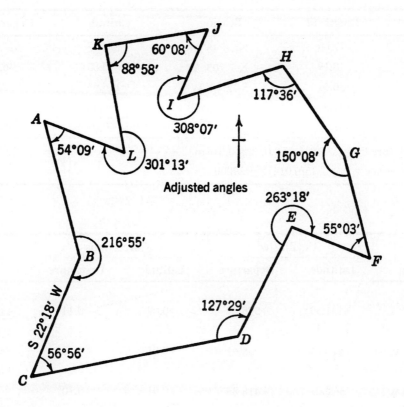

Station	Field	Correction, minutes	Adjusted	Course	Bearings
A	54°08′	+1	54°09′	BC	S 22°18′ W
B	216°54′	+1	216°55′	CD	N 79°14′ E
C	56°55′	+1	56°56′	DE	N 26°43′ E
D	127°28′	+1	127°29′	EF	S 69°59′ E
E	263°17′	+1	263°18′	FG	N 14°56′ W
F	55°02′	+1	55°03′	GH	N 44°48′ W
G	150°07′	+1	150°08′	HI	S 72°48′ W
H	117°35′	+ 1	117°36′	IJ	N 20°55′ E
I	308°06′	+1	308°07′	JK	S 81°03′ W
J	60°07′	+1	60°08′	KL	S 9°59′ E
K	88°57′	+1	88°58′	LA	N 68°46′ W
L	301°12°	+1	301°13′	AB	S 14°37′ E
	1795°288′		1795°300′		
	+ 4°−240′				
	1799°48′				
	−1800°00′				
Error	−12′				

6.

Course	Length, m	Bearing	Latitude	Departure
1-2	77.69	N 16°48′ W	+74.37	−22.45
2-3	48.19	N 77°03′ W	+10.80	−46.96
3-4	136.31	S 32°03′ W	−115.53	−72.33
4-1	144.96	N 77°55′ E	+30.35	141.75
	407.15		−0.01	0.01

Error of closure $E_c = \sqrt{0.01^2 + 0.01^2} = 0.014\,\text{m}$

Relative accuracy $= 1:(407.15/0.014) = 1:29000$

8.

Station	Bearing	Unadjusted Latitude	Unadjusted Departure	Corrections Latitude	Corrections Departure	Adjusted N	Adjusted E
A						868.59	461.57
	N 76°17′ E	+131.39	+538.29	+0.02	+0.14	+131.41	+538.43
B						1000.00	1000.00
	N 9°17′ W	+419.74	−68.61	+0.01	+0.10	+419.75	−68.51
C						1419.75	931.49
	N 79°27′ W	+78.01	−418.85	+0.01	+0.10	+78.02	−418.75
D						1497.77	512.74
	S 22°57′ W	−317.95	−134.64	+0.01	+0.09	−317.94	−134.55
E						1179.83	378.19
	S 14°59′ E	−311.25	+83.30	+0.01	+0.08	−311.24	+83.38
A						868.59	461.57
		−0.06	−0.51	+0.06	+0.51		

$$\frac{0.51}{2073} = 1:4100$$

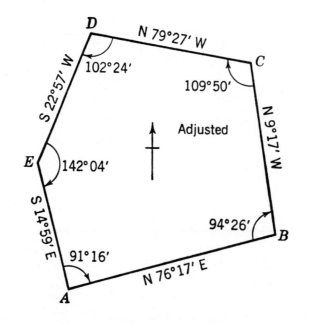

10.

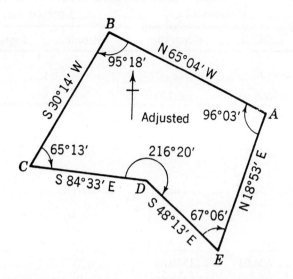

		Unadjusted		Corrections		Adjusted	
Station	Bearing	Latitude	Departure	Latitude	Departure	N	E
A						1425.55	1145.65
	N 65°04′ W	+236.19	−508.05	−0.08	+0.08	+236.11	−507.97
B						1661.66	637.68
	S 30°14′ W	−418.32	−243.79	−0.07	+0.07	−418.39	−243.72
C						1243.27	393.96
	S 84°33′ E	−35.66	+373.72	−0.05	+0.05	−35.71	+373.77
D						1207.56	767.73
	S 48°13′ E	−207.52	+232.23	−0.04	+0.04	−207.56	+232.27
E						1000.00	1000.00
	N 18°53′ E	+425.62	+145.58	−0.07	+0.07	+425.55	+145.65
A						1425.56	1145.65
		+0.31	−0.31	−0.31	+0.31		

$$\frac{0.44}{2181} = 1:5000$$

12.

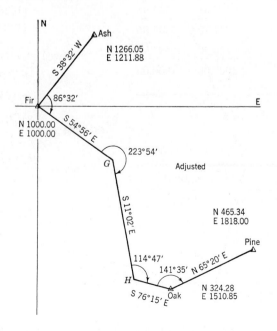

Station	Bearing	Unadjusted		Corrections		Adjusted	
		Latitude	Departure	Latitude	Departure	N	E
Ash							
	S 38°32′ W						
Fir		1000.00	1000.00			1000.00	1000.00
	S 54°56′ E	−199.45	+284.14	−0.13	0.00	−199.58	+284.14
G						800.42	1284.14
	S 11°02′ E	−441.51	+86.09	−0.17	+0.01	−441.68	+86.10
H						358.74	1370.24
	S 76°15′ E	−34.41	+140.61	−0.05	0.00	−34.46	+140.61
Oak						324.28	1510.85
	N 65°20′ W						
Pine							
		324.63	1510.84	−0.35	+0.01		
	Oak	−324.28	−1510.85				
		+ 0.35	− 0.01				

$$\frac{0.35}{942} = 1:2700$$

14. (Refer to Problem 9.)

Station	Transit Rule Corrections		Adjusted Coordinates	
	Latitude	Departure	Northing	Easting
E			1000.00	1000.00
	+0.04	−0.03	−442.63	+79.89
A			557.37	1079.89
	+0.00	−0.19	+40.87	+558.59
B			598.24	1638.48
	+0.05	−0.00	+484.14	+9.44
C			1082.38	1647.92
	+0.02	−0.11	−150.68	−343.96
D			931.70	1303.96
	+0.01	−0.10	+68.30	−303.96
E			1000.00	1000.00
	+0.12	−0.43		

16. (Refer to Problem 9.)

Course	Bearing	Length, ft
EA	S 10°13′ E	449.79
AB	N 85°49′ E	560.17
BC	N 1°06′ E	484.21
CD	S 66°20′ W	375.48
DE	N 77°20′ W	311.50

18.

Course	Bearing	Length
1-2	S 65°51′40″ W	1760.08
2-3	S 42°03′40″ E	380.64
3-4	S 87°26′54″ E	1691.68
4-1	N 19°56′28″ W	1431.50

20.

$$\frac{1000.00 \quad 557.35 \quad 598.25 \quad 1082.37 \quad 931.69 \quad 1000.00}{1000.00 \quad 1079.83 \quad 1638.50 \quad 1647.84 \quad 1303.92 \quad 1000.00}$$

$$\Sigma(\text{up}) = (1000.00)(557.35) + (1079.83)(598.25) +$$
$$+ (1638.50)(1082.37) + (1647.84)(931.69)$$
$$+ (1303.92)(1000.00) = 5\,816\,018$$

$$\Sigma(\text{down}) = (1000.00)(1079.83) + (557.35)(1638.50)$$
$$+ (598.25)(1647.84) + (1082.37)(1303.92)$$
$$+ (931.69)(1000.00) = 5\,321\,882$$

$$\text{Area} = \frac{5\,816\,018 - 5\,321\,882}{2} = 247\,068\,\text{ft}^2$$

$$\text{Area} = \frac{247\,068\,\text{ft}^2}{43\,560\,\text{ft}^2/\text{ac}} = 5.67\,\text{ac}$$

22.

$$\frac{2345.67 \quad 1357.91 \quad 1075.31 \quad 1000.00 \quad 2345.67}{3456.78 \quad 2000.00 \quad 2255.00 \quad 3945.00 \quad 3456.78}$$

$$\Sigma(\text{up}) = (3456.78)(1357.91) + (2000.00)(1075.31)$$
$$+ (2255.00)(1000.00) + (3945.00)(2345.67)$$
$$= 18\,353\,284$$

$\Sigma(\text{down}) = (2345.67)(2000.00) + (1357.91)(2255.00)$
$\qquad\qquad + (1075.31)(3945.00) + (1000.00)(3456.78)$
$\qquad\qquad = 15\,452\,305$

$\text{Area} = \dfrac{18\,353\,284 - 15\,452\,305}{2} = 1\,450\,490\,\text{ft}^2$

$\text{Area} = \dfrac{1\,450\,490}{43\,560}\,\text{ft}^2/\text{ac} = 33.30\,\text{ac}$

24. $\text{Area} = 15\left(\dfrac{4.1 + 2.1}{2} + 8.9 + 15.8 + 28.4 + 39.6\right.$

$\qquad\qquad\left. + 47.2 + 41.5 + 31.8 + 24.6 + 9.1 + 4.0\right)$

$\qquad = 3810\,\text{m}^2$ (from Equation 7.9)

Triangular end areas $= \dfrac{1}{2}(15 \times 4.1 + 8.7 \times 2.1)$

$\qquad\qquad\qquad - 40\text{m}^2$

Total area $= 3850\,\text{m}^2 \times \dfrac{1\,\text{ha}}{10000\,\text{m}^2} \approx 0.39\,\text{ha}$

26. Area of trapezoid $= \left(\dfrac{270 + 90}{2}\right) \times 240 = 43\,200\,\text{m}^2$

Area of segment $= \dfrac{60}{360}(\pi)(300^2) - (300^2)\dfrac{(\sin 60)}{2}$

$\qquad\qquad = 8153\,\text{m}^2$

Total area $= 43\,200 - 8153 = 35\,047\,\text{m}^2 \approx 3.5\,\text{ha}$

28. Azim $SR = 155°45' + 180°00' = 335°45'$

Azim $S\text{-}S10 = 335°45' + 233°15' - 569°00' = 209°00'$

Latitude $S\text{-}S10 = -148.35\cos 29° = -129.75$

Departure $S\text{-}S10 = -148.35\sin 29° = -71.92$

Northing $S10 = 500.00 - 129.75 = 370.25$

Easting $S10 = 500.00 - 71.92 = 428.08$

Coordinates $S10$ are N 370.25/E 428.08

30. $AB = \sqrt{(500 - 300)^2 + (500 - 200)^2} = 360.551$

$\beta = \tan^{-1}\left(\dfrac{300}{200}\right) = 56.3099° = 56°18'36''$

Bearing $AB = $ S 56°18'36'' W

Angle $A = 56°18'36'' - 12°30' = 43°48'36'' = 48.81''$

Angle $B = 75°00' = 56°18'36'' = 18°41'24'' = 18.69''$

Angle $C = 180°00' - 43°48'36'' - 18°41'24''$

$\qquad = 117°30'00''$

$AC = 360.5551 \times \dfrac{\sin 18.69°}{\sin 117.50°} = 130.26$

$BC = 360.56 \times \dfrac{\sin 43.81°}{\sin 117.60°} = 281.40$

Latitude $AC = -130.26 \times \cos 12.5$
$\qquad\qquad = -127.17$ (south = minus)

Departure $AC = -130.26 \times \sin 12.5$
$\qquad\qquad = -28.19$ (west = minus)

Northing $C = 500.00 - 127.17 = 372.83$

Easting $C = 500.00 - 28.19 = 471.81$

32. $AB = \sqrt{(100)^2 + (250)^2} = 269.26$

$\beta = \tan^{-1}\left(\dfrac{250}{100}\right) = 68.199° = 68°1155''$

Bearing $AB = $ N 68°11'55'' E

Angle $A \cos^{-1}\left(\dfrac{269.26^2 + 206.80^2 - 142.15^2}{2 \times 206.80 \times 269.26}\right)$

$\qquad = 31.396° - 31°23'45''$

Bearing $AC' = $ S 80°24'20'' E

Latitude $AC' = -206.80 \times \cos 80.406°$
$\qquad\qquad = -34.47$ (south = minus)

Departure $AC' = 206.80 \times \sin 80.406° = 203.91$

Northing $C' = 1000.00 - 34.47 = 965.53$

Easting $C' = 1000.00 + 203.91 = 1203.91$

34. $\dfrac{800 - 1000}{1500 - 1000} = \dfrac{\text{Ns} - 1000}{\text{Es} - 1000}$

from which: $\text{Ns} + 0.4\,\text{Es} = 1400$

$\cot 25° = \dfrac{(\text{Ns} - 650)}{(\text{Es} - 1050)}$ and $\text{Ns} - 2.1445\,\text{Es} = -2901.73$

Solution: $\text{Es} = 1179.69$ and $\text{Ns} = 928.12$

36. Equation for line AB: $N_s = 3000 - 2\,E_s$

When $N_s = 1650$, $E_s = 675.00$.

For the circle: $(1650 - 1000)^2 + (675 - E_o)^2 - 1000^2$

From which: $E_o^2 - 1350\,E_o - 121\,875 = 0$ and
$\qquad\qquad E_o = 1434.93$

38. $RS = 64.21\,\text{m}$

40.

	Angles and Sides			Final Sides
CA	375.42			375.40
B-CA	70°08'53''	+2''	55''	
C-AB	48°06'25''	+2''	27''	
AB				297.10
A-BC	61°44'36''	+2''	38''	
BC				351.56
	179°58'114''	+6''	120''	
E-BC	82°36'08''	+1''	09''	
B-EC	48°31'21''	+1''	22''	
EC				265.61
C-BE	48°52'28''	+1''	29''	
BE				267.04
	179°59'57''	+3''	60''	
D-EB	52°04'07''	−1''	06''	
E-BD	49°33'46''	−1''	45''	
BD				257.69
B-DE	78°22'10''	−1''	09''	
DE				331.62
	180°00'03''	−3''	60''	

CHAPTER 8

2. See lot *B*-5 in Figure 8-9 of the text.

4. See Figure Answer Problem 4.

6. Lot *A*-8, situated in Blankville, Blank County, Conn., and bounded as follows:

   Beginning at a point in the southerly line of Somerset Street at the southwesterly corner of the land hereby conveyed, said point bearing N 58°04′ E. 183.05 ft measured along the southerly line of Somerset Street from a concrete monument at the intersection of the southerly line of Somerset Street and the northerly line of Overville Street and running:

   1. Thence, N 58°04′ E, 108.15 ft along the southerly line of Somerset Street to a concrete monument in the northwesterly corner of the land hereby conveyed:

   2. Thence, easterly on the arc of a circle 90 ft in radius curving to the right an arc distance of 124.93 ft, along the southerly line of Somerset Street, the chord of the said arc running S 82°10′ E. 115.14 ft to a concrete monument at the northeasterly corner of the land hereby conveyed:

   3. Thence, S 47°36′ W, 180.00 ft along the northwesterly line of the land of (here insert the name of the owner of lot *A*-9) to a point at the southerly corner of the land hereby conveyed:

   4. Thence, N 42°24′ W, 108.15 ft along the northeasterly line of the land of (here insert the name of the owner of lot *A*-7) to the point of beginning.

All bearings are based on the stated direction of the northerly lines of Somerset Street and Overville Street. (*Note:* NE/SW lot lines are assumed perpendicular to Overville Street.)

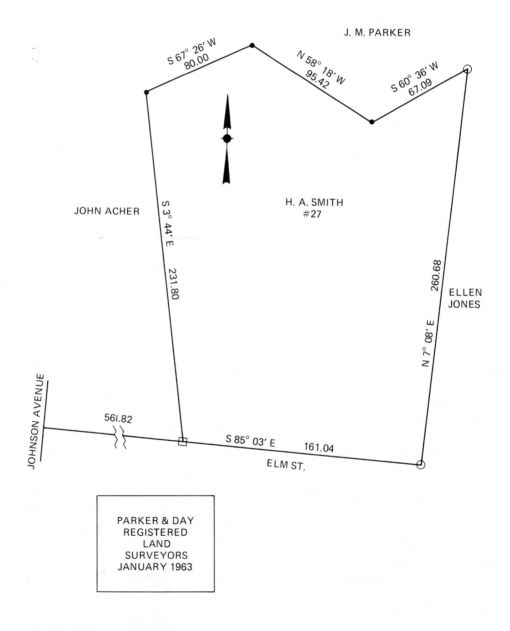

8. Public Land System Descriptions for Figure 8-17:

Parcel	Description
F	E 1/2, SE 1/4, Sec. 9, T 3 S, R 2 W (meridian name); 80 ac
G	S 1/2, SW 1/4, Sec. 9, T 3 S, R 2 W (meridian name); 80 ac
H	SE 1/4, NW 1/4, Sec. 9, T 3 S, R 2 W (meridian name); 40 ac
I	NW 1/4, NW 1/4, Sec. 9, T 3 S, R 2 W (meridian name); 40 ac
J	SW 1/4, NE 1/4, NW 1/4, Sec. 9, T 3 S, R 2 W (meridian name); 10 ac

10. Area $= 0.5 \times 704\ 990$ ft$^2 = 352\ 495$ ft$^2 = 8.09$ ac
    Distance $DG = 587.15$ ft
    Distance $GB = 588.01$ ft:
    bearing $GB = $ N 9°40′01″ W

12. Partitioning boundary line HI: S 14°54′53″ W, 678.53 ft;
    IE: S 81°42′44″ E, 299.97 ft; EA: N 14°54′55″ E, 783.40 ft;
    AH: S 79°49′47″ W, 328.99 ft

14. Area $= 0.5 \times 285\ 443$ ft$^2 = 142\ 722$ ft$^2 = 3.28$ ac;
    $BG = 182.84$ ft; $GE = 592.48$ ft at S 83°57′02″ E

16. Partitioning boundary line HI: N 73°20′50″ W,
    577.10 ft; IC: S 3°10′12″ E, 276.98 ft;
    CD: S 73°20′48″ E, 425.96 ft; DH: N 29°02′14″ E,
    266.77 ft

18. Northing PC 15 $= 610.10$; easting PC 15 $= 792.43$
    Northing PC 16 $= 576.79$; easting PC 16 $= 820.49$
    PC 15-PC 16: S 40°06′38″ E, 43.55 m

20. 63.86 ft

CHAPTER 9

2. RF $= 1:2400$
4. 1 in $= 0.789$ mi; 1 cm $= 0.5$ km
6. 18 ft: 2080 ft; 1200 ft; 15 300 ft
8. 1 in $= 10$ ft
10. 1:200
12. **a.** See Figure Answer Problem 12*a*
    b. See Figure Answer Problem 12*b*

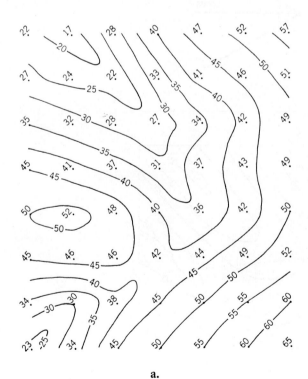

a.

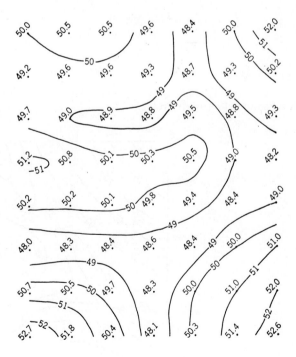

b.

14.

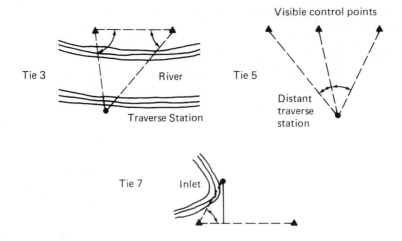

16.

a.

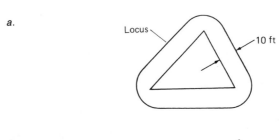

b.

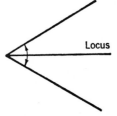

18. See Figure 9-40 Answer Problem 18

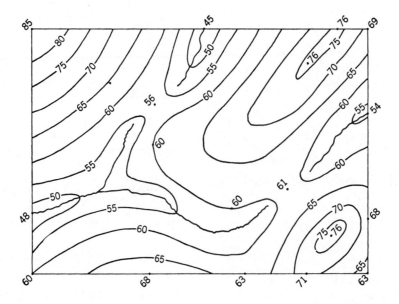

20. 3.6 km

22. 1:3000

CHAPTER 10

2. $T = 125 \tan\left(\dfrac{105.66°}{2}\right) = 164.88$ m

$L = \pi \times 125 \times \left(\dfrac{105.66°}{180}\right) = 230.53$ m

$LC = 2 \times 125 \times \sin\left(\dfrac{105.66°}{2}\right) = 199.22$ m

$E = 125 \times \dfrac{1}{\cos\left(\dfrac{105.66°}{2}\right) - 1} = 81.91$ m

$M = 125 \times 1 - \cos\left(\dfrac{105.66°}{2}\right) = 49.48$ m

4. $D = \dfrac{5729.578}{125}$

$= 45.8°$ (subtended by $100 - $m arc length)

6. $35 = R \times \dfrac{1}{\cos\left(\dfrac{80}{2}\right) - 1}$

$R = \dfrac{35}{0.3054} = 114.60$ m

$D = \dfrac{5729.578}{114.60}$

$= 50°$ (subtended by $100 - $m arc length)

8. $R = 2R \times \sin\left(\dfrac{\Delta}{2}\right)$

$\dfrac{1}{2} = \sin\left(\dfrac{\Delta}{2}\right)$

$\Delta = 2 \sin^{-1}\left(\dfrac{1}{2}\right) = 60°$

10. Station PC $= (12 + 00) - (1 + 64.88) = 10 + 35.12$

Station PT $= (10 + 35.12) + (2 + 30.53) = 12 + 65.65$

12. $R = \dfrac{5729.578}{6} = 954.93$

$\Delta_1 = 49°00' - 33°30' = 15°30'$

$T_1 = 954.93 \times \tan 7.75° = 129.96$

$L_1 = \pi \times 954.93 \times \dfrac{15.5}{180} = 258.33$

$\Delta_2 = 49°00' + 14°30' = 63°30'$

$T_2 = 954.93 \times \tan 31.75° = 590.93$

$L_2 = \pi \times 954.93 \times \dfrac{63.5}{180} = 1058.33$

$PC_1 = (15 + 75) - (1 + 29.96) = 14 + 45.04$

$PT_1 = (14 + 45.04) + 258.33 = 17 + 03.37$

$S_1 = (2300 - 1575) - 129.96 - 590.93 = 4.11$

$PC_2 = (17 + 03.37) + 4.11 = 17 + 07.48$

$PT_2 = 17 + 07.48 + (10 + 58.33) = 27 + 65.81$

$S_2 = (3800 - 2300) - 590.93 = 909.07$

Equation of chainage $= (27 + 65.81) + (9 + 09.07)$

$= 36 + 74.88$

14. $R = \dfrac{5729.578}{12} = 477.46$ ft

For $16 + 00$: $a = \left(\dfrac{75}{477.46}\right)(1718.87)$

$= 270' = 4°30'$

For $16 + 50$: $a = 4°30' + \dfrac{12}{4} = 7°30'$

For $17 + 00$: $a = 7°30' + 3°00' = 10°30'$

Chord PC $16 + 00$: $2(477.46)(\sin 4°30') = 74.92$ ft

Chord $16 + 00.16 + 50$: $2(477.46)(\sin 3°) = 49.98$ ft

16.

Station	Chord	Deflection	Curve Data
+50			
+26.94 PT	26.94	33°09'15"	$R = 400'$
50 + 0	49.97	31°13'30"	
			$\Delta = 66°18'24"$
+50		27°38'45"	
			$\Delta/2 = 33°09'12"$
49 + 0		24°03'45"	
			$= 33°09.2'$
+50		20°29'00"	
+25.32 Pl			$T = 261.29$
48 + 0		16°54'00"	
			$L = 462.91$
+50		13°19'15"	
47 + 0		9°44'15"	
+50	49.97	6°09'30"	
46 + 0	35.96	2°35'00"	
+64.03 PC		0	
+50			

18.

Station	Chord	Deflection	Curve Data
+50			
+49.48 PT	49.45	21°17'15"	$R = 600'$
30 + 0	49.97	18°55'30"	
			$\Delta = 42°34'28"$
+50		16°32'15"	
			$\Delta/2 = 21°17'14"$
29 + 0		14°09'00"	
			$= 21°17.23'$
+50		11°45'45"	
+37.42 Pl			$T = 233.78$
28 + 0		9°23'30"	
			$L = 445.84$
+50		6°69'15"	
27 + 0	49.97	4°36'00"	
+50	46.33	2°12'45"	
PC + 03.64		0	
26 + 0			

20. $\Delta = 43°45' + 39°30' = 83°15'$

$$T = 1200 \times \tan\left(\frac{83.25}{2}\right) = 1066.35 \text{ ft}$$

$$L = \pi \times 1200 \times \left(\frac{83.25}{180}\right) = 1743.58 \text{ ft}$$

$$\text{PI to } A = \frac{987.65}{\sin 83.25} \times \sin 39.5 = 632.61 \text{ ft}$$

$$\text{PI to } B = \frac{987.65}{\sin 83.25} \times \sin 43.75 = 687.74 \text{ ft}$$

Station PC $= (115 + 00) = (1066.35 - 632.61)$
$= 110 + 66.26$

Station PT $= (110 + 66.26) + (17 + 43.58)$
$= 128 + 09.84$

22. Plus PI $= 1287.93$
Less $T_1 = -\underline{407.14}$
Plus PC $= 880.79$
Add $L_1 = +\underline{326.26}$
Plus PCC $= 1207.05$
Add $L_2 = +\underline{379.49}$
Plus PT $= 1586.54$

24. $\Delta_1 = 80°35'14''$; $\Delta_2 = 61°20'24''$
Plus PC $= 1532.71$
Add $L_1 = +\underline{172.75}$
Plus PRC $= 1705.46$
Add $L_2 = +\underline{131.49}$
Plus PT $= 1836.95$

26. $g_1 = \dfrac{49.25 - 73.00}{950} = -0.0250$

$g_2 = \dfrac{93.00 - 49.25}{2225 - 950} = 0.0343$

$g_3 = \dfrac{105.00 - 93.00}{2900 - 2225} = 0.0178$

28.

Station	Tangent Elevation	Curve Elevation
PVC 12 + 50	68.64	68.64
13 + 00	70.34	70.11
13 + 50	72.04	71.13
14 + 00	73.74	71.69
14 + 50	75.44	71.80
15 + 00	77.14	71.44
15 + 50	78.84	70.64
16 + 00	80.54	69.38
16 + 50	82.24	67.66
PVT 17 + 00	83.94	65.49

High point: Station 14 + 36.59, elevation 71.81

30.

Station	Tangent Elevation	Curve Elevation
PVC 7 + 50	62.71	62.71
8 + 00	61.11	61.33
8 + 50	59.51	60.41
9 + 00	57.91	59.93
9 + 50	56.31	59.91
10 + 00	54.71	60.33
10 + 50	53.11	61.21
11 + 00	51.51	62.53
11 + 50	49.91	64.31
12 + 00	48.31	66.53
PVT 12 + 50	46.71	69.21

Low point: Station 9 + 27.78, elevation 59.87

32. $R = 150.65$ ft

34. $L = 1162.35$ ft

36. 186.52 ac

Station	Elevation	Station	Elevation	Station	Elevation
0 + 00	73.00	11 + 00	54.40	22 + 00	92.13
1 + 00	70.50	12 + 00	57.83	23 + 00	94.32
2 + 00	68.00	13 + 00	61.23	24 + 00	96.10
3 + 00	65.50	14 + 00	64.69	25 + 00	97.88
4 + 00	63.00	15 + 00	68.12	26 + 00	99.66
5 + 00	60.50	16 + 00	71.55	27 + 00	101.44
6 + 00	58.00	17 + 00	74.98	28 + 00	103.22
7 + 00	55.50	18 + 00	78.41	29 + 00	105.00
8 + 00	53.00	19 + 00	81.84		
9 + 00	50.50	20 + 00	85.27		
10 + 00	50.97	21 + 00	88.70		

38. 222.22 ha

40. 1542.70 ac

42. Station 39 + 50: area = 914 ft^2

Station 40 + 00: area = 588 ft^2

Volume = 1390 yd^3

44.

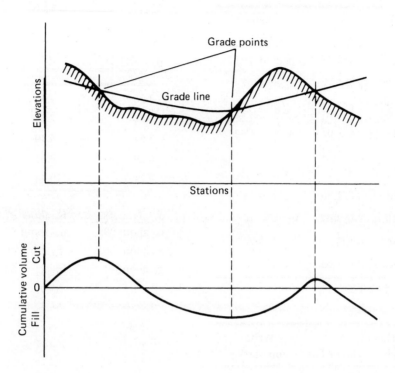

46. 15 squares 15 m × 15 m: corner sum = 73.3

Volume = $\dfrac{73.3}{4}$ × 15 × 15 = 4123 m^3

2 rectangles 7.5 m × 15 m: corner sum = 13.7

Volume = $\dfrac{13.7}{4}$ × 7.5 × 15 = 385 m^3

4 triangles: Volume = $\dfrac{1}{2} \times \left[\left(15 \times 15 \times \dfrac{1.9}{3}\right) \right.$

$+ \left(15 \times 7.5 \times \dfrac{4.9}{3}\right)$

$\left. + (2)\left(7.5 \times 7.5 \times \dfrac{7.5}{3}\right)\right]$

= 304 m^3

2 five-sided figures: area = 196.88 m^2

Volume = 2 × 196.88 m^2 × $\dfrac{9.7\,\text{m}}{5}$ = 764 m^3

Total volume = 5576 m^3

CHAPTER 11

2. $D = 200.00 \tan (40''/3600'') = 0.039$ m = 39 mm

4. $\dfrac{21.23}{5.868} = +3.6179$

$0.203 \times 3.6179 = 0.7344$

$0.50 \times 3.6179 = 1.8090$

$0.165 \times 3.6179 = 0.5970$

Station	Grade	Grade Used	Station	Grade	Grade Used
6 + 29.7	51.26	51.26	+ 50	62.8484	62.85
+ 50	51.9944	51.99	10 + 0	64.6574	64.66
7 + 0	53.8034	53.80	+ 50	66.4664	66.47
+ 50	55.6124	55.61	11 + 0	68.2754	68.28
8 + 0	57.4214	57.42	+ 50	70.0844	70.08
+ 50	59.2304	59.23	12 + 0	71.8934	71.89
9 + 0	61.0394	61.04	+16.5	72.4904	72.49

6. $GR = 123.45 - 121.87 = 1.58$ m

8. $GR = 60.05 - 53.72 = 6.33$ ft

Rod reading $= 10.93$

$F = 10.93 - 6.33 = 4.60$ ft

10. a.

Station	Grade	Elevation Mark	Cut or Fill	Write on Mark
0 + 0	35.64	35.27	F 0.37	F 0′ − 4½″
0 + 50	38.64	39.42	C 0.78	C 0′ − 9⅜″
1 + 0	41.64	46.25	C 4.61	C 0′ − 7⅜″
1 + 50	44.64	47.31	C 2.67	C 2′ − 8″
2 + 0	47.64	46.22	F 1.42	F 1′ − 5″
2 + 50	50.64	47.38	F 3.26	F 3′ − 3⅛″
3 + 0	53.64	55.20	C 1.56	C 1′ − 6¾″
3 + 50	56.64	59.71	C 3.07	C 3′ − 0⅞″
4 + 0	59.64	59.64	G	G
4 + 50	62.64	64.28	C 1.64	C 1′ − 7⅝″

b.

Station	Grade	Elevation Mark	Cut or Fill	Write on Mark
0 + 0	47.28	46.17	F 1.11	F 1′ − 1⅜″
0 + 50	45.28	41.62	F 3.66	F 3′ − 7⅞″
1 + 0	43.28	45.10	C 1.82	C 1′ − 9⅞″
1 + 50	41.28	40.83	F 0.45	F 0′ − 5⅜″
2 + 0	39.28	36.15	F 3.13	F 3′ − 1½″
2 + 50	37.28	42.14	C 4.86	C 4′ − 10⅜″
3 + 0	35.28	34.75	F 0.53	F 0′ − 6⅜″
3 + 50	33.28	35.29	C 2.01	C 2′ − 0⅛″
4 + 0	31.28	32.67	C 1.39	C 1′ − 4⅝″
4 + 50	29.28	33.48	C 4.20	C 4′ − 2⅜″

12. a.

7.21	3.44
4.81	8.72
5.64	9.34
6.41	2.54
4.28	10.65

b.

2.56	4.51
1.84	7.24
3.64	5.40
6.29	8.61
9.71	10.44

14. a. about 48   **b.** about 82.5
    c. about 88   **d.** about 53
    e. about 56.5   **f.** about 86.5
    g. about 91   **h.** about 62

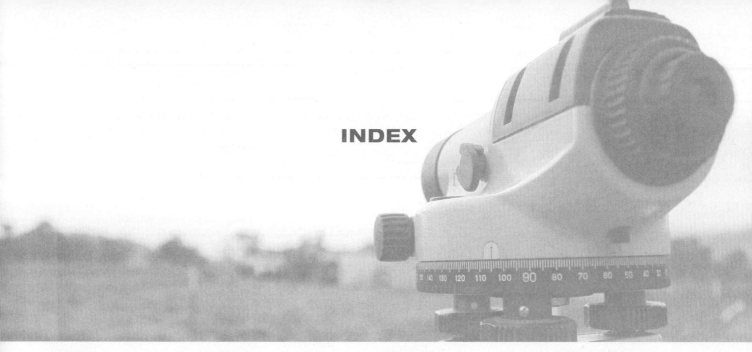

INDEX